P9-DFC-697

DREAMERS WHO LIVE THEIR DREAMS:

The World of Ross Macdonald's Novels

FINKELSTEIN
MEMORIAL LIBRARY
SPRING VALLEY, N. Y.

Dreamers Who Live Their Dreams:
The World of Ross Macdonald's Novels

Peter Wolfe

Bowling Green University Popular Press
Bowling Green, Ohio 43403

850765

Copyright © 1976 by The Popular Press

Library of Congress Catalog Card Number: 76-47226

ISBN: 0-87972-081-6 Cloth bound
0-87972-082-4 Paperback

Artwork by Gregg Swope

To the memory of my mother,

Mae Salius Wolfe
1905, Torrington, Connecticut-1960, New York City

and her little sidekick, Snubs

ACKNOWLEDGMENTS

The author and publisher join in expressing their thanks for permission to quote copyrighted passages from Ross Macdonald's work to Ross Macdonald and his publisher, Alfred A. Knopf, Inc.

Special thanks are owing to Barbara Bullock for typing the manuscript; to the Graduate College of the University of Missouri-St. Louis for grants to cover expenses connected with the manuscript's preparation; and to Margaret and Kenneth Millar for their detailed sympathetic comments about crime fiction in general and Ross Macdonald's artistry in particular.

The combined help of the following people amounts to a major contribution: Janice Montgomery, Thomas Jordan, Robert Markland, Murray Edelman, Linda Gugel, Irene Underwood, Ceola Breckenridge, R. W. Lid, Elizabeth Leopold, and P. K. Savoir.

Contents

1

Ross Macdonald (Kenneth Millar in private life) has been called "the thinking man's crime writer and the street reader's intellectual."[1] It is easy to justify this high claim. His novels are well-built, suspenseful, and easy both to read and enjoy. His best work gives equal weight to invention and execution. His intellectual power, social conscience, and bright, crisp style promote both impact and resonance. He has something to say, knows how to say it, and deserves to be heard.

Like Dickens, he has tried to express his deepest feelings while reaching a wide readership; primitive terror shudders through his Los Angeles as it did through the London of *Oliver Twist*. The goal of forming and then holding a readership he views as conviction and artistic challenge rather than as concession:

I have a very strong feeling that it's the duty of a writer, or at least of this particular writer, to write popular fiction. Ideally, a community tends to communicate with itself through its fiction, and this communication tends to break down if there are Mandarin novels written for Mandarins and lowbrow novels written for lowbrows, and so on. My aim from the beginning has been to write novels that can be read by all kinds of people.[2]

A good example of his ability to write books that everybody can read inheres in his treatment of sex. He never denies the force of sex; sex always plays a large part in the troubled lives he depicts. But because erotic descriptions would cut the range of his readership, they never appear in his work. Nor does he let his preference for searching out criminal causes, rather than merely recording crime's sensations, outrank his sense of mission as a storyteller. Whereas many mainstream novelists since Henry James have subordinated storytelling to giving anatomies of the inner man, Millar/Macdonald translates motive into both physical *and* psychological act. In depicting the inner man, he does not forget the outer man—how he looks and what he does. He tells how characters have become the way they are; he reviews his main issues; he will remind you of the main currents of his sometimes highly complex plot. Though most thrillers start quickly, his set their own pace, adding characters and information when both reader and plot are ready for them.

Thus the novels give a great deal—action and credibility, sound plotting and something to think about: the meaning and the mechanism of crime. The crime points to serious issues. Almost all his work shows how far society at large, the family, and the individual have veered from what they should be. The idea is neither original nor profound. Ross Macdonald's strength lies not in idea but in his moral seriousness and power to convert idea into sharply observed and well-integrated details. He convinces us, through his artistry, of both the complexity and mystery of life. While persuading us that life is full of meaning, he does not define that meaning; rather, he invests detective fiction with a psychological dimension that fits well with its traditionally complex plot. More interested in private than in public crime, he uses psychology rather than applied science to probe motives and causes. This turning-away both from the gadgetry of the novel of international intrigue and the secular rationalism of the 'tec-yarn helps him reveal his characters through speech and action.

The shaping and development of the novels follow in tandem. Most crime fiction rates dramatic situation, immediacy, and form over character analysis. Because brooding clogs dramatic drive, Ross Macdonald does not analyze or explore motives. He shows, instead, the effects of deeply seated, sometimes obsessional, motives. Characters reveal themselves, if not at their worst, then at their most deeply surprised and tested. What will these nerve-raked souls do next? Who will be their next victims? Ross Macdonald conveys a sense of untold menace lurking behind the reported action. The bipolar pull of conscious and unconscious forces both energizes and controls the blend—the dark subject-matter of the novels resonating against a bright, limber style and Kenneth Millar's use of both a penname and a persona, in his narrator-detective Lew Archer. The tensional field of Ross Macdonald's art hums with imaginative possibilities.

The best catalog of these possibilities comes from John Leonard in the 1 June 1969 number of the New York *Times Book Review*:

These books explore guilt, justice, mercy, exile, new beginnings, the "closed circuit" of time, the "family romance" . . . the tension between causality and revolt . . . and, crucially, the spider web of consequences spun from the abdomen of Oedipus.[3]

Ross Macdonald prefigures Leonard's brief catalog in his insight into James M. Cain's *Double Indemnity* (1936), which also appeared in the *Times Book Review* in 1969: "It isn't an action story. Its critical actions are psychological and moral."[4] What Ross Macdonald says about Cain applies just as strictly to himself. His main subject is the comic one of man against man; nature is a passive victim in *Underground Man* (1971) and *Sleeping Beauty* (1973), which include, in turn, a forest fire and an oil spill—both started by people. From the outset, he rules out any struggle between temporal and eternal; man's soul is no battleground for the clash of metaphysical good and evil. Nor does a foreign enemy threaten civilization. The nucleus of western culture—the family—is so weak to begin with that no international conspiracy need be called in to convey danger. Routine living consists of terror and tension; insecurity is the norm.

Though Ross Macdonald links detection to psychology, he ignores criminal pathology. Crime in Ross Macdonald is usually murder; its motive, always personal and specific. Each book has only one killer, but he will kill three or four times. His motives? Gain and self-protection. Though the first victim dies because he stands between his murderer and something his murderer wants, the other ones die because they have incriminating information. The pattern of murder follows that of *Macbeth* and Graham Greene's *Brighton Rock*—the killer cannot stop killing.

Ross Macdonald works harder to justify the motives of murder than to supply a conventional ending, where the murderer is caught after a setting-forth of the evidence. He cares about telling a good story because he cares about people—even killers and thieves. In *The Far Side of the Dollar* (1965), his continuing narrator-detective, Lew Archer, says, "Other people's lives are my business." When asked if they are his passion, as well, he answers, "And my passion. And my obsession, too, I guess. I've never been able to see much in the world besides the people in it." Archer's detection is neither law-centered (Perry Mason) nor God-centered (Chesterton's Father Brown). His creator shares his compassion and charity. Treating characters with respect, the Archer novels portray wrongdoers but, in recent years especially, no villains. Nobody chooses evil. Violence isn't simple; nor does it lend itself to moral absolutes; *Meet Me at the Morgue* (1953), a non-Archer, speaks of "the moral tightrope that everyone has to walk every day." Love or the loving need to protect can incite murder. The more we learn about Ross Macdonald's murderers and the psychic forces battering them, the easier it becomes to forgive, or, at least, understand. "Passion can cut two ways," says Archer in *The Chill* (1964), and in *The Far Side of the Dollar*, he reminds us, "The things you do in a good cause can slip over into bad." Having slipped over into bad, though, they are still morally redeemable. One of the sanest, warmest disclaimers against violence in the canon comes from Ross Macdonald's nastiest character, Sheriff Duane Ostervelt of *The Doomsters* (1958): "I'm a sharpshooter. I still don't like to kill a man. It's too damn easy to wipe one out and too damn hard to grow one." If a parent, long divorced or widowed, clings too tightly to an only child he raised all alone, as in *Find a Victim* (1954) or *Underground Man*, does the parent deserve our scorn? The murderess in *The Doomsters* and the violent father in *The Zebra-Striped Hearse* (1962) are the books' most sympathetic characters. Though not beyond good and evil, they are beyond blame, calling forth, instead, our compassion and understanding. Fittingly, the killer in *The*

Doomsters goes to a hospital at the end, not to jail or the gas chamber.

The artistic expression of this moral sympathy has not always met friendly criticism. Geoffrey Hartman ties his low opinion of *Underground Man* to what he sees as a built-in cramp of the detective genre: "The mystery story has always been a form in which appalling facts are made to fit a rationalistic moral pattern."[5] This pattern, Hartman goes on, drains narrative strength and paralyzes both incident and idea; popular crime novels, including those of Ross Macdonald, solve, rather than study, moral and social problems. Hartman is only partly right. Though Ross Macdonald's faith in the moral will and in the transcendence of reason does not scale the heights Hartman believes, other landmarks of the Archer novels cast harmful shadows. Ross Macdonald can be rightly accused of stretching probability past the breaking point and also of relying upon contrivances to resolve major issues. Examples to support the charge of implausibility come easily: Archer's habit of eavesdropping on conversations that just happen to deal directly with an important aspect of the case he's investigating; an identity-switch involving two women who look alike; the killing of the Most Likely Suspect soon after he rouses suspicion; the obligatory scene near the end where charges are made, evidence is brought forth, and the killer confesses (*The Zebra-Striped Hearse* comes close to having three of these); the missing-persons case where the m. p. is an only child (in *Sleeping Beauty*, she is an only grandchild as well).

These stratagems, or staples, while not fresh, are usually freshly perceived. What is more, they fit well with both Ross Macdonald's use of narrative form and his overall imaginative intent. Though he documents his settings realistically, Ross Macdonald is not a realist. To complain either that life doesn't repeat itself as often or turn in the tight circles as he says is nearly irrelevant. John Skow grouses in *Time* about the implausibility of centering a novel on "a hideous crime committed a generation before, in the presence of a tiny child."[6] This generation-old crime, together with its nearby child, *has* actuated every Archer novel since *The Instant Enemy* (1968). Skow's disclaimer points to another possible lapse: that the repeated use of the same plotting device suggests either carelessness in execution or a dried-up structural imagination. Here he miscues, overlooking both the cultural and the biographical contexts of the novels. Kenneth Millar, earning his undergraduate degree (from the University of Western Ontario) in 1938 and his Ph.D. (from the University of Michigan) in 1951, grew up intellectually in the full flush of the New Criticism; the first edition of Brooks and Warren's *Understanding Poetry*, the seedbed of New Criticism, came out in 1938. Ross Macdonald's plots often profit from the kind of hermetic reading stressed by Brooks and Warren. Rather than attacking the Archer novels, as Skow does, for repetitive plotting, why not look at plot contextually? Art reorders both moral and aesthetic priorities. The plausibility of a child's involvement in an old crime counts less, finally, than how well the involvement serves as a psychological time-bomb, how well it relays the impact of childhood experience, and also how well it shows the ugly process by which crisis reverberates, sometimes tragically, onto the young.

The novels magnify rather than imitate or copy. Highly compressed, they are metaphors for stress. The characters stand larger than life, and the crises that claw them would wreck most of us. According to Ross Macdonald, his novels do not break away from reality so much as give a poetic documentary: "They are related to what goes on in the world, not in factual terms but in imaginative terms. They are halfway between a sociological report and a nightmare."[7] Their working-out of philosophical principles and their poetic symbolism give them a strong intellectual thrust. But they are not modernist in their irony: Ross Macdonald's irony, unlike that of Joyce and Eliot, is not epistemological. Reality is not only given; it also has shape, laws, and meaning. The problem is not how to find it, but how to cope with it. Though living in the twilight of faith, Ross Macdonald's characters believe certain truths worth living and fighting—even, sometimes, worth killing—for. These truths are given in everyday experience. Nor are they described in night language, dream symbolism, or hallucination. Though the novels use the same filial-sexual materials as Joyce in the Circe ("Nighttown") section of *Ulysses,* Ross Macdonald writes objective narratives in straightforward prose. His style obeys the natural controls of conventional syntax and word choice. The inner world of his characters is intelligible. His plots, though full of strange meanings, are continuous. Without trivializing the complex process of causation, the plots transcribe bizarre events accurately.

But, crackling with ingenious twists and turns, they do not develop simply. While their complex symmetry recalls Dickens, it also summons up the eighteenth-century musical mode called the Invention. The Invention fused mathematical precision of design with effortless drive. The fluid formality of the Archer novels, like the best of Mozart and Haydn, rests on stronger undergirding than a Rococo dexterity. A relentless interior logic and a carefully regulated tempo controls the novels. At the same time, the energy building from their robust style, Archer's moral sympathy, and the mood of desperation cast by murder make them human dramas rather than technical diversions. Their strength stems chiefly from their dramatic force—an intensification of existence. Their gyrating plots mesh well with the larger-than-life impressions created by the characters and their crises. The abundance in each book imparts a sense of peopled space, even, in view of the pent-up energies driving the characters on, of overflowing life. The conjuction of Ross Macdonald's plots with the human drives impelling them also dramatizes today's leading concept, in psychology as well as in literature, of the city as maze.

I

Though this city is American and, more sharply, Californian, it has many British landmarks. Aesthetically, historically, and socially, Ross Macdonald belongs in the private-eye tradition of pulp crime fiction; early Archer is as much the hard-boiled dick as Dashiell Hammett's Sam Spade (*The Maltese Falcon*) and Raymond Chandler's Philip Marlowe. Yet both Kenneth Millar's parents were Canadian; Millar lived in Canada from childhood to early manhood; he studied and taught in Canada; he has a Canadian wife; he still speaks in a Scots-Canadian accent.

The vocabulary of the Archer novels alone should have encouraged more than just one critic to note Ross Macdonald's debt to the English detective story.[8] Dining room tables are called refectory tables; a couch, a chesterfield; headlights, fog lamps; a package is a parcel, and french-fried potatoes are potato chips. An American soldier from Missouri in *Trouble Follows Me* (1946) asks "if there's a place I can post [rather than mail] a letter." The adjective, "bloody," and the affectionate, "old boy," are used regularly by native Americans. Archer buys a return, not a round-trip, ticket to Mexico in *The Zebra-Striped Hearse*. In *The Ivory Grin* (1952), he orders a short rye at a Los Angeles bar, and he drinks his beer by the pint or half-pint. These drinking habits befit an Ontarian, not a Californian. The aesthetic distance between all this and the classic English detective story is not far. A Canadian, Kenneth Millar felt as comfortable intellectually with English as with American literature. His first printed work, "The South Sea Soup Co.," in *The Grumbler,* published by the Kitchener-Waterloo Collegiate and Vocational School (1931), burlesques Sherlock Holmes.[9] Though Archer doesn't resemble Holmes any more than California today resembles Victorian England, Ross Macdonald's language and attitudes still send out English echoes.

W. H. Auden believes that mystery novels must take root in closed, harmonious societies: the detective story needs "a closed society so that the possibility of an outsider murder . . . is excluded; and a closely related society so that all its members are potentially suspect." George Grella's formula for the classic British "whodunit" both endorses and extends Auden's working definition:

The typical detective story presents a group of people assembled at an isolated place—usually an English country house—who discover that one of their number has been murdered. They summon the local constabulary, who are completely baffled; they find either no clues or entirely too many, everyone or no one has had the means, motive, and opportunity to commit the crime, and nobody seems to be telling the truth. To the rescue comes an eccentric, intelligent, unofficial investigator who reviews the evidence, questions the suspects, constructs a fabric of proof, and in a dramatic final scene, names the culprit.[10]

The Maze

Jacques Barzun and Wendell Hertig Taylor's belief that domestic crisis, or "household confusion,"[11] undergirds the English detective tradition welds the link between Ross Macdonald and the Sherlock Holmes school. Having lived in fifty different rooms by age sixteen,[12] Ross Macdonald knows that, for a small child, family love is life's best good and the lack of it, life's worst evil. Both his reading and his often-shattered wish-projection of the family as a social and ethical whole drew him to the tale of detection. *The Ivory Grin* deals with a gangster family fighting to survive. Like it, Ross Macdonald's other work adapts the novel of English village life to American social dynamics. Murder in Ross Macdonald is never ideological or crudely mercenary. The killer will come from the same social set, maybe the same family or street, as his victim and the other suspects.

Archer must find the connection between killer and victim(s). Both the openness and the mobility of America today make his job different from that of the English gentleman-sleuth of Dorothy L. Sayers and Margery Allingham. But the difference may be as much technical as generic. Ross Macdonald's characters are linked in many ways; the principle connecting them can be a U. S. Navy ship on which some of them served during World War II; it can be a long-dissolved marriage. Somebody in *Find a Victim*, from the made-up California town of Las Cruces, tells Archer, "In this town everybody's related to everybody else." Although Archer's search for the connecting principle can take him twenty-five years into the past, once he finds it his case virtually solves itself; he says, in *Instant Enemy*, "If you dig deep enough, you can nearly always find the single bifurating root." The steps in the reasoning also hew to the curve of traditional detective fiction. Like E. C. Bentley's *Trent's Last Case* and Agatha Christie's *Witness for the Prosecution*, the novels often tease out a number of clues leading to only one conclusion and then, in the last chapter, knock the props out from under all of them.

Ross Macdonald breaks from the crime puzzle in his handling of clues—the kind of clues he gives Archer to find and their analysis. And since different kinds of clues call for different investigators, the break widens quickly. The crime puzzle is a problem in formal deduction, or logical exercise, in which reason triumphs. R. Austin Freeman called it "an exhibition of mental gymnastics," and Sayers, following suit, said, "In its severest form, the mystery story is a pure analytical exercise." Ross Macdonald, though, claims, "An unstable balance between reason and more primitive human qualities is characteristic of the detective story."[13] This claim is crucial; for as soon as primitive drives enter in, detection loses its rational footing; its faith in reason drops quickly. Next, scientific detection can no longer explain the newly broadened spectrum of criminal motives. The clues in Ross Macdonald existentialize his books in this very way. Like other good detective writers, he distributes suspicion evenly among the suspects; he displays his clues clearly, so that the reader has the same chance as Archer to solve the mystery; he reasons from the clues. But most of these clues do not come from close study of the physical evidence—a bloodstain, smudged footprint, or an overlooked cigar ash: according to the butler's testimony, Inspector, the murdered man was last seen standing by the French doors leading into the library, a cognac in his hand. The chemical analysis of a dried scraping of vomit in *The Goodbye Look* (1969) is Archer's only foray into scientific detection; and, even here, he sends the scraping to a police laboratory rather than analyzing it himself. Usually, he reasons *a priori* from psychological patterns. His clues are based on behavioral rather than material evidence. Any crime occurring during his investigations comes from an earlier one and may cause others later on. What starts as a missing persons case will end as a multiple murder. In order to stop the killing, Archer has to find both its meaning and interior logic. This search for subjective clues and leads takes him into homes and stores, far afield of the laboratories of ballistics or handwriting experts. The sleuth's bloodhound passion for facts has all but vanished. Logical analysis helps Archer less than a generous heart and an imaginative grasp of the moral complexities of daily life.

As Julian Symons points out, moral complexity has no place in the classic crime puzzle:

In a detective story, good people and bad people are clearly defined and do not change (except for the bad person who is pretending to be good). Policemen will not beat up suspects, nor will the criminal's state of mind be considered interesting, since the policemen are on the side of light and the criminal on the side of darkness.[14]

Ross Macdonald rejects this sharply segmented morality. Finding criminal impulses in all, he shortens the moral distance between murderer and victim, even between investigator and suspect; a popular murder-motive in his book is blackmail. Because we are all capable of crime, he extends both charity and moral sympathy to wrongdoers. This tenderness gives him more heart-knowledge than any of his counterparts today—not only in the area of the British detective story but also in that of the hard-boiled private eye, reaching all the way from Hammett to Mickey Spillane.

Seconding Symons, Erik Routley hears the cry for justice in the classic tale of detection as both morally dogmatic and socially reactionary: "They [the tales] rely on the acceptance of assumptions about law and order, about the rights of property . . . and about the propriety of the punishment of wrongdoers."[15] This harshness is softened not only by Archer's charity but also by the killer's helpless entrapment—shown in the need to keep killing. Evil does not win out in Ross Macdonald. The many last-chapter confessions, besides making for artistic symmetry, relax psychic strain. The killers feel relieved, first, to unload their guilt and shame and, next, to stop killing. Despite the greed and violence they describe, the Archer novels often taper to quiet, even peaceful, conclusions. Yet the fast-changing society the novels accept tallies well with the hard-boiled tradition, which is where most readers correctly place them. "Newgate Callendar," reviewer of crime fiction for the New York *Times Book Review*, speaks of "the American private eye, immortalized by Hammett, refined by Chandler, brought to its zenith by Macdonald"; Macdonald puts his work "right in the main stream of the hard-boiled mystery novel."[16]

He drifted to the hard-boiled tradition because the aims and social assumptions of the crime puzzle did not apply to him. One character in *The Dark Tunnel* (1944), his first novel, says, "Melodrama is the norm in 1943"; when Archer is accused of talking the language of melodrama in *The Chill* (1964), he answers, "We live it every day." Ross Macdonald's Foreword to the 1970 omnibus, *Archer at Large,* carries the point further:

When I took up the hardboiled novel, beginning in 1946 with *Blue City,* I was writing in reaction against a number of things, among them my strict academic background. The world of gamblers and gunmen and crooked politicians and their floozies seemed realer somehow, more central to experience, than the cool university life I knew.

The conscious split from the British detective line he summarizes in a 1971 interview: "As a North American, I couldn't very well follow in the footsteps of the British mystery novelists; it is an entirely different tradition, and it doesn't really apply too well to North American experience."[17] As has been suggested, both the fluidity and speed of North America today have corroded our faith in a just, benevolent society where reason reigns and where every wrong can be righted. Our society lacks the stability required for the comedy of manners. Though the reading public, the hard-boiled school, and Ross Macdonald have all changed since 1946, private-eye fiction has always tried to bring crime close to everyday life and language. Its acceptance of corruption and violence as norms of daily life keeps pace with the jarring rhythms of social change, creates important gradations of moral freedom, and conveys the complexity of cities. As Raymond Chandler said, in his notorious send-up of the "Cheesecake Manor" school of detective writing, murder can explain a great deal about the living as soon as it stops being an intellectual frivolity.

Chandler has also discussed the rise of the hard, cynical detective, who first saw life in the *Black Mask* magazine in the 1920s. As we might expect, the need for a new fictional detective rose from changes in narrative technique. *Black Mask* fiction was both scenic in design and quickly paced in action; no introspection clogged its breakneck narrative drive. Even the solution of the crime counted less than the speedy flow of action-filled scenes. Each scene, in fact, *was* a climax: "The technical basis of the *Black Mask* type of story," Chandler writes, "was that the scene outranked the plot, in the sense that a good plot was one which made good scenes. The ideal mystery was one you would read if the end was missing." This discrediting of the *denouement* changed both the personality and values of the detective hero. He became a man who kept the action hot: he moved quickly and decisively; he accepted brutality so cheerfully that he sometimes blurred the moral distinction between himself and gangsters; he fought more readily with fists or revolvers than his British counterpart.

No reasoning machine, Archer risks danger, even death, at least once in every book. He is often knocked out; he has had teeth broken; bullet wounds have sent him to the hospital. George Grella traces the lonely, battered private dick back to the masculine frontier virtues of James Fenimore Cooper's Leatherstocking:

Living in a lawless world, the private eye, like the frontier hero, requires physical rather than intellectual ability. . . . Philip Marlowe and Lew Archer occasionally shoot and brawl, but more often absorb alarming physical punishment, being variously slugged, beaten, and battered by criminals and police, invariably recovering to continue their investigation. They display the stoic resistance to physical suffering which typifies Leatherstocking. Their insults and wisecracks are the badge of their courage; refusing to show pain or fear, they answer punishment with flippancy.[19]

Grella's summary, while compassing *Black Mask* aesthetics, only explains Archer through 1952 and *Ivory Grin*. As has been pointed out, his more recent cases call more upon female graces like imagination and sympathy than upon crude masculine endurance. Accompanying the fading image of the tough, lonely outsider has been the emergence of women: Ross Macdonald is one of America's few male novelists, let alone male crime writers, who use women as major characters. What interests him more than the hardiness of the Leatherstocking hero is the egalitarianism stretching from the eighteenth century to our day. The carrier of this tradition is spoken language. "Democracy is as much a language as it is a place,"[20] said Ross Macdonald in 1966. Archer's terse, middle-register speaking style confirms his freedom and equality. He communicates easily with witnesses, understanding them and being understood in turn. His street language subsumes both tower and gutter; down-and-outers and college deans come within his linguistic purview. A man who starts out knowing nothing and who knows only what people tell him, he has mastered, in his clear, straightforward speech, the basic working principle of his trade.

And so has his creator. Both the form and the build of a detective novel depend on the give-and-take of dialogue, the checking and rechecking of witnesses' stories, and the exchange of information among investigators. Thus Ross Macdonald writes in an oral, rather than in a literary, register. Fiction, he claims, should be written "more or less" in the rhythms and vocabulary of spoken language:

Hammett and Stephen Crane taught me the modern American style based on the speaking voice. Most modern prose is based on the spoken language. A writer has to learn to listen to the sound of his own voice and other people's voices.[21]

This attention to the speaking voice, while interweaving neatly with the aesthetics of detection, invites comparison with the theater. Ross Macdonald's early ambition to write plays and his admiration for Ibsen and Strindberg explain in part the sharp similarities between his work and the nineteenth-century French stage, the moving force behind modern Scandinavian drama. Like the tight plays of Scribe and, more notably, Sardou, the Archer novels balance literary and social values. The action of both a well-made play and an Archer describes the culmination of an ongoing event. Techniques of the "drama of ripe condition" surviving in Ibsen's *Hedda Gabler* and *John Gabriel Borkman* find their parallel in Archer's practice of entering a twenty-year-old action two days before its end. Intensity comes from the revelation of prior relationships and from the struggle between generations. The swing between moments of high and low fortune creates an emotional rhythm while keeping the solution hidden. Other similarities stand out just as sharply: topicality, if only a concern with money and social rank; an avoidance of philosophical imponderables; a self-contained logic monitoring an elaborate plot; the twin discovery at the end of the wrongdoer and an old family secret.[22]

But the finales of Archer's cases, if rationally satisfying, do not always relax the stridency of what precedes. You don't come away from a Ross Macdonald novel with the sense of having been dazzled by a literary showman. Though evil may have been routed, it has claimed victims, including the evildoer. The bright, pleasing snap with which all the parts of a mechanical revel click into place never comes. Certainly, Archer doesn't feel refreshed or purged. John Paterson's 1953 description of the private investigator's feelings after closing a case applies vividly to the sad, drained bewilderment overhanging Archer at the end of several novels:

What exactly he has gained . . . is not immediately apparent. Certainly it is neither the certitude of victory nor the rapture of victory. Returned to his desk . . . he is in fact a bleak, lonely, and unhappy figure, without home, without love, without community, conscious perhaps that his victory is far from final and that it may have cost him far too much.[23]

The search for literary influences on Ross Macdonald continues to give exciting results. Archer's solving a twenty-year-old mystery, while making him both a catalyst and historian, gives the books a causal structure. Jon Carroll has written in *Esquire,* "Macdonald writes of the forgotten past and how it envelops the present, of moral equilibriums and how they are inevitably maintained."[24] Moral inevitability shows most clearly in life's power to regulate itself. The laws that govern human life, Archer explains in *Instant Enemy,* are intrinsic, not imposed: "There is a kind of economy in life. You don't spend more than you have, or say more than you know, or throw your weight around more than necessary." Life's knowability, though, does not soften its harshness. When the moral equilibrium goes agley, crisis must follow. Crisis comes from the refusal to accept the meaning of what has happened. The economy of life decrees that the future unfolds from the past. Life has no stray threads; sooner or later everything must be accounted for.

Crisis is also the structural linchpin of the novels. Archer says in *Far Side of the Dollar,* "Life hangs together in one piece. Everything is connected with everything else. The problem is to find the connection." Events buried safely for a generation spring to life when he digs in the right places. (The Lazarus motif has infiltrated the later works.) As with Eliot's corpse in the garden in *The Waste Land,* dead bodies in Ross Macdonald are planted rather than buried. The bloodhound sleuth plays the scratching dog, and the corpses sprout. Two unsolved crimes from the past, fifteen and twenty-four years old, surface in *Goodbye Look*; in *Underground Man* a corpse is literally dug out of the earth.

The passions fermenting crisis are often simple and predictable, even obvious. This straightforwardness serves Ross Macdonald well. First, it suits his complex plots. As Chesterton reminds us, in his famous remark about hiding a leaf in a tree, simplicity makes for good detection: the direct explanation works best in crime-solving. Also, the build generated by the causal structure takes on some of the inevitability of tragedy. Narrative continuity becomes clear, swift, and relentless; motives reveal cutting edges. Jilted women, we realize suddenly, do kill out of sexual revenge; rich people, having gotten rich deviously, become blackmail victims, then kill their blackmailers; children kick out against overprotective parents. Because of the close human ties that knit the books, criminal motives often lie deceptively close by. Crime belongs to ordinary people in Ross Macdonald, not to the mob or the spy-ring. Life at its most commonplace can unleash terror. The key to the killings in *Meet Me at the Morgue* turns up in a small rundown neighborhood market owned by the killer's father in San Diego; a humble, remote wooden bungalow contains the riddle underlying *The Ferguson Affair* (1960). Murder stirs the social melting pot, as well. Not only does it ignore social distinctions; it sometimes makes nonsense of them. Rich, morally upright characters, like Colonel Mark Blackwell in *Zebra-Striped Hearse,* Lawrence Chalmers in *Goodbye Look,* and Captain Ben Somerville in *Sleeping Beauty,* emerge as frauds and come to grief, while shadowy, deprived ones show great courage: "Nowadays the low-life subplots were taking over the tragedies," observes Archer in *Underground Man.* The force behind the tainted money in *Black Money* (1966) and the novel's arch-villain is a helpless physical wreck. "You see what I've got on my hands?" says his nurse. "A poor little sick old man. He can't walk, he can't talk, he can't even write his name." Archer says of the killer in *The Barbarous Coast* (1956),

"It wasn't an unusual face. It was quite ordinary. . . . Not the kind of face people think of as evil." The killer of four in *Chill* appears as "just an old lady in dirty tennis shoes" when she first meets Archer. People are not what they appear to be. Ross Macdonald's shrewd use of the seem-be dualism, borne out by these examples, shows how crime often works in a democratic society.

The force with which crime overtakes human life in the novels is relentless. Crime infects whole families, can stain three generations, and cover a spread of miles, as in *Instant Enemy*, where it reaches from California to London. In *Underground Man* and *Sleeping Beauty,* the crimes destroy nature. But Ross Macdonald is not the first detective writer to infuse his work with tragic bite. Chandler's famous essay, "The Simple Art of Murder," calls the detective novel a tragedy with a happy ending. Ross Macdonald modifies the definition. The mandatory scene in which the killer is named, the evil overcome, and social equilibrium restored gives no catharsis. Many have suffered; the suffering brightens nobody's outlook; if Archer has learned anything, he keeps it to himself. The tragic effects Ross Macdonald aims for are darker and deeper than those found in Chandler.

These effects, though, help create the fluid narrative tempo of the novels. Now whereas character prevails in comedy, in tragedy it gives way to passion and violence. The individual has little standing in tragedy, where all rolls to a supreme crisis. Somebody in *Black Money* says, "It's dangerous to get what you want, you know. It sets you up for tragedy." Though many of Archer's clients are rich, they come to him in great need. The crises they face exclude accident and chance and also shear away moral gradations. People driven to the edge clutch at simplified, extremist moralities. Though they have created their predicaments, the predicaments overwhelm them. Relationships become collisions, and personality hardens into a knot of desperate motives. The causal structure of the plots conveys this tragic necessity. Archer plays the catalyst: once he sets the complex mechanism of needs and relationships going, not even he can stop it. Having run its course, the mechanism unearths well-kept family secrets and accumulated guilt. But there is nothing mechanical in Archer's reaction. The killers in both *Doomsters* and *Far Side of the Dollar* are the books' most sympathetic, because most deeply shaken, characters. When Archer discovers the sheriff in *Find a Victim* to be shielding a killer, his wife, he tells him, "I'd have done the same."

But if the refusal to give moral instruction sounds a tragic chord, that chord is minor. For Archer's *ex parte* role makes him more of a *deus ex machina* than a principal. Though his moral sympathy helps the later Archer cope with banality and grime, his accommodation is not tragic. He doesn't suffer enough and, by withholding both moral and emotional response, doesn't share any heightened perception with us (the hero's "tragic farewell"). Moreover, any literary form leaning as heavily as detective fiction does on dialogue comes under the aegis of social comedy. Thus Ross Macdonald excels in the skills that count most in social comedy—quicksilver dialogue, trim, inclusive plotting, and the creation of characters who need no reintroducing. The people and their problems range along the arc of comedy. Though Ross Macdonald looks deeply into character, he does not give many-sided pictures; the crimes energizing the plots call for a sharpening rather than a development of character. Character pre-exists Archer; instead of developing or changing, it struggles to survive. Variety comes from the range of character-types; each figure in a novel differs from all the others in age, job, and social-level. The parent who interferes with his child's love life, as in *Zebra-Striped Hearse* and *Black Money,* is a staple of *commedia dell 'arte.* The dreamer who lives his dream, from Don Quixote to Thurber's Walter Mitty (one character in *Black Money* takes the name, Cervantes), is another stock figure of comedy, even if the comedy darkens, as with Malvolio in *Twelfth Night.*

Does all this make Ross Macdonald a comedian? Or does he still merit the mantle of tragedian? How easily does he shift his weight between the classic English detective story and the hard-boiled novel? These questions, though provocative, ignore his formal training, craftsmanship, and his ability, first, to select from different genres and, next, to use what he selects well. Any artist must be judged on how imaginatively he perceives and then arranges his material. Our discussion of literary strains helps show the strength and scope of Ross Macdonald's art. That various elements serve, rather than fight, each other in a novel bespeaks solid narrative construction. It also mirrors the pluralism of American life today.

II

Detective fiction can only take root in a democratic society. The reason? The democratization of authority—i.e., the fluid interchange between authority and ordinary citizens—is its central nerve. The ordinary citizen has more freedom and, thus, more responsibility in an open than in a traditional society. The law assumes one person to be as self-acting as his neighbor; in democratic societies, the same laws govern everybody, and the courts apply the same criteria to all witnesses and suspects. Archer's social mobility, an offshoot of democracy, lets him question people from all social levels. Like any other good detective, he does not erase social difference so much as refuse to let it influence him. But Ross Macdonald carries his democratic principles a step further. His books don't come alive until working-class characters step into them. The blue-collar class is a source of energy to him; society, as in Chekhov, gets its strength from the lower levels.

The Maze

If the detective and the detective writer both flourish in democracies, so does the criminal. Only in a society which prizes individual freedom can a person muster the freedom of the adventurer. Yankee independence has always scorned official restraints; in the U. S. people may protest, hold unpopular opinions, even bear arms. The frontiersman, now a figure of legendary heroism, got his stake of land through fighting and killing, and he held on to it in the same wild way.

The moral condition of Ross Macdonald's novels, reaching from the frontier tradition, is both lawless and godless. The intricate causality of the novels points to a God-governed (perhaps Deist) universe; the high degree of completion and necessity galvanizing the plots invites a non-secular cause. But the demythologizing of good and evil and our century's legacy of rugged individualism bar the characters from God-consciousness. (The religious people in the novels, fiercely puritanical, are mad, self-righteous fanatics.) Hostility has replaced both thought and prayer as moral guides. Somebody who has been damaged will damage in turn instead of trying to understand or forgive.

Kenneth Millar's first-hand experience with violence stems from his provincial Canadian background and from his having been formed by war. Born in 1915, he attained consciousness in World War I and manhood in World War II, when he served as a U. S. Naval officer in the Pacific. A province of Great Britain, between-wars Canada stood stranded many miles from its cultural center. Raw provincial societies, like those of Alberta, Manitoba, and Ontario, where Millar lived as a boy, lent themselves to violence because they lacked indwelling civilized controls. The burden of starting anew and the traditional Canadian fear of looking backward and crude to outsiders often curdled to self-contempt. Culturally starved outposts, where life counts less than the scramble for goods, also promote crime, a situation worsened by the absence of unwritten social codes. For those sane enough to resist crime, humor and horror become the two stock moral responses in primitive societies. Poe and Melville recorded the horror of living without art, literature, or morality. Twain and Faulkner used humor to make sense of their rough, raw societies; in Faulkner the humor is wild. The novels of the Ontarian, Morley Callaghan, describe psychological horror and dislocation.

The *Time-Life* shooting script, *Ross Macdonald "In the First Person"* (1970), mentions "the intense . . . numbing, blinding, and terrifying pain that life can give you" and also "the atmosphere of violence that everyone in this century has been brought up in." In a 1972 interview-essay for *Esquire*, appropriately called "Ross Macdonald in Raw California," the novelist says, "Archer, I think, is not a hero in the traditional sense; he doesn't rush in there and save the values." There are no values *to* save; North America has not yet carved out a value system:

The essential problem . . . is how you are going to maintain values, and express values in your actions, when the values aren't there in the society around you, as they are in traditional societies. In a sense, you have to make yourself up as you go along.[25]

Ross Macdonald depicts a society-in-the-making, shows how it works, and then criticizes it. Much of southern California was a desert outpost within Archer's memory. A real-estate agent in *The Way Some People Die* (1951) says his housing development is "not exactly a place yet, but it will be." When Archer says it looks like a ghost town, he is corrected, "It's the opposite of a ghost town, a town waiting to be born." His moral world is convulsed because the morality of an uncreated society rests on force. Southern California is merely an aggregate of people. Though brimming with energy and striving, it lives by jungle ethics. Its aristocracy, which may go back three or four generations, is sleazy. Its inhabitants have not built up the civilized reserves to act with taste, charm, or decorum. Male and female principles do not balance. Women have no soothing creative influence on their men; they suppress their sons. As nurses and social workers, they usually give Archer trouble; the killer, in fact, is often female. (If the cover-up murder from *Macbeth* supplies Ross Macdonald's favorite criminal motive, Lady Macbeth, rather than Portia of *Julius Caesar*, provides his model of the matron.)

Because Ross Macdonald's California—his metaphor for North America—falls so systematically short of Kenneth Clark's idea of a civilization, the sociology of the Archer novels sharpens when gauged by Clark's standard in *Civilization*: "Civilization means something more than energy and will and creative power. . . . How can I define it? Well, very shortly, a sense of permanence." This permanence, Clark continues, is spiritual, though usually not religious: "It requires confidence—confidence in the society in which one lives, belief in its philosophy, belief in its laws, and confidence in one's own mental powers."[26] The roots and reserves Clark alludes to also come from public faith in the non-violent solution of problems. In this area North America scores low. The harmonious, mutually bracing interplay of man and man, and also of man and natural setting, clashes with the frontier ethic of taming nature. Ross Macdonald's sociological nightmares describe the pitfalls of new world energy. His characters don't understand freedom because they don't respect the freedom of others. Their freebooting individualism, a romantic perversion of the Protestant spirit, overrides secular, scriptural, and moral law. I feel, therefore, I am, is their guiding principle. What they feel most keenly, in Ross Macdonald's best work, is the loss of security; insecurity charges the novels with crisis. Characters deny the reality of both facts and persons; they twist, suppress, even kill. Violence becomes the natural outlet for insecurity; when force is the only social control, chaos, isolation, and despair follow soon after.

The Maze

Moral and spiritual hunger surge through the trim, tight plots. Even Archer must create himself without help. He has no home-port, family, or, being self-employed, financial security to screen him from the void. In *Sleeping Beauty,* he has just enough money to pay his monthly rent. Logically enough, many of the corpses he discovers turn up in either cars or motels. The shifts and upheavals of our time make the car and the motor-court perfect symbols of rootlessness. Rootlessness and violence define a society that strives to create itself through high-velocity action rather than through thought.

Detective fiction has often pinned this speed and violence to the city. In 1901 Chesterton termed detective fiction an urban literary form, "a rude, popular literature of the romantic possibilities of the modern city." Echoing Chesterton in 1972, George V. Higgins, perhaps the best of America's new crime writers, declared the city both headquarters and hunting-ground for the private detective: "The P. I. is invariably an urban character; the only time you will find him in the woods is when he goes from the City, into the woods, to chase somebody else who has escaped from the City."[27] Ross Macdonald feels the force of this urban tradition: "I think Baudelaire's vision of Paris as [urban] Inferno has followed through in the detective story. You have London as Inferno in Sherlock Holmes, for instance. As T. S. Eliot pointed out, *The Waste Land* drew in part on Conan Doyle's London." But he doesn't detach the unreal, infernal city from the surrounding wilderness. The evil centered in Detroit in *The Dark Tunnel* spreads to Kirkland Lake in northern Ontario; the forest fire unifies the action of *Underground Man* so well because its blasts menace city-dwellers and suburbanites. The unpeopled wilderness of nature tallies in all Ross Macdonald's work with the moral wilderness of the city: "Here in California, what you've got is an instant megalopolis superimposed on a background which could almost be described as raw nature. What we've got is the twentieth century right up against the primitive."[28]

The primitive and the urban collide in Hollywood. In his Foreword to the 1967 omnibus, *Archer in Hollywood,* Ross Macdonald calls Hollywood "our national capital": "It's the place where our children learn how and what to dream,"[29] the nerve center of America's romantic fantasies. If California is the land of wild hopes and smashed dreams, Hollywood choreographs and bloats them to widescreen size. "Find the Woman," a 1946 short story collected in *The Name is Archer* (1955), calls Hollywood "the world's most competitive city." A year or two there can rocket a person from poverty to wealth and then to decadence. Hollywood's continuity with the American experience, especially with the American dream, keeps it from being an urban inferno in the Baudelairean sense; now that mass media have made celluloid emotion public property, Hollywood encourages the same illusions and generates the same nervous strain as other American cities. The film industry merely speeds the pace of life and makes setbacks crueller. *The Barbarous Coast,* one of the works included in *Archer in Hollywood,* describes Hollywood as a diversion turned nightmare:

Hollywood started out as a meaningless dream, invented for money. But its colors ran out through the holes in people's heads, spread across the landscape and solidified. North and south along the coast, east across the desert, across the continent. Now we were stuck with the dream without a meaning. It had become the nightmare that we lived in.

The trivializing of meaning into sensation shows vividly in the living room of a screen actor in the same book. The room contains no human associations or aids, nothing to strengthen our imaginative hold on life. Though tidy and well-stocked, this gleaming product of our instant culture exudes an unreality matching that of its occupant's meteoric career:

The living-room was almost as impersonal as a hotel room. Even the pipes on the mantel had been bought by the set, and only one of them had ever been smoked. The tobacco in the jar was bone dry. There was nothing but tobacco in the jar, nothing but wood in the woodbox. The portable bar in the corner was well stocked with bottles, most of which were unopened.

Unreality wins out and mechanical values drive out human ones when shadow and substance trade places. Archer feels unreal walking through a film set in *The Moving Target* (1949):

I turned right and passed London Street and Pioneer Log Cabin, then left in front of Continental Hotel. The false fronts looked so real from a distance, so ugly and thin close up, that they made me feel suspicious of my own reality.

A Hollywood film writer in *Barbarous Coast* has lost not only his artistic vocation but also his identity. The owner of the Malibu pool club where Archer meets him also owns a nearby sanitarium; as might be expected, his guests have worn a path between the two places.

The unreality and violence that create the need for sanitaria flow inevitably from unbridled change. In *Existence: A New Dimension in Psychiatry and Psychology* (1958), which Ross Macdonald reviewed for the San Francisco *Chronicle,* Rollo May yokes the crisis of existential choice to change:

When a culture is caught in the profound convulsions of a transitional period, the individuals in the society understandably suffer spiritual and emotional upheaval; and finding that the accepted mores and ways of thought no longer yield security, they tend either to sink into dogmatism and conformism, giving up awareness, or are forced to strive for a heightened self-consciousness by which to become aware of their existence with new convictions and on new bases.[30]

Violence, unreality, and May's heightened self-consciousness all bring on

crisis in Ross Macdonald. The denial of the past and its meanings bring
on delusions that corrode and finally overtake daily experience. These
delusions, or dreams, bypassing the censors and inhibitions of waking life,
have little empirical content. Defenses against terror, they usually start
with panic: Lawrence "Sonny" Chalmers is pushed into a swimming pool
twenty-five years before the events of *Goodbye Look*; then he fantasizes
himself a naval officer to fight off the terror of drowning.

Dreams, says Freud, move away from the objective world because of
their unreason, incoherence, and anti-social impulses. Ignoring the restraints of daytime thinking gives the dreamer what reality denies him;
dreams fulfill his secret wishes. (Chapter III of *The Interpretation of
Dreams* has the title, "A Dream Is the Fulfillment of a Wish.") Dreams
also strengthen and comfort, warding off emptiness, self-rejection, and
non-belonging. Goals are reached more easily in dreams than in waking
life. The anarchy of the American frontier relates the outlaw-fantasists in
Ross Macdonald to the classic Freudian view of the dreamer's imagination:

> Dreams are disconnected, they accept the most violent contradictions without the
> least objection, they admit impossibilities, they disregard knowledge which carries
> great weight with us in the daytime, they reveal us as ethical and moral imbeciles.
> Anyone who when he was awake behaved in the sort of way that is shown in situations
> in dreams would be considered insane. Anyone who when he was awake talked in the
> sort of way that people talk in dreams . . . would give us the impression of being
> muddle-headed or feeble-minded.[31]

Dreams in the Archer novels lack the elaborate symbolism, transference,
and reversal found in Freud; no dreams occur within dreams. The tie-in
with the American dream comes with the denial of those taboos that align
our anti-social impulses with what Freud calls "the reality principle." No
mere private person, the dreamer is the arch-individualist in a society
which fosters individual freedom. To take what one wants and then to
defend it with arms, regardless of community ethics, affirms Yankee self-
reliance.

But, predictably, the acute individualism of the dream harms everyone in its orbit. In conversation, Ross Macdonald gave the present writer
the following example of the refusal to deal consciously, if not rationally,
with crisis: A man who lost his leg in combat insisted that the war was
never fought and that he never lost his leg; this man would constantly fall
and blame others for tripping him. Again, Freud explains the harm the
one-legged man does by punishing the people allegedly tripping him. The
rechannelling tool of sublimation, by fending off the dangers of repression,
aids both the community and the individual. But the cooling breezes sent
out by restraint to calm the blood in Freud vanish in the glare of private
fantasy in Ross Macdonald. The dreamer has despotic contempt both for
social organization and private conscience. Thus the dreamlike will to

power is neither transcendent nor joyful. A wise daughter in *Doomsters* tells her mother, "Have sweet dreams. Or no dreams. I wish you no dreams at all."

The dreamer twists and paralyzes reality, becoming reality's enemy. Freud's ego-ridden, childish dreamer and Ross Macdonald's self-deceiving fantasist both defeat themselves. No Hegelian hero struggling against an unjust law, the dreamer in Ross Macdonald clings to the creeds of getting, spending, and self-aggrandizing. He is slavishly conventional. Freud calls dreaming "an example of the regression to the dreamer's earliest condition, a revival of his childhood."[32] Awed by Hollywood's celluloid-and-tinsel distortions of self-reliance, Ross Macdonald's dreamer yearns for the banal. Competitive, commercial societies equate money with happiness; the happy man is the rich man. Thus the pedestrian dream of fast, easy money with which to pamper the self runs through the novels. Archer tells a mercenary character in *Moving Target*, "I think you dream a great deal. . . . I think you've been dreaming about a hundred thousand dollars." And just as dreams safeguard, rather than break, sleep according to Freud, so does the dreamer in Ross Macdonald sink ever-deeper into his criminal dream. A second or third murder-victim, mere logistical necessities, bring no remorse. The hard, messy work needed to keep a dream going has to damage more than the dreamer. His act of living his dream denies the reality of persons. The dreamer knows the high cost of his dream—the truths he must suppress, the questions he must ignore, the lies he must believe. Anybody who has sacrificed himself this totally will sacrifice others without scruple. But he cannot keep it up. Sooner or later, the moral equilibrium will be restored. The meanings of the past will surface and engulf him along with his dream. If satire ridicules wasted effort, then this wreckage, bred by frontier ethics and shaped by the distorting lens of Hollywood, counts as some of the darkest, most detailed satire of our day.

No killer in Ross Macdonald kills just once. Because we all live backward and forward at the same time, other people must live and die a dreamer's dreams; a truth springing inconveniently from the past may need a quick death. This pattern of repetition objectifies a death wish, since any criminal's chance of getting caught and then punished rises in direct ratio to the number of crimes he commits. In Freud the id, or raw instinct, leads to death if unharnessed. Thus the multiple murder, while serving as the butt of Ross Macdonald's dark satire, bears out the Freudian view of repetition as a longing for an earlier, simpler stage of life; even, to trace the connection to its source, as a reversion to inorganic life, where the inert and the inanimate blot out consciousness. Archer's view of the murderer in *Zebra-Striped Hearse* as a desperate dreamer, with its clinching metaphor from *The Waste Land*, conveys the unreason, the cancerous spread, and the punishing recoil of the dream:

The Maze

I was thinking that you could never tell what murderers would do. Most of them were acting out a fantasy which they couldn't explain themselves: destroying an un-lamented past which seemed to bar them from the brave new world, erasing the fear of death by inflicting death, or burying an old malignant grief where it would sprout and multiply and end by destroying the destroyer.

III

Statements made by Ross Macdonald at different times in his writing career make clear the strong autobiographical thrust of his work. That he writes from personal experience he admits cheerfully. His work he views as a progressive self-unfolding which neither disguises nor hides "the perilous stuff" of his past: "If one studies my books, he'll find innumera-ble traces of my life running through them. Most of my books do have to do with a broken family and a lost father."[33] Without his "dual citizen's sense of illegitimacy," his father's leaving his mother when Kenneth Millar was only three, and the "Presbyterian gloom"[34] overhanging the house-hold where he was raised, he would not have written novels. Writing fiction for Ross Macdonald combines motives of self-unburdening and self-discovery. The translation of his troubled childhood into art constitutes the classic Freudian acting-out of smothered needs; it is what Mann did in *Buddenbrooks* and what Lawrence did in *Sons and Lovers*. In 1966 and again in 1972, Ross Macdonald asked to be read autobiographically:

We writers, as we work our way deeper into our craft, learn to drop more and more personal clues. Like burglars who secretly wish to be caught, we leave our fingerprints on the broken locks, our voiceprints in the bugged rooms, our footprints in the wet concrete and the blowing sand.

*   *   *   *   *

What makes the verbal artist is some kind of shock or crippling injury which puts the world at one remove from him, so that he writes about it to take possession of it. . . . We start out thinking we're writing about other people and end up realizing we're writing about ourselves.[35]

But what snaps the family? What drives the father out? And why does the fatherless boy feel homeless and unworthy? How does art help him relate to a world where he feels disinherited? Some answers to these questions lie in the Oedipus myth. Ross Macdonald's belief that crime fiction can include psychology fuels his attack on A. E. Murch's *The Development of the Detective Novel* (1959): Mrs. Murch's "escapist" opinion that "criminal psychology" has no place in crime fiction denies any link between detection and "the realities of modern life."[36] Literary detection and psychology can work hand in glove. But the interplay must be covert. Psychology in Ross Macdonald, criminal or otherwise, does not reach us as applied doctrine. Unless the artist's imagination drama-tizes the doctrine, he cannot make the doctrine live. Ross Macdonald uses

Freud as an idea-bank. Much of the theory he bypasses as artistically un-
usable, unsuitable, or irrelevant. What he keeps he varies, even reverses,
depending on his needs. Freud's influence, though strong, is implicit and
absorbed. The novels do not read like psychoanalytic case studies, and
Ross Macdonald does not explore character with the cold eye of the
analyst. The hard purity of the doctrine is warmed and reshaped by the
artist's imagination, moral charity, and sensitivity to the technical demands of his art.

Freud explains, for example, a good deal about Archer's method of
detection. Empiricists both, Freud and Lew Archer start by accepting
the given. They observe details first-hand, collect them, and then arrange
them to find their meaning and interrelation. Both detective and analyst
have to gather the facts before they can study them. If a theory clashes
with an ascertained fact or a good lead, then the theory is thrown out. As
with Freud's logic of repression, crimes fall into patterns for Archer: there
are no accidents or leftover bits of evidence. All forms a causal sequence:
The detective's job is to ferret out the first cause in the sequence. For this
job, he must use both the epistemology and technique of Freudian analysis.

Surprisingly, Ross Macdonald bypasses the basic Freudian drama—
the sexual rivalry of father and son. The received doctrine distributes
Oedipal crisis over several stages: the young boy's conceding victory to
the father in their battle for the mother's love; the fear that the boy will
be castrated by the father for desiring the mother; generalized fear of
authority; the growth of a conscience, which subdues the pleasure principle. This scheme is too strictly formalized for a novel. The Oedipal wish
to kill the father need not lead straight to the possession of the mother.
The desired goal can be fame, riches, or simply freedom from authority,
which is often female in Ross Macdonald. The killing of the parent, i.e.,
the primal murder, can occur symbolically. Self-liberation need not
include a parent at all, so long as the prodigal's breaking-away aims at self-
assertion and the will to live. The father or father-surrogate's role is just
as open. He can be dethroned, devitalized, or simply denied, without
being killed. *Chill* leaves him out altogether. Roy Bradshaw's marriage to
a much-older woman lets Bradshaw rule as the father without having to
supplant anybody.

The notebook for *The Galton Case* (1959) contains this entry:
"Oedipus angry vs. parents for sending him away into a foreign country."
In both its Freudian and Sophoclean aspects, the Oedipus myth has re-
mained Ross Macdonald's favorite.[37] Certain likenesses between the myth
and the Archer novels come to mind straightaway. Both Sophocles and
Ross Macdonald show good, well-meaning characters coming to grief. (All
Ross Macdonald's killers have their good side.) Both writers build their
works around the discovery of a family crisis that took place many years

before. Neither slackens dramatic tempo or suspense by putting his main action in the past. Retribution may be delayed but not avoided; a net of past evil converges on and then traps the culprit. Like Oedipus, the killer in Ross Macdonald pursues his Nemesis and does himself in by performing self-defeating acts. Though fate in an Archer is not malevolent, giving the killer worse than he deserves, time brings about both justice and retribution. The sequence of the scenes, the logical coherence of the relationships, and the psychological inevitability of the finale all argue a structural control that deserves the term, classical.

A powerful legacy from Sophocles is recurrence: Oedipus is exiled from Thebes as a boy and then, at the end of the play, as a middle-aged man. Stanley Broadhurst and his father Leo (Leo-Laius?) are killed by the same woman in *Underground Man* and then buried on the same hill. Recurrence has permeated, perhaps even obsessed, the western spirit. Freud, we have seen, calling it repetition compulsion, links it to childhood regression and, ultimately, to the death wish; Archer is speaking pure Freud in *Sleeping Beauty* (Chapter 8) when he says that stress makes adults revert to childish patterns. Repetition, or recurrence, also afflicts the weak, the sad, and the unlucky in Dante and Nietzsche. (Sophocles, Dante, Nietzsche, and Freud are all mentioned in the Ross Macdonald canon.) A closed circle of changeless pain describes Dante's Hell, where the racked souls, like Paolo and Francesca, must re-enact eternally the crime that damned them. Nietzsche's doctrine of eternal recurrence has the same sting; the knowledge that they cannot escape misery poisons the future for those lacking the will to power. Ross Macdonald leans heaviest on the recurrence-repetition motif in an early novel, *The Three Roads* (1948). The novel's epigraph comes from *Oedipus Rex*, and the title refers to the intersection of the three roads in Phocis where Oedipus killed his father, Laius, and where the past joins with the future. Like his titanic predecessors, Ross Macdonald uses repetition to signal hopelessness: Bret Taylor and his father both have unfaithful wives. The interchangeability in Bret's mind of the three important women in his life—his mother, his dead wife, and a mistress he is about to marry at the end—augurs badly. He needs to snap this destructive pattern. Trapped in a behavioral cycle, he stands little chance of a happy marriage.

The Oedipus myth takes Ross Macdonald to first principles. It also makes us choke down our bile and take a hard look at ourselves. His belief in the inescapability of the past has led him to seat his characters in the family. The family, even if it compasses only two generations, gives him access to one of the few surviving pasts in the instant society of California. This continuity generates force. The family is the greatest single influence on character in his fiction. People never outgrow or flee the family. They exist either as parents or as children of parents; in the last few novels, the parent, rather than the child, plays the truant who is missed and sought by his forgiving children. In all cases, the family ignites action; loss of the family brings emptiness; family crises bring madness. The family allows Ross Macdonald both to explore and connect character at a deeply felt level. The rhythm generated between the persistence and the breakdown of the family sounds responsive chords in all.

The prodigal is a stock figure in Ross Macdonald. But whereas parents usually hire Archer to find their missing children, the father-searchers in *Goodbye Look* and *Sleeping Beauty* work alone. A young husband in *Underground Man* sacrificing both job and family, advertises in newspapers and keeps up an extensive index-file, to look for a long-lost father. A wife of forty in *Goodbye Look* also neglects her home to search for a father she hasn't seen since childhood. The eroticism and guilt informing her search both stab out of her description of her mission-like quest:

"I'm going to find my Daddy," she said. "I'll find him dead or alive. If he's alive I'll cook and keep house for him. And I'll be happier than I ever was in my born days. If he's dead I'll find his grave and do you know what I'll do then? I'll crawl in with him and go to sleep."

The father-quests of this woman and of the young husband in *Underground Man* both end in death; ironically, both questers die pursuing men long dead. Others have better luck: Larry Seifel in *Meet Me at the Morgue* is haunted by a lost father and smothered by a strong mother. Discovery of the father not only frees Seifel from his mother but also improves his professional ethics and gives him the self-acceptance to marry.

Characters with fathers close at hand, i.e., those to whom the father-search does not apply, will defy their fathers. The absent parent is only loved because of his absence. The steady, stay-at-home father is smirched and ignored. This defiance expresses household conflict. Ross Macdonald does not fix his characters supernaturally; nor does the father-image lead regularly to the growth of a social or moral conscience. Little intimacy or affection nourishes either the father-son or man-God relationship. Fathers will use sons to beat back guilt and the fear of personal failure. Sons will rebel. Notwithstanding their protests, rebellion touches them deeply. Freud's preface to the second (i.e., the 1908) edition of *The Interpretation of Dreams* calls the death of a father "the most important event, the most poignant loss, of a man's life."[38] Ross Macdonald records this jolt. A dormitory supervisor in a boarding school in *Far Side of the Dollar* tells Archer, "I'm the authority figure . . . and when I'm attacked it's just like killing their father." When the runaway student in the novel learns that his mother's husband is not his natural father, it becomes hard to know what motivates him more—the father-search he embarks on straightaway or the gleeful denial of the adoptive father. A son in *Instant Enemy* beats and nearly kills his father; sons in two novels published twenty-five years apart, *Dark Tunnel* and *Goodbye Look*, do kill their fathers.

An authority-figure who always gets rough handling is the oil executive. Reasons for the punishment he absorbs come easily to mind. The oil industry, working its will on the countryside, offends some of Kenneth Millar's favorite causes: the welfare of birds (the first victim of the oil spill in *Sleeping Beauty* is a bird), the preservation of natural landscape, the control of big business. It also expresses his love-hate attitude toward money. His only sympathetic oilman, Ian Ferguson of *Ferguson Affair,* suffers deeply before given his chance for happiness. By nature, the oilman, whether as investor, refinery executive, or field hand, is a plunderer and despoiler. The parallel with the colonial imperialist is nearly exact. His one extractive aim is to turn a fast profit; so he drills mindless of the welfare of his crew or of the surrounding area. Then he moves on, leaving the earth gaping and bleeding, his drills at the ready. His wildcat denial of the interchange between man and environment, and also between man and man, denies life. One thinks of Yeat's "The Second Coming": Oil derricks stand like skeletal robots surveying passively and patiently the land they will claim and drain of its energy. The derricks looming on the first page of *Wycherly Woman* (1961), "an abstract forest casting no shade," also convey the discontinuity and lack of civilized process—i.e., the unreality— of the profit motive. A natural corollary of this buccaneering comes in *Ferguson Affair*, when the title character impregnates a salesgirl and then leaves her. The profit motive denies process in all its forms. Appropriately, the oil industry merges with the dream in *The Way Some People Die* (1951): "On both sides of the road, the oilfield derricks marched like platoons of iron men across the suburban wilderness. I felt as if I were passing through dream country, trying to remember the dream that went along with the landscape and not being able to." The frontier encouraged change and movement. But now that it has closed, change recoils on itself; the snake starts to swallow his tail. If somebody mines the earth for oil, somebody else must restore the ecology. The failure of the petroleum industry to strike this balance both bewilders and belittles.

The damage can be assessed. The derricks, cranes, and jerrybuilt lodgings where the work-gangs live all deface the landscape, leaving it worse off than the invading gangs found it. The roustabouts making up the gangs are usually whoring, boozing roughnecks who menace the nearby townsfolk. The carelessness of the workers and their chiefs cause the installation of faulty pipelines, which crack and leak oil. Like the leaking oil that infects the nearby wildlife, a brutal morality emanates outward from the oilfields. In *The Drowning Pool* (1950), a large refinery organizes a lynching party; corrupt oilmen cause much of the evil in *Moving Target, Drowning Pool, Instant Enemy,* and *Sleeping Beauty*; a narrow, cranky oilman, Frederick Kincaid, thwarts Archer in *Chill.*

This conflation of money, power, and corruption shows how the writer interweaves Oedipal and North American themes. Other Oedipal

currents dart into the novels, leaving equally strong impressions. Sometimes characters discuss these currents, as in *Meet Me at the Morgue* and
Galton Case:

"Oedipus," Helen Johnson said from the inner doorway. "Larry's as Oedipal as all get
out. We were just discussing it before you arrived. Abel was Larry's father-image, he
says. Now that his father-image is kaput, Larry has an irresistible urge to possess the
father-image's wife-image."

*   *   *   *   *

"John had an Oedipus theory of his own, that Oedipus killed his father because he
banished him from the kingdom. I thought it was very clever." Her voice was brittle.

Sometimes the currents reverse: *The Wycherly Woman*, a book about
hidden parentage, shows "clefts of pain like knife-cuts . . . before [the]
eyes" of a young woman kissing her father rather than the blasted brows
or eyes of the Oedipal son embracing the mother. The characters' closest
ties exist outside their generation, and the parent-child tie continues to
grip the characters more tightly than the sexual one. Outside the family,
the tie exerts its force as Oedipal sexuality. Examples of this include the
humorous, the subtle, and the overt. In a wry self-spoof, Ross Macdonald
has a character in *Instant Enemy* say, "She is the seductive mother. The
soft-boiled eggs are symbolic. Everything is symbolic!" Oedipal sexuality
can motorize a plot: Ian Ferguson believes that he may have married his
daughter; his wife's mother, the first female he ever tumbled, he met while
buying a gift for *his* mother. As if the most insipid of mothers exists
supremely, the title character in *Wycherly Woman* turns out to be a
middle-aged woman, not her clever, beautiful daughter. Word choice, or
the notorious Freudian slip, can bring home the Oedipal paradigm: Chuck
Begley, or McGee, returns to California in *Chill* to be with his daughter for
the first time in ten years. "I'd certainly like to put my hands on her," he
tells Archer, instead of saying that he'd like to see or say hello to her.

Logically enough, most of the marriages in the canon have a ten- to
thirty-year age difference; the much-older marriage partner *in extremis* is
a popular client of Archer. A college dean in *Chill* has married a woman
twenty-five years older, convinces everyone she's his mother, and even
calls her "Moms"; a woman in *Black Money* calls her older husband
"Daddy." The marital career of another woman in the book is summarized, "Her first husband had been too young, her second was too
old." The statements, "She's practically old enough to be his mother"
and "The woman must have been old enough to be his mother," describe
two intrigues in *Far Side of the Dollar*. Archer, too, having been drawn
into the maternal-erotic orbit, knows its dangers well. A female in
Wycherly Woman who tires to coax information out of him says, "Come
on. . . . Tell Mother." In the next sentence, Archer reports, "She
pressed herself against me," adding soon after, "Her pointed breasts were

like soft bombs against me." These dangers come from the incest-craving and guilt that follow when the symbolic son or daughter becomes the lover. Every off-age marriage both beckons and perpetuates them. Yet, one can't help noticing, the on-age marriages of George and Hester Wall in *Barbarous Coast* and of Tom and Laurel Russo in *Sleeping Beauty* don't work well either. Young men, especially young husbands, are either proto-hoodlums or, aggressively wholesome and wide-eyed, proto-Boy Scouts. Ross Macdonald *has* called his books "quite pessimistic."[39]

The dangers of sex, defying mechanical cause-and-effect, demand psychological explanations. Since so many crimes also have psychological origins, psychology accounts for both the intellectual drive and the economy of the novels. The first Archer, *The Moving Target,* as if taking an intellectual weather-reading, refers several times to psychology in its opening chapter. Archer wonders who his client's analyst is; the client's husband, twenty years her senior, supposedly "wants to be a little boy again. He goes looking for a mother type or a father type to blow his nose and dry away his tears and spank him when he's naughty." A woman wonders about her sweetheart in *Three Roads,* a non-Archer published the year before *Moving Target,* "Could he have confused his mother with his wife? Stranger things had happened in case histories she had read." Crude textbook speculations like these offend as much as the psychology thronging the first chapter of *Moving Target.* Ross Macdonald's early work often leaves big gaps between drama and doctrine, so that its intended effect can differ widely from its actual effect. Characters in *Three Roads* chide each other for mouthing Freudian jargon but go on mouthing it anyway because the novel's framework needs the ideas contained in the jargon. Ross Macdonald's problem was clear: though his plots called for psychology, the presence of one or more psychiatrists threatened to flatten the other characters into cardboard case studies. What is worse, a novel might break into two sets of characters—one acting and one choric, unless, as in *Three Roads,* an astute person with a fine memory could apply her random reading in psychology to the problem at hand. Ross Macdonald does not solve this structural problem until *The Doomsters* (1958), where Archer's client is a mental patient. Rose Parish, a psychological social worker in the hospital where the client lives, makes clinical observations and uses therapeutic techniques beyond the layman Archer's intellectual scope. But she also has a place in the plot—a place whose importance becomes clear once you try to imagine the book without her.

The diagnoses of Drs. Godwin in *Chill,* Smitheram in *Goodbye Look,* and Sherrill, a sanitarium director in *Wycherly Woman,* impart the same theoretical force without weighting the plot. Godwin and Smitheram, in particular, are two clinicians whose troubles merge with those of their patients. The blurring of the cold, hard line between investigator and investigated reorders narrative form along with idea and character deployment. Brecht has vindicated the technique of flawing the personalities of his spokesmen. Ideas must be felt as well as perceived intellectually to deliver an impact in literature. The thawing of the linear structure of the standard crime novel into a warm mosaic adds realism, creates new outlets for the plot, and gives the detective a chance to respond emotionally, a major breakthrough for the sympathetic Archer—all without any intellectual slackening.

From the start of his writing career, Ross Macdonald has tuned his work to the goals and techniques of psychosexual study. The wandering old men who dot his landscapes serve as exiled Oedipus-figures as well as the detritus of free competition. Meanwhile, the detective climbs and descends staircases, then slips through dark corridors and tunnels. *The Dark Tunnel*, reprinted (in 1950 by Lion Books) as *I Die Slowly*, equates immersion in the clammy tunnel with death. Symbols of sexual calamity throng the book, which opens during a hot, sticky Detroit summer. To escape his pursuers, the main character enters a dark underground steam tunnel, where he perspires freely while his shoes hiss along the slippery walkways. The tunnel leads the hero to a zoo, in whose reptile pit he nearly dies. Other Freudian symbolism and name-choice deepen the novel's portrayal of sex as death; the novel's first fatality dies just before his marriage to a Miss Madden by falling from a window. Does Ross Macdonald intend the death as a quick reprieve from the slow decay of sex marriage?

Archer has also been stung by sexual frustration—both with younger women and women his own age. There is, first and unforgettably, his divorce from Sue. Ever since *Drowning Pool* (1950), he has been fighting the psychological backlash of this disappointment. *Doomsters* refers to his "quasi-paternal instinct," and he is often asked, starting with *Wycherly Woman* (1961), if he is the missing girl's father. Though no father, he knows well the libidinous pitfalls of fatherly love. The frequent accusation made against him in recent books of "fatherizing" stems in part from his failure to keep his ties with young women strictly professional. The sexual heat these women fan in him makes good their accusations. Starting with *Zebra-Striped Hearse* (1962) and Harriet Blackwell, who, at twenty-four, could easily be his daughter, runaway or missing girls take the part of erotic daughter-surrogates. His sexual self-control, both with these women and others—he rejects numerous sexual overtures—serves him well. For sex has not brought him close to a woman. The first time he sees a woman in *Sleeping Beauty* after going to bed with her, she greets him "without warmth." Within two pages he finds himself "angry with her now, furiously angry." In *Goodbye Look*, too, he finds himself at odds with a woman he had slept with the night before.

These sour experiences bear out Ross Macdonald's opinion, dramatized more sharply elsewhere, that sex puddles the primeval ooze humanity once rose out of with supreme effort. The paradox from Norse saga, "Them I loved best, I treated worst," gauges the short space between love and hate and between attraction and revulsion. (The beloved often disgusts and repels in Lawrence.) Catullus's maxim, *Odi et amo. Excrucior* (I hate and I love. And it hurts), is quoted in *Wycherly Woman* and *Sleeping Beauty* and acted out in all the other novels. Desire is fleeting, a lawless, disruptive emotion. The wheel of love can be a rack that breaks people with its tyranny and caprice. Physically, love demands a total, unguarded self-giving and abandonment. Morally and socially, it rides herd over our civilized arrangements; psychologically, it releases but also creates deep need. In *Ivory Grin*, it uncoils as a madness that subverts both reason and responsibility. Dr. Samuel Benning, knowing he can't win the heart of his much-younger wife, murders to shock her into loyalty. Similarly, a man tells Archer in *Wycherly Woman*, "You start out with an innocent roll in the hay, and you end up having to kill people." A wild emotion touching us in our most hidden and vulnerable places, sexual love completes a natural circuit with death. Sexual love and the death-drift have a common source. A character in *Sleeping Beauty*, describing a lovers' spat, says, "I wasn't sure if he was talking about killing a woman or making love to her, or possibly both." In *Underground Man* a man is shot to death during sex. The title, *The Drowning Pool*, refers to the whirling, down-pulling dangers of sex; a wave thrown back by the pool stuns Archer when a girl picks his pocket while kissing him. The molecular union of sex, crime, blindness, and death, from Sophocles, holds solid. The brutal chemistry of love is to be feared, perhaps even avoided. It is no wonder that, during a discussion of sex in *Doomsters,* the apple Archer is eating suddenly tastes like ashes. Too often has he seen the bright round succulence of sexual promise beckon and then corrupt.

If sex and crime fuse easily, depravity is often a function of sexual looseness, even of sexual indiscretion. Ross Macdonald has complained of the simplistic parallel drawn in Chandler's early fiction between criminal and sexual impulses:

The people of Chandler's early novels . . . are divided into two groups by an angry Puritan morality. The goats are usually separated from the sheep by sexual promiscuity or perversion. Such a strong and overt moral basis actually interferes with the broader moral effects a novelist aims at.[40]

He might have been writing about his own early work, where highly sexed and homosexual characters always have warped hearts. Evil characters, if not highly sexed, often don't keep their private lies private. Like the cads in Christie and Sayers, they will discuss sex freely, make rough sexual passes, and exude, in general, an animal rankness. In all cases, any kind of sexual excess or irregularity spells downfall elsewhere. J. D. Weather, the narrator's father in *Blue City* (1947), was a corrupt city boss whose marriage broke "because he couldn't keep his hands off women." The killer in *Three Roads*, another book published under authorship of Kenneth Millar, papers the walls of his room with autographed nude photos. Nude photos also cover the walls of a room of an unsavory character in *Drowning Pool*. Ross Macdonald's attitude toward sex in these early works is as angrily puritanical as early Chandler's. A young woman having an affaire with a married naval officer gets killed in the first chapter of *Trouble Follows Me*. Just before her death, she is seen quarrelling with her lover. Besides supplying a murder suspect, the quarrel gives the impression that Ross Macdonald is not content to punish her by killing her early on; he won't even let her enjoy her affaire. He also punishes Anne Meyer in *Find a Victim* for committing adultery with her sister's husband by killing her before the book opens. This moralizing harshness persists into *Zebra-Striped Hearse*, where the parents of an illicitly got child meet inevitable doom.

The homosexual phobia that goes with the hard-boiled pose also filters into Ross Macdonald's apprenticeship. A pseudo-intellectual gentleman-bitch contrasts sharply with the manly, down-to-earth heterosexual detective. The conversion of dramatic to moral contrast is a short, easy step. Usually, the reader's self-image or perhaps the writer's ham-fisted projection of the reader's self-image, bridges the short gap. The soft, girlish mouth and the dainty hands and feet of one Garland, an epicene gang-killer in *Blue City*, fuse killing and homosexuality. That Garland and another prissy homosexual thug in *Moving Target* are both expert pistol shots segments the morality more sharply. Despite their well-bred Anglicized airs, these killers have only one skill, a skill, moreover, whose obvious sexual symbolism invites the same moral condemnation as homosexuality. The detective hero, on the other hand, cast in the solid, free-standing Hemingway mold, is an all-purpose man. Four-square and forthright, he doesn't pretend to be what he isn't. Knowledgeable in a broad human sense, he need not parade his book-learning. But he can best any homosexual wit at repartee *or* at gunplay. He can reason or fight. Women like him; he enjoys normal sex with them. His energies merge with those of the commonweal. Homosexuality symbolizes the sickness, rather than the brawn, of the megalopolis. Crowding too many people into too tight an area blocks the energy needed for health and growth. Ross Macdonald's homosexuals resemble plants who have tried to grow without sunshine and fresh air. Dowser, a racketeer in *The Way Some People Die*, is a physical grotesque, and he supports his spongy, out-of-drawing body on sandals with two-inch heels. It is as if his bizarre footwear and physical handicap mirror an inner depravity which finds natural outlets in crime. George Stade sees the routing of evil in crime fiction as a defeat of both intellectual pride and sexual perversion:

The Maze

The major antagonist is often a connoisseur, a gourmet, an esthete. He has a taste for esoteric learning, dangerous liquors, suspicious tobaccos. If he is not perversely sexless, he is simply perverse. . . . Around him hangs the savor of ruined twelve-year-olds, of either sex. He and his colleagues are negative definitions of middle-class morality; that is why they are sinister.[41]

Experience has taught Ross Macdonald to shun the homosexual villain. The hard-boiled tradition has changed; his vision has deepened; his style has acquired new skills. His readership has also grown more sophisticated. But the old puritan condemnation holds, taking the form of scornful disregard. Despite the technical problem of portraying a decent homosexual, Ross Macdonald's disregard has no technical basis. He has coped brilliantly with more exotic problems of character and form. The reticence is intrinsic, perhaps involuntary. He hasn't put homosexuals into his recent books because he doesn't respond to them imaginatively. Yet, as a seasoned, self-critical professional, he will not revert to the homosexual caricatures of his first handful of books. The absence of homosexuals is worth noting if only because, the taboo against homosexuality having largely disappeared, his imaginative failure weakens the blasts given off by the urban inferno.

This falling-off in urban realism is perhaps balanced by the psychological realism centering on the great sexual success of rogues. *Drowning Pool, Way Some People Die, Galton Case, Ferguson Affair,* and *Black Money* all portray rich, young, sometimes beautiful women falling slavishly in love with heels or cads; Archer tells a young woman in *Galton Case* that she is worth five of the opportunist who dropped her. In "The Wild Goose Chase" (1954), the rogue succeeds so well that, artistically, he bilks Ross Macdonald of his chance for moral retribution. In order to punish Glenway Cave, he must add a pat, moralizing paragraph to the tightly built story, which makes Cave a highway victim "a short time" after the recorded action. The success of Cave and his fellow tom-cats spells out the ugly truth that we often love people either unworthy of us or who feel indifferently toward us; in the latter case, we create rogues out of virtual bystanders. A jilted lover like Anne Castle in *Zebra-Striped Hearse* won't resent the hell her cavalier suitor puts her through but, rather, that the hell has stopped. Both the title and epigraph of *Find a Victim,* from Stephen Crane, endorse this idea—that we gravitate to people from whom we can expect only trouble:

> A man feared that he might find an assassin;
> Another that he might find a victim.
> One was more wise than the other.

Ann Devon hates herself for loving a dishonest, mother-ridden lawyer in *Meet Me at the Morgue*; harboring no illusion about his moral character, she goes on loving him and outraging her conscience. Sometimes, characters deceive themselves for the sake of love. Ella Barker, a young nurse in *Ferguson Affair*, projects a love-ideal which she fastens to the burglar, Larry Gaines. Gaines, whom she never sees as a person in his own right, does not fit the ideal. As is usual in Ross Macdonald, the dream lashes back cruelly against the dreamer:

He was like a sickness I had—a sickness pretending to be something else. All my dreams coming true in one handsome package. I knew it couldn't be real, I just wanted it to be, so bad.

Goodbye Look varies the pattern again. "Women don't always go for the solid virtues," a wise woman tells Archer. What they do go for, she might have added, is the chance to make their men both solid and virtuous—i.e., to control and reform them. This version of the dream turns men into tractable boys who can be saved, remade, and then protected, mainly from themselves.

Is there another explanation covering these one-sided loves? In most of them, we have seen, the beloved has little concern either for the lover or the lover's plans for his moral reform. He is passive and thus innocent. The busy, anxious lover, on the other hand, acts from need. Underlying the need may be a secret wish to fail or to be punished. Ross Macdonald's people are terrible self-blamers. Their violent society often breaks the circuit between repression and work-release. This lack of higher, socially approved goals in which to sublimate instinct causes a lot of the self-blame. Most of the love-fantasists—and these include men in *Moving Target, Ivory Grin,* and *Sleeping Beauty*—are attractive, well-liked, and productive. Is it bad luck that these superior persons all defeat themselves in the same way? Nothing except guilt, over having better than they deserve, accounts for their disastrous choices of mates.

This guilt, besides killing the joy and spontaneity of sex, makes marriage the supreme dream. Marriages in Ross Macdonald often start badly. Ian Ferguson (*Ferguson Affair*), Bobby Doncaster (*Wycherly Woman*), and Alex Kincaid (*Chill*) all marry on impulse. "I decided right away," says Bobby; "Something clicked . . . the first time I saw her." Now love at first sight and the instant decision to marry both affirm some of the wild impulsiveness of sex. But, in Ross Macdonald, anyway, they don't make for happy marriages. Writing for teenagers as well as for adults, the novelist bypasses graphic sex; nor does he show the steps by which sexuality either mellows or stales into domesticity. What does emerge is the weakness of the marital tie. Crisis will wreck a marriage faster than it will any other close relationship. Unfaithful husbands are not rare, and two of the three women Archer sleeps with are married. By slow, minute steps, marriage partners move away from each other. Only in crisis or shock do

The Maze

they see the gulf that has opened between them. The frequent age difference between couples symbolizes major differences in outlook as well as an inability to communicate. Married love, we have seen, always falls short of parental love; in *Galton Case*, it carries less force than the fraternal; in *Goodbye Look* and *Underground Man*, it lags behind the filial. The friendship between an ex-Navy captain and his former ship's steward runs "stronger and deeper" in *Sleeping Beauty* than the ex-captain's marriage. Crowning Ross Macdonald's skepticism, the same novel combines the erosion of three generations of Lennox marriages with an investigation conducted by a divorced man.

The color that expresses both the lure and the mad, careening dangers of sex is red. Red is Ross Macdonald's obsessive color. The color of blood, the fluid and faculty of life, it also designates Christ's Passion, i.e., religious suffering. The range of this hard, emotionally charged color makes it glint, flow, and clot; lets it convey beauty and danger; even instils it with Satanic malevolence. The frenzy emanating from a Nazi rally in Munich in *Dark Tunnel* appears as a waving wall of red and black flags. By analogy, the good looks of a killer in "The Bearded Lady" (1948) dissolve in a rank red blur. Red can suggest sexual cruelty as well as sexual devitalization. Often related to nail polish and lipstick, glaring reds have a razor edge. Blood often traces a worm-like path across human faces; lipstick gleams like fresh blood; *Ferguson Affair* mentions "the . . . feral odor of sex that has grown claws." A woman in *Dark Tunnel* is called "poison with a red label"; blood sparkles "like rubies" on the breast of a murderess in *Trouble Follows Me*, and two pages later she dies, "grinning a shining red grin"; the man killed during sex in *Underground Man* is later buried in a red Porsche. Sue Archer and a castrating mother named Maude Slocum in *Drowning Pool* both have red hair. Finally, the narrator of *Ferguson Affair*, a non-Archer, mistakes the polish on the toenails of a murdered woman for blood. Knowing how both to dramatize and extend a good motif, Ross Macdonald then mentions that, as a girl, the murdered woman went to a school called the Sacred Heart. Red can suggest sexual degradation: a prostitute in *Trouble Follows Me* rouges her nipples, and a red bedroom with a mirror set in the ceiling in *Moving Target* is called "the inside of a sick brain." Chipped nail polish and dyed red hair with gray roots will indicate a woman whose middle-aged lust repels more than attracts.

As in Joyce's "Ivy Day in the Committee Room," red, symbolizing the lurid flames of hell, helps give the modern city its hellish glare. But Joyce also accepts red as the traditional symbol both of Christ's suffering and the Catholic Church in Ireland. Blood is vitality; its loss means death. Fire, one of the basic elements, can both help and harm man. Sex, though dangerous, undergirds animal life. Red in Ross Macdonald reflects both this universality and propensity for either good or hurt. More dramatic than judgmental, red transmits color along with terror. The heightened reaction it sets off in the writer carries richly into his work.

Another heightened psychological reaction shows in his portrayals of mothers and mother-surrogates. Geoffrey Hartman alerted us to it in a May 1972 number of the New York *Review of Books* with his throwaway, "I suspect Macdonald is not too fond of mothers and likes to give them bad nights."[42] Hartman's wise hint needs modifying. For, according to the evidence in the novels, the bad nights plague Macdonald. Everywhere, mother-figures crowd and claw their men. No strengthener or comforter, the mother in Ross Macdonald is Uroboros, the ancient, devouring mother of nightmare. A perfect example of maternal voraciousness comes with a brothel madam in *Doomsters* who supports a young man's drug habit to insure his dependence on her. Besides her and the occasional castrating mothers, there are also the harpy-like social workers and nurses. Women who fill positions of professional power like these are Archer's anathema: "Tall women behind desks had always bothered me," is one way he phrases this enmity in *Doomsters*. Female social workers are usually moralistic busybodies whose careerism can't mask the void in their private lives. Nurses, because of their healing mission, can do worse harm; the beautiful killer of three in *Way Some People Die* conveys this vampirism. The white, starched uniform of the nurse seems to fend off human touch. *Dark Tunnel* mentions "the evil whiteness of Melville's whale, the whiteness of sunless plants . . . the white look of death." In the book's last chapter, the killer tries to murder the hero while garbed in nurse's uniform.

Archer's role in all this sharpens the contours of the pattern. In *Goodbye Look*, he summarizes an essential feature of his life style: "I like to move into people's lives and then move out again. Living with one set of people in one place used to bore me." Any control, male *or* female, hobbles him. Even his dreams (*Doomsters* opens with one) rebel against organized authority. This rebellion is no mere gesture. The tough pose and terse voice reaching from *Black Mask* aesthetics hide a fear of society in general: the lonely, proud detective who knows how to take care of himself, thanks anyway, suffers separation anxieties. Exclusion haunts Archer. He constantly avoids the adult responsibilities of marriage, family, and a job that makes him answer to a system. His line of work makes him a constant target for blackjacks, bullets, and kidnappings. These dangers he accepts like any other good professional. But by opting for them to begin with, isn't he also inviting pain and death? *Way Some People Die,* the title of the third Archer novel, throws a net around Archer's whole career. His divorce from Sue and his leaving the Long Beach Police Department in the 1940s have pulled away the reserves he needs to cushion adversity. In *Doomsters* he says wearily, "It seemed that my life had dwindled down to a series of one-night stands in desolate places." A disbeliever in accident, this highly aware, well-spoken man has made himself the natural prey of guilt and repression.

The authority that threatens him is often masculine—various policemen, doctors, and corporation executives. Icarus, the west's prototype of the father-denying son, comes into two of the novels tangentially: in *Doomsters,* with the Joycean, "Brightness had fallen from my interior air," and in *Galton Case,* during a conversation with a poet. Female authority, though not as widespread, scorches Archer more deeply. Mothers, nurses, and social workers are not his only female enemies. The menace need not be institutional or familial. The short-story title, "The Bearded Lady," pictures a woman usurping one of the badges of male sexuality, even though it also mocks her in the process. A waitress in *Chill* is "so efficient that she threatened to take the place of automation. She said with a flashing smile that this was her aim in life." Archer never seeks her out again. Nor need he; the waitress, having no place in the story-line, contributes her share to the moral and psychological atmosphere and then drops from sight. The short story, "Find the Woman" (1946), not only describes Archer's first case as a private eye but also states his fear and distrust of strong women. To begin with, the title is ironic: for, once found, the woman reveals herself as ugly, cruel, and vindictive. The first five pages swarm with predatory female images. Archer mentions "the scarlet-taloned fingers" and "fierce . . . purring smile" of his first client, "an expert bitch" and "female spider who eats her mate." This danger muddles Archer; soon after leaving his office, he feels both fascinated and terrified by the ("anti-human") sea, universal symbol of motherhood.

The reason for this fear of mother-figures has been hinted at several times in Ross Macdonald's non-fiction. The writer's complex hero-worship of his father, John Macdonald Millar, a Scots-Canadian sailor-poet-journalist who left the family when the writer was only three, gave rebellion a sweet-sad glamor.[43] The "whiff of tobacco, sea water, sweat, and . . . odor of masculine loneliness" rising from the suitcase of a homeless old man in *Galton Case* (Ross Macdonald's attraction to old wanderers has already been mentioned) repeats little Ken Millar's charged sensory response to his father's leave-taking.[44] The combination of a romantic outcast father and a mother who tried to put her only child in an orphanage when he was six could easily ignite fears of female repressiveness. The experience of growing up among women—his mother, aunt, and grandmother—in a stern religious home gave this repressiveness the added weight of organized religion and even of God. Because novels are imaginative works, it is both misleading and unfair to interpret them autobiographically. Yet Ross Macdonald, a specialist in Romantic poetry, responds to his surroundings with the intensity of a lyric poet. While not bearing directly, certain tensions rooted in his boyhood could not avoid coloring his imagination. Could he avoid fearing a female authority that ripped him from his native country, threatened to institutionalize him, and rattled him between fifty rooms in his first sixteen years—all with divine sanction? Could marriage to a brilliant novelist fail to worsen the dread of female suffocation?

But the ordeal that doesn't break the individual strengthens him. Ross Macdonald's fears gave shape to a two-way tension that energizes much of his work—the need to escape and the need to establish roots. This tension, mirroring that of his chief literary influence, *Oedipus Rex*, and stretching back to his "episodic and unpredictable"[45] childhood, unifies the public and private lives of Kenneth Millar/Ross Macdonald. Like Dickens, he would have never written novels unless he first had a troubled childhood. Self-exploration and social criticism fuse in both writers. This unity of method gives Ross Macdonald the confidence to control his many subplots and to impart a wide geographical sweep to some of the novels. Narrative structure doesn't get out of hand. The moral equilibrium created by the past and the toil of solid literary craftsmanship weld the rich variety of the Archer novels. Little more can be asked of any novelist than that he control his deeply perceived and clearly realized materials. This strenuously achieved razor-balance of penetration and control, effortless look and all, has made Ross Macdonald an important novelist.

IV

Ross Macdonald puts the mainspring of his art right here—in the counterforce between impulse and formal design:

In fiction nothing is accidental or unconnected. Description becomes a significant part of the action and blends with it. And style turns out to be structure on a small scale, little things related to the big things, physical things taking on human meaning.[46]

He has the Dickensian gusto—the stamina, curiosity, and genius for organization—both to create a megalopolis and to pull it together. For all its variety and its variety and sweep, California rides easily on the narrative rigging of the Archer books. The job of communicating with the reader claims equal rank with subject and idea—that which is being communicated. The bestowing of equal priority upon different narrative elements is, in fact, one of his leading aesthetic tenets:

I see plot as a vehicle of meaning. It should be as complex as contemporary life, but balanced enough to say true things about it. The surprise with which a detective story concludes should set up tragic vibrations which run backward through the entire structure. Which means that the structure must be single, and *intended.*[47]

The Maze

Artistic practice squares with critical preachment. Ross Macdonald's well-built books glow with bright inter-scenic commentary. We are never put into a room without knowing how we got there and what the room looks like. The room takes shape through well-observed details carefully chosen both for atmosphere and idea. The rundown frame shacks, the stucco ranch houses, and the elegant mansions Archer visits have the same authenticity. Often Ross Macdonald will insert a retrospective passage which reviews and summaries the plot for the reader's benefit.

This solidness comes from careful planning. "Before I actually start writing," he says, "I sometimes fill three or four notebooks; as much as two hundred pages. I sometimes make notes almost as big as the novel and I spend more time on the preparation than I do on the writing." But the preparation does not exhaust the narrative, or he would have known how to end *Underground Man* well before fifty pages from the end. The extensive notebooks deal only with "structure and relationships between people and events," which, he insists, are "subject to change right up to the end."[48] Now the difference between an artist and a craftsman or entertainer is that the artist does not know how his work will turn out. The glinting exactness of Ross Macdonald's art, always capable of surprising, does not clot into repetition or self-imitation. The Oedipal paradigm has not shut out new experience. Not written to formula, the Archers all give something different.

At the top of their form, they vibrate with suspense, undertones, and classical inevitability. The success of most crime fiction depends on plot, and nobody builds a plot more ingeniously than Ross Macdonald. Far into a novel—like the shuddering three-page last chapter of *Chill*—we don't know where it is heading. Everything before is so unforced that the resolution surprises us. The form of an Archer stays hidden until the novel is over. His own ideas about plot bear out Ross Macdonald's rare ability to describe a reality, to weave rich inter-scenic embroidery, and to mount surprise all at once:

Detective novels differ from some other kinds of novel, in having to have a rather hard structure built in logical coherence. But the structure will fail to satisfy the mind, writer's or reader's, unless the logic of imagination, tempered by feelings and rooted in the unconscious, is tied to it, often subverting it.[49]

Suspense builds from the steady unearthing of a buried past—usually an unsolved crime of fifteen to twenty-five years before that relates to a current crisis. The beauty of the narrative construction lies more in its process than in its conclusion. The inclusiveness of the dialectic—the many-sided plot and Archer's method of finding out and then using information—depicts the vitality of life. The cases move forward with the precision, gait, and confidence of *Bleak House* or a Simenon. They make us feel we are in the hands of a master; we may be tricked but not mocked.

For this reason, the plots grip us: we warm to the play of mind, the nimbleness of the dialectic, and the delicate orchestration—amid violence—of the denouement.

The plots gain speed and poise from their use of time. It has been said that, though a plot can reach thirty years into the past for its impetus, its chronology will be straightforward. There are no flashbacks (*The Spy Who Came in from the Cold*), time-warps (*The Lime Twig*), or long historical recitations (*The Sign of Four*). Time acts as a structural control in Ross Macdonald. The time span of an Archer usually comes to two or three days; in Chapter 26 of *Barbarous Coast*, a thirty-two chapter book, Archer mentions that he has been working on his case for twenty-eight hours. This tight time frame owes much to his ability to work non-stop, skipping meals, driving through the night, and sleeping only two or three hours at a time. The benefits gained by this tightening are felt strongly: the novel which compresses time can unleash a whiplike recoil, bringing the reader to the moment of experience. The source of this recoil lies in the seedbed of Ross Macdonald's intellectual growth—nineteenth-century European drama. Ross Macdonald told the present writer that he started out wanting to write plays, not novels. What impressed him most about the drama was its power both to create and to criticize life within a two-hour time span. In *Ghosts* and *Miss Julie*, playing time nearly equals lapsed chronological time. Ross Macdonald's novels of continuous action stand closer structurally to Ibsen and Strindberg than to Victorian fiction. The chronicle, or traditional, novel imitates the passage of time with its bulk and detailed recording of both social and personal change. An Archer imitates the psychological effects of time. Time makes itself felt through its effects rather than through its passage.

One of the author's friendliest critics, William Goldman, has noted the difficulty of discussing the plots of the Archer novels:

Telling the plot of any novel is unfair. Telling the plot of an Archer is impossible. The books are so ramified, Delphic and dark that you either give a one sentence synopsis, or just hand over the novel and say "Read!": nothing in between.[50]

This dark ramification has caused other problems. Some readers are worn down by the cleverness in plotting. Their formalized neatness and condensation, it is alleged, make the plots one-man shows rather than dramas of lived experienced. Caught up by the dazzle of the plotting, we work hard to keep up with Ross Macdonald. The answer to this disclaimer? Writers who put more into their books have always made us dig harder and longer. Aside from revealing the cunning gyrations of the sub-plots, a re-reading will show that the plots grow more complex in direct ratio to the characters steering them: character determines event and is then changed by it. The self is a mystery, a knot of psychic drives, gaining facets and tints as it reveals itself amid an undulating causality. Ross Macdonald respects his characters too much to explain them fully. The adding of new data doesn't exhaust character; rather, it deepens it.

Intricate plotting can flatten characters into cardboard cutouts, Archer's ability to ask the right questions has helped Ross Macdonald avoid this trap. His witnesses are carefully stitched into the novels in which they appear. Some of them are designed small-scale, and with good reason. The gathering of evidence from different places in detective fiction demands that many witnesses speak out but once; though they should be vivid, they must not take over the plot. They do their brief turns, giving or concealing evidence, and then leave the action. Many of these turns are brilliant. The characters stand on tiptoe, anxious to build mood and to add to the quick, unhurried plots. Their brilliance comes from what they say, how much they suggest, and how well they move the ongoing drama. Thanks to Archer, the need to establish character quickly does not often betray the novels into caricature or hyperbole. The ability to fix a character in a few scraps of dialogue and revealing incidentals makes Ross Macdonald an excellent miniaturist.

A structural innovation that creates new opportunities in character-painting is the off-center focus. Ross Macdonald's novels are designed eccentrically because their chief movers rarely appear. The classic British mystery usually starts with a murder. The missing person, a standby of the Archer canon, may be a better plotting device. Not only does he motivate detective action; he also differs from a corpse in his possibly being alive. Thus he can be both found and returned to his family. He touches our hearts and creates suspense in ways no corpse can. (Recent Archers have enriched this emotional pattern by questioning the supposed abductor's guilt.) The missing person or prodigal will usually appear in the first chapter or two; unless we live with a character for a spell, we can't care whether he's lost or found. Mostly, though, the little child who leads the others exerts force by touching the hearts of those who love him. Regardless of whether he has run away or been kidnapped, he exerts his force as an imaginative, not a physical, presence. Embodying his parents' thwarted hopes and stake in posterity, he would not strengthen the plot by appearing in it. Wisely, Ross Macdonald limits his appearances—making them as brief and delaying them as long as possible. Jamie Johnson, the four-year-old missing boy in *Meet Me at the Morgue*, a twenty-eight chapter book, leaves the action from Chapters 2-21. The prodigals in *Find a Victim* and *Underground Man* appear only once—and as corpses, at that; the lost son in *Galton Case* died fifteen years before the book opens. Phoebe Wycherly does not come into *Wycherly Woman* until three chapters before the end; Laurel Russo does not re-enter *Sleeping Beauty* after Chapter 3 until the book's next-to-last page, where she is asleep.

The emotional gap created by the prodigal's absence fills quickly and then shimmers with life. Ross Macdonald's mind is a card-file of character-types, architectural details, and sociological naunces. He describes life in America at a given moment; he has mastered the art of selecting and then dramatizing the revealing detail; he interweaves the bizarre and the prosaic. Agile and well-schooled, he knows the skills of the storyteller's art. A paragraph of physical description gives you the personality, topography, and socio-economic range of a city you can hear and smell:

I drove south through Long Beach to Pacific Point. Crossing the mesa that flanked it to the northwest, you could see the town spread out, from the natural harbor half-enclosed by the curving finger of land that gave the place its name, to the houses on the ridge above the fogline. It rose from sea level in a gentle slope, divided neatly into social tiers, like something a sociologist had built to prove a theory. Tourists and transients lived in hotels and motels along the waterfront. Behind them a belt of slums lay ten blocks deep, where the darker half of the population lived and died. On the other side of the tracks—the tracks were there—the business section wore its old Spanish façades like icing on a stale cake. The people who worked in the stores and offices inhabited the grid of fifty-foot lots that covered the next ten blocks. On the slopes above them the owners and managers enjoyed their patios and barbecue pits.

This drypoint sharpness, from *Way Some People Die*, does not thicken into gimmickry or mannerism. The moral, aesthetic, and logical dimensions of most of the Archers blend. Ross Macdonald no more bullies language than he pistol-whips character and event into the death-clamp of a pre-ordained plot. His prose snaps and sparkles and also, thanks to its poetic symbolism, resonates. Prizing suavity and finesse as much as vigor and drive, he has an almost feminine sensibility to tone, inflection, and facial expression. The salt edge of his prose flicks you like a whip; the flashing image of a man "with the blaze of white like a lightning scar on the side of his head," from *Ivory Grin,* cuts to the quick of both the man and his madness. Mobile as well as marksmanly, Ross Macdonald's lyrical prose can move from soft muted pastels to hard primary colors; bright threads fan into walls of overwhelming brilliance or burst into showers of stressed syllables. He takes special care with verbs, which he selects for cadence, motive force, and metaphorical bite. Will the verb move the sentence quickly? Or slow it down for purposes of reflection? Often, he will put his metaphor into the verb, a difficult but effective and economical stylistic tool: Archer tells us in "Gone Girl" (1953) that a car "looped past . . . in an insane arc, tires skittering, and was sucked away into darkness"; of a man in *Galton Case,* he says that "the events of the day . . . had honed his profile sharp."

Ross Macdonald could always write this flaring, energized prose. The early "terse, highly figured"[51] style, though, is often ridden by the hard-boiled stance, especially in its side-of-the-mouth dialogue. Human warmth is sacrificed to verbal wit; compassion will not stop him from completing a parallel structure in *Drowning Pool*:

The Maze

I parked in front of a restaurant near the courthouse and went in for a cold lunch. The waitress had a red-checked apron that matched the tablecloth, and a complexion that matched the coffee.

The fresh, vivid early style lacks control. The images in the following passage from "Find the Woman," though apt, crowd each other, clogging sentence flow and confusing the reader: "Nothing could have looked more innocent than the quiet cove held in the curve of the white beach like a benign blue eye in a tranquil brow." Yet the same page contains one of Ross Macdonald's boldest but also most delicately cadenced similes: "The waves came up towards us, fumbling and gnawing on the beach like an immense soft mouth." Ross Macdonald's style has always had this range and power. To define late from early style as a difference in execution rather than perception, compare these two passages. The first shows Hitler's SS troops marching through Munich in *Dark Tunnel* (1944): "I had a grotesque vision of radio-controlled robots in field grey . . . bleeding black oil." The opening page of *Sleeping Beauty* (1973) contains the following image: "An offshore oil platform stood up out of its windward end like the metal handle of a dagger that had stabbed the world and made it spill black blood." The artistic seasoning behind the second quotation evokes a Conradian word music and a dramatic foreshadowing not found in the first.

Both quotations, though, show a tendency to use imagery as moral commentary; Ross Macdonald has both the flair and the verbal imagination to convey imagistically ideas he doesn't want to labor in philosophical argument. His strong, sensory prose fills his books with exciting, original images. But, also borne out by the quotations above, his favorite literary device is the simile. Metaphor he uses seldom because his books are metaphors themselves. His first novel, *Dark Tunnel*, a simile in its opening sentence, introduces phrasing that will recur in more polished, fully developed form: "Detroit is usually hot and sticky in the summer, and in the winter the snow in the streets is like a dirty, worn-out blanket." Both polish and development can come quicker than expected. This striking simile flashes across the novel's first chapter: "He seemed astonished and his eyebrows jumped like black mice." Part of the force of the simile, though, is blunted by what precedes it. The mature Ross Macdonald, instead of reporting the man's astonishment directly, would have let the simile do the whole job. Instead of saying, "My eye was bleeding," in *Find a Victim* (1954), Archer tells us, "Liquid warmth ran into one of my eyes and turned the day red." The suddenness of the sensory jolt more than justifies the added words.

Ross Macdonald makes simile dramatic and integral as well as descriptive. Though not as detonative as metaphor, it embodies the distance required for criticism. Ideally, it combines the coerciveness of metaphor with a critical detachment. The braids of an ageing, possessive mother in *Wycherly Woman* "twitched like dying grey snakes on her breasts." While the main verb, "twitched," makes the woman's physical reaction look involuntarily, even spastic, the simile gives her act a context that fuses motherhood and, since the braids are gray, ancient evil. A man's dark hand gripping the clad upper arm of a woman in *Black Money* (1966) "against her light gray sleeve . . . [looked] almost as dark as a mourning band." Besides remind us of the man's non-Caucasian origins, the simile, like the novel's title, with its phonic resemblance to the term, "Blood Money," prefigures several dark turns in the action, including the man's death. Three straight sentences in *Black Money* end in similes. But thanks to Ross Macdonald's skill in varying both sentence length and movement, no monotony jades the freshness:

The white and purple flowers on the brush gave out a smell like the slow breath of sunlight.

When I stopped my car at the Bagshaw mailbox, I could see the ocean below, hung on the horizon like unevenly blued washing. I had climbed only a few hundred feet but I could feel the change in temperature, as if I had risen much nearer to the noon sun.

The simile is both the clincher and the glory of Ross Macdonald's style. Agile phrasing lets him use it in crucial passages without straining or risking clutter. Simile, freshly combined with metaphor, brings the key event of *Underground Man*, the forest fire, to magnificent, unforgettable life:

The fire appeared at the top of a hill like a brilliant omniform growth which continued to grow until it bloomed very large against the sky.

*　　　　*　　　　*

It made a noise like a storm. Enormous and hot and wild, it leapt clumsily into the trees. The cypress that had been smoking burst into flames. Then the other trees blazed up like giant torches in a row.

In a sociological shadow-play on Gresham's Law, the simile ending the following description of the Los Angeles Freeway at night in *Sleeping Beauty* infers a weakening of both moral and intellectual fiber (i.e., light):

I drove up the ramp into the freeway. The traffic going north with us wasn't heavy. But an unbroken stream of headlights poured toward us from Los Angeles, as if the city was leaking light through a hole in its side.

Ross Macdonald responds keenly to Californian themes. (On the other hand, his descriptions of Nevada and Mexico are dim and arbitrary.) One of adventure fiction's great phrasemakers, he often uses descriptions of local scenery to connect dramatic events. These connective passages have the color and shape, the heft and texture, to sustain the drive mounting from the fast-moving plots, as this passage from *Chill* proves:

> She rose and went to the glass wall that faced the mountains. They had turned
> lavender and plum, with dark nocturnal blue in their clefts and groins. The entire
> evening, mountains and sky and city, was inundated with blue.

Energizing a sensory passage with active verbs can create a whipcord
sharpness without any loss in evocative power. The only link verb in this
description of a boatwreck comes in the short concluding summary—a
summary which, incidentally, the preceding simile makes unnecessary:

> Where the surf boiled whitest on the jutting black basalt, the boat lay half-capsized.
> Wave after wave struck it and almost submerged it, pouring in foam-streaked sheets
> down its slanted deck. The boat rolled with their punches, and its smashed hull
> groaned on the rocks. The outriggers flopped loose like broken wings. It was a total
> loss.

Other high stylistic moments in Ross Macdonald stem from his descriptions of the way bodies under psychic stress give off colors, even smells;
of the way stress and terror yank the face apart; of the numbing, reeling
sensation of being knocked out; of fighting: he knows techniques of
fighting, the reaction of different nerves and muscles to physical strain,
and, most important, the psychology of blood anger—how it feels to be
cut and beaten by another man's fists. While telling and accurate, his
descriptions of physical bodies in motion can also rise to poetical beauty.
The candencing of a description of a high dive in *Barbarous Coast*, with its
self-embedded phrasal modifier and concluding spondees, blends the soar-
ing, looping arc of the dive and its fast downward curve:

> I was stopped by one of three divers . . . taking off in unison from the high tower.
> Their bodies hung clear of the tower against a light summer sky, arched in identical
> swan dives, caught at the height of their parabolas before gravity took hold and
> snatched them back to earth.

Ironically, Ross Macdonald, chronicler of movement and change in
southern California's freeway society, uses some of his most memorable
images to describe immobility. Two of his best novels, *Chill* and *Sleeping
Beauty,* convey immobility in their titles. The skeleton at the end of *Ivory
Grin* and a fur coat lying at the bottom of a filled swimming pool, a
jewel box at its collar, in *Underground Man*, inspire some of the novels'
boldest stylistic flights. Chapter 31 of *Underground Man* ends with the
discovery of a corpse. Not content to simply display the corpse, Ross
Macdonald, in the chapter's last two paragraphs, moves toward it, backs
away, and then, after a carefully timed delay, flings it, or rather what
remains of it, into view. He has drained every drop of thematic goodness
out of the moment. The irrelevant-sounding physiology in the next-to-last
sentence, the refusal to say straightout that Leo Broadhurst is dead, and

the quietness of the final periodic sentence all work together at top form:

> I cleared the left front window and smashed it with the spade. The odor of corruption came out, dry and thin and shocking. In the hollow of the car's body something wrapped in a rotting blanket lay on the front seat.
> I stretched head down in the dirt and peered in at the dead man. The flesh was always the first to go, and then the hair, and then the bones, and finally the teeth. Leo Broadhurst was all bones and teeth.

These stunning descriptions of death and calm refer subtly to the rampant change of modern life. Their restrained phrasing provides the same critical perspective as does the simile. The quiet immobility of death is as real as fast change. Death, as life's opposite number, exists in bipolar tension with life. Unchecked life, or violence, brings death; Apollonian balance and order promote life as much as the instincts and the blood. Ross Macdonald conveys this lesson as an artist should—with images that not only describe states of mind but also reveal universal truths.

To crown our discussion of Ross Macdonald's style by praising the style's ability to combine topicality and timelessness would add a nice, and not undeserved, crescendo. But the crescendo would grate. The style has flaws and blemishes, some of which come from his use of stage, rather than narrative, techniques of plot-structure. These, built into the brickwork of the novels, could not be smoothed without a major dismantling. The novel is not a stage play; it uses different rhetorical conventions to generate a quite different illusion of life. The need for the detective to collect evidence from many different people crams most detective fiction with more dialogue than it can bear. Ross Macdonald, too, has a topheavy proportion of dialogue to narration. This imbalance squeezes the characters into the shrill, small spotlight of present time, a handicap offset in part by the presence of old letters, old photographs, and old people (*Underground Man* contains a map dated 1866). A flaw just as serious is that the characters sometimes talk like novelists. The too-sharp eye for detail, the encompassing summation, the measured speech—these all violate the realism of spoken language. The following passage from *Barbarous Coast* shows the speaking voice strangled by Ross Macdonald's refusal to relax authorial control:

> "It was a cold winter," he said. "The snow creaked under your feet and the hair froze in your nostrils. The frost grew thick on the windows. The oil furnace in the basement kept going out."

A third stylistic failing—narrowly grammatical and thus not damaging thematically—rises from Ross Macdonald's practice of omitting the word, that, to introduce the second of two noun phrases governed by a single main verb: "It probably meant that the body had been found and [that] they were tracing my call" (*Way Some People Die*). The failing, though minor, haunts the writer's whole career. Both in dialogue and in narration, it slips into each of his books at least three or four times. A person in *Doomsters* says, "I know what you're thinking—that Carl is crazy . . . and [that] I'm twisting the facts"; "A woman told me in a foreign accent," Archer explains in *Instant Enemy*, "that her husband wasn't home but [that] she expected him any moment." *Goodbye Look* (1969) alters the pattern; Chapter 26 contains the perfectly balanced, "She believed or suspected that Nick had killed both Harrow and Mrs. Trask, and that she herself had acted as a catalyst." Yet two chapters later, Archer tells his client, "Consider the possibility that Swain took some of the bank's money and [that] Rawlinson caught him." This pattern has persisted since *Goodbye Look*; sometimes the adverbial conjunction is included; sometimes, left out. Though no major blemish, the omission does distract. Even more distracting is the fact that no style editor has caught it after twenty-three novels.

On balance, the beauties of Ross Macdonald's style far outweigh the faults. As has been stated, he is one of adventure fiction's great phrasemakers. What is more, he is acknowledged as such. Richard Lingeman's parody in the New York *Times Book Review*, "The Underground Bye-bye: Still Another Lew Archibald Novel by Ross Macdonald," laughs mildly at the writer's fondness for symbolism; his use of facial resemblances between women in the same family as a plotting device; his yoking ecological to social contamination; the long hours Archer spends driving, often accompanied by the beautiful runaway daughter of rich California parents; Archer's faith in truth-telling: "Truth? That's my kick, my high. You might, in fact, call me a twentieth-century Odysseus, cruising the winedark seas of life, in search of the great good place where truth resides."[52] The 400-word parody, no voguish send-up, lights on the recurring subjects and themes of a long artistic career. This inclusiveness makes good the old equation of parody and praise. Though his influence on detective fiction has not yet been assessed, Ross Macdonald has attracted imitators galore, all of whom try to copy Archer's unique voice and stance. None succeeds. Having rung the changes of the hard-boiled novel and of psychological urban realism, Ross Macdonald's style has the precision, strength, and flavor that come only after years spent mastering the difficult art of prose.

2

Lew Archer, Ross Macdonald's detective-narrator, is the cornerstone both of the novels' plot-construction and, by supplying a safe remove from the tensions of the writer's life, a "protective interface." "Archer makes it possible . . . to dredge up material I wouldn't be able to dredge up writing in my own person," said Ross Macdonald in 1971, adding, "The whole apparatus and tradition is to provide what I once described as a welder's mask which enables you to handle dangerously hot material."[1]

Once a writer decides to speak through a character, he must select one that lets him describe outer reality, his thoughts and feelings about that reality, and then his thoughts and feelings about himself. "The decision on narrative point of view is a key one for any novelist. It determines shape and tone, and even the class of detail that can be used,"[2] wrote Ross Macdonald in 1969. Thus Archer needs a sharp eye, an instinct for moral atmosphere, and a compassionate grasp of human motives. His lack of a pronounced personal style lets him recede into the role of passive recorder whenever someone else moves center stage. Though the technical and psychological cornerstone of the novels, Archer, insists his creator, is not what the novels are about:

These other people are for me the main thing: they are often more intimately related to me and my life than Lew Archer is.

*　　　　*　　　　*

Archer is not the main object of my interest, nor the character with whose fate I am most concerned. He is a deliberately narrowed version of the writing self, so narrow that when he turns sideways he almost disappears.[3]

This now-famous disclaimer, though an exaggeration, helps define Archer. Though necessary, he is more of a device than a character; more of a narrator than an author. He doesn't write the books, nor does he enter the causal change he describes, as do the narrators in Henry James. In that he states the problem and then, after finding the clues, solves it, he resembles a *deus ex machina*. Yet his investigative role also makes him a catalyst. (Chandler called the fictional detective "a catalyst, not a Casanova.")[4]　To begin with, by helping his author cope with life's frustrations, instead of giving into them, he gives the novels moral and psychological depth. By fitting his author's private stresses to the pattern of detective fiction, he shapes them dramatically. This shaping function is what makes him more of a plotting device than a free-standing character. Though his values reflect those of his author, his humanity counts less than his instrumentality. Ross Macdonald has described Archer's instrumentality and its benefits not only to his own work but also, possibly, to the art of detective fiction:

> Archer is a hero who sometimes verges on being an anti-hero. While he is a man of action, his actions are largely directed to puting together the stories of other people's lives and discovering their significance. He is less a doer than a questioner, a consciousness in which the meanings of other lives emerge. This gradually developing conception of the detective hero as the mind of the novel is not new, but is probably my main contribution to this special branch of fiction. Some such refinement of the conception of the detective hero was needed, to bring this kind of novel closer to the purposes and range of the mainstream novel.[5]

An aesthetic contribution Ross Macdonald doesn't mention, but one that reaches past the purview of detective fiction, is his working concept of Archer as an "open narrator." The open narrator is a corollary of the continuing detective. He is easily recognizable and needs no reintroducing; since we know basically what to expect from him, we can watch his personality unfold in its own good time without growing anxious. The conventional character gets used up in a book, or even in a short story, like Salinger's Seymour Glass in "A Fine Day for Shooting Banana Fish." Archer develops much more slowly. By adding to him in each book, Ross Macdonald keeps options alive; Archer reveals himself over many novels and remains fluid, besides. As with Anthony Powell's Nicholas Jenkins (*The Music of Time*) and C. P. Snow's Lewis Eliot (*Strangers and Brothers*), a real self emerges from the Archer novels without dominating any single action.

Archer's obedience to his author's will lets him soar lofty heights. If this reversal is a paradox, it is paradoxical in the spirit of New Testament ethics. The hint for Archer's apotheosis comes from Ross Macdonald's use of him as a secondary novelist or moving proscenium arch. The narrative frame Archer sets around the action controls the other characters; he first limits character response and then channels it into a plot whose movement he determines. Recalling Joyce's God of the Founding Pen, his divine attributes outnumber those of Ross Macdonald. He is, first, a dimension (Lew-Fr. *lieu*) in which other dimensions exist. He has the mobility to range freely through many-tiered California society. A licensed private detective, he stands for authority, or the father. His reordering of time to the logic of detective-work enables him, first, to stop time and, supremely, to connect far-flung events; he becomes both the connecting principle and justicer in the lives of people he has only known for two or three days.

Some of Ross Macdonald's projections of him as God or man-God are more pointed. At different times, he is called altruist, do-gooder, Crusader, a zealot in his trade, even Mr. God. In *Doomsters,* he is asked, "Who do you think you are? God?" He says in *Way Some People Die,* "I like to pretend I'm God"; in *Find a Victim,* he speaks of "my Messianic complex"; he denies in *Chill* that there's "much difference" between "the Good Lord" and himself. Many of his virtues, though human in principle, becomes saintly or divine in practice: his siding instinctively with the underdog, his belief in the innocence of suspects till proved guilty; his dislike of intolerance, snap moral judgments, and mass psychology. These virtues he directs to the Godlike task of satisfying both mercy and justice. In *Way Some People Die,* for instance, his sympathy for a killer of three runs so strong that he gives her $500 and the chance to hand $30,000 in stolen money to the police in order to strengthen her legal defense: "I know she's guilty, and I can't pretend I don't. But I feel responsible in a way. For you, if not for her," he tells the killer's mother. His sense of responsibility encroaches upon the metaphysical. Metaphysical echoes reverberate. His helping arrest Galley Lawrence and then testifying for the *defense* in her trial tallies with Christian paradox. The overriding of both secular good and evil in order to give a sinner better than she deserves copies divine grace. His gift comes as a miracle to the Lawrences: "Impossible things are happening all the time," is his response to their, and perhaps his own, bewildered joy. He plays God again at the end of *Drowning Pool, Barbarous Coast* and *Wycherly Woman* when he lets killers go unpunished. (Sherlock Holmes lets killers go free in "The Abbey Grange" and "Charles Augustus Milverton.")

Archer's fate is that of all man-Gods. Though physically damaged, he stays spiritually whole; his professional honor and compassion, if dented, will serve him again. Though he pays compliments graciously, he doesn't like to receive them. Though he stops crime, he often gives the police the credit. His clients do not know how hard he has worked or what risks he has taken for them. Yet his modesty and professional stoicism do not wane into quietism. The West's twentieth-century man-God cannot reign or preside. Of our time, he must certify his divinity in movement and action.

I

Lew Archer's surname comes from Sam Spade's partner, Miles Archer, who gets killed early in Hammett's *Maltese Falcon.* The exact similarity between his initials and those of the city where he works and lives is also worth noting; like Los Angeles, his life has no nucleus, pivoting, instead, on many far-flung centers of significance. Just as thematic is his connection with the Archer of the Zodiac. The Archer, or Sagittarius, is, in fact, the sun sign of Kenneth Millar, born 13 December 1915; curiously, though the dates 12 and 14 December recur often in the work, 13 December never comes up. But Millar/Macdonald does put his astrological sign into his fiction at least twice. It is mentioned in *Moving Target* (Chapter 4), and Archer is asked in *Ivory Grin* (Chapter 16) if he was born under Sagittarius. The question is not gratuitous; several of the Sagittarian's traits fit him well. The Archer is a romantic figure. He sets and tries to meet high standards, except sometimes in marriage; the divorce rate for Archers is high. He is drawn to danger. His love of travel chimes with a dislike of authority and confinement, especially around hospitals. He has marvelous aim: "His arrows never miss their mark."[6]

Nor does he waste them on imaginary targets. Of the many summaries of the thriller hero, the one that suits Archer best comes in Ralph Harper's *The World of the Thriller*:

There is something in him for everyone. He is a very private man who is used to privacy; he is self-reliant, proud, and at home with self-reflection. He is always honest, candid, and loyal, a man of honor. Put all this side by side with a sustaining energy above the average, and we can see the basis for his resilience, even toughness. . . . His existence guarantees excitement and explosions. Evil is attracted to him as flies to flypaper. But with the innocent and gentle, natural victims of this world, he is himself gentle, chivalrous, full of compassion. No wonder he is attractive to women. His integrity is complete.

Harper's technical observation, on the next page, fits not only Archer but also Ross Macdonald's use of him as an open narrator: "The genius of the writer is to avoid making his hero display all the virtues with equal splendor, and yet at the same time all the virtues must be active in him."[7] Thus Archer will lie to or threaten a suspect. He is a man, not a reasoning machine or an angel. His goodness can accommodate some bad without being spoiled by it. A capacity for evil must function as vitually in him as a capacity for virtue. He merges well with the private-eye tradition of the tarnished knight who wears rusty armor and carries a bent lance. He doesn't share Philip Marlowe's zest for women and whiskey or the sadism of Sam Spade and Mickey Spillane's Mike Hammer. But he lives cleanly from habit, not from conviction. His stoicism is inherent, a function of good street-sense. He claims no credit for it.

Like Sherlock Holmes, another crime-stopper who stays relatively unsmirched, he is a consulting detective with an urban background; he has a Victorian faith in proper moral conduct; he moves freely and confidently among his social superiors. Yet he doesn't share Holmes's faith in reason. No logician, he sees reason as regulative but not constitutive; though it can illuminate the darkness of our nature, it cannot stave it off.

Unlike the crime-puzzle sleuth who defeats crime with reason alone, Archer summons both muscle and mind. As has been said, he has taken a great deal of physical punishment. He is nearly drowned in *Moving Target* and *Drowning Pool,* burned in *Doomsters,* and run over by a truck in *Instant Enemy.* In *Find a Victim,* he has eight stitches sewn into his face; *Wycherly Woman* brings six more and a concussion; in *Galton Case,* bullet wounds put him in the hospital for a week. When crime-fighting tests all the detective's powers, as it does Archer's, the stakes rise in proportion. Murder becomes a human problem rather than a plotting device or logical exercise.

But Archer never complains of his knocks. He abides by a silent male fellowship akin to the unspoken decency of the Anglo-Saxon abroad ("our side"). His practice of keeping his thoughts to himself, while honorable and manly, makes him a mite shadowy. Though portrayed realistically, he generates a realism bound up with his professional skills. Ross Macdonald neglects many aspects of his character because of their irrelevance to detective fiction. Because he is rarely seen off duty, for instance, he says little about his dreams or personal opinions. He has little existence apart from the crimes he investigates. Though certain biographical features rise from his past, they play little or no part in his work. He belongs, by temper and by choice, in the ranks of the normal centrist detective, like Ngaio Marsh's Roderick Alleyn, as opposed to the eccentric sleuth tradition of Christie's egg-domed Hercule Poirot and Sayer's flibbertigibet Lord Peter.

The novels merit praise for their happy union of form and content. Archer's professional reason for merging with his urban background carries as much weight as Ross Macdonald's artistic one. The skilled detective need not distract or overwhelm, as R. Austin Freeman's scholarly Dr. John Thorndyke has proved. A businessman who supports himself by private investigation, Archer has only his services to sell. These would drop in value if he cultivated uniqueness. Though a strong personal style would give him color, it would also stop him from gaining people's trust and getting them to talk. His clientele also accounts for his lack of special knowledge. Because no master technicians come into the novels, the materials and techniques of detection he uses don't come from science; he analyzes motives and instincts, behavioral patterns and the stirrings of the heart, not physical clues. He speaks some Spanish because, based in southern California, he sometimes interviews Chicanos. Though he likes sports, the only exercise we see him take is swimming. And, except in *Drowning Pool,* he only swims to save somebody from drowning or to find a piece of evidence, not for fun. He attends no sporting events, films, or plays. He doesn't go to museums, zoos, or concerts. He has no books on his night table; visits no friends or relatives; worships at no church; belongs to no political party.

The Man in the Maze

But he has the experience and skill to steer both the moral and actional currents of a novel without hobbling the other characters. He needs no freight of physical or biographical impedimentia. The lightly furnished hero of obscure background comes straight out of America's pioneering past. The line of literary descent joining Archer to J. F. Cooper's Leatherstocking has been traced by George Grella:

> His [the private eye's] loneliness is characteristic of the Leatherstocking hero who must proceed through moral entanglements unencumbered by the impedimentia of social or sexual alliances. Nothing, not even love, must prevent the detective from finishing his quest. Without antecedents, unmarried, childless, he is totally alone. Archer's symbolic maladjustment as a divorced man emphasizes this alienation from human beings and human institutions.[8]

Though alienated, Archer is no misanthrope or recluse. He does not flee personal relations so much as keep them from controlling him. No angry rebel or reformer, he takes life as it is: society is neither a conspiracy nor a jungle of suckers and hustlers. But, if not hostile, society is unquestionably other; Archer does not fit in. He has built a moral world round himself with the same sturdy diligence as the early Yankee settlers. Police corruption drove him from the Long Beach Police Force, and he has remained anti-establishment and anti-institutional since he started freelancing in 1946. The Archer novels form an extended act of pioneering self-discovery in the tradition of Cooper. A tracker like Natty Bumppo, Archer pits his skills against the megalopolis rather than the wilderness. (In *Zebra-Striped Hearse* he tells someone that his name is Natty Bumppo; he says in *Drowning Pool* that his name is Leatherstocking and that he should be wearing a coonskin cap.) He personifies new world energy as vividly as Bumppo, for his efforts symbolize the strivings and stresses of human endeavor. But now that the maze has replaced the open frontier, his tracker's job has become one of stalking the corridors of psychic disorder.

Perserving his moral integrity is harder work for Archer than for Leatherstocking. As society grows more complex, the open-air male virtues of bravery, physical strength, and rough-and-ready camaraderie shrink in import. In a review of three books on recent French Literature, Ross Macdonald praises Proust—son of a highly sophisticated and involute culture—in terms relevant to Archer: "His greatness consisted in his willingness to live with despair and study its habits, without becoming its devil's advocate."[9] Archer, too, lives with despairing, nerve-raddled people. His excavations unearth greed and cruelty. He deals, in short, with situations so ugly that nobody could reasonably hope to emerge clean from them. Yet his private sense of justice is not primitive, but compassionate. The chance to vindicate a moral principle or support a public cause moves him less than helping a stranger with a problem. In *Zebra-Striped Hearse* he lists the attributes of a first-rate detective: "honesty, imagination, curiosity, and a love of people." These attributes shine through his self-imposed mission of relieving suffering. He doesn't trivialize moral conflict by dissolving it in the details of detection, the received doctrine of a creed, or witless do-goodism. The withholding of moral judgment is, for anybody, an act of love. Archer's lack of a home life makes him a man with love to give. His strenuous attempt to love people without using them has probably been best summarized by Eudora Welty. According to her, Archer's measured understanding has humanized detective fiction: "As a detective and as a man he takes the human situation with full seriousness. He cares. And good and evil both are real to him." The sensitive, lucid reading continues, "He is at heart a champion, but a self-questioning, often a self-deriding champion. He is of today, one of ours."[10]

Ross Macdonald would agree with this reading. He lists among Archer's "internal qualities" an "intelligent humaneness, an interest in other people transcending" self-interest and "a toughness of mind which enables [him] to face human weakness, including [his] own, with open eyes."[11] Archer also invites definition by negation. He is not funny, angry, jaded, self-belittling, or introspective. Though an occasional reference to painting or literature will pepper his speech, he is neither aesthetic nor intellectual. He has no grand ideas about human nature or about himself as a crusader. He can't be called an anti-hero—cowardly, greedy, or bad-tempered; he doesn't think, talk, or act like a criminal. Nor is he a one-man army, equipped with all the moral values plus superb courage and strength. A cautious professional, he uses no tricks; he rarely tries to disarm anybody pointing a gun at him, and he carries no hidden weapons or cameras. His investigations include a sensible mix of seven or eight parts legwork and questioning to one part intuition. His values and attitudes are as conventional as his manner. He has faith in due process: the police are mostly honest and thorough; law and order have not broken down in the court. He judges every case on its own merits; works hard; keeps faith with his clients. He believes in the value of justice—which he rates below mercy but above the law. A man of professional pride and honor, he sees his cases through. He continues working in *Chill* and *Goodbye Look* even after his paymasters fire him. In *Find a Victim*, a page after resigning from an employer who won't let him work freely, he is warned by a sheriff to drop the case altogether. But he does not quit easily. Though lonely and tired, he has not swerved in his belief in the rightness of relieving suffering.

Nor has this belief grown sullen or chic. His blend of sensibility, sobriety, and professional instinct helps him deal with the most delicate and profound of human problems. These gifts he directs to every stage of his work. Several times men he has knocked out slump unconscious at the base of a wall. Forgetting the man as an enemy and seeing him as another confused, struggling human, he will loosen the man's collar button and pull him away from the wall in order to clear his breathing. His job has neither hardened him nor made him complacent about death. In *Doomsters*, he respectfully covers a corpse with a blanket, "as if that would do any good," and then, still deeply moved, loses his meal. But perhaps his most thoughtful, charitable moment comes in *Black Money*: He takes his pistol-harness out of his car-trunk but, because children are playing nearby, ducks into a building to strap the harness on. As is typical with him, he plays down his achievement. His stroke of moral sensibility is reported with such quiet, matter-of-fact modesty that it nearly escapes us. The refusal to take credit or raise his voice makes us respect him all the more.

II

Though no full picture of Archer's past emerges from the novels, certain scattered facts help rough out a profile sketch. The first problem comes at the very outset—with his name and date of birth. Twice identified as "Lewis Archer," he signs a hotel register, "Lew A. Archer," in *Drowning Pool*. Though his birthday falls on 2 June (Margaret and Kenneth Millar's 1938 wedding date), the year of his birth remains hidden.

He seems to have spent his early years in northern California. He lived for a spell with his grandmother in Martinez, in Contra Costa County, northeast of San Francisco, at the junction of the San Joachim River and and Bay. The grade school he attended in Oakland might have been a parochial school; in "The Sinister Habit" (1953), he credits his smattering of Latin to his Catholic mother. His tie to his mother, his life in the Church and Church schools, and his stay in Oakland are all obscure. He speaks of having been brought up in "a working-class tract" in Long Beach, where he went to Wilson Junior High School. Besides this scrap, what little else survives from his Long Beach youth is sordid. In *Doomsters,* he remembers himself as "a frightened junior-grade hood in Long Beach, kicking the world in the shins because it wouldn't dance for me." He bucked authority in the home by taking his father's strap when his father threatened to whip him.

The Far Side of the Dollar mentions his first sexual experience at age seventeen at a dude ranch in the Sierras, but doesn't give the girl's name or any other details of Archer's relationship with her. Then the record thins even more. He never made it to college. But his five-year stint in the Long Beach Police Department was distinguished enough to earn him the rank of detective-sergeant. Though graft drove him from the force, the specific reasons why he turned in his badge are unclear. In *Moving Target* he says he was fired; in *Drowning Pool* in claims he quit. *The Way Some People Die* parts the mists as much as they have been parted. According to a report given here, a local mobster with other policemen on his payroll forced Archer out because he refused bribes. In any case, his police service may have won him an army commission; he served in Okinawa as a U. S. Army Intelligence officer. (Kenneth Millar was also stationed off Okinawa, but as a lieutenant in the U. S. Navy.) Right after his discharge, he went into practice as a private detective. The first paragraph of "Find the Woman" (1946) refers to his sitting in his "brand-new office" on Wilshire Boulevard, "all dressed up in civilian clothes." The story doesn't mention his marriage. But by *Moving Target* (1949) he and Sue have already separated.

Our first look at Archer comes early in this first Archer novel:

I looked at my face in the mirror behind the bar and didn't like it too well. It was getting thin and predatory-looking. My nose was too narrow, my ears were too close to my head. My eyelids were the kind that overlapped at the outside corners and made my eyes look triangular.

Three years later, in *Ivory Grin*, the face peering back at him from a mirror is "a big man's face, too sharp and aggressive." Other physical descriptions come but rarely and are usually brief and impromptu. This reticence owes more to Archer's modesty than to his creator's reluctance to use the ancient trick of describing character through a mirror impression. In *Way Some People Die,* Archer weighs 185 lbs. In *Doomsters* (1958), published seven years later, his photostat describes him as six-foot-two, 190 lbs. His craggy face probably hasn't softened in the interval. Solidly built, he is mistaken for a professional athlete in *Wycherly Woman*. He has dark hair and blue-gray eyes. A large wad of his mustering-out pay bought him a new wardrobe. In *Ivory Grin*, he is praised for his natty dress. He is still playing the dandy in *Barbarous Coast* (1956), where he spends $125 for a suit and owns a sport jacket handsome enough to win a compliment. In recent years, he has let his appearance slide. He feels ashamed both of his shabby living room and raincoat when Laurel Russo comes to his apartment in *Sleeping Beauty*; his wardrobe has dwindled meanwhile to a few lonely-looking suits.

This seediness comes more from choice than from need. Archer has presumably no savings account; the funds in his checking account barely meet his $200 monthly rent and the price of a week's vacation in Mexico in *Sleeping Beauty*. Yet he earns enough to live comfortably. He charged $50 a day plus expenses in 1949; these rates have doubled in recent years. (Philip Marlowe earned $25 a day plus expenses in 1939 and *The Big Sleep*.) He pays no alimony, child support, or it would seem, heavy medical expenses. In *Ivory Grin* (1952), the waiting room of his West Hollywood office, in the 8400 block of Sunset Boulevard, is "neither large nor expensively furnished." But it does contain built-in microphones; by *Barbarous Coast*, he is making enough money to hire a telephone-answering service, which he has continued to use. His plain, simple life style extends to his food. His standard breakfast, when he takes the time to eat it, comprises bacon, eggs, and black coffee. For dinner, he likes rare steak, potato, a salad, and beer. Only once does he order fish (in *Sleeping Beauty*), and he leaves most of it on his plate. He has no favorite drink. He may have a Gibson or a martini before dinner; in *Chill*, he drinks gin, scotch, and bourbon. Handling liquor is no problem for him. Though he will even drink on duty, except before lunch, he has never been drunk in a novel.

His age, as has been said, remains dark. In *Moving Target*, he has a boyish grin, "a little the worse for wear." This self-estimate is plausible. By his own reckoning, he is fifteen years older than his client's missing daughter of twenty. In *Way Some People Die*, he admits to thirty-seven, but in *Barbarous Coast*, published five years later, he describes himself as "pushing forty." A sure sign of middle age enters the novel in his failure to react quickly to danger. He is knocked out by a flailing poker he would have dodged in earlier books, and then he moves too slowly to avoid a kick in the head. *The Doomsters* marks the onset of both his middle-age paranoia and improbable rejuvenation. He has finally reached forty. And while he refers to himself in *Far Side of the Dollar* (1965) as "good old graying Lew Archer," he musters the strength and spring of youth. In *Chill* he outpunches an ex-collegiate football star fifteen years his junior, and his swimming heroics in *Instant Enemy* (1968) and *Sleeping Beauty* call forth the same energies as the ones displayed in *Moving Target* and "The Suicide" (1953). The remark in *Sleeping Beauty* that he left the Long Beach Police "twenty years before" updates the chronology that held good from *Barbarous Coast* to *Black Money*, where he claimed he was not yet fifty. Though he began police work in 1935, Archer's year of birth has jumped from c. 1914 to c. 1920. He ages very slowly because, unlike Christie's Hercule Poirot and Jane Marple, who were always old, he has to exert himself physically. His job keeps him fit and trained. It has also seasoned him morally. Now that Ross Macdonald has achieved in him a near-perfect balance of the physical and the psychic, he can't be blamed for resisting change. Archer has become more exciting and more instructive to watch in the last ten years than in the first fifteen.

His tenderness, it bears repeating, was a long time nurturing. In 1966, Ross Macdonald discussed his literary origins:

Archer in his early days, though he was named for Sam Spade's partner, was patterned on Chandler's Marlowe. Chandler's Anglo-American background and my Canadian-American one gave our detectives a common quality: the fresh suspicious eye of a semi-outsider who is fascinated but not completely taken in by the customs of the natives.[12]

Marlowe voices his suspicions in sour wisecracks and a tough, knowing posture. He has been there before and knows what it is like; art and fist-fighting are the same to him. His reaction to a woman of forty-five or so in *Farewell, My Lovely* captures his cynicism: "She's a charming middle-aged lady with a face like a bucket of mud and if she has washed her hair since Coolidge's second term, I'll eat my spare tire, rim and all."[13] Early Archer has the same jaded arrogance. He too has seen the underside of humanity: no situation is new to him; nothing can surprise him, either. His blunt no-nonsense judgments assess people quickly. He says of Maude Slocum, on the first page of *Drowning Pool*, "About thirty-five . . . and still in the running." On the next page, he tells her, "I am rhinceros-skinned and iron-hearted. I've been doing divorce work in L. A. for ten years. If you can tell me anything I haven't heard, I'll donate a week's winning at Santa Anita [a local race track] to any worthy charity." When he says his wife divorced him for extreme mental cruelty, Maude answers, "I think you might be capable of it." Early Archer will talk tough to any-body—a client, a policeman, or a thug whose loaded pistol is pointing at him. These heavy attempts at man-talk from *Drowning Pool* and *Way Some People Die* complete the hard-boiled pose:

Seven men stopped me. . . . They knocked me out. Then they ventilated Reavis with a dozen slugs and gave him a gasoline barbecue.

*   *   *

You have me. Hearthstone of the Death Squad, I presume. . . . Accompanied by Deathstone of the Hearth Squad. Where's Squadstone of the Death Hearth?

This forced humor grates. One can sympathize with a police lieutenant who tells him, "Soft-pedal the repartee." Suitably, Archer's only three killings belong to this period: in *Moving Target*, he accuses his captor, one Puddler, "a trained beast of burden, a fighting machine," of being afraid to fight fairly, and then drowns him after a spectacular free-for-all. (Elsewhere in the book, he shoots an unarmed man and then pistol-whips him.) He shoots a lesbian through the temple near the end of *Ivory Grin* (1952), after seeing her murder her ex-lover. "Gone Girl" (1953) shows him shooting a man with the slow sadistic relish of a righteous avenger:

I sighted carefully . . . until the black bar of his eyebrows was steady in the sights of the .38. The hole it made was invisible. Gino fell loosely forward, prone on the floor beside the man he had killed.

Early Archer, if brutal, can also surprise us with his compassion. In *Drowning Pool*, he shields the corpse of a woman with his body to stop the woman's daughter from seeing it. He also gives another young woman $10,000 without pretending that the money will strengthen her moral character: "The money wouldn't do her any permanent good. She'd buy a mink coat or a fast car, and find a man to steal one or wreck the other." The response is typical. His loving acts are always either undercut by self-protective cynicism or tied to a pious morality. His compassion, it seems, needs an extrinsic basis; to feel a spontaneous twitch of tenderness or charity is to "go soft" in a hard, fast world. William Goldman has explained how today's Archer differs from the tough private eye with all the answers of *Moving Target, Drowning Pool,* and *Way Some People Die:*

> That's the great thing about Archer—he's done it all and he knows that we've fallen into a rotten place. Still, he plods along, a modern Diogenes who makes his money from other people's suffering, a nosy guy with a passion for mercy who likes to move into other people's lives and then move quickly out so he won't get bored. Nothing surprises him. Nothing shocks him. And he is continually horrified at the things we do to each other.[14]

Ross Macdonald's early tendency to judge can convert dramatic events into moral issues. Sometimes he moralizes through Archer. Accused of having "the Victorian hangover" in *Moving Target,* Archer shuckingly admits, "I'm developing into quite a moralist in early middle age." "The new-type detective," he refuses a pre-luncheon drink. And though he admits having gone to a bordello in Mexico City, he adds smugly, "on a case." Archer loses us when he does these moral calisthenics or when he turns a case into a crusade. He is a much better Leatherstocking than an evangelist. In *Ivory Grin,* not content to bring the killer to boot, he shakes an angry moralizing finger at him:

> It's not just the people you've killed. It's the human idea you've been butchering and boiling down and trying to burn away. You can't stand the human idea. . . . Even a dollar-chaser like Max Heiss makes you look lousy. So you have to burn his face off with a blow torch. Isn't that what you did?

Always ready to sermonize, the early Archer doesn't shrink from reminding people of their moral duties or from telling them, especially policemen, how to do their jobs. But one wonders whether some of his cocksureness comes less from within than from his author's artistic unreadiness. If Ross Macdonald has become an important novelist, his growth has been slow. His first seven or eight titles, though rich in lively characters and scenes, creak with implausibility. Archer's double role as narrator and plot-mechanism makes him, unfortunately, the focus of the novels' structural flaws. A great eavesdropper, he always overhears conversations just when the participants happen to be discussing something central to his case. (In *Moving Target* he is eavesdropped upon.) When he doesn't want people to know he's a detective, he will pretend to be somebody else, like an insurance auditor; or he will disguise his telephone voice; in "The Sinister Habit" (1953), he does three telephone impersonations in three pages. The last chapters of *Drowning Pool* and *Way Some People Die* both resort to the ancient device of pairing Archer, held at gunpoint, against a confident criminal who tells all. Early Archer lacks the human appeal of Philip Marlowe because Ross Macdonald took longer learning fictional technique than Chandler.

But not all Archer's personal failings come from problems in narrative form. He is often priggish in his own right; he stretches and even breaks the rules. Known to bully and to threaten witnesses, he is capable of brutal sadism. Not all his work is clean. In *Barbarous Coast* he mentions helping a friend divorce his third wife; in the same book, he punches the jaw of a man offering to shake hands. In *Way Some People Die,* he snatches a newlywed from a husband who makes her happy in order to stow her in her mother's house, where she doesn't want to live. His judgment and ethics have remained spotty. Though no longer reveling in sordidness ("Night streets were my territory," he says in *Drowning Pool,* "and would be till I rolled in the last gutter"), he still oversteps both legal and moral limits. In *Ivory Grin* he breaks into a house and steals a telegram addressed to somebody else; in *Sleeping Beauty* he rifles a doctor's private records as soon as the doctor's secretary turns her back; again in *Sleeping Beauty*, he feels "a little ashamed" of browbeating a witness. Coinciding with these misdeeds are several acts of downright stupidity. At least once a novel he will blunder badly—misjudging a witness, mixing sentiment with detection, even exploiting people. In *Find a Victim* he is duped by a gangster's moll scarcely out of her teens. In *Wycherly Woman* he is fooled by a woman pretending to be twice her age.

On balance, though, Archer can be forgiven his miscues. First of all, he suffers more from them than anyone else—they make his job harder and, owing to his self-critical nature, give him guilt-pangs. Next, his proneness to guilt and self-criticism has thinned both the number and the gravity of his miscues. Owning up to his mistakes has helped him overcome many of them. He knows that a man can stay honest if he works at it, but his moral imagination exceeds his moral grasp. This situation couldn't be otherwise. Were Archer either a scoundrel or a saint, he couldn't sustain the weight of a novel. He must occupy an ethical middle ground. Actor rather than spokesman, he must also carve out his midway morality in deeds rather than assertions. In *Sleeping Beauty* he refers to "the megalopolis which stretched from San Diego to Ventura," adding, "I was a citizen of the endless city." The addendum needs qualifying: Archer is *both* citizen and pilgrim; Eudora Welty's view of him as "one of ours"[15] holds good. But in order to qualify as Everyman, even a morally aspiring Everyman, he has to share some of the faults of his counterparts. His moral struggles resemble theirs and ours. We believe in the reality of these struggles because we never know how well Archer will cope. We believe in Archer because we know that he will try to cope, even if he fails.

The hub of his self-mending, self-building morality is the ability to resist the lure of money. Though he may muscle a witness or hold back information from the police, he will not let money tempt him. We have already seen him giving away $40,000 in *Moving Target* and *Drowning Pool*. He also rejects offers as high as $100,000 to walk away from an unsolved case. He will not collect twice for doing one job, even when somebody other than his client profits from his labors. He will ignore overbids —a high offer from a would-be client whose interests clash with those of a client who is paying him less. But why should this immunity from financial contamination count in his favor? Why does he deserve acclaim for resisting something he doesn't want? The answers to these questions stem from both his job and his Everyman status. He is a merchant in a mercantile society—one of consumers, where freedom and even selfhood have a basis in money. The ability to fight back greed lifts him above most of his fellow bread-winners. Knowing that people are the best that life offers has made him a man with money to give away, or even burn. Also, as a private detective, he would endanger his career by compromising himself for money. A detective's reputation, both with the police and the public at large, hinges on his honesty. The ability to resist a bribe is a moral imperative for Archer. Money costs a detective more than anybody else. Once it dents his honesty, it can put him out of work in no time. Any detective who trades his honesty for money will soon be controlled by the mob. For a man who lives his work, like Archer, this control would be fatal.

Like most authority-figures since Jupiter toppled Saturn, Archer lacks the proper moral credentials for his job. His self-honesty, though, helps him correct the equilibrium. His moral arrears have helped him respond imaginatively to the mendacity of others. He recalls in *Find a Victim*, "I'd been a street boy in my time, gang-fighter, thief, poolroom lawyer." The memory of his brawling youth, by putting him on a moral par with other offenders, promotes compassion. Like Chesterton's Father Brown, he participates imaginatively in the crimes he investigates; he sins psychologically but not materially. But he doesn't recreate crimes from the criminal's mental standpoint; he never becomes the criminal. The technical side of his sober, practical detection reveals no special imaginative powers. What his imagination does is to convert his own narrow escape from crime into the moral sympathy he extends to all sufferers and wrongdoers.

Though he catches criminals, he also tries to stop crimes before they happen. He lives and works in the open. No secret agent, he offers his services to the general public. He needn't like his clients; he can't choose them any more than a teacher can choose his students or a physician, his patients. Though he may not accept every prospective client, he gives all of them a fair hearing. Nor will he encourage one to chase empty hopes even if those hopes could bring him a fat fee; for instance, he tells Maria Galton not to waste her money looking for a son gone fifteen years. Cautious and honest, he won't guarantee results or make promises he can't keep. The same stubborn pride demands that he handle all cases in his own way. If a client interferes, like Maude Slocum in *Drowning Pool,* he will drop the case and refund his advance. Once he does accept a client, though, he works with diligence, energy, and imagination. He reports regularly, shares his findings, and prepares his clients for the worst without force-feeding them with grief. A guilty client will gain from his legal knowledge and moral sympathy. Though he can't hide guilt, he will try to get a client's sentence reduced. He will, in fact, advise *any* guilty person to give himself up to the police in the hope of gaining clemency. There is much more to criminals than the crimes they commit. No crusader or scourge, he saves what is worth saving without needing to satisfy the letter of the law.

Once called in, the police work quickly and capably. Ross Macdonald's policemen are neither corrupt nor stupid, and Archer has a good working relationship with them. In *Galton Case* and *Far Side of the Dollar,* he cooperates with the law from start to end. Sometimes, the police act badly. Sheriff Ostervelt in *Doomsters* is the scurviest person in the canon. Yet Brandon Church of *Find a Victim* and Pike Granada of *Ferguson Affair* reverse their bad early impressions and turn out to have been first-rate cops all along. Wayne Rasmussen, a junior plainsclothesman in *Black Money*, stays abreast of the more experienced Archer throughout. The mistakes Rasmussen's brother officers make are no more serious and come no more often than Archer's. Policemen usually judge wisely, avoid bribes and graft, and neither fake evidence nor beat up witnesses. Ross Macdonald is a moral relativist. A crooked policeman appears no more often in his work than, say, a crooked doctor or lawyer.

The law also has the wit to respect Archer. As early as *Moving Target* and *Drowning Pool,* members of the Los Angeles Police Department have been sending him clients. Any detective career as long as his will have its bad days with the police. He does not always agree with them, tell them all he knows, or find them cooperative, especially when he leaves Los Angeles. His failure to report a death in *Way Some People Die* nearly costs him his license. Nor does he always obey police orders, as in *Galton Case*, where he takes hold of the hand of a corpse a local sheriff warned him to leave untouched. And like any other good detective who loves to break a case, he captures the killer, as well as the most likely suspect, in *Zebra-Striped Hearse* without calling in the police.

This independence comes much easier to the freelancer than to the policeman. "Speaking as a policeman, I am shocked," says a police inspector in Sayers's *The Nine Tailors*; "Speaking as a human being, I have every sympathy for you."[16] The rift between human and official reaction troubling Sayers's inspector doesn't exist for Archer. Policemen have different goals from private detectives. Often pressured by crowded dockets or angry media, they close cases as soon as possible. The freelancer

The Man in the Maze

doesn't feel the same prods as the elected public official and his circle. Responsible only to his clients, he can ignore vested interests and chains of command. A police detective tells Archer in *Instant Enemy*, "There are places you can go, things you can do, that we can't." He might have added that suspects will tell the freelancer things that, fearing arrest, they keep from the law. Archer can work more slowly, speculate more, and approach witnesses off-limits to the police. Despite his advantages, though, he doesn't try to outsmart the law. In *Way Some People Die*, he says, "I always believe in giving the police an official priority when they get there first," and in most of the books he advises his clients to take their worries to the police. Careful not to overreach himself, he admits in *Instant Enemy*, "The case is too big for me to handle alone." Thus he calls in the police; he confers with lawyers; he co-opts detectives in other cities, like Willie Mackay in San Francisco and Arnie Walters in Reno. This call for outside help serves him well; in *Zebra-Striped Hearse* the police find an important lead he had overlooked.

III

As shown in his professional courtesy toward the police, Archer keeps his mind open and avoids hasty answers. What looks like a side issue often turns out crucial. He welcomes the seeming irrelevancy; you need the pieces of the puzzle before you can put it together. These can lie in obscure places. The four novels preceding Archer's debut (all published under the name, Kenneth Millar) feature evils Archer doesn't come up against—dope rings, slot-machine syndicates, abortion, and prostitution. The crime Archer fights is usually not professional; outside of *Moving Target*, *Way Some People Die*, and *Galton Case*, he never takes on the rackets. His on-the-spot impersonations, which have vanished with the years, are simple. Except for a couple of times when he flashes a bogus business card, he will only disguise his voice on the phone or behind a closed door. He uses no costumes, make-up, or wigs.

Sometimes—in *Drowning Pool*, *Wycherly Woman*, *Far Side of the Dollar*, and *Instant Enemy*, for instance—witnesses will block lines of investigation. Some have information they consider irrelevant; some want to hide an old family secret; most want to protect a child or spouse. Archer will always encourage candor in the refractory. He stands for plain dealing and clear speaking, not because of any blind trust in the truth, but because lies multiply and recoil on the liar; a nice application of this law comes in *Sleeping Beauty*, when a witness he has lied to lies to him, in turn. Truth he approaches from different sides. Though he doesn't ask elaborately detailed questions to break down alibis and discover motives, he practices great patience: "My job was a walking job and a driving job, but mainly a sitting and watching job," he says in *Ivory*

Grin. In *Goodbye Look*, he waits nearly an hour in a ditch for a man to come out of hiding two hundred yards away; he doesn't clockwatch his progress. And once he discovers the truth, he will not lose it in a private grudge or watch it boil off in the fumes of melodrama. He will fight if he must, but he prefers peaceful means, quelling a family crisis in *Underground Man* and a rising mob scene in *Sleeping Beauty*. He forgives his persecutors more quickly and cheerfully than most. He goes on searching for the prodigal in *Instant Enemy* after the prodigal beats him up; in *Sleeping Beauty* he helps a man who had just insulted him while digging a revolver into his kidneys.

Charity, thoroughness, and control of this kind infiltrate Archer's procedure. As has been seen, he follows up every lead in order to get close to the missing person's life. Knowing that he must ask annoying questions, he doesn't mind making a nuisance of himself. To learn about the personality and habits of the missing person, he talks to family and friends, to teachers, doctors, and lawyers; he will ask to see photos and letters, which he sometimes puts in the evidence case he keeps in his car-trunk. Once on the scent, he writes down the license-plate numbers of cars belonging to witnesses or suspects; when he can, he will take information from the registration cards strapped to steering posts. Resourceful and methodical, he inspects a house in *Chill* where a woman was killed ten years before and finds an important clue. He knows the law, especially the rights of the police to hold and question suspects. He has a Sherlockian knowledge of his beat—greater Los Angeles—its freeways, neighborhoods, topography. No armchair sleuth, he will visit the murder site, handle the murder weapon, look at and perhaps even touch the corpse; several times, he hauls corpses from the sea. Physical danger he accepts as a normal business risk. He knows how to fight and to fire a pistol, not because he likes violence, but because he has to master these skills if he is to survive. (In *Find a Victim*, to divert suspicion, he tails a suspect from the front.) Trained by professionals, he keeps fit; good physical conditioning helps him vault a seven-foot fence and then race a man fifteen years younger in *Ivory Grin*. A woman asks him in *Wycherly Woman*, "Are you a professional athlete? You seem to be in very good trim for a middle-aged man." Archer not only fights well, but, thanks to his author's descriptive power, convinces us, too, that fighting takes speed and skill, timing and balance, as well as strength.

A leading motif of Freudian epistemology is connection; the analyst must connect the strong feelings troubling the patient's unconscious. The search for a first cause, Freud says, has both diagnostic and therapeutic value:

> When in the course of a piece of scientific work we come upon a problem which is difficult to solve, it is often a good plan to take up a second problem along with the original one—just as it is easier to crack two nuts together than each separately.[17]

The Man in the Maze

Archer, too, with his belief in the vitality of the past and disbelief in coincidence, uses a comparative method. In *Find a Victim*, he is told, "There's too damn many coincidences here. You make a habit of finding murder victims in pairs." Aware of the cancerous spread of killing, he notes in *Galton Case*, "In murder cases, there are usually more victims than one." As has been said, no killer kills just once in the canon. The dialectic generated by setting a recent murder against an old one reveals the strangeness of life in all its hidden linkages. This technique not only solves murders but also gives a glimpse of obscure undercurrents, setting forth hidden meanings without arrogantly defining them.

His helpers come from all over. He questions bartenders, rooming-house clerks, and, quite often, gas-station attendants: now that the American life style is built around the automobile, the gas-station attendant or garage mechanic makes an excellent witness. Archer visits shanties, bars, and all-night restaurants; *Black Money* takes him to a hobo jungle, or tramps' bivouac. But he also goes to the mansions and private clubs of the mandarin class. He will hold his style in these places and also in the clinics of angry physicians and psychiatrists. Because crime and its detection are social levellers, the search for motive, means, and opportunity supersedes class differences.

Interviewing is the most important part of his job. This he prefers to do in person rather than on the phone, where a witness can be more evasive and curt. Though witnesses don't have to talk to him at all, they usually ask him into their homes and speak freely; even uncooperative ones will give him a scrap of useful information. Most people, in fact, enjoy helping; most like to see crime stopped or punished. Once they trust a questioner, they will help him all they can. When asked in *Goodbye Look* how he makes people talk, he answers, "I don't. People like to talk about what's hurting them. It takes the edge off the pain sometimes." His job as an interviewer, in short, is to win and then hold a witness' confidence. Since he cares about people, he does the job well. He makes his witnesses feel strong, important, and knowledgeable; he calls them by name; he convinces them that he and they are working together. He will do his best to protect their confidence, too. Because a frightened or hostile witness can't help him, he puts the witness at his ease. Knowing how to handle people, he controls the flow of an interview. He listens patiently and carefully; he changes pace when the interview is going badly; he changes the subject or answers a pointed question vaguely if the need arises. He can talk a great deal without saying much. One character in *Barbarous Coast* calls him, "Mr. Questionnaire," and another tells him, "You're a hard man to get information out of." Some of his witnesses don't surrender information easily, either. The duels of wit, flashing insights, and conversational nuances flickering over an interview with a reluctant witness can turn the interview into a little drama.

But Archer prefers to bypass dramatics. He is an investigator, not a showman. He needs his witnesses' help; everything he knows comes from them. Angering or arguing with one is counterproductive. Thus he doesn't use a relentless Socratic questioning technique to confuse or tie a witness in logical knots. On the other hand, inconsistency will not get by him. His good memory and his alertness to gesture and vocal inflection may help him to use it later on. But he is also realistic enough to know when even the baring of new evidence won't open a witness's lips. When this happens, he grows more coercive, often reminding the witness of the advantage of talking to him rather than to the police. The coercion can be gentler. *Find a Victim* shows him rolling a cigarette with the paper and tobacco belonging to a man he wants information from. Sometimes five or ten dollars will improve a hotel clerk's memory. But, just as Archer will only strongarm underworld people, he will only buy information from working-class people (and usually only when they are at work), never from children or pensioners.

His ability to gauge a situation quickly and then react has helped him in many ways. Living in an instant society can call for the instant response. *Doomsters* opens with Carl Hallman knocking at his door at first dawn. Archer's reaction, if grumbling, is gracious and self-sacrificing:

A pre-breakfast client was the last thing I needed that morning. But it was one of those times when you have to decide between your own convenience and the unknown quantity of another man's trouble. Besides, the other man and his way of talking didn't go with his ragbag clothes, his mud-stained work shoes. It made me curious.

Archer stays up, invites Hallman in, and then makes him a breakfast of coffee and eggs even though he has never seen him before. In *Find a Victim*, his capacity for self-sacrifice touches on the saintly. He sees a stranger bleeding from bullet wounds along a highway in the opening paragraph. By the fourth paragraph, he has stopped his car, gotten out, and then bound the stranger's wounds with his own jacket, shirt, and tie. His remark about the bleeding stranger, "He's nothing to me. I found him on the highway," touches a core reality of his job: no sooner does he meet someone than he finds himself closely tied to him. He must be ready to sacrifice comfort and property at a moment's warning. If this readiness falls short of Whitmanesque compassion, it carries Whitman's moral requirement. Later in *Find a Victim*—and the situation recurs in *Wycherly Woman*—the news of the death of a young woman he had never met makes him cry. These tears, which help melt the private eye's tough shell, are genuine. As his name implies, Archer darts in and out of other people's lives. His reluctance to stay long anywhere, though, does not weaken his bond to those he is with at a given time. His friendships live fully, if briefly; he feels strongly and gives a great deal of himself, serving his fleeting friends to the limit of his physical and imaginative powers.

The Man in the Maze

Is this goodness innate or acquired? Although the question remains open, the bombshell of his divorce sent shock waves through him from which he still hasn't recovered. His downstairs neighbors in *Underground Man* (1971) call him "a lonely man," and nobody meets him at the airport when he flies back from a Mexican holiday in Chapter 1 of *Sleeping Beauty*. A sudden insight in the same books shows guilt over his wrecked marriage still riding him after twenty-five years: "He's a willing man," Archer says of his client, "If I had been half as willing, I could have held on to my own wife." Though he enjoys tumbling Ada Reichler (*Galton Case*), Moira Smitheram (*Goodbye Look*), and Elizabeth Somerville (*Sleeping Beauty*), he doesn't try to sustain a relationship with any of them. The guilt that keeps stabbing out of his past could explain not only his faint-heartedness but also his preference for fleeting friendships in general.

A survey of the spread of years since his separation and divorce shows these setbacks to have injured more than his vanity. The past-tense verb in this sentence from *Moving Target* shows that, though still married, Sue and Lew Archer no longer live together: "She didn't like the company I kept," he tells a friend. By the next novel, *Drowning Pool*, published a year later (1950), they have divorced: "My wife divorced me last year. Extreme mental cruelty." In *Zebra-Striped Hearse* (1962), he admits, "I treated her badly." Other explanations for the divorce in *Find a Victim* (1954) and *Goodbye Look* (1969) swing enigmatically between his job and his person:

> She said she couldn't stand the life I led. That I gave too much to other people and not enough to her. And I guess she was right in a way. But it really boiled down to the fact that we weren't in love any more. At least, one of us wasn't.
>
> *　　　*　　　*
>
> She divorced me. . . . I don't blame her. She wanted a settled life, and a husband she could count on to be there.

The certainties rising out of the fog belt of twenty-five years are that Archer's work routine blunted Sue's love and that the divorce was her idea, not his.

But *Moving Target* suggests that Archer's job was not the only raw spot in the marriage. Right after he refers to "building up my virility" by eating oysters at the end of Chapter 11, he goes to bed "without looking at the empty twin bed on the other side of the room." Why should the Archers have twin beds at all? Judging from his Army tour, which lasted till 1946, and from the absence of children in the marriage, sex may have hamstrung them from the start; for whatever reason, the marriage seems to have soured quickly. In *Way Some People Die*, he is still living in the home he had with Sue, "a five-room bungalow on a middle-class residential street between Hollywood and Los Angeles." But the home, "the end of a journey from nowhere to nowhere," gives little comfort, strength, or security: "Since the divorce I never went home till sleep was overdue." *The Barbarous Coast* both says that Archer has moved and tells about his new home, "a two-bedroom stucco cottage on a fifty-foot lot off Olympic":

For a while the second bedroom hadn't been used. Then for a while it had been. When it was vacated finally, I sold the bed to a second-hand furniture dealer and converted the room into a study. Which for some reason I hated to use.

Did Sue occupy the other bedroom? As a way of easing back into marriage, did she and Archer agree to live together again but in different rooms? These questions can't be answered. What can be said is that Archer's strong efforts for other people's happiness might well carry over to his own. His avoidance of the converted study makes Sue a likely occupant of the other bedroom, as does his self-protective haste to sell the bed. A male lodger Archer may have taken in to relieve a financial pinch wouldn't provoke an emotional reaction; a female lodger would, in all likelihood, stay in Archer's room. Also worth considering, though five rooms is too many for most bachelors, is the chance that Archer bought the cottage because he thought a reconciliation easier to bring about in new surroundings. A trier, he didn't walk away casually from Sue. He recalls in the last chapter of *Doomsters*, "my latest efforts to effect a reconciliation with Sue" three years before. The stiff, defensive "effect a reconciliation" shows the persistence of his pain and regret.

This effort, which took place around 1955, was probably the last. By *Zebra-Striped Hearse* she was remarried and had two children. Two novels later, *Far Side of the Dollar* (1965), Archer has moved into the West Los Angeles flat where he still lives, "a fairly new, two-story building with a long roofed gallery on which the second-floor apartments opened directly. Mine was the second floor back." Descriptions of Archer's neighborhood, building, and apartment come seldom; nor does he exchange frequent visits with his neighbors. Since 1965, he only accounts for his surroundings in *Goodbye Look*, where he says, "I lived in a quiet section, away from the main freeways," and in *Underground Man*, where "rather worn furniture" occupies his "shabby" living room.

Age has made him slower, drier, and more restrained. The compassion for human suffering he has acquired—his way of relating to a world that does not include him—makes him more of a rounded character than a mere unraveller of other people's problems. But what of his own problems? In *Black Money* (1966) he says, "I started out as a romantic and ended up as a realist." What reality means in the deep places of his heart is a starved lust he usually crushes because it fastens to women half his age. A subtle but persistent erotic gleam flickers over his first impression of Laurel Russo in *Sleeping Beauty*: "Her narrow feet left beautifully shaped prints in the wet sand." Chapter Three, which refers to "her dirty elegant feet," shows Archer foolishly taking her to his apartment: "I caught an oblique glimpse of myself as a middle-aged man on the make. It was true that if she had been old or ugly, I wouldn't have brought her home with me. She was neither." He questions his motives with bleak honesty: "I don't want anything from you," he tells her in the next paragraph, "asking myself if I was telling the truth." With the slightest encouragement he would try to take her to bed. He can't stay away from beautiful young women or from inviting danger once they come near. His craving for beauty has sharpened in direct ratio to his loneliness and powers of observation. Only self-respect and, perhaps, fear of another sexual failure blocks an unsolicited pass.

The outcast or exile, who, for reasons known to himself, deserves to be cast out, runs through western literature. Perhaps Archer's self-exile, like that of Oedipus, stems from sexual guilt. But his secret sorrows have not been wasted. Rather than watching them erode him, he has rechannelled them. The rechannelling goes beyond textbook sublimation because it refers only slantwise to socially approved goals. Archer acts from conviction, and his work, like that of God, mirrors him. Lew Archer has a firm sense of himself—moral integrity as well as moral passion. He has tried to heal himself by fitting his needs to those of others. His charity is rooted in pain. Born too of pain, Lazarus-like, is the overarching virtue irradiating the novels.

3

The four novels Ross Macdonald published before 1949 and *The Moving Target* look to the more accomplished work which followed. These four, published between 1944-48 under the by-line of Kenneth Millar, introduce the family as a major influence; both family conflict and the repetition of obsessive behavior by members of the same family in *The Dark Tunnel* and *The Three Roads* prefigure similar struggles in *The Underground Man* and *Sleeping Beauty*. Introduced, too, in these four fledgling works is the idea that crisis engulfs whole families, not just individuals. Any unit comprising sub-units will be controlled by the least stable one. Accordingly, anybody drawn into a crime will draw in others. As his family rallies round to protect him, normal work routines break, trips are made, and long-dormant relationships revive. The nightmare reunion of Dr. Herman Schneider and his son, a Nazi intelligence officer in *The Dark Tunnel,* causes the same havoc as that of the elderly Macready sisters in *The Chill,* a work published twenty years later.

The first quartet of novels also establishes the importance of the Midwest in Ross Macdonald's thought. *The Dark Tunnel* and *Trouble Follows Me* both take place in Detroit; *Blue City* is set in a small city near Chicago; the hero of *The Three Roads* grew up in Michigan and studied at the University of Chicago. Although known as a California writer, Ross Macdonald grew up in the Midwest; the Midwest is the source of some of his biggest experiences. He has continued to draw on both the Canadian and American Midwest. George Wall of *The Barbarous Coast* once lived on the same Toronto street as Ross Macdonald, and the main character of *The Galton Case* grew up in southern Ontario and then went to the University of Michigan; the moral struggle at the core of *The Ivory Grin* was hatched at the Great Lakes Training Center, near Chicago; the killer in *Black Money* both studied and taught at the University of Illinois, Urbana. Besides storing many indelible memories, the Midwest, because of its conservative tradition, also symbolizes the buried past where the California detective sometimes digs for answers to old mysteries.

Ross Macdonald and his California sleuth, Lew Archer, have both traveled their own tacks since 1949. The end of the war killed the market for spy novels like *The Dark Tunnel* and *Trouble Follows Me*. The high-speed extroversion and the crudely applied Oedipal psychology of the next two works mellow into the controlled unity of the later Archers. Basic attitudes emerge early, together with the moral passion to give them force. What remained in 1948 was for Ross Macdonald to find a persona through which to voice his commitments. But the slow steps by which Archer helped both develop and shape the writer's deepest feelings will be discussed in their place. Meanwhile, a look at the novels preceding Archer will beam in on Ross Macdonald's early growth and also display some effects artistically exciting in their own right.

I

Recalling *The Dark Tunnel* in 1971, Ross Macdonald said, "My first novel was written in Ann Arbor in the fall of 1943. I worked on it at night in one of the offices of the main classroom building, and the book preserves some of the atmosphere of that empty echoing pile."[1] This atmosphere stems in part from the false security given off by academe during wartime. *The Dark Tunnel* (1944) occurs in September 1943, mostly on or near the campus of Midwestern University in Arbana, some fifty miles from Detroit.

The main character, Robert Branch, Ph.D., teaches English at Midwestern. As his name suggests—if not his deeds—he is but a branch or offshoot, rather than the main stock. In fact, he seems attached to no stock or bole at all. At thirty, he has no parents, wife, child, or ruling purpose. Though anxious to help America's war effort, he has been turned away by both Army and Navy recruiters because of a weak left eye: a Nazi officer clubbed him in Munich, where he was researching his doctoral thesis six years before the time of the book. Munich 1937 also introduced him to Ruth Esch, whom he then knew for a month, fell in love with, and has spent the intervening six years wondering about. The symbolic, retrospective, and actional currents join neatly. Like other living branches, Bob Branch can sprout leaves and flowers; he is also an artery—a carrier of blood and channel of communication. This life-giving potential, though, he can't fulfill on the concrete pavements of Detroit or mid the campus politics of Arbana. His rejection by the armed services on account of his damaged eye also makes him a Joycean, rather than Oedipal, outcast, whose handicap both divides him from his kind and causes him bodily anguish. This manifold pain of not-having, not-belonging, and physical suffering persists. Branch is sorely tested time after time. The girl he loves has vanished inside Hitler's Germany, his best friend dies mysteriously, and Branch is accused of killing him. What develops, besides the hot action of gunplay and a manhunt, is the education of Bob Branch.

The September time-setting coincides with the start of the 1943-44 academic year, with Branch unknowingly giving up his teacher's role to be taught. The instruction he needs most doesn't come from books. His heart wants activating. His dearth of heart-knowledge shows in the remark, "A man will trust another man further than he'll trust a woman—women are a different kind of animal." The book's symbolism gauges his unreadiness. His escape from his murderous pursuers takes him down into the hot, clammy steam tunnels which heat the University; this great female symbol scares him as much as his pursuers do. In the last paragraph, he emerges, thanks to his immersion in danger, from the symbolic birth canal, primed for manhood.

The book opens well. Chapter One, where Branch is rejected by the Navy, gives the wartime mood, the Detroit setting, and the friendship of Branch and Alec Judd, an English department colleague at Midwestern and chief of the local War Board, whose V-12 program he helped start. Detroit's U. S. Naval Recruiting Office, where Judd and Branch go to enlist, was located, incidentally, in the Book Tower Building. This midtown setting not only embodies two of Ross Macdonald's abiding concerns —struggle and intellectual pursuit—in an urban context; the Book Tower was also to become, twenty-eight years later in 1971, the home of the first bibliography of his work—Matthew Bruccoli's *Kenneth Millar/Ross Macdonald: A Checklist.*

Spying enters the book when Judd says that important secrets have leaked from the War Board to Nazi agents in Detroit. Soon emerging as the Most Likely Suspect for causing the leakage is Dr. Herman Schneider, "until 1934 . . . the greatest Shakespearean scholar in Germany":

Schneider was a German, Doctor of Philosophy of Heidelberg and head of the Department of German at Midwestern since 1935. He had left his chair at the University of Munich in protest against Nazi philosophies of education soon after Hitler rose to power. His classic letter of resignation to the Chancellor of the University of Munich had been published in translation in the United States, and made several hundred dollars in royalties for the International Red Cross.

The same evening Branch is invited to Dr. Schneider's dinner-table, he learns that Ruth Esch has taken an instructorship at Midwestern's German department and will arrive in Arbana in a few hours. Having roused our curiosity, Ross Macdonald deepens it in Chapter 2, which goes back six years to Munich 1937. The episode, the only historical time-glide and only European setting in the canon, starts when Branch's English briar, symbol of sociability, is snapped from his mouth by an angry German who then savages him for smoking near the *Führer.* Stunned and frightened, Branch tries to explain that he didn't know the passing military parade included the *Führer.* He is soon rescued by Ruth, a passerby, who tells his persecu-

Four Before Archer

tor that, as a foreigner, Branch can't be blamed for dishonoring the *Führer*. What threatens the novel here is the Hollywood cliché of an American graduate student who meets an anti-Nazi *Fräulein* with a background of English (maybe even American) travel and a fine command of English. But the novel steers clear of this cliché. Ruth not only speaks English fluently; she also displays her wares as a Shakespearean actress. Now since he must hide Ruth's loyalties till the end, Ross Macdonald does well to put her on the stage. An acting career makes her capable of dissembling and thus morally suspect. Her playing the role of Cressida, which she manages triumphantly, carries an added hint of falseness and faithlessness. Ross Macdonald also maintains the excitement created by the novel's strong start by giving Hitler, Göring, and Goebbels walk-on roles. Matching this audacity is his tact in parading the three Nazi leaders before us without giving them anything to say and without having them notice Branch. They are only in the book to justify the near-sexual frenzy they exude, and this job they do effectively and economically. Quiet economy also sends a chill through the description of a murdered Jewish scientist which ends the chapter. Because Ross Macdonald doesn't shout, he makes us listen: "Most of Dr. Weiner was lying on the next bench, but parts of his head and face were missing."

Chapters Three and Four keep the action moving with both control and intelligence. In Chapter 3, Branch eats with Dr. Schneider and his son, Peter, and then goes to their fencing room, where he is nearly butchered in a saber duel. Dr. Schneider then tries to kill him on the way to the train station by jamming his door, so he can't get out, and then running the car toward a cliff. Without knowing why, Branch sees clearly that the Schneiders want him dead. Explanations for this and for other mysteries surface in Chapter 4. Branch goes back to the Schneiders' home, bringing Alec Judd, and looks into the fencing room, where Peter is dueling with somebody that looks like Ruth Esch. Then, after a passionate kiss broken by a fuming Dr. Schneider, Branch enters the home. The person Peter was fencing with and then kissing was not Ruth but her brother Carl, who had truncheoned Branch in Munich and who has just fled a German prison camp in northern Ontario. But Branch's poor sight, unhelped by eyeglasses, which broke during the fencing match in Chapter 3, mistakes Carl for Ruth. This mistake Carl gladly encourages to divert suspicion.

Chpater Five brings more violence. Early into it Judd hurtles to his death from the window of a locked room he had been in alone. The belief that Judd did not kill himself makes Branch, first, a man with a mission and, next, the target of a manhunt by Peter Schneider and Carl Esch, who engineered Judd's death. The link between the death and the suspicion of an information leak from the War Board brings in the FBI. But even the FBI agent, backed by Judd's former fiancée, believes Judd a suicide. As with a Hitchcock hero, all the evidence and sentiment go against Branch. Contending most fiercely against him is the novel's antagonist, Peter Schneider, described thus when he came into the book in Chapter 3: "His face and hair were very blonde, almost albino, and his eyes were as pale and empty as the sky." This description recalls the priests with no-color eyes and drab, parchment skin in Joyce's *A Portrait*. Leached out and morally inert, Peter serves the snow-swept creed of national socialism. His Nordic whiteness a badge of depravity, he has carried Hitler's Aryan ethic to its logical non-human extreme. He argues that we exist to serve the state and that the good of the state sanctions forced labor camps and secret police.

Fiendishly clever, Peter always outwits the more-educated Branch, who admits, "He had taken me in three rounds and I was waiting for the fourth." Three times he has Branch at his mercy; three times Branch is saved by luck. An engineer and highly skilled spy chief, he recalls the ruthless efficiency of the Walter Slezak role in Hitchcock's *Lifeboat* and the Fifth Columnists in Greene's *Ministry of Fear*. Even when Peter is out of the action, Ross Macdonald's warnings of the Nazi menace sometimes sound like sermon and propaganda:

It's the Nazi principle that killing people is less complicated than living with them. If they were allowed to carry it to its logical conclusion, the world would be populated by the 6,600,000 members of the Nazi party and their women and children and some slaves.

Much of this criticism has a sexual basis. Peter is not just a Nazi; he is also a homosexual and a parricide. Carl (von) Esch is another Nazi homosexual who violates nature by trying to kill his sister Ruth. The bullet from Peter's revolver that hits Branch in the thigh was aimed at his genitals. A well-schooled propagandist as well as a budding master of narrative form, Ross Macdonald doesn't miss his chance to tie Nazi politics to a deranged psychosexuality:

I thought of Roehm, the homosexual chief of the SA whom Hitler murdered with his own talented hands in the bloodbath of 1934. I thought of the elegant Nazi boys I had seen in the Munich nightclubs, with their lipstick and their eye-shadow and their feminine swagger, and the black male guns in their holsters.

The fourteen-chapter book splits neatly in half. At the end of Chapter 7, Branch is alone. His only helper, Alec Judd, is dead, and nobody else beside Peter Schneider, Judd's killer, believes Judd a murder victim. In Chapter 8, the war secrets are stolen from Judd's office. With Peter and Carl at large, Branch's life is in danger. Carl's disguising himself as Ruth has both confused and upset Branch. On the first page of Chapter 8, he admits, "Maybe I was all wrong and maybe Alex had been all wrong," and also, "I didn't know what to think." He needs to recover grip. The second half of the book starts with him playing the double role of detective and fugitive, on the run from both Peter, his potential killer, and the police. The hunt, comprising Chapters 8-10, is the best part of the book. It takes some exciting twists; several rural grotesques flash across the action; the literary allusions Branch drops compulsively vanish altogether. His run through the steam tunnel—the dank coils underlying the airy, light-filled campus—copies the epic hero's descent into the underworld, which also comes midway through the action, as a rule.

The chase sequence comes just at the right time. At the start of Chapter 8, the plot has all the imponderables and moral issues it needs, with Judd dead and Ruth apparently mad. What it needs to give the second half a good push is some action. Branch goes to Judd's office, finds the missing war secrets, but also finds himself held at gunpoint by Dr. Schneider. Tricking him, Branch disarms and then knocks Dr. Schneider out. But while Branch goes looking for a policeman, Peter steals into the room, kills his father, and pinches the war secrets. Branch is quickly taken as a murder suspect. Unwisely, he steals the arresting policeman's gun, locks him in a room, and runs away. Chapter Nine shows him on the run; he says here, "I felt more than ever like an outlaw." Like Greene's heroes in *This Gun for Hire, The Confidential Agent,* and *Ministry of Fear,* he has to catch the criminals before the police catch him. Remarkably athletic for a sedentary man, he is hard to catch. He runs and scrambles, then jumps and flings himself over fences with daredevil abandon.

Images of sickness and mutilation along the countryside bring in a mood of hectic desperation which combines with the fetid mists of the steam tunnel—a man at a barn dance who once shot off part of his foot, a noseless man, a customer called the Tube, whose throat rotted away from cancer. This desperation grips Branch. At the end of Chapter 9 some information given him by a local cabdriver inspires him to call in the police. But this he can't do. As soon as he gets up to leave, Peter and Carl, disguised again as Ruth, walk into the saloon, pistols in their coatpockets. From the start of Chapter 11, where Branch is saved by an FBI agent, the moral and legal balance shift in his favor. Yet, to avoid too sudden a shift, Ross Macdonald wisely ends Chapter 11 by having a policeman handcuff Branch, if only to free him early in the next chapter.

As has been said, the chase is the best part of the book. Without warning, it will stall, dart ahead, change direction. It even changes principles; sometimes Branch is chased by the police, sometimes by Peter and Carl. It moves easily from indoors to out; from University campus to back country; from flatland to bluff; from dark to light. Distance between pursuer and pursued will widen, shrink, or disappear. Some rural folk turn Branch away; some, like a pair of rabbit-hunting deaf mutes, help him. But as soon as the FBI rescues Branch in Chapter 11, the literary references start anew. We know that the chase has ended. When asked if he's feeling better, Branch replies, "Yes, thanks. But my neck is somewhat chapped. Bring me my honey and almond cream. Also my bow of burning gold. I'm on a hunting trip." And Ross Macdonald needs a walk in the fresh air. These references ring false, coming from a character who has just awakened after being drugged, strangled by a rope, and then pinned under a heavy beam. They cause regret, not only because of their unnaturalness, but also because they yell out at us that, the chase now over, we are in for something less exciting.

The action of the next two chapters is solid police procedural. The last chapter includes a flight from Detroit to Toronto and then a fourteen-and-a-half-hour train ride to Kirkalnd Lake in the far north. Ruth is cleared—morally and politically. Her brother, having escaped Bonamy, the nearby prison camp, took her clothing and, then, with Peter's help, tried to kill her. The trans-sexual identity switch between look-alike brother and sister holds the plot together. But does it work? It fools almost everybody, including Branch, Judd, and a hotel detective in Arbana. It squares with the political satire. It puts no strain on the story. When Ruth, whom Carl had beaten and then left for dead, reappears, she is lying unconscious, like the heroine of Ross Macdonald's latest novel, *Sleeping Beauty,* published twenty-nine years after the first. Shocked and concussed, she nevertheless awakens to speak gently to Branch. The novel ends here—in a hospital, emblem of a sick world. A first-chapter reference to a Detroit bar as "the twentieth-century urban inferno," the terrifying steam tunnel, and characters like the Tube, the noseless man, and the homosexual Nazis all prefigure this last-chapter setting. Like the Naval recruiting office and the steam tunnel, the hospital winds with passageways. But Branch's initiation ordeal doesn't end with his passing through them. He must also accept Ruth's dangers as his own. Before his arrival, Peter had marked Ruth's room with a vase of roses, hoping to come back after dark and kill her. Branch, detecting Peter's plan, has her moved to a different room, wraps his head in bandages, and takes her place as Peter's intended victim. The finale, where Branch gets his man— dressed as a nurse—ties all in a neat package.

Neatness also shows elsewhere in the structure. *Tunnel*'s first sentence mentions Detroit's "hot . . . sticky" summers, and its last sentence refers to the crisp brightness of northern Ontario in the fall. Branch has caught one of Hitler's best spies; in the book's symbolic last paragraph, the moist menacing tunnel warms and dries, and Ruth stands waiting for him in the sunlight. Yet the real Ruth lies unconscious in a raw mining town unconscious of itself and bracing for a long, heavy winter. Branch's relationship with Ruth is an open question. The moment they spend together at her bedside is their first together in six years. Thus the book avoids a romantic finale. War is more pressing than

Four Before Archer

heterosexual or filial love. The German prison camp lies close by, both night and winter draw on, and the roses in Ruth's room waver between red and black, the two main colors of the Nazi flag. Branch's final vision of Ruth in sunlight is wish-projection. The reality is war, death, and the coming winter. Though the last chapter sharpens the moral and political issues, it refuses to resolve them.

One unresolved issue is Branch's capacity for evil. Branch and Peter turn up in many of the same places—Dr. Schneider's home, Alex Judd's office, the tunnel and museum of the University, a rural bootlegger's, and the hospital at Kirkland Lake. Peter's evil shadows Branch so closely that it looks like a part of him. The ending, where the two men fight, looks like a routing of Branch's evil side, even though Branch is less wicked than unready. His role in the plot needs better planning. Also, Carl Esch fits clumsily into the action. Captured offstage in Chicago, he never reappears after the chase of Chapters 9-11. All the tensions of the novel must sharpen to a one-on-one struggle between hero and villain, who are always alter-egoes. But since Carl smashed Branch and clouded his sight, he bids stronger as Branch's double than Peter; Branch and Peter never meet before September 1943. The novel's structure blocks narrative outlets. As Branch's prospective brother-in-law, Carl couldn't have played the villain without also inviting identification as Ruth's alter-ego. For this doubling to work, Branch would have had to show homosexual traits. Besides, a last-chapter defeat of Carl would have recalled the closing scenes of Greene's *Ministry of Fear,* published the year before *Tunnel.*

The characters, Peter included, represent a solid achievement in their range of background, interest, and social level. They have personalities, not just peculiarities. They don't mumble or rant. Something is going on inside them all the time, though we must wait to learn what it is. Certain characters exist to move the plot; these, Ross Macdonald has the good judgment to keep shadowy and to remove from the novel once they do their essential work. They are not missed after they leave us. A colleague named Hunter, whom Branch happens upon in a coffee shop in Chapter 2, supplies the ear into which Branch tells the details of Munich 1937. The chance meeting justifies the inclusion of information the reader needs to make sense of what follows. Moreover, Hunter is the ideal silent listener. Branch couldn't have told his twenty-page story to Alec Judd, because Judd, as his close friend, would have already heard it. He couldn't have told it to a woman, because the first breath of a liaison would weaken Ruth as an imaginative presence. Nor could Branch detain a senior professor like Dr. Schneider long enough to tell it to him. An FBI agent named Fenton helps the plot in the next-to-last chapter in the same way Hunter did in the second. Fenton is brought in to give important background information about Peter Schneider and his spy ring. His recital, though not dramatic, promotes drama, by leaving the last chapter free for the renewed chase, the capture, and the surprising end.

Tunnel has three elements—espionage, which includes Judd's mysterious death and the theft of the war secrets; melodrama, or the chase, which occupies the middle part and then comes on again at the end; finally, the love interest, reaching from six years before the action and extending indefinitely into the future: included here are the riddle of Ruth's whereabouts since 1937, the vexing change in her personality, and her perplexing love for Peter Schneider; even Branch refers to her twice as "the Esch woman." These elements mix well; *Tunnel* is not random or thin. But its treatment of homosexuality gives the mixture a cheap patina. There is, first, the facile equation of Nazism and homosexuality. This equation goes beyond propagandizing into commercialism. Ross Macdonald flits Peter's gay Detroit roommate across the action for a few pages; smuggling transvestitism into the book, he reveals Ruth near the end wearing her escaped brother's clothes. And even *she* is indirectly accused of being homosexual by a hotel detective in Arbana. The accusation is unwarranted. Like everyone else, the detective mistakes Carl for his sister, in whose name he has checked into the hotel. A homosexual, Carl wouldn't prefer women to men, as the detective alleges. The allegation—keeping the issue of homosexuality before us without dramatizing or explaining it—only makes sense as crude commercialism.

No profit-motive mars the language of the novel. The style of *Tunnel,* besides moving briskly, soars and resonates. Branch, dog-tired from the chase, says, "I tried to lengthen my stride, but tiredness hung around my thighs like hoops." Ross Macdonald's description of an exchange between two deaf mutes registers freshness and force without resorting to simile:

I took two twenties out of my wallet and handed the card and the bills to the young man. He read what I had written and looked at me in smiling surprise. Then he turned to the other hunter and talked to him on his fingers. The other man's fingers began to talk.

Though Chapter 3 includes two high-velocity attempts on Branch's life, its real subject is Ruth, who never appears. Ross Macdonald knows the uses of flat, bald statement. The simple, straightforward phrasing of the last sentence of the chapter reasserts Ruth's importance to Branch. Of the nineteen words comprising the sentence, only two have more than one syllable: "Ruth Esch did not come on that train and nobody I knew was at the station to meet her." The dialogue, furthermore, is tight, clean, and plausible; characters speak to converse, not to tell the reader things or to advance the plot.

What clouds the novel's clear, strong voice is its pretension. Because most of the literary flights are launched by the narrator, Branch, they fly from all sides. *Tunnel* is both a spy thriller and an academic novel. The two fictional strains don't fit well because Branch's voice wavers between the bookish and the hard-boiled. He tells another character, "You mingle philology with homicide and espionage." The same charge can be made against Ross Macdonald's own intellectual gunplay. The writer won't let you forget that he knows his intellectual history, giving Branch speeches only a professor or a literature student would say: "Your character is your fate"; "Arbana is the Athens of the West and McKinley Hall is its Parthenon and I am Pericles"; "Those whom the gods wish to go to sleep, they first make sleepy." Branch has a literary quotation for every occasion. Many come at dangerous moments, when his instincts should turn to survival, not to Shakespeare. He also has the habit of working a literary reference into a sarcasm or a private joke with the reader; at times, he'll display the academic temper and then belittle it.

The reason for all this? Ross Macdonald conceived of Branch as an all-purpose man—an impromptu patriot-sleuth with the fast fists and street sense of the private eye and also the thoughtfulness of the college professor. Had his eyeglasses not shattered in the fencing match against Peter Schneider, he would have spotted Carl's drag impersonation of Ruth right away, even though it fools everybody else. Besides, how could Ruth have sunk to loving Peter when Branch's falling in love with her confers supreme sanity, sense, and health upon her? Ross Macdonald's own attempts to confer superiority upon Branch fight the plot. Here is Branch's explanation for failing to see through Carl's disguise:

I saw Peter Schneider kiss him. That's what buffaloed me from the first, more than my bad eyes, I think. I've seen men in women's clothes in Paris, in the hole-in-the-wall dancehalls around the Place de la Bastille. But I forgot there were such things.

But of course, he has seen men dressed as women before; of course, he has seen them in Paris, where seeing them counts more than in Detroit; why, he can even pinpoint the area. Carl's female impersonation is the hinge of the plot, as has been said. If Branch could normally detect it, then we, who have gone step by step with him all along, should detect it, too. The impersonation is the shakiest part in an otherwise tight, firm plot. Ross Macdonald should have played it down, rather than reminding us of it. *Tunnel* gets his writing career off to a good start. Though it sacrifices plausibility to the image of its narrator-hero, it both seizes and holds us at a high dramatic pitch.

II

Trouble Follows Me (1946) resembles its predecessor. First, it brings back the foreign setting—Hawaii and Mexico. The same tension prevails in wartime Hawaii as in 1937 Munich. The Nazi philosophy of Aryan supremacy and the master race comes back as racial prejudice: a black American sailor named Hector Land is insulted, betrayed, and ultimately killed, along with his wife and brother, by whites he had trusted. Like Alec Judd's death in *Tunnel,* the first killing in *Trouble* both takes place from a window and looks like suicide. The narrator-hero, like Bob Branch, comes close to death in a murder stage-managed to look like suicide. Also like Branch, he discovers the murder victims, rejects the official account of the deaths as suicide, and then becomes a somewhat inept one-man attack squad—looking foolish in public and walking into traps. Yet the tighter time scheme and widened geographical sweep of *Trouble* make for a new technical maturity.

Ross Macdonald's handling of Sam Drake, his narrator-hero, also reflects a maturity in technique, if not in attitude and outlook. In principle, anyway, the intellectual and the athlete in Drake do not obtrude as in Branch. Drake is touched but not tainted by commonness; he doesn't parade his humanism or patriotism as Branch did. He is a journalist by trade, not a Ph.D. in English; in fact, a career officer in the U. S. Navy, he may never have gone to college. His crime-hunting takes less agility, endurance, and physical strength than Branch's did. Yet, in spite of this restraint, Drake, too, comes across as an all-purpose man, gratifying the reader's moral superiority. He says, "I'm an intellectual among roughnecks and a roughneck among intellectuals." His choosing duty over love affirms his manliness as do his Hemingwayish references to Midwestern towns, as if the Midwest had a corner on tough-minded, grainy honesty. But Drake's references do not end with Detroit, Kansas City, and Topeka. He is forever trotting out literary allusions; in two sentences he mentions Morpheus, Cuchulain, and the poet Stevie Smith. Two pages later, alluding to Eliot's "Hollow Men," he says, "The party started out with a bang but it ended up with a whimper." The warning, "Block that metaphor!" given him in jest by another character, is too mild. Drake is sententious: "Murder is always incredible. . . . That's why it's a crime and punishable with death." He is long on epigrams: "Too much drinking can explain anything. . . . But it requires explanation in turn." His moral will can turn nearly any human situation into a lesson in character building.

Given his unimpeachable ethics and wide experience, he is astonishingly naive—and lucky. Warned to keep out of an all-black bar in a Detroit ghetto, he says, "This is a democracy, isn't it? They drink the same liquor we do, and it makes them drunk just like us." Later, he goes back to the same bar alone, innocently believing that the black bartender will tell him, a white man, about a black militant gang. Then he fearlessly chases a young black thug through the ghetto. Unadorned luck stops his being killed, first, by the thug's friends and then, by falling into

Four Before Archer

the basement of a burnt-out tenement the thug lures him to. Only after these lucky escapes from death does he ask the FBI's help.

Homeless and confused, Drake, when we first meet him, has just spent a year in combat. He has no family or close friends; his ship was blown up; waiting for the shock to subside, he doesn't know his next posting:

Ever since I left Detroit I had felt dislocated, and after my ship went down it was worse. Sometimes I felt that all of us were adrift on a starless night, singing in the dark, full of fears.

The action starts when Drake and his friend and fellow officer, Eric Swann, go to Honolulu House, "a decaying mansion" turned into a cabaret. They are joined by Sue Sholto, a young Jewish American who works at the local radio station and is Eric's sweetheart. While discussing the leak of war secrets to nearby Japanese submarines, they invite Mary Thompson, another local disk-jockey, and her escort, a successful journalist named Gene Halford, to join them. The first chapter ends with a jolt. The nervous strain caused by the war and by Sue's affaire with Eric, who has a wife, flares into a drunken lovers' quarrel. Sue storms out of the cabaret and is next seen hanging from a window by a rope, choked to death. Her killer? There are many suspects but no leads. Though many had good opportunity to kill her, nobody had a clear motive.

Trying to tie Sue's death to the war, Drake follows his skimpy clues to Detroit and back across the continent to southern California and Mexico. Each part of this four-part novel contains a murder; each victim is killed differently. The victim in Part II, "Detroit," is Bessie Land, wife of Hector, a suspect in Sue Sholto's murder and a steward on Eric Swann's ship in Oahu. The case has taken shape. Bessie's murder is the second inflicted upon a woman sexually linked to a crewmate of the same ship and the second made to look like a suicide. Part II also broadens the thematic base of the plot; for Bessie's death ignites a search both for her killer and for information about Black Israel, a secret society of black militants presumably infiltrated with enemy spies. The end of Part II speeds the action as did that of Part I. Mary Thompson, who has become Drake's girlfriend, announces that she has taken a job at the Naval Supply Depot in San Diego, where Hector Land—Bessie's widower, a Navy man, and possibly a Black Israelite—was seen three days before.

Part II, "Transcontinental," the longest section of the novel, occurs on the Grand Canyon Limited, which takes Mary and Drake from Chicago to Los Angeles. Though he describes the passing landscape, Ross Macdonald doesn't draw on many of the artistic possibilities created by the moving train—the combined sensation of ceaseless motion and closure, even entrapment; the dramatic use of engine noise and smoke, scenery, and the jets of light squirting from the train's wheels; the instant society of strangers. Drake does reach both a destiny and destination. But little surprises us; the action never lurches into the surreal or the fantastic as in other novels featuring train rides, like Greene's *Orient Express* (1932), Patricia Highsmith's first novel, *Strangers on a Train* (1946), and Rebecca West's *The Birds Fall Down* (1964).

But neither is the action prosaic or predictable. The apparent blanket catch of strangers drink and talk to pass time. But the tedium of turning wheels and dark, lonely stations unleashes terror. A sailor who remembers knowing another passenger named Anderson dies from drinking ether disguised as whisky. Drake nearly dies twice—by drinking from the same deadly bottle and by being dragged unconscious under the train during a stop in Emporia, Kansas. Fortunately, he had only swallowed enough ether to pass out briefly, and so he wakes before the train crushes him. He then learns that the mysterious stranger on the train—the one nobody else can account for—has been Chet Gordon, an FBI man, and that Gordon, who saved Bob Branch's life in *Tunnel,* has been protecting him the whole trip despite his refusal to cooperate. Before Part III ends, both Gordon and one Anderson, whom the poisoned sailor remembered but couldn't name, leave the train mysteriously.

In Part IV, "The End of the Ride," Gordon the professional and Drake the clumsy amateur ("My melodrama had descended into farce") join forces. Gordon explains that he left the train to follow Anderson, who had bolted suddenly in New Mexico. The Detroit police, the Military Police, and the Mexican Border Patrol also enter the search. Chapter Thirteen opens with Drake spotting one of Anderson's cohorts, a Miss Green, in San Diego and then chasing her black Cadillac limousine across the border in a cab. The chase ends in a brothel, which Miss Green, an ether addict, operates. A new character, simply called the Baroness, enters the book to give this depravity an old-world patina. Drake is knocked out twice—by a blackjack and by ether. He is taken to a lonely ranchhouse where Hector Land, waiting in the wings since Part I, has been stationed. Anderson tells Land to strangle Drake so that when they burn the house with Drake, who is about Anderson's size, inside it, the police will think Anderson dead. But Drake convinces Land that Anderson killed Bessie. What follows is melodrama. Anderson shoots Land and, having emptied his revolver, fights Drake, who snaps his larynx. Then Land, six bullets in his body and streaming with blood, kicks Anderson to death. The last chapter restores Drake's sweetheart, Mary Thompson. Her driving to the ranchhouse, when supposedly she didn't know Drake's whereabouts, puts her in the Anderson camp. Amid a welter of painful recognitions and angry moral judgments, she admits killing both Sue Sholto and Bessie Land. Hector's wife had to die because she knew too much about the spy ring, and Sue had discovered Mary to be an enemy spy. Mary offers Drake his life provided he join her organization. But her pleas are cut short. Hector Land stumbles in again, having heard Mary's murder confession. Before killing himself, he shoots Mary, thus freeing Drake from killing the girl he loves. A shocked and reeling Drake leaves the blood-spattered ranchhouse, noting the first rays of dawn lighting the withered mists.

Hector Land, ex-prizefighter, ship's steward, and Black Israelite, remains Ross Macdonald's only portrayal of a black American. Much of his brawn and biddability stems from the pseudo-scientific notion of post-Darwinian man. Like O'Neill's Emperor Jones and Hairy Ape, Land shows more intellectual development than a gorilla, but less than a human. Even more important than Ross Macdonald's conception of him as an evolutionary throwback or "missing link" is his place in the plot. Land is a good bad man, whom Ross Macdonald neither patronizes nor uses as a peg on which to hang his views on racial injustice. But without intending it, he makes Land his main character. Drake's ubiquity makes the book's title a misnomer. Drake is not singled out for trouble or bad luck; he goes to great lengths to win Mary, and the corpses he finds are not planted for his benefit. Because he is no fugitive, *Trouble* lacks the tension and drive of *Tunnel.* The suspense it does rouse comes largely from Land. Although neither hero nor villain, he's the novel's title character, embodying both the heroic and the base. He is more oppressed than Dr. Herman Schneider, the outsider-suspect in *Tunnel.* Racialism killed his brother, drove his wife into the streets, and sent him to jail. He is maligned by his naval officers and betrayed by his fascist paymasters, one of whom kills his wife. Trouble marked him down long before Sue Sholto's murder.

Like Ross Macdonald's other missing persons, he spurs a great deal of activity from behind the scenes. He serves the theme with the same craftsmanly economy he brings to the plot. Though he is more hectored to than hectoring, his last name suggests the corrosive effect both his gambling and his spying have on his shipmates. He no more belongs aboard a ship than another black sailor *manqué,* Conrad's James Wait in *The Nigger of the* Narcissus. Though several of the men in the book are sailors, all four murders and both suicides happen on land (land-Land). Surviving the wreckage and the shame, Drake says in the book's last sentence, "I wanted to get to sea again." His remark chimes with the book's setting and character-deployment. Unlike Hector Land, the good sailors, Eric Swann and Sam Drake, have aquatic surnames. And like Land, whose bankroll fattens as his hopes thin, the land brings them woe when it glitters most brightly. Part I takes place in the false earthly paradise of Oahu, setting for treason and murder. Drake senses terror along the curve of one of Hawaii's most beautiful beaches:

I'm beginning to feel that nothing good can happen here. There's something ominous and anti-human about those mountains, and the clouds, and the bright green sea, and a climate that's too good all the time.

Continuing the pattern, Part II takes us to an anti-Paradise, the black Detroit slum called Paradise Valley. More subtly, a Laura Eaton of Santa Barbara, who gets a letter from the sailor poisoned aboard the Grand Canyon Limited, puts forth the California of Part IV as another false paradise (Eaton-Eden). Drake prefigures this motif on the first page of Part IV, saying that Santa Barbara reminds him of both Oahu and the Midwest, where the first three parts of the novel took place. The pattern is generalized with the moving rain in Part III. Ross Macdonald describes not merely the train's sleeping coach but rather the North American continent as a dark tunnel—mazelike purview of the rat. Ratlike bustle and decay both show brilliantly in the events of the trip. The symbolic portrayal of the passengers and what happens to them as a microcosm of America deepens the pessimism. Drake's hurt and hollowness at the end are well justified.

The morality of *Trouble* is not cheap or trite. Ross Macdonald never presents Negroes or Jews as the oppressed noblemen of nature. Sue Sholto is an adulteress and communist sympathizer. On the payroll of his country's enemies, Land is a traitor. Minorities like Negroes and Jews, though expected to fight their nation's enemies, had little say in their nation's politics in 1941-45. Though Ross Macdonald doesn't sympathize with the methods they used to get into the political mainstream, neither does he favor the white Christian society that made communism and black nationalism last refuges for the powerless. This complex political attitude he conveys as a novelist should—through character, incident, and setting rather than manifestos. The international intrigue ends without fanfares in an out-of-the-way ranchhouse; the key figure has been an uneducated, put upon black man; key testimonies come from black witnesses both on the train and at navy headquarters.

But this indirect plea to look for meaning and value in neglected places leaves out women. Sue is morally and politically smirched; the manager of Honolulu House, Mrs. Merriwell, is a racial bigot; Bessie Land divides her energies between alcohol and prostitution; Miss Green, the enemy spy, runs a brothel and inhales ether; Drake's sweetheart, Mary Thompson, turns out to be an adulteress and a bigamist, a traitor and a killer. These moral lapses determine the characters' worth for Ross Macdonald. The moral identity he foists on his women is as shabby as the political identity he accuses the white establishment of foisting on blacks.

But no lowering comes from Ross Macdonald's style. The bright, crisp language of *Trouble* reflects both a sharp eye and tender heart; the

Four Before Archer

narrative materials are well selected, imaginatively perceived, and carefully arranged. Ross Macdonald homes in on his subject and conveys it livingly. The first look he gives us of Hector Land registers pity and shock:

> His ears were convoluted and frayed like black rosebuds after a hailstorm. His nose was broad and saddled, his eyes bright black slits between pads of dead tissue. It was an old boxer's head, powerful and scarred as if it had once been used as a battering ram. . . . But there was no power in the posture of his body. His shoulders drooped forward and his belly heaved with his breathing. . . . He looked like a frightened bear caught in a dog-pack.

Simile gives this descriptive power the ring of lyricism when directed to natural landscape. The following account of a Hawaiian roadside effortlessly combines the massive with the sheer:

> The air was suffused with light, the tender green of the young pineapple shoots was like a whispered promise in the fields, the palm-trunks rose straight towards the sun like a high song. But here and there along the rocks . . . were ribs and boulders of volcanic rock, as if hell had thrust a shoulder through the earth.

Ross Macdonald moves from island to mainland and from country to town without dimming his bright prose. His descriptions of Detroit black slums wring social injustice and economic stress from physical details like sagging roofs, cracked heating systems, and rotten plumbing. The same variety and technical skill show in his presentations of the murder victims. Not only does each victim die differently; the death of each reaches us from a different angle. Instead of saying that Sue Sholto died at Honolulu House, Ross Macdonald shows the physical effects of her death by hanging. The second murder, that of Bessie Land, he conveys outright, ending his description with a strong tactile impression that clinches the foregoing visual imagery:

> I saw that Bessie Land's throat was deeply cut. The pull of the skin had made a raw ellipse in her darkly glistening neck. A wavy-edged bread-knife rested on the quilt beside her head. She had her coat on, but it did not prevent her from being terribly cold.

The prose only flags when characters feel grief or physical pain. Eric Swann says over Sue's dead body, "Darling, you shouldn't have done it. I'd have done anything." Smacking just as much of women's magazine fiction is Mary Thompson's response to being shot in the chest: "My breast is a nasty mess. You liked it for a little while, didn't you, Sam? You thought my breasts were beautiful."

The structure of the novel embodies many of the strengths reflected in the style, but, along with them, a still higher proportion of the blemishes. Mindful of his reader, Ross Macdonald both relates the murders to each other and makes sure that none outranks the others in gore or moral blame. Drake surveys the suspects, reviews the events leading up to the murders, and looks for connections. Together with his growing love for Mary, his search for evidence and motives reminds us that *Trouble* is an organized narrative rather than a series of killings. Drake's relationship with Mary also knits the four parts. Part I has a strong sensory ending. The lovers have gone swimming. Excited by the tracers shooting into the night from an anti-aircraft drill nearby, they kiss passionately, "until the sound of the guns and the beating of our hearts were a single clamor." Part II opens, "Five thousand miles and two weeks later I met Mary again." The sentence shifts both space and time without slackening the human drama. Mary and Drake, though divided, have not been out of our sight since our last look at them. Everything and nothing have changed. Part II restores most of the people from Part I—Mary, Eric Swann, and Drake; Hector comes back as his wife, the alcoholic prostitute, Bessie, and the browbeating he got as Sue's suspected killer recurs as Bessie's murder. Eric's mistress, Sue, now dead, Eric takes his wife drinking and dining. But his appearance in Part II, as in Part IV, is window dressing. His shock and guilt over Sue's death both fade quickly into the ongoing drama. As a person with needs and fears he is forgotten.

Eric is not the only character who unbalances the book. The journalist Gene Halford also moves the plot in Part I and then drops out. Drake envies him first his success as a syndicated columnist, and next the pretty girl—namely Mary Thompson—he brings into Honolulu House. His dual envy gives the book an incipient dramatic conflict with which to grip the reader until Sue's death provides a real issue. As a holding action, the Drake-Halford rivalry works well. But Halford leaves the action until Part IV, when his return means nothing. Another mismanaged character is Mary. The last-chapter confession Ross Macdonald puts on her lips violates our imaginative commitment to her; it changes a heroine into a heavy within a few paragraphs. Though she does act suspiciously a few times, beautiful women have always cloaked themselves in mystery. Besides, the suspicion comes from her lover, Drake, who is admittedly irrational toward her and thus an unreliable judge of her motives; he says in Chapter 9, "I felt that she was more precious to me than a part of my own body." The only clue to her villainy comes from her author's angry sexual Puritanism. Sex is the giveaway. Aboard the Grand Canyon Limited, she invites Drake into her bed. Her rutting invitation gainsays not only restraint but also proper womanly submissiveness. To poison our hearts against her, Ross Macdonald piles on the sexual misdeeds. She admits being Anderson's wife and sleeping with Drake at Anderson's request in order to distract Drake from the chase. The moral inference is clear; no decent girl would ask a man to her bed. But even Ross Macdonald doubts the conviction both of her confession and of the inferred tie between sexual looseness and moral degradation. Otherwise, he wouldn't have groped so wildly for a motive to pin her evil to; in the last pages, Drake accuses her of being mercenary, amoral, and simply depraved. Had any of these accusations carried force, neither Drake nor Ross Macdonald would have needed to multiply them.

The writer's powers of observation excel in his second novel, but his dramatic motivation falls short. A good example of this shakiness comes from his use of cryptology. Mary had used a time code to relay war secrets to the Japanese submarines lurking in nearby waters. Now in a time code, the lapse between the signals, not the signals themselves, gives the meaning. Mary's marking of the studio's phonograph records at preordained intervals is solid, plausible spying. But this believability doesn't carry into the plot. By coincidence, one of the train-passengers in Part III was a vaudeville magician who used a time code in his act. The old showman, quite without motivation, explains the technique to Drake, who later uses it to uncover Mary's guilt.

The novel's other evildoer, Mary's husband, also suffers from poor narrative technique. Under the name of Anderson, he enters the book in Part III, too late to qualify legitimately as the book's arch-villain. Ross Macdonald's failure to establish Lorenz Jensen as a possible suspect in the first or second chapter breaks a cardinal rule of literary detection. Instead of prefiguring Jensen-Anderson's guilt dramatically, the writer asserts it by giving him a German-sounding first name, by making him an oilman, and by arbitrarily making him physically repellent:

His plump, uncertain joviality, his carefully cut and thinning hair, his healthy shoulders becoming infiltrated by fat, his thick silk ankles crossed in front of him, his severely pressed and already crumpling grey pin-stripe suit, and his expensive and passionate tie announced: I am a successful American business man.

Jensen-Anderson is not a contending force, never appearing for as long as three straight pages until the closing scenes, when he drives Drake to the ranchhouse. He can't carry the heavy plot-burden shoved onto him. One snag in the novel's motivational fabric appears when Drake wakes up in the back of his car after being knocked out: "I could see over the back of the front seat the upper half of a man's head wearing a chauffeur's cap. I knew that the head . . . must be Anderson's because I hated it so much." Drake's intuitive stroke is both right and wrong. The head seen silhouetted above the steering wheel *is* Anderson's, but because the melo-dramatic finale requires that it be.

The plot depends throughout on a great deal of surmise and offstage action. Both Anderson's infiltration of and Hector Land's membership in Black Israel are merely asserted. Nor is Land ever seen collecting or passing on information to other agents. Though the first-person narration limits the novel's dramatic range to Drake, the more flexible, open narrations of Archer manage to include key offstage events as felt experience. A slow developer, Ross Macdonald will spend several more novels attuning narrative point of view both to his materials and to his attitude toward those materials.

III

Johnny Weather is on the warpath, and anybody in his way can look for insults, angry moral instruction, and a pounding he'll never forget. The time is early spring, 1946. Weather is hitchhiking to Blue City, his home town, which he left ten years before, first to get an education, and then to serve as a combat infantry sergeant in Germany and France. After cracking a couple of skulls, he learns that his father, a local city boss, was killed; that the killer is still at large; and that the town, a middle-sized community near Chicago, reeks with graft.

This corruption comes from *Red Harvest* (1929), where Hammett's Continental Op cleans up the town of Personville, or Poisonville, amid the gore and spatter of twenty-five killings. Though no detective, Weather works with professional control and efficiency. He is not tempted by money and will only risk sex and sentiment after disparaging them. The human form is as ugly, motives are as debased, and society is as foul in *Blue City* (1947) as in Hammett's first book, which also has a primary color in its title. Weather has come to town unwashed, unshaven, and rumpled. His homecoming jars him. Though the buildings and streets are the same as before, they look shrunken. Though crime is still rife, the criminals have changed. His first stop is a tavern, where he insults the bartender and then drinks beer with a sixty-six-year-old pensioner named McGinis. Like Weather, McGinis, who has no birth certificate and only one functioning arm, is an outsider. The town's mayor, Freeman Allister, has just found him a place to live and a slot on the social security payment lists. Their common exile and return make it fitting that McGinis and Weather, two Oedipus figures, become friends straight-away.

McGinis excuses himself from the table. Then, hearing shouts for help from the men's room, Weather rushes in and beats up two local men who have attacked and robbed McGinis. At the end of Chapter 1, he puts the older man in a cab and heads for Weather House, a town landmark renamed the Palace Hotel since his father's death. He talks to his father's widow and to an industrial magnate and former friend of J. D. Weather. Though he learns that his father was not "the straightest man in the Middle West," as he had thought, but a slot-machine racketeer and police briber, Weather rejects all pleas to forget the unsolved murder. He had come to town looking for a job and, a few hours later, finds one— to hunt down his father's killer and then clean up Blue City.

Four Before Archer

In Chapter 5, he meets and befriends another older man and exile—the Marxist refugee, Kaufman, from whose used-goods store the pistol that killed J. D. Weather was stolen. He then goes to the Cathay Club, a cabaret-brothel, where he meets Carla Kaufman, the Marxist's prostitute-granddaughter. As he did with old Kaufman, he gets along well with Carla from the start. After trading sarcasms to beat back romantic sentiment—the worst crime in this gritty world of suckers and hustlers—they make love. Their reaction recalls the scene where the ground moves underneath the lovers in Hemingway's *For Whom the Bell Tolls.* He gives her her first orgasm; she refuses his money. And the flat, predictable morality of the book joins them forever, even as she paints and powders herself for the next customer. The bond is stronger for being unspoken. In another part of the club, Weather soon works his way into the private office of Roger Kerch, the club's owner and the town's biggest racketeer. To get closer to the nerve-center of Blue City's evil, Weather asks Kerch for a job and, to prove his worth, outfights Kerch's bodyguard, a hulking ex-boxer. But Weather is spotted by one of Kerch's other henchmen as J. D. Weather's son and an upstart troublemaker. Helped by a bribed police detective, the gang beats, robs, and then runs Weather out of town.

But he comes back to Blue City fighting—going straight to Mayor Allister, whom he wakes up in the middle of the night, lectures on municipal reform, and talks into handing over $50 and an automatic pistol. Weather believes that Kerch, "evil through and through," had J. D. Weather killed because he wanted to control Blue City's crime himself. He then follows the drug-pusher, Joe Sault, Carla's first lover and ex-pimp, to Floraine Weather's house at four o'clock in the morning. He overhears his stepmother, Sault's paramour, ask Sault to kill Kerch and then remove an envelope from the safe of the Cathay Club. But Weather is not the only gatecrasher at Floraine's. Kerch has also overheard the murderous dialogue. He and his mob take the lovers to a deserted roadhouse six or seven miles out of town, with Weather secretly following them. Eavesdropping for the second time in as many chapters, Weather sees Floraine and Sault murdered. He, too, is captured and slated to die but escapes, snapping a wrist of his "murderous, cheaply elegant, and epicene" guard. Then he drives back to Floraine's, where the mob had taken her body, to make Weather look like her killer. He is seen bending over the corpse, and a chase—perhaps the longest and most elaborate in Ross Macdonald—begins when a robed suburbanite with a razor in his hand and shaving cream on his neck starts running after him. Suddenly, the hunter has become the hunted. Weather eludes his pursuers by foot, car, bicycle, and delivery truck; he passes through a barber shop and a library, where he vents some ideas about literature, before reaching Carla Kaufman's apartment, his projected hideout. Carla, his only friend in the crisis, gives him food and shelter.

She then telephones Kerch and, in her most seductive tones, dupes him into meeting her at the Cathay Club, where Weather will be hiding in ambush. The trap works as planned. Carla, the decoy, escapes, and Weather—beating Kerch bloody—makes him hand over the envelope Floraine had wanted from his safe. The envelope contains a marriage certificate joining Floraine and Kerch in Portland, Oregon in 1931. The certificate, proving Floraine a bigamist, automatically transfers her share of J. D. Weather's estate to her son. But before the son can think about his inheritance, he is arrested and taken to the police station, where the police kick, club, and beat him with brass knuckles. Police Inspector Ralph Hanson, the only decent cop on the force, comes in and releases Westher. As in *Tunnel* and *Trouble,* the loner-hero leagues with the police at the end. In the last chapter, Mayor Allister confesses to the murder of J. D. But he doesn't condemn the murder, claiming instead to have killed J. D. for the public good. Weather lectures him again on political morals, unravels some remaining mysteries, and decides to marry Carla. With her help, the boy wonder—Weather is only twenty-two—will reform Blue City: "You couldn't build a City of God in the U.S.A. in 1946. But something better could be made than an organism with an appetite for human flesh. A city could be built for people to live in."

Allister's guilt tallies with both hard-boiled ethics and aesthetics. The Least Likely Suspect, the mayor took Weather into his home, gave him $50, and then drove, in deepest night, to get him a revolver. He had helped old McGinis get his social security payments, and another character says of him, "I've seen him help more than one fellow out of a bad spot." But his omissions invite suspicion. Though he campaigned for and became mayor as a municipal reformer, he hasn't torn down the slums, banished the slot machines, or wiped out prostitution. The explanation for his errors both of omission and commission comes in the disclosure, in Chapter 18, that he keeps a mistress. Sex, as usual, is the giveaway. As in all these early novels, a person who misbehaves sexually will also lie and steal, even kill. And keeping a mistress is worse than an occasional rut or even a steady arrangement in which no cash changes hands. Allister is of the devil's party.

Like old Kaufman, he is an idea-ridden ineffectual. Ideas and ideals run to waste in hard-boiled fiction, substituting thought for action, and *Blue City* hews to the usual curve. Thought must not pre-exist action. When an intellectual tries to convert political theory to deeds, he causes disaster. Yet Ross Macdonald extends more compassion to Allister than Weather does. This spoiled dreamer couldn't get a commission after Pearl Harbor because he was classified psychoneurotic. Then his wife rejected him sexually, and he turned to a mistress. Reforming Blue City crowned his romantic fantasy. The mob learned of his affaire and black-mailed him into cooperating with them. Rather than victimizing his

Four Before Archer

townsfolk, he should have resigned. But living a dream took away his judgment. Accused of sacrificing both the law and the public to his ruling passion, he cries out, "You'd throw filth on every dream I ever had."

A character who gives and asks no compassion is John Weather. Like the weather itself, he is an elemental force; nobody can do anything about him. One character says of him, "You never stop fighting, do you?" Very hard-boiled, this brash boy has no social conscience. He fights crime alone, demanding a wide berth from the police and town fathers. Fast with his words, temper, and fists, he backs down to nobody. And why should he? He has great self-command, both verbal and physical. He can withstand enormous physical punishment. Star quality all the way round, he beats a local poolroom hustler at rotation, and he knows literature, geography, and political science. Called "a man who knows ideas" by old Kaufman, the town's old world intellectual, he holds his own in a political discussion which starts with his recognizing a lithograph of Friedrich Engels in Kaufman's store window. Later, he psychoanalyzes Kaufman's tough-tart granddaughter, Carla:

Once upon a time you let a dimwit with sideburns take advantage of you. You woke up from love's young dream with a hangover. . . . You knew damn well you were a romantic sap, so you set out to prove the opposite. You'd been too soft, so now you'd be too hard. You'd been tumbled once, so now you'd get yourself tumbled ten or twelve times a night. All to show yourself, and your dimwit with the sideburns, that you're a hard girl and can take it.

But the boy wonder's greatest gift remains his unshakable self-confidence. Everyone he deals with he stares down, outargues, or offends. Dauntless in his rectitude, he will scold anybody. He tells the town's leading industrialist, "You'll excuse my sitting down. I've been running around all night trying to clean up your lousy town. It's tiring." A page later, he lashes out, "You can't snub me. . . . You didn't get where you are by talking with six-syllable words at pink-tea parties." He first accuses Police Inspector Hanson of shielding J. D. Weather's killer and then patronizes him, "You could have the makings of an honest man, Hanson." In Chapter 19, he is hit with a pistol, a blackjack, and brass knuckles. The beating is so brutal that it would throw anybody else into shock. Yet, when Hanson rescues him, Weather thanks him with threats, insults, and commands:

To hell with you Hanson. . . ! Beat me up and toss me in a cell, you rotten, lily-livered grafter. I'll get the best lawyer in the state and tear this reeking town wide-open from gullet to gut. Get somebody to take me away, for Christ's sake. You stink in my nostrils, Hanson.

Weather's heroics foul both the book's dramatic motivation and style.

Ross Macdonald is capable of subtle discriminations. His yoking of simile and an active verb within a short sentence produces a sharp jolt: "A swart automatic hopped into his hand like a toad." His skill at impressionistic description makes for the same immediacy: "Rusty's third swing made the floor stand up vertically and bounce the back of my head." But how acceptable is this vivid rhetoric in context? A reference to "A Turk in a sack on his last ride to the Bosphorus" doesn't sound plausible when spoken by a one-man riot force of twenty-two. No real person, Johnny Weather is a metaphor for a kind of simplified maleness. His heroics belong in rod-and-gun pulp magazines. The unrealistic claims made for his powers rule out dramatic conflict. Nobody stands a chance against him. He says in the first chapter, "I hadn't had a fight for a long time, and I was spoiling for one." Three pages later his wish is granted, when he disposes of two local bruisers in the men's room of a bar. Other fights take longer to win, especially when, as in the case of Mayor Allister, he first needs to discover his opponent.

But he's so pugnacious and right minded that he needs no reason to fight. Unfortunately, he rarely gets a credible one. His revenge is unmotivated. He hadn't seen his father in ten years, when he left home after a falling-out, and he learns soon after his arrival in Blue City that his father had disinherited him. He never missed his father's love and sneers at his money; J. D. opens no scar tissue. Either McGinis or Kaufman, who fills in the political background on Blue City and then sends Weather to Carla, *could* stand as a rallying point. Weather could serve either man without healing the Oedipal split between himself and J. D. But both elders appear but once and thus can't bear a heavy motivational load.

In 1971 Ross Macdonald said that *Blue City* was about "the underlife of an imaginary American city, abstracted from the several cities the war had taken me to."[2] The key word here is "underlife." The book takes a very low view of people and their purposes. All of life is ugly. The town's biggest industry, a rubber factory, fouls the air, kills the local vegetation, and sickens the people. Like Charley Summers, the returning veteran in Henry Green's *Back* (1946), Weather comes home from the front to find civilian peacetime life as deadly as the military during war. Organized society is a corrupt, repressive monolith. Nearly every policeman, business leader, and politician has been bought by the mob. The strong men are brainless; the smooth ones are gutless or perverse. Most of the townsfolk are pimps, whores, grafters, or drug addicts. Setting is also rundown and sordid; most of the action taking place in slums or dives. Weather notes, "Nearly everybody I met bore the stamp of poverty on faces strained thin or coarsened by the exigencies of modern life." Drunks sleep in doorways; lovers embrace against tenement walls; the spring rains, normally life-renewing, run "in the gutters like a swift, foul stream." In Chapter 11, Weather hears a tap on the window above him: "It was only a late whore holding out her heavy breast the way a butcher holds up a steak for the customer's approval." Human faces and bodies are ugly; expressions are grotesque and cheap. Here is Weather's impression of the woman who finds him bent over Floraine Weather's corpse in Chapter 16:

I . . . saw in detail the unplucked eyebrows raised on her lined forehead, the lines that ran down from the fleshy wings of her nose, deepened and curved by her smile of terror, the tense wrinkle across her hairy lip, the false upper teeth that slid down into the space between her parted lips and made even her fear ridiculous.

Animal imagery heightens the brutishness. At the start of Chapter 17, Weather calls himself "the rat in the maze." A dried-up abortionist and radio preacher with urine-yellow eyes is called Professor Salamander. A Judge Simeon is mentioned several times. Roger Kerch, whose name also suggests spiritual defilement (Kerch-Church), has a bovine face, and people call him "frog," "rat," and "a gone gosling."

The word, blue, in British English, often denotes lewdness, as in Graham Greene's short story, "The Blue Film." Correspondingly, much of Blue City's evil has a sexual basis. Sex brings about Mayor Allister's moral and political collapse. His dream of reforming Blue City exploded when the mob learned of his adultery and threatened to broadcast it unless he left them alone. Floraine's bigamy has the same cancerous effect. Once J. D. is shot, her first husband, Roger Kerch, blackmails her into turning over her property and business interests, which he absorbs into his already large and powerful vice ring. And when Kerch stabs Floraine, his wife, the murder parodies the act of sex:

I couldn't see Floraine's face, but I could see the vigorous movements of his right arm and shoulder up and down, back and forth, as he worked on it with the knife.

This heavy charge of sexuality goes with the book's rank mannishness. Weather grieves that his father's hotel, a dim, shaggy place with heavy oak doors and deep leather chairs, has been prettified under its woman-owner. His description of Floraine, the woman-owner, the first time he meets her, is nearly pornographic in its detached carnality. He surveys her breasts, hips, legs, mouth, and hair; then he compares her to "a seal in water." A page after entering the hotel, he says, "I weighed a hundred and eighty stripped and was almost as fast as a welterweight." The male readership the novel aims at knows of course, that welterweights weigh between 135-147 lbs. The novel's extroverted brutality crowds out tenderness. Boy does get girl. But no sooner does Weather say he's going to marry Carla than he hangs up the phone, as if ashamed of his declaration of love.

Blue City mars its *verismo;* the slice of life it serves up is locker-room fare. Though it has a rough strength, it lacks any offsetting humor, irony, or comparison. The wit is malicious, not affectionate, absurd, or funny.

The blunt, cynical tone takes charge from the very outset. The first twenty-three words of the book have only one syllable apiece, and the following simile fumes up at you from the next page: "I caught a whiff of the rubber factories on the south side, corrupting the spring night like an armpit odor."

How can this rankness harbor gentle feelings? Weather's cynicism and breakneck life style rob the book of a humanizing perspective. *Blue City* is too closely tied to the cult of the hard-boiled. Its evil characters are neither understandable nor sympathetic. Though it has some good scenes, its characters lack life. Carla Kaufman says of her grandfather, "He's supposed to be pretty clever, but he gets all tangled up in words." She is right; her grandfather *is* all talk and abstractions. But she is the other side of the mind-body dualism. She earns her livelihood with her body, and she relates physically to Weather, as well. To stage the showdown between him and Kerch, her boss, she uses her sexuality again. Carla marks no advance from Ross Macdonald's portrayals of Ruth Esch and Mary Thompson in the first two novels. And though Weather's stepmother and dead father give Weather more family background than Branch or Drake had, the background exerts no psychological force. Weather's individualism has no ancestry.

IV

The move from hyper-masculine police drama to psychological realism brings both a slowing of pace and more introspection. *The Three Roads* (1948) includes only two killings, one of which is done by the police. The main character is an amnesiac, his memory having been shattered by the bombing of his ship in the Pacific and by the unsolved killing of his wife. Like John Weather, Bret Taylor is an actionist, a doer rather than a thinker or talker: "I can't rest until I find the man that killed her," he says of his dead wife:

That makes no sense to you, does it? What makes no sense to me is your idea that I should waste my time telling my dreams to a psychoanalyst, instead of settling the trouble at its source.

This actionism pays dividends. Like his brutal counterpart, Weather, Taylor finds out more in a day than the police do in months. Yet, though police corruption is no issue in *Roads,* other similarities between the two books come to mind. The characters, if not sexually determined, are sexually explainable; most of their problems springing from a troubled libido. This sexuality isn't treated commercially, as in *Tunnel.* Though there's a mystery whose solution depends on sex, the book is no whodunit, either. The solution forms but part of the hero's search for wholeness. Again following *Blue City,* the family crisis and unsolved murder

Four Before Archer

carry the action into the past. The most overtly Oedipal of Ross Macdonald's novels leans most heavily on events that took place before the
dramatized action begins.

The book opens in February 1946. Paula West is making her weekly
visit to Taylor, her fiancé, a U. S. Navy lieutenant, and a patient in a La
Jolla hospital for nine months. As often happens in Ross Macdonald, the
woman protects and the man rebels. Paula, a divorced Hollywood script
writer of twenty-nine, which is also Taylor's age, takes her protectoress's
role seriously. On the first page, she remarks inwardly, "It was her job to
bring reality to him. She was his interpreter of the outside world, and
she musn't forget its language." More educated, older, and inwardly
scarred than the lovers in *Blue City,* Paula and Taylor must surmount
more dangerous hurdles if their love is to thrive. Some of the reasons for
his amnesia come out in an interview between Paula and his psychiatrist
in Chapter 2. Late in 1944, Taylor had met a slattern of nineteen or
twenty in a San Francisco bar, got drunk with her, spent the night, and
still drunk, married her the next day. Though he regretted his marriage
as soon as he sobered up, he determined to make it work. His sexual
innocence, fostered by a stern, moralistic father, explains much of his
conduct. His psychiatrist talks about him in terms applicable to two
other spoiled idealists, Hawthorne's Chillingworth in *The Scarlet Letter*
and Mayor Freeman Allister in *Blue City:* "He's an idealist all right. And
that's all very well, but when idealists break down, and they nearly always
do, they tend to go to the opposite extreme."

Taylor has always been ridden by his father's moral Puritanism.
Thus his sudden marriage both defies his father and releases his longstanding sexual inhibitions. But the release isn't total; nor is it meant to
be. Unable to break from his dead father, Taylor rejects his act of
paternal defiance while performing it. His choice of Lorraine Berker, so
alien from him morally as well as socially, contained its own punishment.
But what of the shy, monklike father who studied for the ministry before
settling on an academic career? Why should he distrust sex so much? And
why should his influence persist so long after his death? It comes out
later that this morality-obsessed man, limiting sex to procreation, refused
to bed his wife after complications in young Bret's birth stopped her
having any more babies. After four years of celibacy, his wife had an
affaire with a student-boarder, was caught *in flagrante* by both husband
and son, and then left with her lover, whom she married at first chance.
Though Taylor has blocked out the memory of his mother's adultery, it
has nonetheless filled his unconscious with contempt for women, with
dark self-doubts, and with an inability to give or receive sexual love.

After a few sessions with psychiatrists, where some of the effects of
these realities are described, Paula drives Taylor to Los Angeles for a vaca-
tion. But he upsets her holiday plans by deciding to search for Lorraine's

killer: "My wife was murdered. God knows our marriage never amounted to much, but I owe her something. The least I owe her is some attempt to find the man that killed her." He bolts from Paula to go to the Golden Sunset, where, according to a newspaper story, Lorraine was last seen alive. To block a lead, Paula meanwhile calls Larry Miles, or Harry Milne, a rutting opportunist, ex-prizefighter, and borderline gangster. Miles was with Lorraine the night she died, and Paula bribes him to keep away from Taylor. Although he agrees to take $200 in traveling money, Miles heads straight for the Golden Sunset, where he watches Taylor get drunk and then brawl with another drunken sailor. Then he takes Taylor, knocked unconscious, home with him and puts him up for the night in order to watch him more closely. The next day, wearing Miles's clothes, Taylor asks more questions around town; he keeps tracking Lorraine's killer despite Paula's entreaties. All her plans for him, like her attempt to keep him and Miles apart, seem doomed. But even though his battle-cry for justice defies her, it takes him, oddly, to several places she had already visited before him. One of these is a motel where he overhears her talking to Miles and gathers mistakenly, from the talk, that Miles killed Lorraine with Paula's knowledge. (The novel's only foray into eaves-dropping does not play Ross Macdonald's artistry false; for, no sooner does Taylor eavesdrop than he is eavesdropped upon in turn by the motel manager.)

The last chapters revive the past in unexpected forms. Taylor's mother is not dead, as we had thought, but living in greater Los Angeles with her lover and bridegroom of twenty-five years before. Revenge, moral contempt, and personal hurt had driven George Taylor to tell his four-year-old son that his mother died, and the son has insisted ever since that he found his mother dead. But, as has been suggested, his unconscious has rejected this fiction, and the rejection accounts for his abiding distrust of women, his yoking of sex and death, and, most recently, his confusing his mother with his dead wife. The plot tightens in Chapter 18. Paula's visit from Taylor's mother is interrupted by a phone call from Larry Miles; meanwhile, Taylor is sitting in a parked taxi a hundred yards from Paula's house. But Ross Macdonald relaxes the tension; the drama mustn't peak too early. Taylor's mother's resurrection is followed by analysis and theory. An interview between Paula and a psychiatrist brings out that Taylor has evolved a pseudo-memory of his mother's death in order to fend off guilt for wanting to kill her for committing adultery:

It is easy for a child to suppose that he has committed a wrong. The line between wish and responsibility, between intention and guilt, is very thinly drawn in a child's mind. I do not insist that he believed he killed his mother. The possibility would be enough.

Four Before Archer

The next-to-last chapter, restoring movement and dramatic drive, contains the obligatory fight between Taylor and Miles; a knife, a revolver, and flailing fists make for an exciting brawl. But when he has Miles helpless, Taylor finds he can't shoot him even though he believes him his wife's lover and killer. His moral forgiveness proves costly. Miles clears his head and, a page from the end of the chapter, points Taylor's own revolver at him while Taylor watches helplessly, holding Miles's knife. The mirror-like reversal is short-lived, though. The police arrive and shoot Miles, both saving Taylor and carrying out his revenge. Their arrival creates the best possible outlet for the scene's tensions: justice is served, and Taylor will live with clean hands because somebody else kills his tormentor for him.

The last chapter points the moral and partly reunites Taylor and Paula. She admits that Miles, after learning of her tie to Taylor, blackmailed her; unless she paid heavily, he would tell Taylor that, before fainting from shock, he murdered his own wife. Paula finally tells Taylor that he killed Lorraine and that, to protect him from this ugly truth, she lied to him, to the police, and to the examining psychiatrists. The revelation makes us reinterpret everything preceding it. Like his father, Taylor had an unfaithful wife he caught being unfaithful to him. But, still judging himself by his father's rearguard morality, he turns his mother's invented death into a real one; his repressed wish to kill his mother, long festering, explodes on his wife. Mother and wife have traded places in his mind. He still retains an image of his living mother's corpse but has no memory of the dead Lorraine's. Taylor has a great deal of sorting-out to do. But this task must wait. The book ends with him and Paula—who have slept together—on the way to bed. Ross Macdonald doesn't concede to a happy ending. Taylor is still reeling from Paula's disclosures, and she doubts whether she can break down his longstanding condemnation of sex as a faithless, death-dealing act. Ending the book before the couple go to bed sidesteps these problems, which, while external to the plot, give the reader plenty to ponder. Wisely, Ross Macdonald doesn't try to say everything about his people.

Like Sam Drake and John Weather before him, Taylor is a combat veteran. A full lieutenant and air intelligence officer, he spent a year at sea which ended, as has been said, with the bombing of his ship. Belying his name, he runs counter to Kierkegaard's tailor (Kierkegaard is mentioned in Ross Macdonald's next novel, *The Moving Target*)—the plain man indistinguishable in the crowd who has, nevertheless, made the leap of faith. He has the looks and build of an Adonis. His past clamors with success: "boxing championship in college . . . *summa cum laude* . . . the publication of a book on the Age of Reason." Offsetting this achievement is an anti-social streak, whose origins are already clear. Taylor calls himself "a lone wolf": "Even my profession—I don't believe I told you I write history, or used to—was a one-man sort of thing. I never did much in team games, but I was good at boxing and swimming." This solitariness has become aggravated since his attack of battle fatigue and the death of his wife. The first time he sees Paula in Chapter 1, he holds her "in a grip that almost hurt," giving physical form to his inner stress.

The novel's opening image shows a one-armed golfer. Like him, Taylor is trying to overcome a handicap. Unlike him, his handicap is more emotional than physical. A selective amnesiac, he wavers between a need to face his guilt and a need to forget it. Recapturing the past could establish his autonomy and self-worth. But, his unconscious warns, it could also crush him. Thus he has lost his memory because he wanted to, blocking out certain events and twisting others to save his sanity. So long as he lacks the information on which to base choice, he can postpone choice. The novel seizes him at a crucial moment. He is bracing himself for a leap into self-acceptance and self-renewal. One embodiment of the self must die so that another can be born. The materials for this painful process lie at hand. He has been in hospital for nine months, and his clothes no longer fit him. He calls himself Lazarus and also says in Chapter 1, "I guess I'm partly dead" and in Chapter 15, "It was a hard rebirth into the adult world." Another sign of this hard rebirth comes a page from the end of the book, when his head lies on Paula's breast.

Ross Macdonald states the realities of his world directly. *The Three Roads* is his first California novel and also his first novel which stresses the vitality of the past. As we have seen, Taylor can't wipe out his early conditioning. He knows that the meaning of his life lies in the past, even though he can't cope with it. His entrapment in a cycle of sexual betrayal, murder, and self-loathing recalls Nietzsche's cyclical doctrine of eternal recurrence, where the weak must undergo the same painful ordeals again and again. The Golden Sunset Cafe, where Taylor meets Miles, is located on Round Street, and Taylor, going there, sees himself "caught in a closed circle only death could open." The mirror behind the bar reminds him of "an archaic proscenium through which he watched the tragic life of the world." Endorsing eternal recurrence, the novel has a classical flow, in which acts of passion and retribution occur.

To symbolize this necessity, one character is called Mustin; another comes from Syracuse, New York, with its classical echo; and part of the action occurs on Los Angeles's Caesar Street. In addition, both the novel's title and epigraph come from *Oedipus Rex*. The three roads in Sophocles converge on Phocis, the place where Oedipus killed his father. Oedipus's horrified discovery of his patricide at the junction of the three roads provides the novel's epigraph:

For now am I discovered vile, and of the vile. O ye three roads, and thou concealed dell, and oaken copse, and narrow outlet of three ways, which drank my own

Four Before Archer

blood. . . .

But what bearing has this vision of horror on the book? The answer to this question has already been implied. The convergence of the three roads in Sophocles, giving them a common source, makes them one road; past, present, and future are one. Accordingly, the three loves in Taylor's life—mother, dead wife, and fiancée—are also one. We have already seen what Taylor's mind makes of the first two women, who die in different ways in his presence twenty-five years apart. But what of Paula, whose hair reminds him of his mother's? How does she become the third spoke of the wheel that will either roll him deeper into the tangle of repression or break through to the open road of freedom and rebirth? And how will she influence the wheel's course?

Ross Macdonald's problem in portraying her was this: she had to play the antagonist, suppressing Taylor's killing of his wife, and also, by acting on motives of love, hold the reader's sympathies. The problem proved too much for his powers. For Paula is as much a patient, or case-study, as Taylor. Her last name, West, suggests promise and renewal; at one point, Ross Macdonald uses the phrase, "the westering dream." Very enterprising and managerial—she earns $750 a week in 1946—she gladly takes charge of Taylor; she arranges a furlough for him with his senior officers, packs his luggage, and drives him from La Jolla to Los Angeles, where she has planned a holiday. If sex has hostile associations for Taylor, for her it rouses impulses of protectiveness:

She . . . went down on her knee, holding his head to her breast. She felt his body shaking and held him tighter. She would have liked to be able to divide her own flesh, to take him inside of her and shield and comfort him.

This protectiveness has a blind, amoral urgency. Taylor is her project and obsession. Without his pain and loss, she'd have nothing to do. But withholding his past from him does her no good. He is more of a truant or a prodigal than a lover; indeed, though he keeps deserting her, he has never taken her to bed. He spoils her plans, disobeys her, and postpones their time together. Denying the meaning of his past, while unfair and dishonest to him, darkens her hopes, too. But she can't break out of the cycle. Nor is she blind to her entrapment. She admits having "a fractured mother complex," and she asks a psychiatrist if he thinks her a masochist.

In her favor, it must be said that she is sorely tried. Loving Bret Taylor forces her to wait longer, doing nothing, than any woman should be asked to wait. Her waiting takes different forms. She waits for him to come back from the war. After learning that he has married a younger woman on less than a day's acquaintance, she waits for his marriage to shake itself down. Then, bearing alone the heavy burden of her knowledge of Lorraine's death, she waits for him to recover his sanity. Finally, she must wait till he finds Lorraine's killer—a mission which, if successfully carried out, may leave her with nothing. It is a desperate gamble all the way through. Paula West is one of the most patient, put upon young women in recent American fiction.

But her ordeal is voluntary. She keeps insisting that her love for Taylor is not sick but healing and strengthening to both of them. And she doesn't make unfair demands on it. On the last page, she notes sensibly, "Things would never be as good as they might once have been, but they would be good enough." We can believe in the honesty of her efforts to make a good marriage with Taylor. What we can't accept is the effort itself. Certainly, an able and attractive young woman need not settle for a wraith like Taylor. Surely, she shouldn't have to work so hard for such a dubious goal. And she *must* doubt his love for her. That she rouses no deep need in him shows through in the ease with which he thwarts her and casts her aside. Marrying her could be his crowning act of self-destruction rather than the happy unknotting of his Oedipal cramp. She'll go on managing him, and his resentment will build. Perhaps some resentment has already set in; she has to ask him twice in the novel's closing pages to come up to bed. If he doesn't resent her, neither does he display the hunger and urgency befitting a young man about to make love to his fiancee for the first time.

Bret is still unborn. But if his psychosexual future resembles that of his past, then his marriage looks ominous. For he can't accept the reality of a woman. His mother, whom he had believed dead for twenty-five years, has been alive the whole time. Lorraine only stirs him deeply after her death. Where does this death-drift leave the serviceable, eminently available Paula? Though she has worked and suffered for Taylor, she exists marginally for him. He hunts his wife's killer, he tells her, because, "we can't set up housekeeping on an open grave." His male tendency to sacrifice love to a private sense of duty stems logically from his highly developed super-ego. He claims "that without Paula his world would turn gray again and bleed away to dust." But Paula brightens nothing. The closer she moves to him, the further he pushes her away. Toward the end, she worries about him: "Where was he now? Wandering somewhere in the city, utterly vulnerable to evil." She overrates his vulnerability. Her compulsive need to protect could well spur in him the same will to punish that he felt toward his mother and wife. A psychiatrist in the novel points out, "The line between wish and responsibility, between intention and guilt, is very thinly drawn in a child's mind." Taylor is both childish and self-blaming. Wishing Paula dead might fill him with as much guilt as killing her. His practice of finding scores to square, by lessening her importance to him, will hasten, rather than retard, this doom. Her claiming more importance in his life will only whip her out of it and ride him with so much guilt he won't be able to accept himself.

Four Before Archer

This struggle grows out of the novel's structure. Parts I and II, "Saturday" and "Sunday," give the background. In Part III, "Monday," signalling the start of the work week, Taylor's chores begin. In Part IV, "Doomsday," the search leads him, like Oedipus, back to himself. This fourth and last part runs as long as the first three combined; being reborn is long, hard work (Paula's married name was Pangborn). Now the Old English word for the verb, to judge, is *deman,* which survives in the Doomsday-Judgment Day parallel. Ironically, Taylor learns in Part IV *not* to judge, most of all himself: "He could say the word 'murderer' to himself and answer to the name. He could see it was not justice but mercy that he needed." He has learned of his guilt and passed judgment. But his sudden reluctance to sentence himself to Oedipal exile knits with his inability to shoot Larry Miles in the previous chapter.

His hesitancy comes from his forgiving Miles for tumbling and then killing his wife; heretofore, he had always punished adultery. The forgiveness matters structurally because he and Miles are doubles, as always holds good with hero and villain. Forgiving Miles becomes both a necessary corollary to and preparation for self-forgiveness. Morally, Taylor has been foursquare, whereas Miles has lacked scruples. Yet Taylor's fastidiousness has caused worse grief than his double's cheap opportunism. This moral reversal occurs honestly. Both men are about the same size. Indeed, Taylor sleeps off a drunk in Miles's pajamas and, the next morning, borrows a pair of Miles's slacks and his topcoat. Both men know Paula well. Both keep doing the opposite of what she asks— Taylor by going in circles to find Lorraine's killer, and Miles by staying in Los Angeles after Taylor arrives and then going to the Golden Sunset, the one place in town Taylor is likely to be. But the two men have an even closer tie with Lorraine than with Paula. Taylor has only been drunk twice in his life; once he goes to a hotel with Lorraine, and the next time he goes home with Miles. Taylor and presumably Lorraine have slept in Miles's apartment. Analogously, both men, husband and lover, have spent nights in Lorraine's bed. Both cause her death; both may have seen her die.

The closeness of the two men to Lorraine gives one hint of the closeness between *The Three Roads* and Greene's *Ministry of Fear* (1943). (Ross Macdonald has admitted his great debt to Greene in the early fiction.)[3] The villain in both books has information that might crush the hero were he to learn it; the heroine in both books works long and hard to keep this crushing information from her lover. One can see why. Both heroes are amnesiacs who killed their wives. Finally, the beginning of *Roads* comes straight from the scenes at the rest home in *Ministry* where the amnesiac-hero is visited by the woman who loves him and is keeping back from him the knowledge that he killed his wife. The debt to Greene is clear. But does Ross Macdonald improve on Greene by changing the mercy-killing into a crime of passion? The *crime passionel,* while relieving Taylor of the tremendous pity that hobbles Greene's hero, fits the novel's psychological theme, meshes with Taylor's personal history, and brings Lorraine's death closer to North America's tradition of violence. It also relates the killing to the worst fears of servicemen returning home in 1945-46. These fears could serve as subject matter without giving offense in 1948, when *Roads* came out.

But the adaptation, or borrowing, doesn't work. Greene's plot doesn't allow for Ross Macdonald's belief in the danger of suppressing the past. The idea hardly exists in Greene. His characters have their hands full coping with the everyday, and their exertions mean more when viewed timelessly, as phases in a metaphysical drama, than chronologically. Ross Macdonald's arbitrary grafting of his beliefs about time on a novel which uses time differently explains several problems of character and plot—most significantly, perhaps, the inability of Paula to stand in proper narrative focus. Her denial of the past weighs more heavily against her than does Anna Hilfe's in *Ministry,* even though both women act from similar motives.

A formal element that works better than time is the third-person narrative—the only instance of it in Ross Macdonald's twenty-three novels. The technique allows for a many-sided look at the action, while also freeing the author from the burden of choosing a narrator. This burden Ross Macdonald wisely left alone; both subject and character rule out a central intelligence. Neither Paula, because of her vested interest, nor Taylor, because of his shattered memory, is reliable. Shifting the point of view between them and several other characters, like Miles and then Taylor's mother, prevents a thinning-out of thought and emotion. The different voices, backward looks, and interpretations of the past both deepen and enrich the action. The variety of perspectives also keeps the action fresh—or at least less stale and flat than might have been had it stayed trapped inside the murky hollows of Taylor's Oedipal fixation. The novel's shifting narrative focus scores high, not only as technique but also as shrewd literary judgment.

A letter of 21 July 1972 from Ross Macdonald to the present writer says that *Roads* was planned as a realistic social novel as well as a psychological thriller. The letter adds that the book originally ran a hundred pages longer than the printed version but that it was cut "for the market." Editorial lopping explains some broken scenes, some characters who seem stranded from the main action, and others whose thematic functions overlap, like the two psychiatrists, Wright and Klifter. It does not explain other blemishes. Anxious to test his skills, Ross Macdonald moved too far in *Roads* from the hot surface action and extroversion of *Blue City.* As a result, he deprived *Roads* of a rich inspirational source. An anomoly, it is not a novel of character or of place; its incidents are contrived and

Four Before Archer

its motivation, stiffly formalized.   The Oedipal paradigm, rather than
energizing the action, flattens it into case study.   Taylor is nothing more
than a mental patient.   The diagnosis and therapy doled out by psychiatrists exhaust his background and personality:

> Taylor would rather suppress certain memories than live with them. . . . But
> so long as he suppresses those memories of the past he can't make a healthy adjustment
> to the present. Past and present are so intertwined that you can't abandon one without
> losing your grip on the other.

*   *   *

> Suppose that he desired his wife's death. Though he was innocent in all but wish, her
> death, satisfying as it did his unconscious or partially unconscious desires, might very
> well leave him with an overpowering sense of guilt.

Paula, too, though a richer and more sustained characterization than Carla
Kaufman in *Blue City,* never rises far from the psychiatrist's couch.   Her
unswerving devotion to Taylor only makes sense as a subject for clinical
analysis.

   Motivation gives even more trouble in the case of Larry Miles.   Miles's
staying close to Taylor, his dead paramour's husband, defies both reason
and self-preservation.   Taylor had already caught Miles with Lorraine
just before killing her.   Despite his amnesia, which Miles, in any case,
can't judge, Miles is taking a great risk by presenting himself to Taylor.
His motive?   Again, we rush to the psychiatrist's file cabinet.   If Taylor
is Oedipal, then the same self-destructiveness prods Miles, his alter-ego.
This reading of Miles's character, unfortunately, doesn't work.   Though
structurally and clinically plausible, it goes against Miles's opportunism
and animal vulgarity.   If his unconscious harbors archetypal drives, they
should have come out earlier.   Poor preparation also shows in the
smuggling of a new major character, Taylor's mother, into Chapter 18
of a twenty-two chapter book.   She does not fit well into the plot,
appearing only once and then dropping out of sight.   Even if editing
may have reduced her role, it does not account for Ross Macdonald's
inability to resolve the novel with his basic materials.   One can argue that,
since she exists so vividly as a psychological force, her material appearance
is neither cheating nor smuggling.   But the argument neglects the author's
obligation to convey her as a living person.   She *had* to appear in the
novel, and she had to appear late, else she make the plot peak too early.
She is a creature of the plot.

   And so is Ross Macdonald.   Formal psychology and the influence of
Greene's *Ministry of Fear* didn't rouse his best efforts.   Dimly perceived
materials give any book an arbitrariness that can't be offset.   Withholding
the key event of Taylor's marriage retards his recovery.   But it also
degrades the plot.   When the disclosure does come, it shows all too clearly
that *Roads* contains no chain of events or pattern of relationships that

justifies its conclusion. Drawing on personal experience rather than on his reading made Ross Macdonald's first two novels, *Tunnel* and *Trouble,* better than the next two. The shuttle asserted here between successes and misfires will haunt his whole career through 1969 and *The Goodbye Look.* *Blue City* and *Roads,* though, while regressing artistically, have a breadth in both character and idea that signals, however costingly, new strengths.

4

No book on Ross Macdonald should bypass his Ph.D. dissertation, written around the time the first three Archers were breaking into print. Kenneth Millar's "The Inward Eye: A Revaluation of Coleridge's Psychological Criticism," University of Michigan, 1951, announces its twofold aim straightaway: "to mine Coleridge's critical work for a psychological theory of poetic, and to relate this theory to the psychological tradition in European and English thought" (p. 2). A 455-page work of scholarship and invention, Millar's study could stand as a doctoral dissertation in philosophy, psychology, or linguistics as well as in English literature. It surveys Aristotle, Augustine, and Aquinas, among earlier wrtiers; Kant and Hartley, among Coleridge's contemporaries; and also some of today's leading critics, like I. A. Richards, Wellek, and Bate. But Millar's critical skills go beyond intellectual history. Millar analyzes passages from Shakespeare. After giving, in passing, a pocket history of psychology, he shows the impact of Cartesian dualism upon Renaissance and Enlightenment aesthetics. He provides learned, meaty footnotes. He assaults us with audacious paradoxes: "The internal contradiction in Hobbes's psychology is its saving grace" (p. 241). Through it all, he imposes both historical and conceptual order on his multiform material: "At the [eighteenth] century's very outset, the Hobbesian and Lockean strains were brought together and cross-fertilized in the criticism of Joseph Addison" (p. 277).

Millar hasn't just read widely; he has also thought about his reading. No blind worshipper, he notes his subjects mistakes along with his merits: "[Dr.] Johnson anticipated Coleridge's 'willing suspension of disbelief,' and Coleridge should have known it" (p. 306). But "The Inward Eye" usually supports both Coleridge's aims and methods. Balancing his cognitive and creative faculties, it shows Coleridge freeing art from the mechanical behaviorism of the eighteenth century; his anti-determinist psychology made perception a transforming and organizing process rather than a passive recording of sense impressions. In Millar's words, "Coleridge's main problem as a psychologist . . . was to rescue mind from the dominance of senseless matter, and to restore it to its ancient position as originator and arbiter of its own activity" (p. 197). The activity of the perceiver accounts for much of the dynamism of artistic creation. Art, in turn, affirms both the drama and autonomy of the imagination.

But what is the tie between Coleridgean psychology and literary detection? Besides ordering shoals of richly varied material, Millar/Macdonald's crime fiction and scholarship have little in common. The only mention of crime in "The Inward Eye" comes in a footnote reference to Coleridge's "intellectual larcenies" (p. 317n.). Yet a knowledge of the history of psychology had to help this budding psychological novelist. Coleridge didn't only break open modern psychology. He also contributed heavily, both as a poet and critic, to the Gothic tradition in which Ross Macdonald writes; Poe, the founder of detective fiction, a version of Gothic, acknowledged Coleridge as his master. Other, less apparent, influences are just as important. Since plotting requires verisimilitude, the theory of probability, reaching from Aristotle to Coleridge, should be understood by any fiction writer.

These lines of fertilization give rise to an enigma. We shall never know if Ross Macdonald's true writing vocation lay in criticism and scholarship. Such speculation isn't idle. "The Inward Eye" has the best style the present writer has seen in any Ph.D. dissertation, and it both perceives and presents ideas as a high intellectual plane. The novels of the period, though promising, lack this force, freshness, and distinction. In 1951, Kenneth Millar was a better academic writer than a novelist.

I

Archer turns up the first page of *The Moving Target* (1949) in Cabrillo Canyon, a rich housing estate of "ordered palms and Monterey cypress hedges" in Santa Teresa. Because this imaginary town recurs as a setting in nearly half the Archer novels, it is worth pointing out that, though still lacking a personality in 1949, Santa Teresa lay along the California coast some two hours' drive north from Los Angeles. Archer has made the trip to talk to Elaine Sampson, whose husband has vanished. Like the opening of *The Big Sleep* (1939), Chandler's first Philip Marlowe novel, the first Archer starts with the detective-narrator calling on an invalid client from the mandarin class. It also sends out the same chisel-like jabs. Elaine, "a figure carved from mahogany" in a wheelchair, hasn't summoned Archer out of love or charity. "I want my marriage to last," she tells him. "You see," she continues with deadpan earnestness, "I intend to outlive my husband." Nor does she want his fortune diminished. Twenty years younger than Ralph Sampson, Elaine, grown vain and greedy since her crippling accident on a horse, stands to inherit two and a half million when he dies. Sampson, from all reports, doesn't deserve to be loved or missed for himself. Alcoholic, sexually warped, and—the clinch-er—a wildcat oil operator, he has bullied everyone in his orbit ("Sampson made anyone who worked for him feel like a valet"). Yet Archer, who need not like or approve of his paymasters, has a job, and the novel has a missing person worth wondering about.

Archer was recommended to Elaine Sampson by Albert Graves, an ex-District Attorney of forty, the family's lawyer, and worried suitor of Miranda, the missing man's twenty-year-old daughter by his first marriage. Graves's place in the plot sends out important signals. Because of him, a tight, shapely narrative structure has already started to emerge. The first chapter of *Target* contains several staples of Archer canon: the missing person; the sexual relationship with a twenty-year age difference; the unlikeable female client; the neighbor, close family friend, or in-law who manages the family's business or legal affairs. Chapter Two introduces Miranda, "a tall girl . . . the kind who developed slowly and was worth waiting for," and handsome, athletic Alan Taggert, her father's pilot and her own neglectful lover. Joined by these two, Archer finds a photo of an ageing film starlet later identified as Fay Estabrook in Sampson's bungalow. He then goes on his own to Telepictures, a small independent film studio in Universal City, where Fay is shooting a film. After watching her play a scene on the set, he follows her home, through Los Angeles County and along the Pacific Palisades, thus giving his author the chance to scene-paint the local landscape in some of his freshest, most pulsing prose.

Masquerading as a termite-control expert, Archer reconnoiters Fay's home but soon runs afoul of her tough protector-friend, Puddler, in whose beetling eyes he squirts oil before leaving. When night falls, he comes back to watch for Fay. He follows her into Swift's, a chic bar near Hollywood and Vine, meets an acquaintance who introduces him to her, and, after some drinking, leaves with her on a pub-crawl. His attempt to learn her connection with the missing man, Ralph Sampson, takes on a new urgency when word arrives that Sampson has written his wife for $100,000. Archer drives Fay home, where she passes out from drink, and then rifles her personal belongings. No sooner does he find $10,000 in cash at the bottom of a dresser-drawer than a phone-caller, mistaking him for a Mr. Troy, warns that Fay has been drinking with someone who could be a policeman. The real Dwight Troy walks in, a pistol in his hand. Unshaken, Archer insults and matches wits with the epicene Troy, an excellent pistol shot. But he does leave Fay's, as ordered. His next stop is the Wild Piano, the local bar from which the warning phone call came. He spots the caller, a boogie-woogie and blues pianist, Betty Fraley. Betty, though brain-fogged by drugs, has also spotted Archer as a detective: "You could be a cop. . . . There's something about the way you look at things, wanting them but not liking them." She calls for the club's bouncer, the gorilla-like Puddler, who, with relish, knocks Archer unconscious.

Archer's first sensation, upon waking up, is seeing Alan Taggert fell

Puddler from behind. Some gunshots and a charging truck, which nearly hits Archer, follow quickly. This danger sends him to the police, namely Peter Colton, formerly Archer's chief in Army Intelligence and now a senior investigator for the D. A. Colton names Troy—ex-gambler, bootlegger, and brothel-keeper—the owner of the Wild Piano. Colton and Archer, having a common purpose, join forces. A by-product of the missing-persons case has become the job of closing the Wild Piano and jailing its owner. But first Archer, kindly and workmanlike, drives back to Santa Teresa to report to his client, Elaine Sampson. He advises her to send her husband the $100,000 but also to call in the police. Chancing to look out the window, he sees several black disks skimming into the sea. But an overhang stops his seeing the thrower of the disks.

While he tries to puzzle out the thrower's identity, the novel moves from the sea to the mountains. Chapter Sixteen, occurring midway into the action, takes place at the Temple of the Clouds, a mountain hunting lodge which Ralph Sampson drunkenly gave to a Mithraic cultist named Claude for his sun-shrine. Like Professor Salamander in *Blue City*, the womanish Claude is a spiritual fraud. But Archer's success in ferreting out Claude's charlatanism has no counterpart. The detective finds no clue of Sampson in the shrine and returns empty-handed to Sampson's family in Santa Teresa, where he inspects the ransom note sent by the kidnapers. Sampson's chances, as he sums them up here, are nearly hopeless:

This is the situation. Even if we obey instructions to the letter, there's a better than fifty-fifty chance that Sampson won't come out alive. He must be able to identify at least one of the gang. . . . That's bad for him. You'll make it worse if you try to trip the money pickup. You'll have a kidnaper in the county jail, and Sampson lying somewhere with his throat cut.

The appearance of the novel's first corpse in Chapter 18, well beyond the halfway mark, deepens the gloom. The dead man in the rented car used to pick up the ransom money is identified as Eddie Lassiter, small-time criminal and brother of jazz pianist, Betty Fraley. Eddie, Archer reasons, was killed for the ransom money. Following his leads, Archer goes back to the Temple in the Clouds, where a dozen small brown attackers, their teeth flashing, storm him and knock him out. Troy re-enters, his revolver again trained on Archer. The detective is knocked out a second time, stuffed into a car, and driven somewhere. Awakening, he finds himself guarded by Puddler near a pier and some oil pumps. As happened so often to Hector Land in *Trouble*, an earlier specimen of pre-Darwinian man, Puddler is easily tricked. Archer, rating survival over combat ethics, kicks him in the stomach, rakes his forehead with a file, and, after a furious underwater struggle, drowns Puddler. Anxious to get away from his victim, he returns to Santa Teresa. But, once there, he dives into the same sea that is decomposing Puddler's body. His purpose? To

Debut

look for the black disks careening into the sea from beneath the second-story overhang of the Sampsons' house the day before. He does find a phonograph record with its labels scratched out and confronts Alan Taggert with it as proof that Taggert kidnaped Ralph Sampson:

You had more opportunity than anyone, and more motive. You resented Sampson's treatment of you. You resented all the money he had. You hadn't much yourself—

*   *   *

Nobody else could have known that Sampson was going to phone the Valerio [a local establishment]. Nobody else knew when Sampson was going to fly in from Nevada. Nobody else was in a position to give Eddie the tip-off the night before. Nobody else could have made all the arrangements and run them off on schedule.

This allegation stems from sound detection. First, Archer collects the evidence, and then he reasons from it. The record scooped from the sea floor, when played on Taggert's phonograph, turns out to be the piano music of Betty Fraley, sister of the dead pick-up man of the ransom money. Unable to explain why he threw Betty's records away, Taggert pulls a gun on Archer and, just as he is about to kill him, is shot to death by Albert Graves, who has materialized.

An interview with the local police follows. Though no nearer to Sampson or the stolen $100,000, Archer learns that Troy has been using the Temple in the Clouds as a way station for illegal Mexican immigrants. He follows Troy and some of his gang to their canyon hideaway, where Betty, Troy's prisoner, explains, first, that she killed her brother and, next, that she has the ransom money. His gun smoking, Archer rescues her in exchange for a promise to deliver Sampson and the $100,000. She leads him, next, somewhat reluctantly, to a disused beach club about forty miles north of Santa Teresa. When he reaches the club, he notes with dismay that Albert Graves, whom he had called to bring food and first aid to the kidnaped man, has not preceded him. Then he is knocked out from behind. But he is soon revived by the dilatory Graves, allegedly summoned to a county hospital since Archer's telephone call. The two men find Sampson strangled to death. The novel, without fatalities its first half, has suddenly sprouted corpses. For Betty Fraley dies after a car-wreck some fifteen miles away from the beach club, having fled in Archer's car.

But the resolution is not *Grand Guignol*. The last chapter beams in on Graves, who married Miranda and, the same day, killed her father. A pattern forms. Making the killer the same person who saved the detective's life is good literary detection. Graves, an excellent pistol-shot, could have saved Archer without killing Alan Taggert; at point-blank range, a leg shot would have been easy for a sharpshooter like Graves. Archer accuses him of killing Sampson in order to convert Miranda's million-dollar inheritance into a dowry for himself. Yet money is a poor motive. Graves earns a good salary; furthermore, Miranda says she always admired him because he never cared about money—a judgment seconded by a long-standing business acquaintance. Archer is wrong to say of Graves, "It must have galled him to work for millionaires and handle their money and have nothing of his own." Graves have nothing of his own? From the look of things—an office in a good building, a personal secretary, an established clientele—his practice is thriving. He also has a first-rate name in legal circles, which has earned him the confidence of the rich and the powerful. Any lawyer with rich, powerful clients pockets large fees.

A better motive—but one the plot slights—is that of sexual jealousy. Possessiveness and insecurity led Graves to kill Taggert, whom Miranda was in love with. Sampson, fanatically devoted to her, was another rival who had to die; since his son's death in the war and the wasting of his marriage to Elaine, he had clung to Miranda more and more for emotional support. Miranda's own competitive relationship with Elaine gave the girl another motive to look after her father. The book ends with a flurry of reversals. Graves, who dreamed for months of marrying Miranda, turns from her within hours of their wedding. Sick of dreams and violence, he gives himself up to the police. Miranda, who thought she knew him, is stunned by Archer's disclosures. Elaine Sampson has come into a fortune and ridded herself for good of a husband she hated. But, without anybody to share her life, her freedom and inheritance both ring hollow. She and Graves have gotten exactly what they want but reject it flat out. (Living the dream, however briefly, proves unbearable.) Miranda, who has lost a lover, a father, and a husband within a day, emerges stronger than either of them.

Graves is the book's least plausible character. Like the killers in Hammett's *The Dain Cruse* and *The Thin Man*, he is an old friend of the detective. But because the detective doesn't mix reason and sentiment, his killer-friend must be punished. The novel's chief weakness centers not just on Graves's evil, but also on Ross Macdonald's presentation of it. Graves, heir of the Midwestern dream of money and romance, has always struggled. Son of an Ohio farmer, he worked in a tire factory before putting himself, first, through college, where he made Phi Beta Kappa, and, then, through the University of Michigan law school. As has been said, skill, experience, and honest hard work have already made him one of southern California's leading lawyers: "His courtroom work had been cited by a state-supreme court judge as a model of forensic jurisprudence," Archer recalls of his old friend. In addition to the two last-chapter statements that money meant little to Graves, only a law-respecting penitent would turn himself into the police as Graves does.

Graves has neither the need nor the temperment to kill for money. Even sexual love, if plausible psychologically, doesn't carry much probative impact. Though strong, intelligent, and well-informed, he always feels clumsy around Miranda. As Archer says of him, "At forty he was drunk on love." The trouble with Graves is that Archer misreads his motives and needs. A Midwesterner like Ross Macdonald, Graves could be the novel's main character. But he never moves from under the shadow of Archer, who doesn't understand him; he appears rarely, and Archer always has a facile explanation for his deeds. Like Mayor Allister of *Blue City* and Bret Taylor of *Roads*, he is a spoiled idealist. Yet Ross Macdonald only shows the effects of his corruption; his fall from virtue occurs out of view. Neither his evil nor the forces that created it are dramatized. That he repents the evil so soon after performing it suggests that Ross Macdonald didn't believe it himself.

A more believable moral collapse happens to Ralph Sampson and his troubled house; as is usual, the family jogs Ross Macdonald's imagination much more than the private individual. Elaine Sampson may have faked her paralysis; she acts like somebody with a mental, rather than a physical, disorder. Miranda's expulsion from Radcliffe, like her falling in love with the opportunist Alan Taggert, represents a turning-away from received values. The Sampson family undergoes a constant rhythm of breakdown and renewal. The breakdown of unity and collective moral fiber dates from the death of Miranda's brother during the war. Sampson feels guilty for having made money from the same war that took his son. Without ever appearing alive, Sampson is the book's most fascinating character. His guilt shows in his alcoholism, his bullying of anybody who can't fight back, and his newly acquired sexual irregularities. The twelve-sided bedroom in his bungalow, fitted with a circular mirror in its red ceiling, strikes Archer as "the inside of a sick brain." Sampson's knack for money-making gives only an illusion of freedom; his growing dependence on Miranda brings both his guilt and his erotic vagaries back to the family hearth, where they fester and fret. This contagion infects everyone in the Sampson orbit, including Taggert and Graves.

The process is inevitable. Nothing can stall the family tragedy set into motion by Bob Sampson's death in the war. The doom is deepened by numerous primitive and classical references. A local cabdriver says of Cabrillo Canyon, the Santa Teresa neighborhood of the Sampsons, "This is where the cavemen live," and Archer mentions the Stone Age, "when men stood up on their hind legs and began to count time by the sun." Human life is as savage in postwar California as in primitive jungle cultures. The Sampsons and their set abide by social restrictions as rigid as they are vague. Pain and death join people. Taggert's death wins Graves a bride and saves Archer's life. So long as Ralph Sampson is alive, his wife will never walk. Despite their money, the Sampsons can't reverse the death drift that has caught them up. Miranda fails to win the love of the working-class outsider, Taggert. Her hope for happiness at the end—bought by the arrest of her husband and the deaths of her lover and her father—looks more like punishment than promise.

Though the references to Theseus, the Zodiac, and Shakespeare's *Tempest* fit no pattern, their accumulated force lends weight to the action. Some of this intellectual undergirding is recast to suit the contemporary setting. Sampson's non-appearance leaves the book without a Prospero, or guiding spirit, in spite of all the riches the family enjoys. The Ferdinand-figure, Taggert, won't play his role, ignoring Miranda for another woman, Betty Fraley. Instead of marrying Miranda, he kidnaps her father and then performs the Prospero-like act of drowning, not a book, but some phonograph records. One of these, though, refuses to stay drowned. Suffering no sea change, it surfaces to bring about Taggert's death. Taggert, ironically the book's first corpse, may be the only non-self-destructive person in the Sampson set. Ralph Sampson's kidnaping and murder only externalize a death wish that expresses itself in alcoholism, religious cultism, and sick sex. Betty Fraley and her brother, Eddie Lassiter, are both killing themselves with drugs. Puddler, the book's Caliban, lacks the wit to survive. Elaine Sampson is said to have caused the horse-riding accident that paralyzed her legs. Though Albert Graves stands to profit from Sampson's death, he advises Elaine to hire Archer, i.e., a detective whose skill at finding missing persons and tracking criminals he knows well. These examples prove one thing. The source that explains *Target* best is Ross Macdonald's standby, the Oedipus myth: most of the characters harm themselves more than others could do.

Archer, the catalyst, hastens rather than causes the downfall of the guilty. He stands outside the deathly process. Like the other early Archer books, *Target* features the staples of the realistic action-thriller—tough talk, tough characters, tough factual writing. Though a questioner, Archer sometimes acts as if he already has all the answers he needs. His toughness, vehemence, and arrogance rival those of John Weather in *Blue City*. He spouts mannish slang: "Douse the muggles, Marcie. I want you to talk some sense." Unflinchingly, he invokes the letter of the law against his old chum Graves, once he finds out that Graves killed Ralph Sampson; obnoxious in his moral rectitude, he even forbids Graves to call him by his first name. Holding human purpose cheaply, he reduces most human conduct to motives of sex and money. But the famous Archer compassion and moral sympathy soften the brutality. Before starting the hour-and-a-half drive to where Sampson has been stashed by the kidnapers, he phones ahead to get Sampson food and first aid. Ross Macdonald has troubled to give his detective both a personality and a set of moral values. Archer's recitation on the rift between making moral judgments and the law's need both to judge and to punish sounds like a personal and professional manifesto:

When I went into police work in 1935, I believed evil was a quality some people were born with, like a harelip. A cop's job was to find those people and put them away.

But evil isn't so simple. Everybody has it in him, and whether it comes out in his actions depends on a number of things. Environment, opportunity, economic pressure, a piece of bad luck, a wrong friend. The trouble is a cop has to go on judging people by rule of thumb, and acting on the judgment.

The manifesto, pitched between Victorian confidence and existential doubt, suggests an intention to use Archer as a continuing detective. But perhaps the art form Ross Macdonald had in mind for him was the film rather than prose fiction. In 1966, the novelist said, "*The Moving Target* . . . is a story clearly aspiring to be a movie. It was no accident that when Warner Brothers made it into one last year they were able to follow the story virtually scene by scene."[1] The only novel our writer published under the name, John Macdonald, conveys psychology through gesture and movement rather than thought. Its cinematic technique, avoiding analysis and introspection, inculdes a great deal of dialogue, action, sharply realized settings, and, a standby of early postwar film thrillers, a small, lithe, inscrutable Filipino servant with pointed ears. Certain scenes are photographed rather than narrated. For instance, a camera homing in and then fixing on a doorknob introduces Dwight Troy in Chapter 9:

The knob of the front door rattled slightly behind me. I froze with my hand on the telephone and watched the cut-glass knob as it slowly rotated, sparkling in the light from the living-room. The door swung open suddenly, and a man in a light topcoat stood in the opening.

Even when he goes into a character's mind, Ross Macdonald describes visual images rather than ideas or emotional states. In Chapter 2 a series of montages and dissolves throngs Archer's half-conscious mind after he is beaten and knocked out:

On the threshold of consciousness my mind swarmed with images from beyond the threshold: uglier faces than I'd seen in any street, eviler streets than I'd seen in any city. I came to the empty square in the city's heart. Death lurked behind the muttering windows, an old whore with sickness under her paint. A face looked down at me, changing by the second: Miranda's brown young face sprouting gray hair, Claude's mouth denuded to become Fay's smile, Fay shrinking down, all but the great dark eyes, to the Filipino's head, which was withered by rapid age to the silver head of Troy.

But a novel consists of words, not visual impressions, and no novelist can neglect narrative technique. Also, some of Ross Macdonald's main ideas and arguments don't convert to cinema. His frequent shifting between cinematic and novelistic strategies probably hurt *Target*. The pace and texture of the novel are both smooth. Scenes at the elegant Sampson estate follow ones occurring in primitive or rundown settings; quiet scenes follow violent ones. But some of these add nothing—failing to bring Archer closer to his quarry, to show how southern Californians live, or to bolster the plot. The episode in Chapter 6 where Archer masquerades as a termite exterminator could be lopped, for instance. In fact, everything between his discovery of Fay Estabrook's photo in Sampson's bungalow and Troy's discovery of him in Fay's home needs trimming. Betty Fraley is also disposed of clumsily; the book must introduce a new character, a highway patrolman, in the last chapter to report the death.

Another blemish, not structural, comes from the author's not having done his homework on drug addiction and traffic. Ross Macdonald misjudges nearly everything connected with drugs. That a seasoned professional racketeer like Troy would join forces with a hard-drug addict like Betty Fraley defies both reason and experience. The discovery of marijuana butts in her brother Eddie Lassiter's rented car rivals in implausibility the hopeless shuddering of two tarts deprived of their weed in *Blue City* and *Find a Victim*. Non-addictive, marijuana doesn't produce painful withdrawal symptoms, and a skilled, high-speed driver wouldn't smoke it on a job, especially one as big as that of collecting $100,000.

These flaws, though, don't pit the handsome sheen of the novel. *Target* isn't just the first Archer; it also introduces the process, or dialectic, associated with both Archer's detection and the narrative form that describes it. The search for the missing person, growing into a multiple-murder case, takes Archer through many byways and yields many by-products, like family stress, drug addiction, and the smuggling of Mexicans across the border. Archer turns up these surprising developments by tracing his leads to characters carefully selected for age, job, and social background. There is little misspent effort. Rather than straying from his purpose—to find Ralph Sampson—he gathers the material needed both to carry out and understand his purpose. Ross Macdonald believed in *Target*. And he made good his belief by staking his future writing career on the book's detective hero and narrative form. Its search for meanings rather than sensations gets the Archer series off to a fine start.

II

The Drowning Pool (1950) starts when Maude Slocum, an attractive matron of thirty-five, asks Archer's help with a poison-pen letter she intercepted before it reached her husband, to whom it was sent. The mention in the letter of "your wife's amorous activities" makes Archer suspicious when Maude refuses both to discuss her private life and to let him meet her husband. Another problem—domestic, financial, and moral—comes in with Olivia Slocum, Maude's mother-in-law and "the central figure" of her marriage. Maude and James Slocum live in Olivia's large house and, because Slocum doesn't work, depend on Olivia for money as well as shelter. Still worse, Olivia has always disliked Maude and wants James to divorce her.

Chapter Two carries the action to Quinto, a fictional town an hour north of Santa Monica, where, after checking into a motel, Archer goes to a local community theater. Masquerading as a literary agent for a Hollywood film studio, he watches a rehearsal of a play written by a local playwright, Francis Marvell, and starring his client's husband, James. The rehearsal stops when the Slocums' chauffeur, Pat Reavis, makes a rough pass at Slocum's sixteen-year-old daughter, Cathy, in the darkened auditorium. Though Cathy had welcomed Reavis's advances the night before, she now rebuffs them. In a fury, Slocum leaps from the stage and fires Reavis. The offstage drama, Archer notices after Reavis's angry leavetaking, is more exciting than the one being played on the stage. But he still has no contacts or leads. Convincing Maude that he can't help her unless she puts him closer to the things she lives by, he talks his way into a cocktail party she's giving later that day. The chapter ends with tenderness followed by turmoil. Archer overhears Cathy and her effeminate father voicing endearments: "They could have been two lovers of the same age," he notes uneasily. Then Maude storms in, warning her husband to leave Cathy alone. Her warning gives the chapter a sharp sensory ending that keeps us reading: "The throaty whisper made the short hairs prickle at the back of my neck."

Archer recalls that Cathy isn't the only quarrelling-point in the troubled Slocum home. Slocum's mother Olivia, hasn't forgiven Muade for marrying her son and refuses to sell her home—worth millions because of the rich oil deposits underneath—in order to control him. As in D. H. Lawrence, modern man is too weak and modern woman, often too strong in the Archer canon. Jobless, Slocum lives spinelessly in his mother's home and takes her money. The denial of work routine has sapped his pep, ambition, and independence, plus wrecking his marriage. Appropriately, when Olivia, the castrating mother, enters the book, she is holding garden shears, as will two other domineering women—Tish Bradshaw in *The Chill* and Rita Chalmers in *The Goodbye Look*. Showing the main cause of the Slocums' marital trouble soon after the trouble is made known tightens the plot. The party in Chapter 5, an excellent device for bringing people together, introduces Police Lieutenant Ralph Knudson, Nopal Valley's Chief of Police and an invited guest. Although we don't know it, the action is well under way. Knudson, it is later divulged, is Maude's longstanding lover and Cathy's natural father. Muade had met him at a students' rooming house Knudson operated with his older wife in Berkeley many years before. The wife's spiteful refusal to give Knudson a divorce, even after learning that Maude was pregnant, caused two upheavals; it sent Knudson to the Midwest and threw Maude together with James Slocum, who married her, ignoring the improbability of Cathy's birth seven months later. Maude kept faith with Slocum for twelve empty years. Then she saw a news photo from Chicago praising Knudson for his police work. The Midwest revives the past. Maude, finding that she still loved Knudson, called him and flew to him in Chicago. When Nopal Valley needed a new police chief, Knudson, his wife still refusing to divorce him, applied for the job and got it. Slocum, content with his own social routine, has kept his back turned on the renewed intrigue.

Chapter Seven brings on the violence. Olivia Slocum is discovered drowned in her private pool. And a flock of likely murder suspects emerge straightaway. Slocum's lover, Francis Marvell, would profit from Olivia's death because her son's legacy could take Marvell's new play, along with the son and heir, his star, to New York. The Pacific Refining Company, or Pareco, wanted Olivia dead to better their chances of mining her property for oil. Maude Slocum's long-festering resentment of her mother-in-law gives still another murder-motive. Pat Reavis, just rebuffed by Cathy and fired by her father, has his own private grudge. Where does Archer start looking for clues and leads? From the spacious elegance of the Slocum estate, he goes to the dingy, noisy jazz cave, the "Romp Room," where a combo, the Furious Five, is blaring to a crowded dance floor. His purpose is to meet Gretchen Keck, a B-girl, semi-prostitute, and sweetheart of Pat Reavis. Pretending to be an ex-Marine cohort of Reavis, Archer drives Gretchen to Reavis's trailer. Though he doesn't find his man there, he does get his Hollywood address, where he heads straightaway. By chance, he arrives just as Reavis is leaving in a chauffeured limousine for Dennis's Hunt Club, a seedy cabaret. Reavis soon departs the cabaret with Mavis and Walter Kilbourne, owner of Pareco, the large oil refinery determined to drill the Slocum acreage. Once on the Freeway, Kilbourne's massive Cadillac loses Archer's modest cab, and the detective must start afresh unriddling the Kilbourne—Reavis entente and its link, if any, to Olivia Slocum's death.

The unriddling starts out badly. Driving back to Reavis's apartment, Archer is set on, knocked out, and tied up by some of Kilbourne's henchmen. But Mavis, Kilbourne's wife, comes in to save Archer. Her motive is clear. She wants Archer to crack a safe and remove a roll of film. Doing as she asks, he no sooner sees that the film shows Mavis naked than she grabs it and tries to burn it to stop Kilbourne's blackmail scheme. Archer takes the film before it burns, but "the whirling vortex . . . the drowning pool" of Mavis's embrace sends his reason awash, and the next thing he knows, after Mavis's long goodbye kiss, is that he has been pickpocketed.

After a couple of reconnoiters, he drives to Las Vegas to look for Reavis, whom he finds at his prostitute-sister's rural cabin. He listens in on a hot quarrel between brother and sister based on a news report of the brother's involvement in Olivia Slocum's death. Then he captures Reavis and begins driving back to Quinto with him. A package containing ten thousand dollars in cash found in Reavis's pocket makes him the leading murder suspect. But—as will often happen in Ross Macdonald—the person suspected of doing the first murder is often the second victim. Archer's call to Lieutenant Knudson at the Nopal Valley Police Station is taken by a desk sergeant. Some time later, six men, using their truck for a road-block, stop Archer's car and tell Archer that they want Reavis. The detective's attempts to ward off the vigilantes go astray when Reavis unexpectedly attacks him, his protector, from behind. Archer is quickly swarmed and knocked out. Waking up, he learns that Reavis was shot, doused with gasoline, and then incinerated. Archer returns to the police station in Quinto, but finds no record of his phone-message to Knudson regarding Reavis's return. Correctly, he reasons that, besides failing to relay the message, the desk sergeant alerted the gangsters who organized the lynching party.

A third reversal in as many chapters occurs back at the Slocums', when Knudson explains Reavis's death as an execution rather than a murder. Reavis deserved to die, says Knudson, because he killed Olivia Slocum; marks on her body prove she was pushed into her drowning pool, and Reavis's cap turned up near the pool the night of the drowning. Yet Archer, who drove Reavis back to town from the Slocums' the same night, uses the timing of Olivia's death to prove the chauffeur's innocence. Reavis was riding in Archer's car about a mile from the estate when Olivia was heard to splash into the water. Having ruled out Reavis's guilt, Archer then tries to connect the murder with the poison-pen letter that brought Maude to his office to begin with.

The case is breaking. When one of the lynchers turns out to be on Pareco's payroll, Archer draws reasonable conclusions:

From where I sat it looked as if Kilbourne had sparked a double play that would never be recorded on the sports pages: paid Reavis to dispose of Mrs. Slocum, then paid to have Reavis disposed of before he could talk.

But instead of breaking, the case lurches into violence and mystery. Archer finds Maude Slocum dead of strychnine in her bed. He also finds her suicide note and the poison-pen letter of Chapter 1 to have both been typed on Maude's typewriter. Knudson upends him again by destroying this evidence. Knudson then blocks the detective's protests by reminding him that his carrying Reavis, or Ryan (the dead man's alias), across a state line under duress could lead to a long jail term. Archer's helplessness and frustration soon dissolve in a strange development. Though it is nearly four o'clock in the morning, Mavis Kilbourne telephones to ask him to meet her on Quinto's pier. A half hour later on the pier, she confirms his suspicions about her husband's part in Pat Reavis's death. Mavis also recounts through a morphine mist the sordid details of her courtship and marriage, a love affair with Reavis-Ryan, then her husband's chauffeur, and the husband's photographing the lovers in bed together to stop Mavis from getting a divorce and then divulging the graft at Pareco.

The morphine Kilbourne shoots into her bloodstream has worked as a truth serum, making for the quick, ample filling-in of vital background. Both the information and its speedy setting-forth lend urgency to new developments. Mavis and Archer are taken prisoner aboard Kilbourne's yacht, where an interview between the oil titan and Archer deepens as many mysteries as it resolves. Kilbourne admits getting Pat Reavis a job as the Slocums' chauffeur to learn of any offers other oil companies might make the family to dig on their property. But while confessing both to industrial espionage and moral responsibility for Olivia Slocum's death, Kilbourne denies having told Reavis to kill her. Archer believes him; trusting an indiscreet dreamer like Reavis *would* have been foolish. Then Kilbourne's reasoning spins into darkness. Still denying that he ordered Olivia's death, he does admit killing Reavis:

Ryan saw an opportunity to tap me for a very great deal of money. . . . By killing Mrs. Slocum he placed me in jeopardy along with himself. His jeopardy was also mine. I had to help him out of it, and he knew it. . . . When he was careless enough to allow himself to be captured, I had to take other measures. . . . In the end my hand was forced. So while I can't claim that my motives in this sorry business were wholly pure, neither have they been entirely black.

Kilbourne then offers Archer $10,000 to forget the whole Slocum-Reavis-Pareco embroilment. When Archer balks, he is knocked out, straight-jacketed, and driven to a nursing home owned by Kilbourne. Kilbourne's evil has reached beyond cars and petroleum to doctoring. Running his sanitarium are an unlicensed doctor and an imbecilic nurse. With Kilbourne's approval, these two bruise and blister human flesh rather than heal it. Chapter Twenty-two, which supplies one aspect of the novel's title, gets much of its sting, literally, as we shall see, from the cruelty of Melliotes and Miss Macon.

Taking Archer "to a room like a burial vault," the two give him what they gleefully call "the hydro treatment"—a roaring blast of water that knocks a victim off his feet and slams him into the far wall. The next torture, Melliotes's "prettiest fountain," consists of a single needle-stream that prints the letter M across the victim's, i.e., Archer's, chest in six inches of blood. What follows is even more lurid. On his own, Archer fills the room with water, hoping to escape through the overhead skylight. Water, the element that had stung and smashed him a few minutes before, could now save his life; Archer has both the speed and control to turn a threat into a friend. But the threat befriends him in an unexpected way. Though he can't punch through the reinforced glass overhead, he escapes drowning when the weight and pressure of the rising water break the door of his water chamber.

Mavis, freed by Archer from a padded cell, then shoots her husband dead. Just as Chapter 22 showed Archer's grit and decisiveness, the next one features his tender heart. Human enough to be tempted, he ponders

Mavis's offer of marriage, ten million dollars, and "fine warm fishing waters . . . high sea-cliffs, and . . . long slow tequila nights." But, like Sam Spade in *The Maltese Falcon*, he turns down the murderess's offer of love, fortune, and ease to arrest her, instead. Though no relationship builds between the two, as with Spade and Brigid O'Shaughnessy, Archer exercises loving tact by having Mavis tell the police she killed her husband in self-defense. The next chapter—the next-to-last in the book—also subordinates action to tenderness. It introduces Maude Slocum's former college roommate, Mildred Fleming, who tells of Knudson's bad marriage, his wife's refusal to give him a divorce, and the many ramifications of his affaire with Maude. His heart and his professional integrity both stirred, Archer determines to find out why his former client died. A dusty bus takes him back to Quinto. But before going to the Slocums', he visits Gretchen Keck, first, to tell her that Reavis said he loved her just before he died, next, to give her the $10,000 Reavis took from Kilbourne as a fee for drowning Olivia Slocum, and, last, to explain that, though he took Kilbourne's money, Reavis never killed Olivia.

The killer and the poison-pen letter-writer both turn out to be sixteen-year-old Cathy. Her motive? As in *Roads*, the punishment for adultery in Ross Macdonald, when detected by a household relative, is harsh. Cathy found her mother with Ralph Knudson, whom she didn't know was her natural father, and sent the letter both to scare and hurt Maude. Seeing that she couldn't end the liaison, Cathy killed her grandmother to drive the disinherited Maude out of the house and thus get James Slocum, the only father she ever knew, all to herself. This arrangement would have given everybody—Cathy, Maude, Slocum, and Knudson—what he wants. But its mainspring was murder. Cathy's private crime moves us more than the public crime of Walter Kilbourne, who, along with his helpers at Pareco and the rest home, is portrayed with simple malice throughout. Like the later novels, *Pool* shows family-centered, rather than professional, crime as Ross Macdonald's true subject. The family or the closed social circle is what Ross Macdonald knows best and writes about best. His books work when he sticks to what he knows. *Pool* succeeds because its underlying family crisis and Midwestern background (Gretchen Keck, Knudson, and Kilbourne have all lived in the Chicago-Detroit area) fueled his creative energies.

Like him, Cathy has the burden of a smothered paternity. Yet she accepts Ralph Knudson and goes to Chicago with him to start anew. Archer is glad to give her this chance. Though she confesses her guilt within the shadows of cypress trees—symbolic of death—he doesn't exercise the deadly letter of the law against her. Instead, he gropes for Knudson's hand in the looming darkness of the Slocums' lawn to wish him and Cathy luck in their new life. His charity and the joint agreement of Cathy and Knudson to fight the cypress-hung darkness with their love make the ending Ross Macdonald's strongest to date. The symbolism generated by the scene sorts with the novel's underlying realities. *Pool* is shrouded in ambiguous grays; sometimes flecks or streaks of light interrupt a black field. Francis Marvell, James Slocum's lover, is mocked throughout for his poofish, prissy ways: "Murder is such a perfectly dreadful thought," he says breathlessly. "It was bad enough when I found the poor woman's body. Now I simply know I shan't sleep a wink tonight." Yet Marvell is also praised by the local police for having the courage to haul Olivia from her drowning pool.

The home of the Slocums seethes with ambiguity. Olivia can't be faulted for refusing to sell the property she bought with her husband thirty years before. But her refusal may come from the selfish impulse to control her son and to spite his wife, not from a loving memory or the public spirited wish to save the land from despoilation. Wisely, Ross Macdonald doesn't resolve the ambiguity. Maude and James Slocum resent each other's treatment of Cathy, accuse each other of sexual failure and betrayal, and, knowing the accusations to carry force, shoulder enormous guilt. Yet the complex needs created by marriage keep Maude and Slocum together, as in Albee's *Who's Afraid of Virginia Woolf.* Maude will betray her husband but can't leave him. After her death, Archer notes of her, "Hers was one of those stories without villains or heroes. There was no one to admire, no one to blame. Everyone had done wrong for himself and others. Everyone had failed. Everyone had suffered."

Both suffering and failure darken the future of Cathy Slocum, the book's youngest character, who must give up a father she has always loved for one she has never even liked or accepted. The motivation in *Pool* is more complex than that in *Target*; conveying it is a plot not only elaborate but also tight and believable. *Pool* has structural flaws—frequent coincidences, eavesdropping, and the introduction of a new character, Mildred Fleming, in the next-to-last chapter to give the background of the case. But the book also shows new technical insight and control. Its many good descriptions come to life through auditory, as well as visual, imagery. It surveys Slocum women from three generations, gives each woman valid emotional demands, yet shows each wasting James Slocum. The self-defensive chatter and emotional craving of the guests at the cocktail party in Chapter 5 reach us through a catalog of upper-bohemian motifs that capture the California pseudo-chic of the late 1940s:

I listened to them talk. Existentialism, they said. Henry Miller and Truman Capote and Henry Moore. André Gide and Anais Nin and Djuna Barnes. And sex—hardboiled, poached, coddled, shirred, and fried easy over in sweet, fresh creamery butter. Sex solo, in duet, trio, quartet; for all-male chorus; for choir and symphony; and played on the harpsichord in three-fourths time. And Albert Schweitzer and the dignity of everything that lives.

Characterization in *Pool*, though not brilliant, also marks an advance from *Target*. Women appear more often and act from more complex motives. Pat Reavis, or Ryan, looks back to grabbers like Larry Miles (who also uses an alias) in *Roads* and, more pointedly, to Alan Taggert, who also dies for his dreams in *Target*. But the underlying pattern is different. Taggert, the man who controlled his chief's favorite machine, his airplane, also controlled the chief's most cherished prize, his daughter. In *Pool*, the chief has no money of his own, and the chauffeur hotly pursues the passive debutante. A poor outsider and self-romanticizer hopeful of gatecrashing a rich California family, Ryan looks ahead to the have-not heroes of *The Galton Case* and *Black Money*. His grandiose plans and tall tales of his war exploits with the Marines, from which he was dishonorably discharged, put him in the camp of the self-destructive dreamer. Like his counterparts, he actively defeats himself—throwing in with the mob and then, by attacking Archer, his protector, helping the mob lynch him.

But if Reavis is part of a developing continuum, Walter Kilbourne belongs to a static, simplistic one. Like Anderson/Jensen in *Trouble* and Mayor Allister in *Blue City*, this public enemy is no felt force. We hear much about his evil, and we see its deadly effects. But until Chapter 21 of this twenty-five chapter novel, when he kidnaps Archer aboard his yacht, he is only a walk-on; his sole appearance coming in Chapter 10, where he gets into a limousine after leaving a night-spot. The moral ambiguity addling the Slocums doesn't carry into the Pareco subplot; as has been said, public crime fails to rouse Ross Macdonald's best energies. Kilbourne is the same flat, cardboard villain as Ralph Sampson. Both oil moguls, working through henchman, produce wreckage and distress from behind the scenes. Neither emerges wholly. Sampson only appears as a corpse, and his counterpart exists trivially: he speaks with a false refinement; a physical grotesque, he oozes sexual depravity from a pink, pudgy body set between an oversized head and tiny legs; he has a passion for food:

He ate with a gobbling passion. A piece of ham and four eggs, six pieces of toast; a kidney and a pair of mountain trout; eight pancakes with eight small sausages; a quart of raspberries, a pint of cream, a quart of coffee.

Members of Kilbourne's gang are also depicted in clumsy, lurid strokes. These depictions don't gain from feeble reproductions of rough language like "He advised me to commit sodomy" and "His voice announced clearly that he would not be fornicated with."

The unintended comedy created by these sexual periphrases lighten one of Ross Macdonald's darkest books. *Pool's* running metaphor is that of entrapment—usually in a cold, tight place. "Coffin fear" grips Archer while, stuffed behind the driver's seat, he rides from Hollywood to Glendale in Kilbourne's car. After escaping, he browbeats his former captor,

"You're in a box. You want me to nail down the lid?" In Chapter 22, Archer and Mavis are both locked inside rooms by enemies who want to kill them. Everybody gets trapped sooner or later. Pareco's sulphurous fumes, nodding, clanking oil pumps, and ugly housing developments have ruined Nopal Valley. Archer's swim in Chapter 3 denies civilization as forcefully as Sam Drake's wish to go back to sea duty at the end of *Trouble*:

> I turned on my back and floated, looking up at the sky, nothing around me but cool clear Pacific, nothing in my eyes but long blue space. It was as close as I ever got to cleanliness and freedom, as far as I ever got from all the people. They had jerrybuilt the beaches from San Diego to the Golden Gate, bulldozed super-highways through the mountains, cut down a thousand years of redwood growth, and built an urban wilderness in the desert. They couldn't touch the ocean. They poured their sewage into it, but it couldn't be tainted.

But water, universal solvent, can drown and smash. The bloody monogram Melliotes prints in water on Archer's chest represents not only his initial but also that of Mavis, Muade, Miss Macon, Mildred Fleming, Francis Marvell, Kenneth Millar, and Ross Macdonald. Collecting so much pain and dismay under the rubric of his own initial signals the writer's doubts about the value and aim of human existence. Even Archer, normally poised and controlled, gives in to the gloom. Though he shields the dead body of Maude from her daughter Cathy, on the next page he cruelly tells the girl, since her father won't leave his bed, to "get into bed with him."

Cathy jars Archer's reason throughout. The sexual temptation she poses is more complex and thus more dangerous than that of Miranda Sampson in *Target*; though, at sixteen, Cathy is four years younger than Miranda, she makes deeper contact with the hidden places in the detective's heart:

> She was one of the girls I had watched from a distance in high school and never been able to touch; the girls with oil or gold or free-flowing real-estate money dissolved in their blood like blueing. She was also young enough to be my daughter.

Archer's tightness and defensiveness show clearly even before meeting Cathy. He is sharp and sour with the Nopal Valley police, and he talks so nastily to Maude Slocum in Chapter 1 that he's accused of mocking her. His narration, meanwhile, lapses into a cheap cynicism. Hearing Maude's family problems, he says to himself, "Here we go again. . . . True confession morning, featuring Archer the unfrocked priest." Later, when he tries to coax a woman into waking her journalist-husband, his language becomes self-consciously cute and coy:

> For five minutes of his personal sleeping time, I offer ten dollars in cash. Two dollars a minute, a hundred and twenty dollars an hour. Show me the movie star that gets nine hundred and sixty dollars for an eight-hour day.

His verbal posturing aside, Archer works with his usual nerve and dedication. Encouraging no false hopes, he doesn't guarantee his client, Maude Slocum, positive results within a week or even a month. But, having taken her money, he doesn't let her death stop him from seeing the case through to the end. This integrity inspires more than respect; Mavis Kilbourne and seventeen-year-old Gretchen Keck both ask to go to bed with him; Mavis even proposes marriage. His sexual attractiveness, physical and nervous stamina, and brave defiance of the six-man lynching squad that demands Pat Reavis all bespeak a rare, outstanding nature. Archer both controls *Pool* and gives it, thanks to his keen moral sense, novelistic undertones lacking in its predecessors.

III

The Way Some People Die (1951) begins as a prodigal daughter case. As in most of the early Archers, the private drama is more intelligently perceived and freshly described than the public one; nor are the two dramas threaded together as neatly as in the mature work. The action starts with Archer cutting his car engine in front of the Santa Monica home and rooming house of the prodigal's mother—Mrs. Samuel Lawrence, "a tall woman in her fifties with worried vague dark eyes in a worried long face." Her daughter, Galatea, or Galley, has been missing for three months. Galley's last-known address was an apartment in Pacific Point, a town, some sixty miles south of Los Angeles, which will recur in the novels as often as Santa Teresa. (The towns are different: Santa Teresa, 120 miles to the north on the coastal highway, is much older than Pacific Point—founded, like Santa Barbara and Los Angeles before 1800—and more civilized. Pacific Point, whose population in *Meet Me at the Morgue* [1953] is given as 34,197, lies in Orange County, site of new industrial developments and reactionary politics.)

Archer's first witness, Mr. Raisch, the wheezy, red-faced manager of the apartment court where Galley lived in Pacific Point, prefigures an important element in Ross Macdonald's later work. Raisch not only proves a good witness, telling Archer about Galley's personality and habits; he is also the first of Ross Macdonald's many fine cameo portraits. Like his descendents, he appears just once. More of a lyrical than a sustained dramatic challenge, he embodies some of his author's best effects. These, as in Dicken's memorable minor characters, constitute brilliant verbal impersonations. Both Raisch's outdoorsman's color and blue-collar energy gain voice in his speech. He is a talker. He creates himself by expanding into language, and Archer, drawing him out, asks the questions that promote this verbal expansion. Here is Raisch on the subject of his apartment complex, which he views, characteristically, as an extension of himself and his strong opinions:

I can afford to pick and choose. . . . My place doesn't look like much from the outside, maybe, but she's in absolutely tiptop shape. Redecorated the whole thing with my two hands last year, put in new linoleum, fixed up the plumbing. And I didn't raise the rents a red cent. No wonder they come to me. What did you want to see me about? I don't need a thing if you're selling.

Archer's talks with Raisch and Galley's last room-mate turn up some good leads. Galley's last nursing patient, Archer finds out, was a local pinball merchant, wrestling promoter, and drug dealer, Herman Speed; Galley met Speed while he was spending three weeks in the hospital recovering from bullet wounds. More trouble came to him when one of his aides, Joe Tarantine, now Galley's husband, presumably stole a large cache of Speed's heroin. Tarantine seems guilty by the look of things. A visit to Pacific Point Hospital introduces Archer to his brother, Mario, swollen, abraded, and contused in the face after being beaten by Speed's gang. Getting Joe's address from Mario, Archer goes to Joe's apartment but finds the place stripped, smashed, and gutted. Then many things happen quickly. The inspection of the wreckage ends when an emaciated-looking thug named Blaney takes Archer at gunpoint to the hilltop estate of local mobster, Danny Dowser. Though surrounded by Dowser's thugs, Archer retains grip, neither running from danger nor talking his way around it. He makes Dowser, who outdoes him in bargaining power, accept *his* terms. Making it clear that his first loyalty is to Mrs. Lawrence, Galley's worried mother, he takes a $500 retainer to look for Joe Tarantine.

His destination upon leaving Dowser is Palm Springs, where the bartender of a side-street bar recognizes Galley from her picture. But, after making a phone call, he refuses to say anything more. Like all good hunters, Archer waits patiently. He doesn't stay idle long, though. An incredibly handsome man ("A Greek sculptor could have used him as a model for a Hermes or Apollo") comes in and sits at his table. The stranger, Keith Dalling, identifies himself as an out-of-work radio actor and, more significantly, owner of the desert ranchhouse where Galley and Joe Tarantine are hiding from Dowser. Archer and the alcoholic Dalling drive to the desert hideaway, Oasis. Leaving Dalling in the car, Archer knocks on the door of the ranchhouse. To his amazement, Galley opens it. But before he can talk her into leaving her gangster husband and going back to her mother, he is clubbed from behind.

The mad March night is one of strangers and strange events. Waking up on the porch of the ranchhouse, Archer sees "a large hippy woman in a dark suit" standing over him. The woman, who has "a nice warm prewar midwestern voice," calls herself Marjorie Fellows. Marjorie and her husband, Henry, a retired Army colonel, are honeymooning at the Oasis Inn in nearby Palm Springs. The facts surrounding her appearance at the ranchhouse stir Archer's suspicions: "Her car . . . was parked on the shoulder a couple of hundred yards from the house. She had to use a key to open it. Another thing that puzzled me was the fact that the Cadillac was turned towards the house." But instead of pressing Marjorie for answers, he lets her drive him to the Oasis Inn and civilization.

Archer dislikes her fuming husband straightaway ("I thought of hitting him"). A tall, powerful Army officer of distinguished bearing, Colonel Fellows takes the full force of Archer's dislike of authority figures. Like the physical coward, the authority figure in Ross Macdonald seldom acts from goodness; seldom does he deserve the authority he flaunts; he usually has a shameful past. Fellows acts in line with the archetype. It later turns out that he is Herman Speed, the gangster Galley nursed in Pacific Point Hospital. Speed/Fellows married Marjorie, just divorced from a Toledo businessman, within weeks of meeting her in Reno. Like other Ross Macdonald men who use an alias, he wants to keep part of his life hidden. He only married Marjorie for the $30,000 coming from her divorce settlement; this he immediately used to buy the heroin Joe Tarantine later stole from Dowser. His lawlessness touches all. Crime, rather than another woman or marital unhappiness, took him from Marjorie's side during their honeymoon. Although she didn't know it, crime also sent Marjorie to Dalling's Oasis ranchhouse looking for him the night she found Archer, a victim of criminal assault.

Back in town the next morning, Archer finds Dalling shot dead in his apartment. Dalling's death at this point looks back technically to that of Pat Reavis in *Pool*; as soon as Dalling becomes a leading suspect—owing to his cowardice, his alcoholism, and his disappearance after Archer's clubbing from behind—he gets killed. A sentimental letter found in his pocket makes Archer's next stop the Hollywood radio station from which the letter came. One of the station's programmers, who used Dalling on his radio show so long as he stayed sober, tells Archer that Dalling had been having an affaire with Galley Lawrence Tarantine. The news takes Archer to Mrs. Lawrence's, where Galley had returned briefly the same morning but then left with "a very thin man, a walking skeleton." Archer recognizes the man as Blaney, the hoodlum who took him at gunpoint to Dowser. He goes to Dowser on his own and finds his worst fears confirmed: the racketeer is hostaging Galley in exchange for the $30,000 worth of heroin her husband presumably stole. Persuading Dowser to leave him alone with Galley, Archer hears two important pieces of news: first, that Joe Tarantine's "trick of slapping people" wrecked his marriage and, next, that Joe fled to Mexico carrying "something valuable of Dowser's." Dowser, listening to the conversation from a hidden microphone, then sends Galley home and tells Archer to renew his hunt for Joe.

Mario Tarantine, our next witness, confirms Galley's story that the family's boat, the *Aztec Queen*, has left its anchoring-place. The boat is next seen capsized and smashed near some reefs, and Joe, presumably having piloted it, is feared dead at sea. Mario believes otherwise. Ever since boyhood, Joe has let others be punished for his misdeeds. Thus Mario, beaten up by Speed's gang simply because he was Joe's brother, believes Joe, a crack swimmer, to have wrecked the boat himself and then gone to Mexico. The missing-persons case has enlarged. Witnesses Archer first sees at a brilliantly described wrestling match and then at a cheap dockside hotel send him to San Francisco. Meanwhile Joe, perhaps a murder victim himself, is wanted by the police in connection with Keith Dalling's murder; and Marjorie Fellows, self-styled "an awful dreamer," reports that her new husband has bolted with $30,000 she had given him to invest.

Pretending to be a drug addict, Archer goes first to a San Francisco jazz cellar and then to a ramshackle hotel, where he bullies and beats a hard-drug dealer called Mosquito into taking him to Herman Speed. The two men drive to Speed's cabin. The crude, out-of-the-way cabin where an important mystery unravels had already figured in *Trouble* and *Target*. *Way* hews to the pattern. Archer turns down Speed's offer of a partnership and fortune to get Speed to hand over two kilos, or $100,000 worth, of pure heroin. This he takes to the office of Peter Colton, his former commanding officer in Army Intelligence, now assistant to the D. A. of Los Angeles, and a well-met recurring minor character. But instead of giving Colton the heroin, Archer takes it to Dowser. In Archer's only important out-of-hearing conversation, the detective arranges to plant the heroin on Dowser just before a police raid. This withholding of crucial information doesn't work well, and Ross Macdonald wisely abandoned the device. The brief violation of the partnership between reader and detective-analyst confuses and vexes. For a while, we fear that Archer, who has already acted sadistically, may be conspiring with gangsters. Then we're bewildered by what looks like stupidity. By the time he tells four carloads of policemen, camped a quarter-mile from Dowser's, to make their raid, his tricking Dowser has lost much of its force. Nor do we have the pleasure of watching the police invade Dowser's private fortress, find the heroin, and take their man.

Instead, the private drama reasserts itself. Back on the familiar ground of a missing-persons case, Ross Macdonald writes with renewed vigor. The scene moves to Pacific Point morgue, where Joe Tarantine's body, "roughly used by the sea," had been taken several hours before. After talking to the coroner, Archer, "ready to try a long shot in the dark," finds Galley at Keith Dalling's Oasis apartment. The story of her affaire with Dalling and its ramifications comes to light here. A loaded pistol in her hand, she tells Archer how Dalling killed Joe in order to free her for himself and then how she killed Dalling in revenge. Joe's brother, Mario, comes in, breaking the recitation. Galley, not satisfied merely to kill him before he kills her, empties her revolver into his corpse.

The next-to-last chapter continues the killer's obligatory confession. Galley, or Galatea, completes her transformation from a beautiful healer (her job, once again, is that of a nurse) to a killer. In another reversal of her mythical namesake, a statue who turned into a lovely woman, Galley literally chills her husband to statuesque hardness and immobility by stowing him in her freezer locker. Whereas the original Galatea was given breath and warmth by the man who loved her, hatred, love's opposite number, smothers and freezes Galley's husband. The mythical wedding becomes a multiple murder and probably also a long jail sentence or execution—other forms of immobility. After killing Joe, Galley took the stolen heroin and sold it to Speed for Marjorie's $30,000. To clear herself with Dowser, she put Joe's body aboard the *Aztec Queen*, creating the impression that Joe drowned while escaping to Mexico. Then, to get rid of a would-be husband and partner-in-crime, she shot Dalling.

Following his usual practice, Ross Macdonald extends the novel a chapter after the apprehension of the killer: Meaning follows melodrama. Archer returns to the home of his client, Mrs. Lawrence, where the case began. Although sure of Galley's guilt, he extends charity both to her and her mother. He gives Mrs. Lawrence the $500 he took as a retainer from Dowser, and, doing Galley another favor, leaves behind the $30,000 Speed had paid her for Dowser's heroin; letting Mrs. Lawrence hand over the blood money to the police could strengthen Galley's legal defense and lighten her sentence. Along with his vague promise not to testify against her, the gift partakes of Godlike charity. Getting rid of tainted money, encouraging others to get rid of it, and offering Galley something better than justice, Archer plays God more freely in *Way* than anywhere else in the canon. Freely but not arrogantly; though touching on sarcasm and cruelty, his personal morality hinges on tenderness. He doesn't hit Mosquito, the San Francisco dope peddler, until attacked with a knife; hearing of Herman Speed's death in the last chatper, he says inwardly, "Now there were four men violently dead. . . . Galley and I between us had swept the board clean."

Archer knows himself better in *Way* than in *Target* or *Pool*. As the quotation suggests, much of his self-command comes from a new recognition of his capacity for evil. Awareness of his involvement in crime helps him respond more imaginatively to evil-doers and to a universal drift to evil that catches us all up. For the first time in a Ross Macdonald novel, murder generates moral ambiguity. Apart from the heroin subplot, which isn't Ross Macdonald's true subject in any case, the tight one-to-one correspondence between evil and evil-doer breaks down. These early Archers, to their credit, draw their detective-narrator progressively out of the hard protective shell that encased Chandler's Philip Marlowe. The artistic growth Ross Macdonald attained in the early 1950s fused a deepened vision of evil with a new sympathy and compassion.

But the old *Black Mask* schooling still shows in places. Archer's simple morality has a strength and purity that compel admiration: so long as he believes Galley to be standing by her husband, regardless of Joe's crimes, he stands by *her*. Sometimes, though, a simple morality can't cope with a complex problem; Archer can look crude and naive. In Chapter 9 he asks Galley, whom he has just met, to leave her husband and go back to her mother. He has only Dowser's word that Joe is a criminal; what is more important, he knows nothing of Galley's relationship to either Joe or her mother. Archer needs to mellow his decisiveness. Too many of his responses smack of the actionism of hard-boiled fiction. Characters often exist to flesh out a sociological commonplace. A few sentences formulate the life of a young black janitor and prize-fighter:

After a while he'd be a fighting machine hired out for twenty or twenty-five dollars to take it and dish it out. If he was really good, he might be airborne for ten years . . . eating thick steaks for breakfast, dishing it out. Then drop back into a ghetto street-corner with the brains scrambled in his skull.

But Archer isn't only priggish with the helpless. He'll lecture anybody he thinks needs it. His sarcasm extends to the police, especially when they try to corner him. The news that Dalling was killed with his, i.e., Archer's, pistol and that Archer's failure to report the death could cost him his license meets with a verbal sideswipe. Not content to clear himself legally, Archer must also degrade both accuser and accusation:

I'm very smart . . . and very devious. I saw Dalling for the first time last night and decided that he was too pretty to live, a fit subject for the perfect crime. So I committed it. I shot him with a gun that could easily be identified as mine and carefully deposited it in the nearest drain, where any cop would be sure to look for it. Four hours later I returned to the scene of the crime, as murderers must, in order to admire my handiwork.

Characters not degraded by others usually degrade themselves. As in most of the canon from *Roads* onward, the degradation is sexual: Giving into sexual impulses is the way some people die. Ross Macdonald's 1951 novel, aware of the metaphysical poets' definition of sex as "the little death," shows the pitfalls of erotic abandon. Archer refers to this in a remark about a young drug-pusher and his fifteen-year-old addict-sweet-heart: "He'd started her on heroin, given her yellow fever and white death, so she was crazy about him." This bizarre logic says a good deal about human sexuality. As has been indicated, Ross Macdonald's people fall in love with people who will hurt them—either through indifference or greed. Lovers bring out the worst in each other. Marjorie Fellows represses her doubts about the moral character of Herman Speed, marries him, and soon comes to grief: "I trusted him because I wanted to so badly," and "I don't know who he is or what he is," she admits after the reality of being robbed and walked out on shatters her romantic dream.

This bleak sexual dynamic fits with the novel's overall pessimism.

Debut

Way is one of Ross Macdonald's grimmest books. Nothing in it thrives, fits, or makes sense; all is awry. Galley and Joe's marriage sours right away. Although Oasis, the housing complex where Archer meets Galley, looks like a ghost town, it is, more properly, "the opposite of a ghost town, a town waiting to be born." Appearance belies reality in people as well as places. Speed undoes Herman Speed, who dies in a high-velocity car crash. Ruth, the fifteen-year-old heroin addict, looks "old enough to be her own mother." Later, she is described as "waiting to be born into the world or out of it." Galley, perhaps the most beautiful woman in the canon, performs some of the vilest deeds. This vileness grips us, coming from a nurse and daughter of a doctor. Adding to the pattern of up-side-downness, Galley also reverses Ross Macdonald's usual technique of handling missing persons. First, she appears both early and often, rather than exerting her force from offstage. Next, she is the killer; though Ralph Sampson, the missing person in *Target*, damages many, he never kills. The prodigal in Ross Macdonald can be a small child, a youth, or, as in *The Goodbye Look* and *The Underground Man*, somebody in late middle age. Only in *Way* and, nine novels later, *The Zebra-Striped Hearse*, is she the killer. The fusion of different narrative elements within an overall pattern of reversal shows more innovation than any of his books to date.

But the innovations don't always work. Ross Macdonald said in 1966, "Some of my colleagues . . . think that *Way* is the best of my twenty books. I hope it isn't."[2] He doesn't hope in vain. Several serious flaws grant him his wish. First, there are structural problems. The plot has loose ends. After gaining our imaginative commitment to the two gangsters, Danny Dowser and Joe Tarantine, he whisks them away; Dowser's arrest by the police and the recovery of Joe's body from the sea both take place out of view. Herman Speed is also slighted. Though essential to the plot, he is left out of the resolution, Marjorie reporting his suicide 600 miles away in the last chapter. No such attempt at tidying-up can hide the book's main structural flaw. The novel runs off course in Chapter 15 and never regains its purpose or direction. Here, Joe Tarantine, presumably having run out on both wife and paymaster, takes Galley's place as the missing person, or prodigal. Joe, a heroin peddler and stooge to a local racketeer, stirs neither our hearts nor our imaginations. This small-time thug and wife-beater can look after himself, especially with $30,000 in hand. He faces none of the dangers menacing a pretty young woman on her own. Already an underworld figure, he need not worry about moral degradation. Ross Macdonald remained true to Joe's character when he turned Joe's prodigality into a red herring. But by including it, to begin with, he weakened suspense.

Joe's non-appearance may have another explanation—Ross Macdonald's inability to portray a convincing professional criminal. Danny Dowser, "a fat powerful shark," looks cubical and gives off a fishy smell.

Like Walter Kilbourne of *Pool*, who also tries to snare Archer into *his* mob, he appeals chiefly to the detective's "honesty." He also has the wide hips and womanish ways of several other criminals in Ross Macdonald's early work, including Herman Speed, a man of "feline dignity" who speaks with Dowser's self-conscious formality. Nor are Dowser and Speed the only underworld figures who shun the American idiom. Mosquito, the soft, swaying heroin dealer from San Francisco, calls Archer "old man" just as Dowser does; a jazz pianist with the "sad bad centerless eyes" of a drug addict keeps calling the detective "boy friend." Ross Macdonald's dislike of criminals becomes more moralistic in his treatment of Galley Lawrence Tarantine. Galley possesses the feral elegance of an eagle or panther. But as soon as she reveals herself a killer, she loses her looks: "Her face seemed to narrow and lengthen. I had never seen her look ugly before. An ugly woman with a gun is a terrible thing." Archer even throws her vanished beauty up to her: "You're losing your looks. . . . Murders take it out of a woman. You pay so much for them that they're never the bargain they seem to be." Robbing Galley of her beauty like this rules out all but the most trivial morality. And the robber is Ross Macdonald, not his spokesman, Archer. The charity extended to fifteen-year-old Cathy Slocum Knudson in *Pool* doesn't apply to Galley, ten years her senior. Ross Macdonald's need to punish sexual wrongdoers, by withholding charity, looks shabby besides Archer's godlike compassion in the last chapter.

IV

The Ivory Grin (1952) is a work of solid literary detection. It has a crime with a motive, a detective (Archer) who solves the crime, and a criminal who gets caught and punished at the end. Sticking to the basic format of crime fiction, Ross Macdonald adapts it to his theme. Though the main killing remains a mystery till the next-to-last chapter, at least three characters share the guilt and suffer for it. The conversion of a missing-persons case to a murder case includes five violent deaths amid a tangle of cunningly interwoven subplots. The action starts when "a stocky woman of less than middle height" with a grip "as hard as a man's" comes to Archer's West Hollywood office one September morning. The first-chapter meeting both recalls the opening of *Pool* and looks ahead to similar encounters in the later work. When an Archer opens with a would-be client visiting the detective, the visitor is usually female, and her unwillingness to call in the police, her evasions, and her transparent lies try the detective's patience. As in *Pool* and also *The Zebra-Striped Hearse* and *The Instant Enemy*, where the pattern varies, Archer accepts his visitor as a client with misgivings.

Una Larkin wants him to find a pretty black girl of twenty-five, Lucy

Debut

Champion. Lucy supposedly pinched some jewels when she stopped working for Una two weeks before. Besides needing her jewels back, Una wants
Lucy intercepted before she reveals some embarrassing facts about the
Larkin family. Taking $100 as a retainer, Archer goes to Bella City, "a
sprawling dusty town" two hours inland from Los Angeles. Fortunately,
Lucy is lunching at the diner where Una told Archer to look for her. He
follows Lucy from the diner into a neighborhood of dirt roads, "smashed
windows patched with cardboard, and scarred peeling doors or no doors at
all." Lucy's homecoming embrace with Alex Norris, her college-age sweetheart, is broken by some angry words from Alex's mother. The blustering
Mrs. Norris, who is also Lucy's landlady, then evicts Lucy despite Alex's
protests.

Archer follows the dispossessed girl's taxi to the Mountview Motel
and Trailer Court and then calls Una Larkin to give her Lucy's new
address. Una comes to the motel, and Archer hears her coaxing and then
bullying Lucy in vain to come away with her. Another memorable minor
character in the Dickens mode enters soon after the motel scene—the L. A.
detective, Maxfield Heiss, his "clever dirty eyes" glinting "liquidly, like
dollops of brown sherry." Heiss sees Archer follow Lucy to the local train
station. The nervous, chattering Heiss, who, it comes out, had his detective's license taken away for interfering with prospective jurors in a recent
murder trial, doesn't win Archer's cooperation. Archer bolts from him to
follow Lucy, who suddenly leaves the station in a car driven by Alex
Norris. A long traffic light puts Alex's car out of Archer's scope. The
next time Archer sees Lucy, several hours later, at the motel, she is dead,
her throat slit by a nearby bolo knife.

The plot reshapes itself quickly. A page after the discovery of Lucy's
corpse, a new prodigal, or runaway, emerges. A newspaper clipping found
in Lucy's purse explains that Charles Singleton, a Harvard graduate and
former Air Force lieutenant, has been missing for a week and that his
family has posted a $5000 reward for information leading to his discovery.
Before Archer can work out the connection between Singleton and Lucy,
he sees Alex Norris watching him from the motel gate. Alex explains that
he drove Lucy to the motel to collect her effects before going off to get
married. A Lieutenant Brake, just arrived on the scene, accuses Alex of
killing Lucy. (Blacks exist chiefly as victims in Ross Macdonald.) Unable
to sway the bigoted white policeman, Alex flees, giving the novel still
another runaway youth. The moments following his flight from white
man's justice inspire some of Archer's finest energies: Archer blocks the
line of fire between Alex and the policeman who tries to shoot him; he
scales a seven-foot fence and, still fresh, runs fast and hard enough to pull
even with Alex's moving car. Then, in a well-timed leap, he hooks his arm
inside an open window. The melodrama tests his mental, as well as physical, powers. The excitement of the chase and the bucking of the car,

which soon slams him to the ground, don't stop him from learning the car's license number, which he promptly tells Brake.

Brake, "a rough small-city cop, neither suave nor persuasive," can't badger Archer as he had done Alex. Though admitting that "the physical facts are against Norris," Archer refuses to testify against him. Instead of making an official statement to the police, he goes to his client, Una Larkin, to find out *her* role, if any, in Lucy's death. But Una runs out on him, climbing down a fire escape. Archer is thus stranded, without client or clue, till "the bitch goddess coincidence" puts him in the way of Maxfield Heiss, now calling himself Julian Desmond. From his tavern-booth, Archer overhears Desmond/Heiss talking to the secretary-nurse of a doctor Lucy had gone to a few hours before her death. In a scene that echoes Una's attempt to lure Lucy from the Mountview Motel, the doctor's wife, Elizabeth Benning, orders the secretary-nurse to leave the tavern with her. This development makes Archer's next stop the Benning clinic. Playing the unaccustomed role of housebreaker, Archer looks in vain for Lucy's medical records in the doctor's filing cabinet. His search ends when the lights of the consultation room snap on, and he finds himself looking down the bore of Mrs. Benning's revolver. The incident proves a stalemate. Archer doesn't learn Lucy's reason for going to Dr. Benning, but neither is he arrested or shot at, the news of Lucy's murder having drained Mrs. Benning's force.

Seizing his chance, Archer leaves the surgery to interview the family of the missing Charles Singleton in nearby Arroyo Beach. Singleton's cranky mother offers little help; she resents the implication that her son had a black lover and then connects Archer with Desmond/Heiss, who had already offered to produce her son for $5000. Unlooked-for help comes from her young paid companion, Sylvia Treen, who hires Archer to find Singleton. Sylvia sends him to the mountain cabin of an effete hermit-artist and friend of the missing man. Like Claude, the sun-worshipping mountain recluse in *Target,* Horace Wilding is a posturing fraud. But he gives Archer two important leads: he tells of Singleton's weekend sexual romps in the mountain hideaway, and he sketches Singleton's blonde romping-mate. The blonde turns out to be the same person one Una Durano bought an expensive turban for at a local *couturier* and also, we later learn, Dr. Samuel Benning's much-younger wife.

The first half of the novel ends with the wildest chapter in all Ross Macdonald. The scene, taking place at the Durano estate—as usual, the big-time racketeer lives in splendid isolation—fuses horror, compassion, and a basis of moral judgment. After passing through a set of heavy wrought-iron gates, Archer sees a deranged-looking man straining at the bars on the window of his Spanish Renaissance mansion-prison. "The man with the blaze of white like a lightning scar on the side of his head" starts howling so loud that his orderly turns up the sound on a record player to top volume. Then, after some obscene ranting in English and Italian about sex, crime, and religion (which the novel doesn't reproduce), the madman wrenches a revolver away from his orderly-keeper and shoots both him and Una three times point-blank. Archer doesn't storm into the house and take the man because he had noticed that the revolver was a cap-pistol. Both Una and the orderly get up, ending the mad game, while Archer listens to "the waves playing pattycake in the sand and gurgling rhythmically like idiot children." The universe itself seems mad.

Echoing both the madness of Leo Durano and the idiot slap of the surf, a different hysteria runs through the next scenes. Alex Norris has been hunted down and arrested. His mother tearfully admits evicting Lucy because she wanted to separate Lucy and Alex. Alex is next seen at the Bella City Morgue, hand-cuffed to Lucy's stretcher. But this psychological torture doesn't break him down. Archer, convinced of his innocence, gets the police to remove the cuffs and to leave Alex alone with him. He talks more roughly to Alex than one might expect: "You're worse than a horse. You're a stubborn mule. Your girl is lying dead, and you won't open your mouth to tell me who did it to her." But the rough talk makes sense. Convinced of Archer's sincerity, Alex tells the detective things he holds back from the police. Archer learns, among other things, that Desmond/Heiss tried to force Lucy to tell him what she knew about Charles Singleton, particularly Singleton's death.

The scene shifts quickly. No sooner does Desmond/Heiss become a suspected killer than he is found, a charred corpse wearing Singleton's monogrammed belt, in Singleton's incinerated car. Archer's next stop is the Bennings' shabby home. Now Archer had recognized Elizabeth, or Bess, Benning as the girl in Horace Wilding's sketch of Singleton's weekend lover. His flair for connecting crimes, his ability to use evidence as leverage to get more evidence, and his good looks pry important background facts out of Bess. As is usual in Ross Macdonald, these are midwestern. An ex-juvenile delinquent from the mill section of Gary, Indiana, Bess met Sam Benning while he was serving at a nearby Navy base. She jumped probation, married Benning, twenty years her senior, and moved with him to Arroyo Beach. Six months later, they parted when his transport ship took a two-year voyage. Though ashamed of himself for pressing the interrogation, Archer gets her to admit knowing both Lucy Champion and Una Durano, who, having bought Bess an expensive turban, may have also been her lover.

The recitation saps so much of her energy that Bess pitches forward, and Archer has to break her fall. This same moment, Dr. Benning comes in, fresh from church, a black Bible under his arm. Playing the heavy husband, he accuses Bess and Archer of being lovers. But his anger rings stale ("I gave you a helping hand. I lifted you out of the gutter. You owe everything to me."). The balance of power in the marriage asserts itself straightaway: "Drawing terrific energy from his weakness," Bess easily drives Benning to his knees. Archer halts the sadistic onslaught with a whispered reminder to Bess of his private knowledge of her past. One deathly situation follows another. Leaving the Bennings locked in his imposed truce, Archer goes back to the morgue.

The morgue brings back Leo Durano, "the blasted man with the toy gun" of Chapter 15. Desmond/Heiss's private log of the case explains that Durano, a Michigan numbers runner, had been slowly losing his mind for several years. To keep his madness both from the Detroit police, who want to jail him, and the Detroit underworld, who would soon take over his assorted rackets, Una brought him to California. But her brother, insane and virtually a prisoner—in *Grin* the powerful gangster is both physically *and* mentally isolated—only steers the drama briefly. The news that he had lived with Bess Wionowski, *viz.,* Elizabeth Benning, gives *her* the controlling role. Archer's summary of Bess's importance ends Chapter 25:

> Mrs. Benning is the central figure in the picture. . . . She had three men on the string: Durano, Singleton, Benning. Durano shot Singleton over her. She couldn't face an investigation so she skipped out and came back to Benning for help.

This insight holds good. The rest of the book consists of a motive-hunt and an unravelling of the evidence. Dr. Benning can't explain how his carpet got bloodstained two weeks before. Archer thinks he's protecting his wife, who, in view of her criminal record, doesn't want a police investigation. But Archer changes his mind when Una tells him that her mad brother, Leo, shot Singleton, his love-rival, during a mountain tryst with Bess. Una's story helps clear up other mysteries. Lucy, who worked in the Durano fortress, died because she knew how Singleton died. Desmond /Heiss's death had two causes: aware of Lucy's link with the Durano's, the unlicensed detective wanted Lucy to lead him to the $5000 reward posted by Mrs. Singleton. Even dead, he had a use; dressed in Singleton's clothes and stuffed inside Singleton's burnt car, his face blowtorched beyond recognition, he could sidetrack the police from the real killer.

Back at the Singleton estate in the valley, Archer contacts his client, Sylvia Treen. Sylvia tells him that Bess, apparently leaving her husband for good, has offered to divulge the facts of Singleton's death for the posted reward. Archer tells Sylvia to set up a meeting between herself and Bess at his office the same evening. Several hours later, when Bess parks in front of his building, he orders her from the car at gunpoint. But instead of browbeating her, he offers her the $5000 in exchange for a full confession. The next-to-last chapter confession, neither slick nor mechanical, surprises even Archer.

Ten years before the time of the book, Leo Durano had been sentenced to a mental home for corrupting a minor, Bess Wionowski, but Una convinced the judge that she'd take care of Leo were he released. The following year, Bess married Benning and then met Charles Singleton, who became her grand passion. Though hard and tough, Bess has always thrived on love. Her love for Singleton survived her marriage, a long separation during the war, and, after he cast her off in Boston while attending Harvard Law School, five years with the Duranos in Detroit. Her return to Arroyo Beach, a by-product of Leo's madness, reinstated her affaire with Singleton. The reunion nettled Una. Though she may not have minded sharing Bess sexually with her brother, she resented Singleton. As Archer had believed, she goaded Leo into killing him. But Leo's bullet only wounded him, and Bess rushed Singleton to her doctor-husband, claiming she'd shot Singleton herself for making an ugly advance. For a dark reason—Benning's incompetence; the incompetence of Lucy, who was helping; or the acuteness of the bullet wound—Singleton died in surgery. A swarm of events ends the chapter. Sylvia, crushed to know of her beloved Charles's rutting, faints behind Archer's one-way mirror. Bess tries to cut and run with the $5000. She is stopped by the improbable entry of Una Durano. Una guns down Bess for betraying her to Archer, and Archer, shooting to kill, squeezes off a round into Una's temple.

The last chapter exists chiefly to punish the already whipped Dr. Benning and to account for the body of Singleton. This, Benning reduced to a skeleton, which he hung in a closet to frighten Bess into fidelity. But then, afraid of a police investigation, he put it inside his glowing furance. His moral spirit crushed by loving a woman who has never loved him in return, Benning goes on the last page to the police station to confess to murdering Lucy, Desmond/Heiss, and Singleton. Though the confession never reaches our ears, the thin, wounded voice of the man who loved wife, work, and God haunts us. A healer unable to heal himself, Benning repeats the plight of his two love rivals: like Singleton, he cracks together with his humanitarian ideals; like Leo Durano, he cracks so deeply he loses his mind. He also shows what happens when able, intelligent men like he and Albert Graves of *Target* waste their hearts. Though weaker than Graves, Benning, married to a vain, faithless woman, has suffered more for love. This suffering creates both a dramatic and psychological realism lacking in the earlier novel. The difference between him and his early counterpart, Graves, limns an important aspect of Ross Macdonald's artistic growth. This growth is borne out in the final scene. The closing image of Archer, robust, morally right, but also meanly mindful of the $5000 reward, taking the bent, jerking Benning to the police touches our hearts as no other finale to date.

The condition of this gripping moment and the violence leading up to it is heat. Heat pervades *The Ivory Grin*. Ross Macdonald's control of his governing metaphor makes for both a tightening and an intensity. Lucy Champion, whose first name means light, a corollary of heat, dies in hot Bella City, far from her Detroit home. The last name of Maxfield Heiss means hot in German, and Heiss, in line with the destructive implications of his name, dies by fire and then incinerates inside a burning car. Leo Durano takes his first name from the astrological sign for the hottest time of the year; also, Leo goes irreversibly mad in a Detroit night club, symbol of the red-hot center of the urban inferno in both *Tunnel* and *Trouble*. His sister Una, soon after looking like "a sexless imp who had grown old in hell" in Chapter 8, complains of "this foul heat." And when she runs out on Archer in the same chapter, leaving him without a client, she climbs down the fire escape. Nobody walking "the sun-stopped streets" of Bella City can escape heat. A thermometer found in Lucy's purse reads 107° F., to which Lieutenant Brake replies, "It wasn't Champion who had the fever, it was this bloody town."

On the next two pages, Brake mentions "hot pants" and "hot psychological flashes." Archer notes that the years have scorched Brake's face "like fire-traces on an old tree." One female character has the same name, Florida, as America's hottest state. Her employer's wife, Elizabeth Benning, dressed in a yellow dress with gold buttons, dies clad in the colors of sunshine. When Benning douses the flames in his furnace, where Charles Singleton's bones are decomposing in the last chapter, he only lulls one fire. The urban inferno has driven inland. Crime and impersonality, or facelessness, two enemies of humanity fostered by the North American city, plague Bella City as much as L. A.; five people get killed in Bella City within two weeks, and one of the victims dies without a face. The enormous heat radiated by the novel gives off an apocalyptic blast more menacing for coming in mid-September rather than in dense, clammy July or August. The midsummer madness recounted in *Grin* has no trouble overtaking life in early fall.

The novel's sadistic title neglects this madness. Ross Macdonald's titles lack both the flair and the subtlety found in many of his characters' names. A title like *The Ivory Grin* is flashy rather than original or evocative. Witty, eye-catching titles like *The Zebra-Striped Hearse, The Instant Enemy,* and *The Goodbye Look* neither criticize nor describe. More thematic are flat, serviceable ones—*Blue City, The Galton Case, The Ferguson Affair,* and *The Wycherly Woman. The Ivory Grin* refers to the fully articulated skeleton of Charles Singleton, which Sam Benning hung in his closet to shock his wife. Yet Bess holds his love so cheaply that he couldn't shock or convince her of anything against her will. Singleton's bones serve only to chill Archer's, and the reader's, spinal fluid when they rattle into view for the first time. The title alludes to but fails to comment on the blacks in the novel, who, unlike those in Sherwood Anderson's *Dark Laughter*, don't have the last laugh, or grin, or their white oppressors: Lucy is killed; Mrs. Norris suffers for indirectly causing her death; son Alex, bullyragged by the police, is still in jail at novel's end.

Debut

The craft of *Grin* lags behind the book's searing vision. Even Archer needs help from contrivances to display his remarkable talents. Some of the help comes from coincidence. He also eavesdrops a great deal and assumes different false identities—giving a false name to Dr. Benning's secretary and then pretending to be both an investigator for the hotel association and an agent for a firm making a national radio survey. But his eye is sharp and his heart, warm. *Grin* has a wide scope. Using him to stir the brew, the book mixes psychology, deduction, and slice-of-life realism. This brew has some of the zest of the mature Archers. Clotting it, though, are several street scenes which give the same sordid pictures of society and express the same pat cynicism as the pulp detective fiction of the day:

> It was an early Saturday-night crowd. Farmhands in jeans and plaid shirts, soldiers in uniforms, boys in high-school windbreakers, roved singly and in pairs and packs among women of all ages and all shades. Hard-faced women in hats towed men in business suits. Ranchers hobbling in high-heeled boots leaned on their sun-faded wives. Under the winking yellow lights at the intersection. long shiny cars competed for space and time with pickup trucks, hot-rods, migrant jalopies.

Apart from these *verismo* passages, with their sour detachment, the book contains very little hard-boiled writing. Like its running metaphor of heat, which flickers brightly over the novel, its tight, figured prose aims for more literary effects and, hence, a more sophisticated readership. Sometimes a metaphor will grate: "I didn't know whether the umbilical cord between Mrs. Singleton and her son had stretched and broken and snapped back in her face and knocked her silly." The similes, though, have an effortless precocity that seizes the reader even when they miss their mark: "Lights shone like wit in a dowager behind the windows of the Palladian villa." When they do strike home, their impact transmits shock waves. The one-syllable intransitive verb, falling rhythm, and enigmatic adjective give the description of Lucy's corpse a Conradian ring: "Her cut throat gaped like the mouth of an unspeakable grief."

Ross Macdonald's claim, in a letter to the present writer date 13 March 1971, that *Grin* is "the best of the early Archers" has force. In 1971, he also discussed his intentions in the *Grin* and even granted the novel a key place in his artistic growth:

> In the course of the first three Archer novels, I tried to work out my version of the 'hardboiled' style, to develop both imagery and structure in the direction of psychological and symbolic meaning. In the fourth, *The Ivory Grin* (1952), I extended the range of the form beyond California, touching on Boston and Montreal, Chicago and Detriot; and doing a portrait of a gangster family which was unblurred by any romantic admiration.[3]

A sure sign of artistic seasoning is the characterization of Leo Durano. Durano shows Ross Macdonald's ability to use fictional technique to cover his tracks. Unable to portray a professional gangster realistically, he nonetheless avoids the epicene, false-gentleman frills or his earlier attempts. Durano's madness, though arbitrary, creates bold scenic effects, moves the plot, and points a moral. Technique hides Ross Macdonald's inventive lapse so well that we don't doubt Durano's plausibility.

Less easily hidden is Ross Macdonald's old uneasiness with sex and the need to punish sexual offenders. Bess Benning, an adulteress, dies. The novel's two homosexuals, Una Durano and the artist, Horace Wilding, meet grief, too; Wilding is doomed to a hermit's loneliness, and Una gets a bullet through her temple. Yet any important character in an accomplished novel will resist moral absolutes. Her evil is softened. Perhaps love as well as money took her to California with her brother. She backs up her conviction that Leo shouldn't be institutionalized by cooking his food, by watching the orderlies who tend him, and by keeping his last days free of trouble. Capable of evil, Una is less of a devil than a dreamer. Yet her homosexuality is no dream, but rather the choice of blood and nerves. And Ross Macdonald punishes this choice by making her plain-looking, describing her as "half a woman," and wrecking the structure of her face when Archer accuses her of killing Charles Singleton:

She looked at me with loathing, the muscles weaving and dimpling around her mouth. On the left side of her head where the knotted veins jerked, her face had swelled lopsided, as if moral strain had pushed or melted it out of shape.

The reader, finally, dislikes Una as much as Archer does.

Undermining and rebuilding itself, by turns, *Grin* creates a dramatic tension that holds and expands rhythmically. It asks important questions, and its characters, amalgams of purpose and passion, are worth caring about.

V

Experience with Evil, the title of a shortened version of *Meet Me at the Morgue* that ran in *Cosmopolitan* magazine, March 1953, has an eye on moral absolutes. The novel gains moral depth from incident, idea, and characters with elemental-sounding names like Forest and Snow. Another character whose name has primitive echoes, Howard Cross, gets important help from a blind newsdealer. This Tiresias figure, who, suitably, earns his living by disseminating news, leads Cross indirectly to a crossroads, near which a lost boy is found and because of which love emerges between Cross and the boy's mother. *Meet Me at the Morgue* (1953) expresses Ross Macdonald's interest in syncretism—the use of myths from different cultures. Biblical and Oedipal legend hum through the action. At the same time, the action needn't resort to legend and myth to hold our interest. *Morgue* has both animal vigor and intellectual depth, taking place amid bursts of color, light, and sound. Though no more imagistic than its predecessors, it throngs with noise; leaves crackle under foot; tape recorders purr ominously, car brakes rip the night air. A quayside scene in Chapter 7 shows the force with which sounds assault the reader:

> The Harbormaster's Quonset and jetty lay in the corner of a cove. . . . The blank-walled bath-house in front of it was loud as a monkey-house with teen-age whistles and hoots and ululations Beyond it, across the base of the landspit, deep-sea breakers pounded a steep shore. The desolate beach . . . was closed to swimmers. It pullulated with gulls.

This sound-and-light-show isn't conducted by Archer. For the first time in five novels, Ross Macdonald uses another narrator. The voice and mind of *Morgue* both belong to Howard Cross, thirty-seven-year-old bachelor and probation officer, headquartered in the familiar Orange County setting of Pacific Point. One fine May morning on his way to work, Cross meets a client, Fred Miner. Miner, a former machinist's mate in the U. S. Navy and now a chauffeur for the rich Johnson family, had been convicted of killing a man while drunk in a hit-and-run accident the previous February. Though Miner's jail sentence was suspended, the judge put him on probation for five years. Miner is now reporting to Cross before taking the Johnsons' four-year-old son for a drive in the country.

Crisis erupts suddenly in this tightly built novel. Miner's wife, "aged ten years . . . in three months," visits Cross to say that little Jamie Johnson is missing, that the Johnsons have received a ransom note demanding $50,000, and that Miner is being sought as Jamie's kidnapper. The news hits Amy Miner hard because of the Johnsons' kindness to her husband: Helen Johnson nursed Miner after a combat accident incurred near Okinawa put him in a U. S. Navy hospital, and then her husband hired him as a chauffeur; Abel Johnson also paid Miner's legal costs during the hit-run litigation, even though Miner had taken his car without asking permission. Johnson now regrets helping Miner.

Together with his assistant, Ann Devon, Cross goes to interview Johnson at his redwood-and-stone estate. What he encounters first, though, is danger. No sooner does he close his car door than he finds himself looking into the bore of a shotgun held by a red-headed woman in a green dress. The woman, Helen Johnson, tells him she never authorized Miner to take her son for a car ride. A tender moment occurs when Amy Miner, who is keeping Helen company, offers to make food and coffee both for the visitors and the woman whose child her husband is suspected of kidnaping.

Chapter Five introduces Abel Johnson, "a heavy contributor to local charities and a member of the retired executives' club." Victim of a coronary thrombosis five or six years before, Johnson looks smaller, older, and more worn than the last time Cross saw him. Yet he insists gustily on paying the $50,000 ransom and also on obeying the kidnapers' order not to call in the police. Accompanying Johnson is his attorney,

Larry Seifel, who defended Miner three months before. The novel's complex network of human ties has taken form; the sight of Larry Seifel unnerves Cross's helper, Ann, "a mouse blonde with a recent degree in psychology and large untapped reserves of girlish fervor." The reason for her distress soon becomes clear. The actorish Seifel, apparently motivated "from some internal center of self-love," had lied to break a date with Ann the previous evening. Both this high-handedness and his Anglicized airs repel us as much as they do Cross. Ann's more complex disapproval knifes still deeper. Whatever obscure impulse drove her to Seifel also sealed her unhappiness. Though despising him, she can't stop wanting him. What is worse, she outrages her morals and self-respect gratuitously. Seifel, afraid of angering his prying, domineering mother, gives Ann but little of his time and attention. Her relationship with him frustrates, at best.

But Ann is not the only troubled person in the novel. Johnson leaves the ransom money as told by Jamie's abductors but hears nothing of his missing son. The drama created by Seifel to give the book an issue, meanwhile, transfers to Joe Trentino, a blind newsstand operator who reconstructs reality from sounds and smells. Though Trentino appears in the novel for under three pages, he contributes heavily to both plot and mood. He lacks a distinctive voice, or speaking style, unlike many of Ross Macdonald's other brilliant cameo portraits. But his uncanny powers of perception tell him the height, weight, and age of people and also where the people have just been: "I see with my ears and touch and sense of smell," he says, and his second sight makes him an excellent witness. He says who collected the suitcase containing the ransom money and also where the suitcase was probably taken—the nearby Pacific Inn. Interrogating brilliantly, Cross traces the suitcase through an ageing bellhop to the man who hired the bellhop to pick it up and bring it to him. Cross proves as good a tracker as a questioner, quickly finding both the bellhop's paymaster and the suitcase. But the case is empty, and the man with it, coiled in the front seat of a prewar sedan, is dead, the red plastic handle of an icepick jutting from his neck. Treating the corpse with respect, Cross covers it with a topcoat and gently shuts the car door.

Cross has some solid data to work with by Chapter 7: two unidentified men have died violent deaths involving cars, symbolic of movement and change. Cross takes this mental pattern with him to the Pacific Point morgue, where he meets Helen Johnson and Detective Lieutenant Cleat, a cigar-chewing old warhorse. Cleat bullies criminal suspects and their families as openly in *Morgue* as his counterparts did blacks—i.e., those guilty of crime of blackness—in *Grin*. Whereas he speaks to Helen Johnson, wife of a leading local citizen, with respect and restraint, he calls Amy Miner by her first name, refers to her to her face as "this biddy," and threatens to punch her jaw. But Ross Macdonald has no grudge against the police. This brutality, it needs saying, is balanced by the fatherly forbearance of sheriff's officer, Sam Dressen. The criticism of policemen and their practices, a minor concern since *Blue City*, doesn't resurface with any force until *Find a Victim*, Ross Macdonald's next book.

Following up a lead supplied by Ann Devon, Cross learns that Seifel met the victim of the icepick murder during Fred Miner's February trial. The man, claiming to be a private investigator, told Seifel that he could identify Miner's anonymous manslaughter victim. The talk turns to Seifel's more distant past. Seifel, born and raised in Illinois, explains that his mother divorced his father after the lawyer-father got disbarred for tampering with jury-members. Then, after the mother took custody of little Larry, the father kidnaped the three-year-old. It took the police several days to find the pair, but once they did, they returned Larry to his mother and, on the strength of her family's political clout, had the father committed to a mental hospital. The arrival of Florabelle Seifel at her son's office breaks the recitation. Straightaway, she scolds Seifel for being late to collect her for a party, giving his jacket-sleeve "a violent jerk." The chapter ends with the departing Cross noticing a "bruised and hopeless" look on Seifel's face, "as if the Cuban heels of Florabelle's shoes had been hammering it."

The scene switches to the country courthouse. Cross, keeping the pressure on, learns that Fred Miner's manslaughter victim was wearing a stolen suit. Meantime, the second, i.e., the icepick, victim, is identified as Art Lemp, former employee of the Acme Investigative Agency in Los Angeles. The owner of the agency, a man called Bourke, tells Cross that he fired the sixty-year-old Lemp the previous year for unethical practices. Lemp would maneuver the husbands of jealous wives into compromising positions with his young blonde paramour, Molly Fawn; then a third partner would photograph the pair. Disclosures follow quickly. No sooner does Cross identify the photographer and blackmail partner as Kerry Smith than he learns that Lemp's death-car belonged to Smith, as well. These disclosures speed the ongoing search for Jamie Johnson. For Bourke explains that Abel Johnson, suspicious of his wife, hired Bourke to spy on her. He adds that he unwisely gave the watching case to Lemp, who, after four or five days in Pacific Point, hatched the idea of kidnaping Jamie.

Cross's next scheduled witness is Molly Fawn, Lemp's former lover and co-extortionist. Molly's ex-landlady gives the second half of the novel a good push; first, by producing a camera Molly had left behind bearing the legend U. S. S. *Eureka Bay* and a U. S. Navy serial number; and next, by identifying the owner of the case as Kerry Snow, or Smith, a special friend of Molly's as well as the owner of the car in which Lemp's dead body was found. Most important of all, the landlady identifies Smith, or Snow, from some coroner's photographs as Fred Miner's ex-crewmate and manslaughter victim.

People, places, and events continue to mesh. Molly Fawn accuses Lemp of murdering Snow, her husband, to get her for himself. She and Cross drive to Santa Monica. Molly, who came to Hollywood from Minnesota to star in the movies, tells him how Kerry spent six years in jail for theft and desertion from the Navy. In the meantime, word comes that Abel Johnson is dead from a heart attack stemming from Jamie's abduction. A barefaced father search drives Larry Seifel to Helen Johnson the day after she becomes a widow. Seifel's marriage proposal has the following motives, according to Helen, who rejects it:

Larry's as Oedipal as all get out. . . . Abel was Larry's father-image, he says. Now that his father-image is kaput, Larry has an irresistible urge to possess the father image's wife-image. That is, me.

The shock caused by this announcement subsides into Helen's rehearsal of several key incidents of her marriage. Johnson felt guilty, first, about spying on her and, secondly, about bringing the kidnaper Lemp into his home-life. Knowing the excitement could crush him, he went berserk, tearing apart the furniture in his room, and died of the strain. Helen neither forgives nor regrets his death.

The novel needs movement and dramatic incident to balance this introspection. The search for little Jamie renews as Helen, Seifel, and Cross drive to the Johnsons' desert hideaway. Again, a lonely, rich hermit's landscape plays a key role in a Ross Macdonald novel: as soon as the Johnsons' big Lincoln rolls into view of the hideaway, Jamie materializes. Then many things happen. Surprised by the visitors, Fred Miner comes out of the cabin; Seifel shoots him from the back seat of the car; Jamie, breaking loose from his mother, is confused and upset: "Fred wouldn't hurt me. Fred and me are shipmates," Jamie insists. Also flustered, Miner bolts in the Johnsons' Jaguar, Cross following closely behind. The two-page chase through dusty flatlands and up snow-patched mountains ends with the Jaguar crashing and Miner flying halfway down a slope. "Coughing bright blood and holding his chest," Miner tells Cross before dying that Helen Johnson told him to bring Jamie to the desert cabin. The problem of a mother conniving in her son's abduction is knotted by Helen's denial that she ever gave Miner such an order. Cross challenges her with this discrepancy and also with the story, told him by Molly Fawn, that Kerry Snow had come to Pacific Point to hurt the red-haired woman whose 1946 court testimony sent him to jail for six years. Though Helen admits having red hair, she denies any other tie with Snow apart from owning the car that killed him.

Cross's nerve-fraying interview with Helen is followed by another like it. Florabelle Seifel confronts the probation officer with some nasty words about "this nonsense between my son and your secretary." But no sooner does she begin to complain than Cross throws her long-hidden marriage to George Arthur Lempke back in her face. The disclosure jars her into talking. Besides recounting her marriage to Lempke, or Lemp, at age twenty against her parents' wishes, she says that she'd rather control her son than free him for the risks of manhood. But her long reign of overprotection ends when her son learns—off-stage, so his reaction won't sidetrack the emotional currents of the plot—that Lemp was his father. Seifel's father-search has ended—not by replacing Abel Johnson, a father-surrogate, but by seeing Lemp, his natural father, in the city morgue. Thus the title, *Meet Me at the Morgue*, describes Seifel more accurately than anybody else in the book. Seifel can only know himself by accepting a personal history steeped in crime; the sight of his dead father removes the tension and uncertainty blocking his self-acceptance.

Morgue contains many rises and falls—up and down spirals and straight shafts like staircases, elevators, and hillsides. Near the middle of the novel, Cross says, "I was . . . moving in a long, descending curve toward the heart of the evil." Life itself is a high-wire balancing act; Chapter 1 ends with a reference to "the moral tightrope everyone has to walk every day," and several characters are spoken of as toppling into a moral void. But this symbolism doesn't apply to Seifel, who looks like "a large bird with clipped wings" and whose padded shoulders flop "like clumsy wings." Seifel invites ruin by remaining symbolically aloft; flying for him is coterminous with death. Instead of flying, he has to plummet to the core of himself, where the deep truths of his life lie. Becoming human means accepting his tainted past—or fallen state. Unlike the other characters, he needn't dread falling. The son of an alcoholic, blackmailer, and sexual sadist, he is already steeped in depravity. Acknowledging the depravity sheds the baleful influence of his mother and frees him to appreciate the worth of Ann Devon.

Once humanized, Seifel moves out of the mainstream of the plot. His place is taken, somewhat surprising, by Amy Miner. Amy has been held in jail as a material witness for being the wife of a suspected kidnaper. Three chapters from the end, Cross notes, "she had probably been an attractive girl." Her patience and compassion toward her husband reflect a humanity that impresses Cross still more than her looks. But this high respect vanishes quickly. The book's only instance of flagrant eavesdropping comes in the next chapter; here, Cross overhears Molly Fawn and Lemp's ex-employer, Bourke, planning to rob the woman who killed and then robbed Lemp. The woman, a former redhead turned gray, is Amy Miner. Her motives, as recounted by Molly, sound murderous. Amy wanted Kerry Snow dead because he had spurned her for the much-younger Molly. Art Lemp also suited her needs more as a corpse than as a living man. Besides making her rich, his death would rid Amy of a practiced blackmailer armed with incriminating information about her.

She could pick her time to kill him because, as his spy in the Johnson household, she knew his whereabouts after collecting the ransom money. But Cross must wait before he challenges her with these disclosures. For, as soon as the local Grand Jury acquits her of conspiring in Lemp's murder, Amy leaves Pacific Point for her family in San Diego.

The causes of *Morgue* contrast admirably with their effects. The complex murder case turns on the simple motives of sex and money and then plays itself out in a small working-class neighborhood grocery. Danny's Neighborhood Grocery, owned by Amy's father and "built onto the front of an old two-story frame house, so long ago that it was now old itself," holds the answers to the unsolved mysteries of the case: the missing ransom money and the weapon used to kill Lemp. Cross opens a package containing $50,000 Amy had mailed herself in care of the store, and a display rack full of plastic red-handled icepicks just like the one that killed Lemp hangs in clear view behind Danny's counter. Danny Wolfe confirms the story about Amy's affaire with Kerry Snow, adding that Amy wanted to leave Miner to marry Snow in 1945. Ross Macdonald redeems in part his gimcrack last-chapter introduction of an important character by fitting Danny neatly into the novel's motivational pattern. Danny establishes Amy's evil historically by noting her adultery and proneness to violence: "I always knew she'd come to no good end. She was defiant. More than once she threatened me with my life." Flinging open the door, Amy is soon handcuffed and led away amid a storm of cries and protests. But first she admits killing Kerry Snow after getting her husband drunk in order to fasten the blame on him. Yet Amy doesn't leave the novel as an ogre or a madwoman. She thanks both Helen Johnson and Cross for befriending her and then, just before leaving the action, laments in straight, simple language the loss of love in her life: "I'll never be anybody now. . . . I haven't got anybody left to love me. I'll never get to have a baby of my own."

Ross Macdonald tries to maintain the tender mood created by her soul-searching, getting Helen and Cross to declare their love for each other as soon as they're alone. But we don't believe the mutual declaration. Mood notwithstanding, this romantic resolution rings false on too many grounds. Helen and Cross, who meet the day before her husband dies, have only known each other a week; they've never been along together; nothing indicates their special feelings for each other. Helen, though, as a beautiful mother of a small son, has a double appeal for Cross. And the channeling of most of Abel Johnson's money into a trust fund for Jamie removes money as a motive for a future with Helen. The novel's discreet last sentence, "Her hand touched my shoulder, lightly," following an agreement to wait before marrying, both modulates the romantic finale and conveys a mature accommodation to the everyday world.

Helen's elevation from suspected killer to romantic heroine comes from clever plotting. Her red hair, the shotgun she points at Cross the first time they meet, and her unloving references to her husband are all red herrings. Keeping the reader guessing, Ross Macdonald scatters these carefully. Helen calls her husband "pretty much of a broken reed" in Chapter 5, adding patronizingly, "Not that I blame him. It's not his fault, dear man." Three pages after learning of her husband's death, she calls herself a "non-grief striken widow." Yet her harsh words don't exhaust the impression she gives. Though never describing her in close physical detail, Cross registers the strong psychological effect she has on him:

> Helen Johnson's face was suddenly in my mind. I realized that she was a beautiful woman. Her beauty wasn't dazzling. It was simply there, something definite and solid that had never entirely left my mind from the moment I met her.

This response carries added import. Ross Macdonald dislikes flashy beauty, garish clothes, and heavily applied cosmetics. Helen Johnson's sensible good looks, like her active, friendly son, are a badge of her integrity. Cross's choice of her signals the same integrity, even though it baffles him. In Chapter 23, he admits admiring her but adds, "I'm not sure yet what I admire her for." Understanding, if it comes at all, comes indirectly. At the end of the same chapter, he asks if the keys to her Lincoln are symbolic. Even after quarreling with her and being virtually chased off her property, he says of the keys, "Oddly enough, I liked the idea of having them." The Freudian reading of keys as symbols of male sexual potency conveys Cross's growing awareness of Helen. But the real key to Cross's interest in Helen may be her son, Jamie, of whom Cross blurts out, "I wish he were my boy." To balance the claims of Helen and Jamie on Cross's heart is not possible; the claims may not even be competitive. Ross Macdonald only shows the effects of psychological drives. He doesn't analyze their causes. Cross, an actor rather than a spectator, has moved too close to Helen to account rationally for his attraction to her. His first-person narration makes him the least reliable source of information about his heart.

Another smothered father is Art Lemp. Formerly a lawyer, police inspector, and, for seven years, a jailbird, Lemp peddles his shady wares unsuccessfully either side of the law. Even a wig and an alias don't help his bad luck. Lemp is a petty racketeer who overreaches himself. Poor judgment cost him his license to practice law some thirty years before the time of the novel; accordingly, his highblown scheme to kidnap Jamie Johnson costs him his life. Though mean and self-defeating, Lemp, curiously, controls his son's future. Seifel says of him, recalling their meeting in court three months before, "He talked a great deal without saying much. . . . In addition to which, he had a breath that kept me off. The stink of corruption"; later, Seifel, alluding to his "nose for evil," says of the incident in court, "I could smell the odor of hellfire." The hellish stink is real: Lemp lives by rank, festering things. Yet, to become whole, Seifel must accept the man of whom he says, "I hated that man," and "He represented pure evil to me." Now wholeness to Seifel includes rejecting both his mother and mother-figures like Helen Johnson in favor of Ann Devon. Lemp, obscure, small-time, and foul of spirit (i.e., breath), influences several lives. Like Pip in *Great Expectations*, his son finds the wellsprings of his life hidden and muddy. Seifel's job of accepting a father-criminal is both easier and harder than that of Pip. The convict Magwitch isn't Pip's natural father. Yet, in accepting him as he deserves, Pip must love a living man. Seifel, on the other hand, only learns that Lemp is his natural father after Lemp's death.

The echo from *Great Expectations* isn't random. Grizzled Abel Johnson has the same first name as Abel Magwitch, the father-figure in Dicken's novel. Magwitch's bond with Pip in the opening chapter recurs in the bond between Jamie Johnson and the ex-convict and suspected kidnaper, Fred Miner; Miner, like Magwitch has had a serious physical injury at sea. The main legacy from Dickens, though, is the father in search of a son. This motif outpaces that of the father search or the missing father. Though Larry Seifel is a moral void till he finds his father, he doesn't seek Lemp out. Union with the son generates a greater urgency than any supplied by conscious motives, symbolizing, perhaps, continuity amid change and even atonement. Fred Miner, Abel Johnson, and Howard Cross all love little Jamie as a son; looking at the four-year-old, Cross becomes "permeated with a sense of what I had been missing." Jamie impels Cross throughout—not only to marry Helen but also to find him and restore him to safety. Men whose sons are taken away fall apart. Abel Johnson (also called "Abe," short for Abraham, the name of a famous Biblical father) dies a day or two after Jamie's kidnaping. Lacking a son to come home to, Art Lemp deteriorates—drinking heavily, beating women, cheating his employers, and blackmailing. A pair of bronzed baby shoes in his old canvas suitcase shows that Lemp still remembers his son. His plan to kidnap Jamie follows the memory logically enough. A man whose son was torn from him, he steals another man's son, knowing first-hand that any father would pay a kidnaper heavily to get his son back. As an added fillip, Jamie is about as old as Larry when Larry was taken from Lemp thirty years before.

These repetitions come often. Both George Arthur Lempke and his son practice law. Disbarred in Illinois and then dismissed from both the San Francisco Police Department and the Bourke-owned Acme Detective Agency in Los Angeles, Lemp loses at least three law-related jobs. Two of Helen Johnson's former nursing patients, the wounded sailor Fred Miner and the heart patient Abel Johnson, play a large part in her future. By portraying characters goaded by the same forces and performing the same acts, the novel gains some of the simplicity and drive Ross Macdonald admired in *Oedipus Rex.*

Unity also comes from the first-person narration of Howard Cross, a typical Ross Macdonald narrator-hero. Somewhat displaced and anomalous, he recalls both the newly discharged G-I, John Weather of *Blue City,* and Bret Taylor, who in *Roads* bemoans "my inability to fit into a group, my feeling that I have no definite place in society." Comparisons with Archer run still deeper. His probation officer's job, like that of the private detective, both gives him different aims and lets him use different methods from the police. Detective Lieutenant Cleat says of criminals, "Once a man starts to go bad, he's bound to go all the way." Cross's view is less official and deterministic. Guide, adviser, and friend of men gone wrong, he tries to reclaim ex-convicts. Like the other people in the book, he walks a moral tightwire: "I'm a sort of middleman between the law and the lawbreaker," he says in Chapter 4, adding later, "The criminal is at war with society. Society fights back through cops and prisons. I try to act as a neutral arbitrator." His reference to "the anomaly of my position, halfway between policeman and civilian," says a great deal. Cross's working space lacks sharp definition and so does he. His freedom as both a probation officer and a man stems from his unclassifiability. Though responsible to a system, he owes his first loyalty to the social and moral rehabilitation of his clients. His working materials, the minds and impulses of ex-convicts, free him from formal controls and tight supervision.

Much of his work in *Morgue* is straight detection. He drives to witnesses' homes and places of business; he collects and studies evidence; he shares his findings with the police. This work he does well, for, like Archer, he's not afraid of hard digging or long hours. Also like Archer, he served in the Pacific during the war; physically, he's a strong man who, steering a line between sadism and cerebration, will fight if he has to. He admits his mistakes: "I had come to the wrong place, at the wrong time, and done the wrong thing," he says near the end of Chapter 18. His self-objectivity and middlebrow earnestness generate a work ethic with which Archer would gladly identify: "I've either got to clear Miner, or pin the kidnaping on him. I feel an obligation towards the law, the truth, whatever you want to call the abstractions that keep us going, keep us human. There's nothing personal in this." Cross follows Archer in practice as well as in principle. He knows the law and its applications, and he can work comfortably within the limits set him by his (non-paying) clients. He is also a synthesizer, even an on-the-spot theorist. As early as Chapter 5, he looks for a tie between the kidnaping of Jamie Johnson and Fred Miner's hit-and-run fatality, pointing out, "Miner's in both. The things a man does are always connected in some way." Even Cross's irony can have the same ham-fisted cruelty as that of the early Archer. When Molly Fawn asks Cross about Lemp, whom she thinks is still alive, he gives her answers like, "I saw Art today. He wasn't feeling so well," "He isn't hearing so well," and "He isn't talking."

As a carrier and critic of the action, Howard Cross is effective. But he represents no gain over Archer, whose forte is the missing person's case with criminal by-products. A rewriting of the early chapters to show the Johnsons hiring Archer to find Jamie wouldn't have changed either the plot or the mood of this strong novel. But Cross's efforts both go beyond and fall short of a probation officer's normal work. Assuming Cross to carry a heavy caseload, we wonder how he can neglect office routine, co-workers, and other clients to give so much of himself to the Miner-Johnson case. The question wouldn't arise with Archer piloting *Morgue*. Ross Macdonald's own notion that detection is best left to detectives comes through in his nudging Cross toward the altar and then restoring the wifeless Archer to his next novel with renewed verve.

VI

Find a Victim (1954) touches many nerves. The crime it describes is more shocking than that in any of Ross Macdonald's earlier work; the pity we feel both for criminals and their victims drives deeper; far from Wilshire Boulevard, Archer faces constant danger in a town where he is scorned as a meddling outsider by a morally compromised police chief. Wilfrid Sheed, though qualified in his praise, singles out the book as a break-through performance: in *Victim*, Sheed says, "Macdonald was nudging the form [of the hard-boiled detective novel] into pure fiction, where the metaphysical possibilities of private-eyeness could float loose from police radio naturalism. Unfortunately, he was still stuck with a mess of tired conventions."[4] Macdonald's view of the book is also mixed. In a letter to the present writer, dated 10 January 1972, the novelist says, "It's too action-fraught, the curse of all beginners in this work—but I think the last couple of chapters rise to the wholly human."

The first chapter balances the human and the actional. *Victim* starts more explosively than any other Archer novel. Driving to Sacramento for a conference on drugs, Archer sees on the side of the road "the ghastliest hitchhiker who ever thumbed me." The hitchhiker, with a red smear for a mouth and eyes like black holes in his yellow skin, has been shot in the chest. Archer's reaction to him shows outstanding goodness and a self-detachment approaching that of a mystic. Improvising a tourniquet of his own tie, shirt, and jacket, Archer carries the dying stranger to his car. He then places the man gently in the back seat, "his head propped up on my overnight bag so that he wouldn't smother, and covered him with the car blanket." In the hope of calling an ambulance, Archer drives to a nearby motel, where he hears a onesided quarrel. Don Kerrigan, the worse for drink and lumbering "like an ex-athlete gone to seed," is shouting at his wife, Kate. Kerrigan identifies the dying man, who does die before the chapter ends, as Tony Aquista, a Mexican-American truck driver employed by a Las Cruces hauler named Meyer. Archer shows the sheriff of the imaginary valley town of 50,000 the roadside ditch where he found Aquista. One of the sheriff's deputies is Sal Braga, who, as Aquista's cousin, has strong personal reasons for wanting to find and punish the killer.

Near the end of the chapter, Sheriff Brand Church says something that pertains to Braga, to Las Cruces, and to the strange turns the case will take before being cracked: "In this town everybody's related to everybody else." The tight, nearly closed, social community helps *Victim* the same way it helps other Archers where it appears. First, it brings the investigator close to those being investigated. Including policemen, criminals, and their victims in the same social unit increases the number of suspects; it introduces non-tangible evidence, i.e., the psychological background needed to dig out evidence; as Braga shows, it brings the motive of revenge into police investigation; and because of the strong claims made by family, it helps criminals escape both detection and punishment. The family is a felt force in *Victim*. Besides Sal Braga's blood-tie to Aquista, Sheriff Church's father-in-law was Aquista's employer, and Church's sister worked until recently at the motel where Archer took Aquista. This web of personal relationships and the hostility with which rural police view city detectives both slow Archer in his attempt to find Aquista's killer.

A more pressing problem for Archer at the moment is that of finding a client. Some of this pressure relaxes with the introduction in Chapter 3 of a missing person. The mid-October day is Thursday, and Anne Meyer, above mentioned bookkeeper-secretary at Kerrigan's motel, sister-in-law of Brand Church, and daughter of Aquista's employer, has been gone since the previous weekend. "A hatred that went beyond violence" flares between Kerrigan and Church when Anne is mentioned, giving the novel its third dramatic conflict in ten pages. But Church wisely puts down his wrath and goes away. No sooner is he gone than the genteel Kate Kerrigan tells Archer that her husband is planning to leave town with another woman. Sliding into the room, Kerrigan overhears Kate say that he and the missing woman, Anne Meyer, had had an affaire the previous year. He hits Kate and then, his anger blinding his judgment, foolishly charges Archer. Relying on timing and coordination as much as on strength, Archer knocks out his man easily. He then drives about a hundred yards to a place hidden from the motel, and, two cigarettes later, tacks past the motel just when Kerrigan's red convertible is leaving. He follows Kerrigan to a Chinese restaurant, where Kerrigan has a lunch date with a girl of nineteen or twenty. The girl, identified later as Josephine Summer, complains of severe pains caused by marijuana withdrawal. Though Kerrigan has no weed for her, he does give her some rancid sex, "his fingers plucking at her clothes like a dying man at his sheets." The footsteps of an approaching waiter send Archer from his listening post, and, when he returns a few minutes later, he finds Jo Summer and Kerrigan gone.

Short on aids, Archer goes to Meyer's truckyard, where he gets two big leads—the news that Tony Aquista loved his chief's daughter, Anne, and that Aquista's death-rig contained a shipment of bourbon insured for $65,000. Barbed edges and hidden traps come to light, as well. The sheriff's wife, Hilda, looking "very female, almost too female for comfort," invites Archer into her father's home. Archer relishes the invitation. He wants Meyer to hire him, first, to recover the missing truck and, next, to find Anne. A bull-like widower, Meyer brings him good news. The stolen whiskey, belonging to Anne's former lover, Don Kerrigan, wasn't fully insured. Archer offers to work for ten per cent of the $7000 Meyer stands to lose on the payload. Agreeing to these terms, Meyer starts to talk about his family when Hilda comes in and accuses him of having corrupted Anne. Though Meyer, "a big old wreck of a man," tries to silence Hilda, he doesn't deny her charge. In fact, when she starts for home on the next page, he thanks her for visiting him. Nor does she blame him, pointing out that his wife died during childbirth with Anne, whom Meyer had to raise by himself. Yet something has given Hilda night fears. When Archer drives her to her "good residential suburb," she sees her home as "a dangerous maze" where she doesn't want to be alone. Archer turns down her sexual overture to inspect her sister, Anne's, apartment several miles away. The most revealing effect in the unlocked flat is a letter written Anne by Tony Aquista. Writing from San Diego a year before, Aquista chides Anne for spurning him in favor of the rich Don Kerrigan. But he ends by assuring her of his love, loyalty, and deep wish to be with her.

Archer's inspection of the apartment ends when local sheriff Brand Church comes in with his .45 revolver at the ready. Archer explains his suspicions about Don Kerrigan and the highjacked truck; then, hearing that Kerrigan owns a local bar called the Golden Slipper, makes the Slipper his next stop. After speaking with a bartender, he takes a prostitute to her private room. "I'd rather have information than fornication," he makes clear at the start of their time together. Thus taking charge of the interview, he learns that the girl in the Chinese restaurant with Kerrigan that afternoon was the B-girl and prostitute, Jo Summer. Archer goes straight to Jo's red-appointed flat. Bribing her with some marijuana cigarettes, which the State Bureau in Sacramento wouldn't miss from a cache of several hundred, he loosens her tongue. Like many reefer addicts in Ross Macdonald, Jo sucks the weed with ravenous and unrealistic abandon. Her nerves soothed, she tells of her plan to bolt to Guatamala with Kerrigan, her lover. The reefer also makes her divulge the highjacking plot: Kerrigan robbed his own truck for the insurance money, in order to finance his trip to Guatamala with Jo.

But just as Archer feels informed enough to break the case, he is foiled. Jo, supposedly drugged and not more than nineteen or twenty in any case, decamps while he believes her in the shower. Then, Leonard Bozey, an iron-knuckled thug with red hair and eyes having a "frightened savage lostness in them," knocks him out and steals his wallet. Still hoping to block the Guatamala caper, the battered Archer hauls himself to Kerrigan's elegant home. This chapter screams with implausibility. Archer stations himself both to watch and hear the Kerrigans without being spotted himself. The "beautiful room, white-carpeted and filled with the suave and fragile curves of eighteenth-century furniture," clashes with Kerrigan's vulgarity. The motel-keeper's appeal for his genteel wife, the daughter of a distinguished judge, never surfaces either. Nobody can fault Ross Macdonald for putting so much distrust and resentment into the Kerrigans' marriage. But he fails to show how the pair could have ever loved each other. Kate's indictment, "Your entire life with me has been a lie," has no basis; the marriage never had enough promise to be significantly violated, to begin with. Kate turned to Kerrigan after her lover died in the war, and he married her for her father's money. How a gentle, articulate woman like Kate ever mistook his coarseness for animal spark or his opportunism for energy defies belief. Yet Ross Macdonald mitigates Kerrigan's evil and humanizes the poor communication between the pair. Without denying or pardoning Kerrigan's unfaithfulness, he describes it as an effect rather than a cause:

Maybe you loved me in your head [Kerrigan tells Kate]. Only what good is love in the head? It's just a word. You're still a virgin as far as I'm concerned. Did you know that, Kate? It's been chilly work, trying to be your husband. You never made me feel like a man. Not once.

Kate's feeble retort to this Lawrencean allegation is, "I'm not a magician," and on the next page, Archer notes, "She sounded a little defensive for the first time."

Victim is no forum for resolving marital problems. But if Kate can't give sexual love, then her husband isn't breaking a sexual bond by spending time with other women. Suffering dominates the novel, and the characters' efforts to fend off the pain of routine existence often worsen the pain. The more we learn of these people, the knottier and denser their predicaments grow. Ross Macdonald scrupulously avoids fastening blame and guilt. Apparently an innocent victim of her husband's sadism and wenching, Kate later concedes, "I was cruel, too. It wasn't all one-sided."

Kerrigan leaves Kate the second time that October day with Archer on his heels. Archer watches him take an oblong package from a man waiting in a parked Buick. The man turns out to be Bozey. Tailing him from the front to divert suspicion, Archer finds himself at a disused air-base. Suddenly, a truck roars out of a hanger straight at him. Diving out of its path, he follows it into the foothills. But instead of catching Bozey, he happens upon Sheriff Church, who orders him to drop the case and leave town. Archer, ignoring the veiled threats, drives back to Kerrigan's motor court. To his surprise, he sees Kerrigan's car parked in front of the office. A second, and bigger, surprise comes when he looks through the office window and sees Kerrigan's head blasted open by gunfire. Archer's investigation of the corpse ends with the entry of Deputy Sal Braga, Tony Aquista's cousin. Underterred by Braga's calling him a "smart-cracking L. A. bastard," Archer keeps infuriating the local police. He knocks the deputy unconscious, leaves the motel, and goes back to the Kerrigans' eighteenth-century estate. Though not saddened by the news of Don's death, Kate Kerrigan does deny that her husband staged the highjacking and the Aquista murder. The approach of Sheriff Church cuts the interview short, but not before Archer learns that Kerrigan had given Anne Meyer the keys to his mountain cabin on Lake Perdida the past weekend, since which time Anne has been missing.

A frequent master of indirection, Ross Macdonald adds an uncharacteristic touch by including in the redwood lakeside cabin a bottle of estrogen oil and "a limp, rubber tube," Archer's next crucial witness is Jo Summer's reclusive grandfather, who, by coincidence, lives near Lake Perdida. Like old Kaufman, the Marxist junkdealer in *Blue City*, MacGowan loves a sluttish granddaughter he can't control or understand. Another echo from *Blue City* comes in MacGowan's announcement that, several days before, he saw Anne Meyer digging a grave-like trench, but as soon as he called out, Anne and Don Kerrigan, who was watching her dig, ran away. In a ditch where she stumbled, Archer finds the heel of a shoe later identified as Anne's. Then the pace of the book speeds. Hilda Church—who needs love more than anybody else in the novel—leaves both her husband and her father, the two men closest to her, inside the next two chapters. Other changes come just as quickly: Archer drops Meyer as a principle, and, on the next page, is again told to drop the case altogether by Sheriff Church. A brilliantly described fight between Church and Archer follows. Though the fight doesn't ease the enmity between the two men, it does reconcile Hilda and Church. In a touching reunion, nearly Chekhovian in its understatement and delicacy of feeling, Church takes his wife home, "leaning . . . like a dutiful doll," and promises her to end the killing that has overtaken their circle.

This tenderness proves surprising after his toughness with Archer. The fracas with Church forces Archer to have eight stitches sewn into his face the next day by a local doctor. Another big service is done for him by the local District Attorney, who recounts Bozey's criminal record through a recent $22,000 bank robbery in Oregon. A more important disclosure, from Kerrigan's financial records, proves that Anne Meyer had been blackmailing her former lover while working as his secretary-bookkeeper. Archer and the D. A. interpret the blackmail differently. Though Archer admits that blackmail gave Kerrigan motive enough to kill Anne, he resists naming him Anne's killer. He also doubts that Bozey paid Kerrigan for the highjacked liquor with marked, and thus non-negotiable, bills from the Oregon bank heist and then killed him. Archer's talk with the D. A. both smoothes the book's texture and darkens its mysteries. The rehearsal of the evidence by two experts and the trying-out of different interpretations quiet the furor caused by Archer's brawl with Church. Its professional detachment balances the touching reunion of the Churches and prefigures Kate Kerrigan's emotional outburst in the next chapter.

Dramatic pacing now calls for movement. Taking old MacGowan with him, Archer drives to Bozey's hideout in the Nevada desert, where they hope to find Jo. Jo does turn up on the twisting, chuckholed road. But she's bleeding, bruised, and in shock after being gang-raped by the three men who had come to collect the stolen whiskey. Jo leads Archer to the gutted mining town of Traverse, where more violence occurs. He sees two of the bootleggers unloading whisky from Meyer's truck. Pistols flare and Archer kills the bootlegger-rapists. Then he captures Bozey, who leads him to an abandoned car. The novel's great shock comes here. Inside the "iron womb" of the car's trunk in a foetal coil lies the corpse of Anne Meyer. The buzzards circling overhead in the glare of the "insane red eye" of the sun, with its bloody undertones, help make the corpse the logical offspring of Jo's gang-rape. This part of the book has a wide emotional sweep. Back in Las Cruces, Brand Church breaks down when he sees Anne's corpse, his tears softening the brutality unleashed in Nevada.

But who killed Anne? Ross Macdonald uses scientific detection to find an answer. The date assigned her murder by the coroner's report proves that the woman who lost the heel off her shoe at the shallow gravesite near Lake Perdida couldn't have been Anne. Though the D. A. admits Church was Anne's lover, he rejects Archer's suggestion that he was also her killer. This interview balances the one in Chapter 21 where Archer disproved the D. A.'s belief that Kerrigan killed Tony Aquista. The book's closing chapters, affirming Church's innocence, vindicate the D. A. at Archer's expense. The (always crucial) next-to-last chapter takes Archer back to the Churches' home, where Hilda receives him "looking like any pretty suburban chatelaine." Her appearance runs counter to reality. Denizen of a bleak, hard world where love kills, she admits straightaway that she killed her look-alike sister Anne for deceiving her with Brand and then impersonated her to trick the police. Her life since killing Anne shows her as a Puritan whose cleanliness is worse than other people's dirt:

I've done nothing but think about it since it happened. I haven't even taken time to sleep. I've spent the whole week thinking and cleaning house. I cleaned this house and then I cleaned Father's house and then I came back here and cleaned this house again. I can't seem to get it clean, but I did decide one thing, that it was Anne's fault.

Knowing for months about Anne's affaire with Church, she followed the lovers to the mountains the foregoing weekend. The Sunday morning church bells mingled in her mind with her own wedding bells, whose mocking clamor she could only silence by shooting Anne. Normally gentle and retiring, Hilda proves how quickly evil spreads. She killed Tony Aquista to keep his knowledge of the highjacking from getting out, and she killed Kerrigan to quiet him on the subject of Anne. Brand Church's knowledge of these killings, the focus of the last chapter, also comes out here. More a patient, reproving father to Hilda than a husband, Church confesses that, in not arresting Hilda, he has been shielding a killer.

The confession—an outright declaration of guilt—starts a deeply moving dialogue between the book's two authority figures. Archer, who had despised Church, opens his heart: "You're the sort of conscience-stricken bastard who would get satisfaction out of public disgrace and maybe a term in your own jail." Besides extending this leather-lined compassion and respect, Archer admits that he'd have done as Church did in Church's position. Chief witness in the case, he vows to withhold any evidence damaging to the Churches in any formal hearing or inquiry. A restrained emotional climax crowns the action. Looking like "a ravaged saint," Church makes Hilda's guilt a function of the psychological strain of living with a father who tried to force his other daughter; of her never having borne a son; of his own intrigue with Anne. This explanation creates no catharsis. Instead, it deepens the pain and guilt. Helplessly life-denying, Hilda, though "almost too female for comfort," can't love. Church, no cardboard dreamer, has braved a barren, loveless marriage. Though it gives more sorrow than joy, it means more to him than inner peace and professional integrity. A nerve-raking commentary on his recitation comes in Hilda's last mad act—ripping the grass out of her garden and stripping her lemon tree with torn, bleeding hands. This madness gives physical expression to the psychological trauma rumbling through the chapter. Disciplined but not neurotic, dutiful but not slavish, Brand Church qualifies as a martyr-hero. Archer's ability both to perceive and to value his heroism, furthermore, singals a strengthening of the detective's moral fiber.

Like Lieutenant Ralph Knudson of *Pool*, Church is a tender-tough cop with a guilty past. "A lonely silhouette," yet also a pit of turbulence, he baffles Archer most of the way. Kate Kerrigan calls him "the best sheriff we've ever had in this county"; the local D. A., just as cordial in his praise, says, "He works a sixteen-hour day for less money than I get" and

Debut

"You don't know him or what he's done for the community. . . . Brandon Church is a genuine practical idealist. If there's one man in the valley whose character I'm sure of, he's the man." Church can't be defiled. To his townsfolk, he's the rock on which the moral security of Las Cruces rests. Yet even his admiring neighbors don't know the pressure he lives with each day or the self-control he must exert to hold his life together. Most of the humanity in the novel comes from him, but his clashes with Archer, whom we instinctively side with, veil the fact. Why does Archer clash so inexorably with Church? Normally a fine judge of character, he seems compelled to cut Church down. He tells him how to do his job; calls him "a zombie that takes the public's money"; even accuses him of dishonesty. When offered a friendly truce by Church after their fight in Chapter 20, the detective snubs him. Church can't do anything right in Archer's eyes. Even after he credits Archer for reporting the incident with Bozey at the disused airbase, Archer makes him out a murderer to the D. A.

Archer and Church, whose names sound roughly alike, are about the same size and age. Self-made men, they have both worked hard; both have had bad marriages. Their mutual greeting in Chapter 12—"So it's you again" and "It's also you again"—resembles a mirror meeting. *Victim* is a looking-glass novel. Just as Leonard Bozey is a younger outlaw version of Archer, so is Church, who keeps turning up in the same places as Archer, the detective's double within the establishment. Each man envies the other; each sees in the other several traits he dislikes in himself. To wipe out his smirched counterpart would certify each man's autonomy and worth. Before the big fight in Chapter 20, Archer says, "One of us was going to have to kill the other." The resentment has deep roots. Much of his ongoing conflict with Church and his wish to wreck Church's reputation for moral integrity stem from Archer's anti-institutionalism. Brand Church is the law, or established church, in Las Cruces, California. Like Ibsen's Brand, he is lonely, humorless, and hard-working. No Everyman figure, he takes on greater responsibilities, risks more, and suffers more deeply than his fellows. The parochial view he takes of law enforcement fits both his sense of mission and the religious symbolism evoked by his town's (Las Cruces-the Crosses) name. Such orthodoxy rankles Archer's anti-institutionalism, and the freelancer from the city grabs every chance to thwart the provincial sheriff.

Brand Church lends his share to the search for a son that comes back from *Morgue*. The discovery that his wife couldn't give him a son soured his marriage on the spot. His father-in-law, Meyer, even resents a wife dying in childbed for bearing him a daughter instead of the son he craves. Ross Macdonald's men keep using sons or son-surrogates to square accounts with life. Old MacGowan, the hermit-like grandfather of Jo Summer, had a son who'd be Archer's age had he not been killed in a shipyard accident. The association in MacGowan's mind between Archer and the dead son might explain the old man's willingness to help even more than a concern for Jo or respect for the law. The possibility that MacGowan, an outdoorsman and a loser whose travels have included Scotland and Canada, refers to Kenneth Millar's Scots-Canadian father gives the father-son drama an added charge.

This two-way flow—between wish and reality and also between father and son—follows from the dialectical pull the novel generates at the outset. *Victim* thrums with tension. Archer says of Tony Aquista on the first page, "He was a young man, and he was dying." The next people Archer meets are the brutal Don Kerrigan and his placid wife. The town's police chiefs, Sheriff Church and Captain Danelaw, have names symbolic of spiritual and temporal law. Polarity also dominates action and setting. The vertical and horizontal bars of the crucifix—Las Cruces's totem— encompass all. In Chapter 1, Archer goes to a motel, ordinarily a setting for companionship, and meets rudeness, instead. A hospital, where the sick go to be healed, becomes Tony Aquista's place of death. The death then balances the vivid life arrowing from the chapter's final paragraph: "From somewhere in the murmurous bowels of the building an infant's cry rose sharp. I wondered if it was a newborn baby equalizing the population of Las Cruces."

Archer, too, vibrates to the bipolar tension. In no other book does he span a wider moral and emotional range; he is at his kindest and cruellest in *Victim*. His help to Aquista, a total stranger, in Chapter 1, approaches the saintly. Later he tells MacGowan as gently as possible that the police want to talk to Jo about Kerrigan's death. This tact he also extends to Hilda and Meyer when he states his fear that Anne is dead: "I don't mean to frighten you unnecessarily, but it's a good idea to expect the worst. Then any surprises we get will come as a relief." Yet in the previous chapter, Archer admitted being shop-soiled by his job: "I've been tempted to use people, play on their feelings, push them around. Those are the occupational diseases of my job." *Victim* exhibits these diseases in their most malignant light. As has been said, after his big fight with Brand Church in Chapter 20, he turns down the sheriff's offer of a friendly truce; throughout, he both underrates and disparages Church, ignorant of his suffering.

If Archer acts stupidly with Church, his hardheartedness with Jo Summer amounts to sadism. He questions her closely and scolds her while she's still in shock after being raped by three men and then thrown from a moving car: "All you hustlers get hurt sooner or later. It's fair enough when you make a living hurting other people." Then, instead of rushing her to a doctor, he makes her revisit the scene of the gang rape. Still playing the sexual scourge, he kills two of the men. Something, perhaps Ross Macdonald's inability to resist making sexual judgments, destroys narrative technique in this chapter. Jo speaks too coherently for a very young woman coming out of shock; MacGowan is forgotten in the violence; Archer's daredevil exploits smack of pulp melodrama. Through it all, Archer's sullenness holds—and with good reason. Compassion must wait till the harrowing last-scene encounter with Brand Church. The uplift of spirit experienced here, besides giving the last pages a warm human glow, reasserts the Church-Archer dialectic. But it also resolves the dialectic with kindness and compassion. The last chapter confers a saintliness on Church matching the one Archer rises to in the first. Countertension, a corollary of the tightwire metaphor in *Morgue*, governs both the novel's structure and chief dramatic conflict. The "wholly human" resolution of the last novel Ross Macdonald wrote in his thirties ends his apprenticeship. The works following *Victim*, blending mellowness and tang, take on the vintage Archer flavor.

5

The works Ross Macdonald published between 1956 and 1960 justify Gerald Walker's description of the novelist as "a nice man who happens to know a lot of dangerous truths about people."[1] These novels both probe inward and, owing to their geographical sweep, reach outward. Richer than their predecessors, they dovetail their author's social conscience with the artistic resources of the hard-boiled genre. Finally, they extend the genre to create a new kind of crime fiction. The people in these four novels portray southern California with a new sharpness and economy, their problems often mirroring those of their real-life freeway society. In a 1974 newspaper interview, Ross Macdonald said that a society reveals itself in the acts of its members; he also claimed that hard-boiled fiction captures the shifts and upheavals of modern America better than other narrative modes. Both the materials and intentions of the detective novel lie close to everyday experience:

The American hard-boiled tradition gives us an instrument for exploring society that other fiction doesn't provide. I regard the detective novel as a social novel. Whatever social meaning it has in it is given in action and conflict. That's happening in real life, too.[2]

But rapid movement and change don't forge the link between contemporary America and hard-boiled fiction by themselves; a copy or a report gives but a crude, stunted picture. Interpretive power and rhetorical skill are needed to turn sensational journalism into serious fiction. These, in turn, depend on a controlling intelligence that perceives and then conveys the meaning of what happens. Archer helps Ross Macdonald explore change so well because he has the physical stamina to keep pace with change, the wit to understand the motives underlying it, and the moral sympathy to help those battered by it. Midway into *The Barbarous Coast,* the first novel of Ross Macdonald's middle period, Archer states his personal and professional creed: "The problem was to love people, try to serve them, without wanting anything from them. I was a long way from solving that one."

Like the rest of us, he never does solve that one. But he tries. He perceives hearts and faces in the fraught inhabitants of the urban sprawl. The overbuilt city may be infernal; the hearts of its dwellers, shrivelled; the faces, clenched tight for the onset of calamity. But Archer has both the imagination and the moral energy to refresh this bleakness. Ross Macdonald summarized his detective's humanity in a 1973 interview for *The Journal of Popular Culture:*

He's not a model of morality, but like several good private detectives I know, he's a better man than most of the people he has to work with. That's what makes him effective. He's in control of himself. He's not a moral ideal, not a paragon, but a guy that's fairly trustworthy.

*   *   *

Archer has two aspects. In one aspect he's an ordinary man, a private detective doing a not terribly well-paid job and working hard at it. And there's the other aspect of him where he's the representative of the novelist in the novel, and, in a sense, the mind of the novel. It's his observing mind in which things are put together and in which the whole novel exists, in a sense.[3]

These middle novels bring Archer's perceptions even with those of his creator. Though starting to sag in the body, Archer demonstrates new powers of compassion, braced by fresh insights into the loss of love and security. These novels make him the hero we would secretly like to be.

His moral growth asserts itself both dramatically and psychologically; his job tests him deeply and over a wide range of response. In 1966, Ross Macdonald called *The Barbarous Coast* "my largest book so far. . . . In it I was learning to get rid of the protective wall between my mind and the perilous stuff of my own life." He also called *The Galton Case,* published three years later, "my most ambitious and personal work so far."[4] In both books, Archer helps him get closer to himself and put more of himself into his work. Autobiography also runs through *The Ferguson Affair,* a non-Archer novel which followed *The Galton Case* by a year. The moral complexity described in the books after *Victim* has both a new urgency and control; Archer has to work harder to help people with their problems. To write these novels, Ross Macdonald dipped his pen in dark colors. Held together by a narrator he knows and trusts, they take up new challenges without sacrificing artistic balance or distance.

I

The Barbarous Coast (1956), the first novel Kenneth Millar published as Ross Macdonald, opens with Archer sounding his car-horn at the gatehouse of the exclusive Channel Club on Malibu Beach. But he isn't alone. George Wall, "a big young man . . . with flying pink hair," has come from Toronto, where he writes sports journalism, to see the club's

manager, Clarence Bassett.   Wall, Ross Macdonald's first important
Canadian, suspects that his estranged wife, Hester, and Bassett are lovers
and that Hester is in danger; two nights ago she had phoned Wall to voice
her fear of being killed.   Tony Torres, ex-prize fighter and gatehouse
guard, has orders to keep Wall out of the club.   These he takes seriously.
When the younger, bigger Wall tries to race past him, the one-time
Fresno gamecock stops him with a waistlock and a pistol.

Chapter Two introduces Bassett, a prissy bachelor of sixty with a
Harvard B.A. and an established New England family to go with it.
Bassett wants Archer to protect him from George Wall.   Hester Campbell
Wall, a championship diver, married George after touring North America
with an aquacade, left him within a year, and came back to Malibu to
teach diving at the club.   Though Bassett hired her and even cooked her
several dinners, he denies having been her lover.   What is more, he insists
he hasn't seen her for three months.   The chapter soon works its way to
familiar ground.   Besides introducing a missing persons case, it mentions
one Gabrielle Torres, daughter of gateman Tony Torres, close friend of
Hester, and victim of an unsolved murder of a year ago.   Archer's line
of investigation is clearly marked.   Working within a tight social frame,
in which ties of job, blood, and marriage join the characters, he must
connect Gabrielle's murder with Hester's absence; the connection, once
found, will explain an old grievance whose felonious effects are still at
work.   These effects he must also keep from crashing into violence.
George Wall has scaled the wire fence enclosing the Channel Club and
demands that Bassett, now holding a pistol, take him to Hester.   Archer
convinces Wall that Bassett hasn't seen her for months.   Responding
gratefully, Bassett agrees to hire Archer to find Hester on condition that
Wall keep away from the club.   Characteristically, the counter-suggestible
Wall opposes the plan and makes Archer toss a coin to determine his
client.   Wall wins the coin toss.   Together, he and Archer go to look for
Hester.

Their first witness, Hester's ex-landlady, whom Archer interviews
while Wall waits in the car, explains that she had to evict Hester for
"carrying on": "The girl's a fool about men," the landlady says, calling
one of her visitors "a regular gangster type."   Her judgment proves
accurate.   Lance Torres, former lifeguard at the Channel Club, prize
fighter, and jailbird, *had* been visiting Hester till recently.   That Lance is
the nephew of Tony Torres, who also trained him for the ring, and first
cousin to the slain Gabrielle enriches the plot.   Its first five chapters,
integrating a rich store of well-perceived material, have given *Coast* a good
push.   The momentum carries.   Tony calls his nephew his own worst
enemy, and the evidence supports the claim.   After winning some fights,
Lance wasted his boxing career on women, drugs, and motorcycle crime.
He hired the homosexual gangster Carl Stern to manage him, made some

159

Hollywood-Ontario Shuttle

money throwing fights, and then lost his license and went to jail after drugs were found in his car. Archer's old commanding officer, Peter Colton, newly retired from his post as senior investigator for the District Attorney, tells the detective that Stern's underworld ties in southern California, including narcotics, go back to Bugsy Siegel's notorious Syndicate. (*Coast* is the only Ross Macdonald novel whose felons have worked with real-life gangsters like Siegel, Lepke, Gameboy Miller of Cleveland, and Lefty Clark of Detroit.) Most recently, Stern has obtained a Nevada gambling license preparatory to building a new casino-hotel in Las Vegas with Simon Graff, a powerful film tycoon and Channel Club member.

Stern probably also talked his partner Graff into giving a screen contract to Lance. Archer goes to Lance, who has a new name, Lance Leonard, to match his new career and "raw new" home. The image of Leonard/Torres combing his hair with a sequined comb exudes rank sexual vanity. It also labels him a trouble-spot for Archer. The trouble starts quickly. His refusal to tell Archer anything about Hester leads to a fight, which Torres, younger and more battle-wise, wins easily. Meanwhile, George Wall has left Archer's car and, nervously walking the grounds, spots Hester on Torres's patio. Calling out, he gives chase. But Torres stops him as quickly as he did Archer. Nor has Archer helped his client by throwing his weight around. Though he knocks out Leonard/Torres with a sneak punch, he can't leave Wall alone with the film actor to follow Hester, who has driven away in a Jaguar.

Archer's reasons for staying on the case have changed. The unsolved murder of Gabrielle, an admitted desire to hurt Lance, and the obscure tie joining Lance, Gabrielle, and Hester, who appeared together in a framed photograph in Chapter 2, bring new challenges. He will also help Wall get the explanations he deserves from Hester so long as Wall's hopes stay alive. But first Wall needs a different kind of help. Archer takes him home, battered and dazed, for a spell of therapeutic bed rest, as prescribed by an examining physician. The lives of the characters continue to mesh. Clarence Bassett tells Archer that, like Lance, Hester had a film contract with Helio-Graff Studios; she probably got the contract, Bassett adds, by sleeping with Simon Graff. But he also forbids Archer to question Graff, "the most powerful single member of the club." Having been handicapped by witnesses before, Archer skillfully improvises other leads. A local shopkeeper gives him information that sends him to the "poor street of stucco and frame cottages" where Hester's mother lives. Archer hears that Hester has grown rich on uranium stocks inherited from her dead husband, the Canadian mine-owner, George Wallingford. Mrs. Campbell also mentions her other daughter, Rina, a psychiatric nurse; unlike her impulsive, trouble-prone sister, Rina is sensible and practical.

But Archer doesn't make her his next witness. The action swings from the rundown to the slick and garish. Archer watches Lance drive away from his palm-fringed street in Beverly Hills. The man who had pulled up to Lance's Moorish mansion a few moments before and presumably sent Lance on his errand knocks Archer out after the detective barges into the mansion asking questions. Emerging from the "deep red darkness" of oblivion, Archer finds himself being driven by his attacker, one Theodore Marfield, to Marfield's chief. Although he varies the pattern set by Ralph Knudson in *Pool* and Brand Church in *Victim,* Ross Macdonald keeps presenting guilty policemen. Marfield and his chief, Leroy Frost, both have a police background: Marfield was a Los Angeles County policeman for fifteen years; Frost, chief of police for Helio-Graff film studios, worked in federal security and personnel. The interview between Archer and the corrupt lawman, Frost, reveals the book's delicate, sure-handed command of human situations. Frost's armed cadre, big job, and political influence can't hide the sickness and fret conveyed by his yellow eyes, quilted, baggy flesh, and sharp weight-drop since Archer last saw him. Describing himself as "just another joe working my way through life," Frost gets Archer to admit having made a mistake barging into Lance's home and demanding information. But the duel of wits scores Frost no more points. As usual, Archer won't work with the underworld. Ignoring threatening references to the "accidents" that sometimes happen at big, powerful companies like Helio-Graff, he refuses to trade the name of his client for a free vacation in Italy.

Only a novelist gifted with second sight could have masterminded the coincidence that follows. The client whose name Frost has been trying to coax out of Archer races past Frost's window. Like a silent-film comic, George Wall, his pink hair flying, is seen running across the film lot. But the comedy gives way to gore. Two of Frost's henchmen, catching Wall, pound and pistol-whip him so badly he has to be taken to a hospital in an ambulance. Archer's lot is only slightly better. Soon after his refusal to cooperate with Frost, he is blackjacked from behind. Still a prisoner, he wakes up by a swimming pool to hear his captor talking to Lance Leonard. Before he can learn anything from the talk, though, he is again knocked out. But his outlook soon brightens. As he did with Puddler in *Target,* he tricks his gorilla-like guard, immobilizes him, and escapes.

After thumbing a ride to a hospital, he has some stitches sewn into his head. But he disobeys the doctor's orders to rest for a couple of days ("Call me trouble looking for a place to happen"). A bloodstained carpet and an overheard conversation between Frost and Marfield at Hester Wall's apartment make it clear that two killings have taken place. Like much of the violence-ridden midpart of the book, the scene at Hester's misfires artistically; Archer has gone to Hester's simply to eavesdrop. But the good scene following this badly motivated one gives the novel the boost it needs. The news Archer overhears sends him to Lance's. Death, a reality in both chapters, hits much harder here than at Hester's. The level, easygoing syntax describing Lance's corpse, with Ross Macdonald's pawky editorial intrusion, "he wasn't going anywhere," transmits real shock. The suppression of stylistic heightening forces us to discover the corpse for ourselves:

> Lance himself was just inside the front door. He wore a plaid evening jacket and midnight blue trousers and dull-blue dancing-pumps, but he wasn't going anywhere. He lay on his back with his toes pointing at opposite corners of the ceiling. One asphalt eye looked into the light, unblinking. The other had been broken by a bullet.

That death comes to the highly sexed Lance through the eye prefigures both the Freudian symbolism and erotic motivation of the finale. Daniel R. Barnes has traced Ross Macdonald's eye symbolism to Oedipus: "Archer's eye imagery and blindness motifs thematically support . . . the Oedipal patterns which consciously informs so much of Macdonald's fiction."[5]

This sexual interpretation fits *Coast* perfectly. For Lance's next visitor after Archer is the womanish Carl Stern, Lance's ex-lover. Knocking in vain on the door, Stern then drives to Hester's Los Angeles apartment. The deathliness flooding the previous two chapters spills into Chapter 16. Hester receives Archer, who had followed Stern, in a white blouse; her hair, cropped close to the head, creates a skull-like look; the white leather suitcase gaping open on her bed has a black dress in it. Such sharp contrast isn't lifelike. Archer's first words, "Hello, Hester, I thought you were dead," enforce the macabre mood. Ironically, this thought has hit on the truth. The woman packing the suitcase isn't Hester at all, but her lookalike sister, Rina.

The menace and the mystery hold. The party at the exclusive Channel Club, where Archer goes next and where Gabrielle worked till her death, reels out a good deal of symbolism which hints at the violence lurking beneath. The scene is the author's most ambitious, to date. Characters discuss Freud; a Hollywood script-writer from Galena, Illinois, calls himself Oedipus; Simon Graff performs an alarming act of ritual purification and purgation: still shaken by the death of Gabrielle, his much-younger mistress, Graff pushes a young woman into the water at every pool-party given at the club. His aim? To re-enact Gabrielle's death and, by saving her stand-in, to restore her to life. Gabrielle also dominates the next scene, which takes place elsewhere at the club. Archer goes to the room of gateman Tony Torres, near the boilers which heat the pool and dining room. Though Tony openly mourns his eighteen-year-old daughter's death, a pulp-magazine account of the incident found in his belongings, "The Murder of the Violated Virgin," fends off sentimentality. Ross Macdonald's brilliant evocation of the clichés, the lurid imagery, and the manipulative syntax of pulp journalism makes the passage worth quoting:

> It was a balmy spring night at Malibu Beach, gay playground of the movie capital. But the warm tropical wind that whipped the waves shoreward seemed somehow threatening to Tony Torres. . . . He was not easily upset after many years in the squared circle, but tonight Tony was desperately worried about his gay young teen-aged daughter, Gabrielle.

Symbolism and irony continue to run strong. Though a head shot killed Gabrielle, the discovery of sperm in her body and of another bullet in her thigh, which "bled considerably," again yokes sex to death. The conjunction persists in Isobel Graff's accusation that her film-mogul husband was Hester Campbell's lover. Isobel makes more trouble in the next chapter. The effeminate Carl Stern hits her and then slams her to the ground amid charges that she killed his lover, Lance. Archer steps in and Stern, after trying to bite him, whips out a knife. But before he can cut Archer, he is stopped by a right-left combination to the jaw.

Stern never returns to the action alive. Dominating the final third of the book are Isobel Graff, chattering non-stop about her sad marriage, and mild, retiring Clarence Bassett. Ross Macdonald fills Bassett with drink to get this normally discreet man to reveal his secret heart. Bassett does ramble on about Isobel's long mental illness; then he explains to our surprise that he and Isobel had been lovers but that her father talked her into marrying Simon Graff, "a climber and a pusher and a whoremonger and a cheat." Archer leaves him in a stupor of self-pity. Another loser, the black junior college student and pool hand, Joseph Tobias, making Archer eggs and coffee, explains how he found Gabrielle the night she was killed. The muted inter-racial sex introduced into *Victim* with Anne Meyer and Tony Aquista comes back in the same minor key with Gabrielle and Tobias. Gabrielle never encouraged Tobias's love; though she told him about her sexual bouts with others, lacerating his heart, she wouldn't let him touch her. More relevant to the investigation is his announcement that, although she presumably died on the beach, an ear-ring matching one she was wearing turned up inside the Channel Club. This evidence, if confirmed, means that she was killed at the club and then carried to the beach. But why? Tobias, badly shaken, drives home, and Archer strolls the surf-front to collect his thoughts. The moment isn't one for contemplation, though. What first looks like a piece of driftwood turns out to be, on closer look, the corpse of Carl Stern.

The necessary calls are made, and Chapter 25 opens with a message from Archer's telephone answering service saying that George Wall is in a Las Vegas hospital with concussion. Taking its cue both from this injury and from the sharp head blow that killed Carl Stern, the novel shifts its reference point to the head; i.e., it grows increasingly psychological.

Hollywood-Ontario Shuttle

Visiting his client briefly, Archer then looks for Hester in several nearby inns and motels. His search ends in a rundown stucco cube, the Dewdrop Inn. A young woman answering Hester's description agrees to see him in her room when she learns that the same danger that cracked George Wall's head hangs over hers. But the girl in the upstairs room is Hester's lookalike sister, Rina. Summoned by Stern and Leonard, Rina flew to Las Vegas and checked into a hotel using Hester's name, presumably to spare Hester a jail term. Luckily, Archer found Rina before she left the inn to be taken back to Los Angeles. Shock waves run through her when she hears that Hester is probably dead and that the L. A. police wouldn't ask questions if Hester or somebody impersonating her disappeared in Las Vegas. A more pressing fear overtakes both Rina and Archer when Frost and two of his thugs barge into the room. But Archer fights them off and then makes Frost drive Rina and him to Hester.

The drive ends in grief. But not in meaninglessness: killed in L. A., Hester, like her good friend, Gabrielle, was taken from her death-site. Frost had flown her, brained to death by a poker, to a disused ammunition dump near Las Vegas, where he incinerated her. Sickly in any case, Frost, as his name implies, droops under the ovenlike heat and smell given off by the squat, windowless building. Desperately, he tells Archer that Isobel Graff killed Hester after finding her with Simon: again, a primitive emotion like sexual jealousy actuates a dazzling, convoluted plot. Archer's skill and experience smoothe the convolutions: Carl Stern had been blackmailing the Graffs because he had recovered the pistol Isobel killed Gabrielle with. Isobel's murderousness is then explained as an effect of her schizoid paranoia by Dr. Frey, who runs the sanitarium in Santa Monica where she had been treated. A trained psychiatric nurse, Rina can also speak with authority about Isobel. She helps Ross Macdonald explain Isobel's problem to the reader without resorting to a highly technical vocabulary; here is her novelistic definition of paranoia: "Paranoid people are . . . almost like radio receivers. They pick a tiny signal out of the air and build it up with their own power until they can't hear anything else."

The gathering fog and darkness of the late December day match Isobel's shrouded mind. At the sanitarium, Dr. Frey says that, after he signed voluntary commitment papers for Isobel that morning, she escaped. Archer suspects that somebody must have incited her to murder (as Una Durano did her mad brother Leo in *Grin*). His suspicions are well judged. The book ends where it began—at the Channel Club. Breaking into Graff's cabana, Archer heads straight for Isobel's dressing room, where he reconstructs Gabrielle's murder as Isobel would have committed it. The reconstruction works. Along the edge of one of the louvers runs a row of teeth-marks ringed by lipstick. The image, one of the book's best, catches the emotional stress of a woman seeing her husband deceive her:

Pain jerked through my mind like a knotted string. . . . It was pain for the woman who had stood on this bench in the dark, watching the outer room through the cracks between the louvers and biting down on the wood in agony.

Down on the beach, Archer finds Isobel squatting and shaking her fist at the thudding surf. She rails with good reason. The grief that wrecked her life came early. Like Mavis Kilbourne in *Pool*, another unhappy wife of a racketeer husband, Isobel recounts her past in a delirium. She confirms Clarence Bassett's story—also told semi-coherently—about her father's pressuring her into marrying Simon Graff. The action moves back quickly to the present. Graff comes down to the beach carrying the pistol that killed Gabrielle, which he claims to have just bought from Bassett for $100,000.

The tight last chapter gives Archer both a killer and a moral issue. Again, the incitement to kill is sexual. But rather than blaming Isobel for killing Gabrielle and Hester, Archer unloads the guilt on Bassett. This ageing, mother-fixated Eastern social brahmin first tricked Isobel into killing Hester; then he blackmailed her, manipulated other evidence, and hired Archer to accuse George Wall of killing Hester on the basis of the rigged evidence. Bassett also engineered Gabrielle's murder while protecting his innocence. But he didn't do a thorough job. Although Isobel shot the girl in the thigh, the bullet that lodged fatally in her heart was fired by Bassett. He accused Isobel of the murder in order to blackmail Graff. The book's finale releases other suppressed realities. Tony Torres, hearing that Bassett killed his daughter, comes in and shoots him dead. Keeping his head, Archer acts decisively and humanely. His placing Graff's revolver next to Bassett's outflung hand in order to win Tony a justifiable homicide plea also tones down the melodrama. For all its bloodshed, *Coast* ends on a restrained, positive note.

The characters have kept the action moving. Like Albert Graves and Una Durano, Bassett diverts suspicion from himself by bringing Archer into the case. Hester also has antecedents, most notably Anne Meyer of *Victim*. Like Anne, she never appears alive, having been killed before the action starts. Both young women die indirectly from coupling with a married man. Both are dishonest: whereas Anne blackmailed Don Kerrigan, her lover and employer, Hester steals the wallet of one of the Channel Club members. Her husband, George Wall, has no clear antecedents in the canon. His name has a directness, simplicity, and symbolism. "A natural-born trouble-maker, dangerous to himself and probably to other people," Wall keeps slamming into walls. He has a wife bent on divorcing him. The morning the book opens, he nearly gets shot by two people, Tony Torres and Bassett. He throws his weight around with ex-prize fighter, Lance Leonard. Several hours after Lance takes him out, he gets another beating, from the security guards at Helio-

Graff, which puts him in the hospital for a month.

These knocks don't come to Wall by chance. The unswerving love he extends Hester is so rare that people, Hester included, don't recognize it or know how to handle it. Wall is odd man out in a world ruled by greed and lust. His goodness even baffles Ross Macdonald. He clamors to interview witnesses with Archer. Though denied, he won't stay put. He makes his own inspection of Lance Leonard's property, and then he turns up at Helio-Graff studios despite doctor's orders to spend two days in bed as a result of Lance's beating. Wall gets in everybody's way, like John Galton and Ian Ferguson, two other exiled, somewhat innocent, Canadians from Ross Macdonald's middle period. To keep him from derailing the plot, Ross Macdonald has to send him to the hospital with concussion and fractures.

Archer is consistent with his earlier self. *Victim* had shown him at his best and worst. Moreover, his two alter-egos, Brand Church and Leonard Bozey, added to Ross Macdonald's understanding of him. This enrichment carries into *Coast,* where he acts wildly, even inconsistently, without violating plausibility. He mocks the garbled speech of drunken Clarence Bassett; but within a page, he helps Bassett into a chair and, when he slumps to the floor, turns his head sideways so he won't smother. After being called a sadist by Rina Campbell, Archer admits harboring "cruelty in my will to justice." This cruelty shows most clearly in Chapter 23. Black junior college student and Channel Club menial, Joseph Tobias cooks Archer a delicious breakfast on his own time and, digging deeply, explains his secret unrequited love for Gabrielle. Archer repays Tobias poorly, probing his secret pain for information of border-line value. Tobias finally tells him, "You stirred up a lot of things I want to forget. In fact, you've been giving me kind of a hard time." Chapter Eight adds another ugly twist. Here Archer punches Lance in the jaw after Lance offers his hand in good will. Ross Macdonald accepts Archer's cruelty, cowardice, and vindictiveness. As he said in his 1973 interview for the *Journal of Popular Culture,* he never planned Archer as a moral giant; when Archer acts badly, he doesn't hide or explain away his badness. Yet the badness isn't gratuitous. Archer doesn't see people at their best; they only call on him after they've been hurt, deprived, or threatened. He hears their problems and feels their grief. Working with desperate people can make him desperate, as it can any sensitive person who takes the problems of others to heart.

Coast abounds in desperation, its title and seafront setting both referring to the half-lives led by the characters. A border between land and sea, the beach conveys to Ross Macdonald, a man keenly sensitive to borders, the tension of living near the edge. That this half-life threatens survival shows in the book's rampant animal imagery: characters clutch inhumanly at whatever keeps them human. When asked to explain his presence at the Channel Club party, Archer answers, "Watching the animals." He has plenty to watch, both in and out of the club. Characters with animal names include Hester's ex-landlady, Mrs. Lamb; a Dr. Wolfson; a journalist named Sammy Swift, Rina Cam(pb)el(l), who drives a Jaguar in Chapter 8; Clarence Bassett, who shies "like a frightened horse" in Chapter 3 and reminds Archer of a camel in Chapter 22. In the dramatic last scene, Bassett says he killed Gabrielle (daughter of the once-named Fresno Gamecock) because, "I could never bear to see an animal hurt." Isobel, who also shot Gabrielle, accuses her husband (Graff-giraffe) of treating her "like a chattel-beast."

The pain and the beastliness infect all. Gabrielle was killed on 21 March, the first day of spring; her murder overturning the promise normally connected with youth and the onset of spring. Like her, Hester and Lance, who appeared with her in a photograph diving from a tower in Chapter 2, also get killed; brightness and beauty keep falling from the air. Rina Campbell, also bright and beautiful, only escapes early death because Archer saves her. Joseph Tobias's low-paying job and love for a dead girl's memory creates a wasting-away Archer can't stop. Tallying with this picture of blasted youth and seasonal blight is the novel's time-setting. Though the action takes place 27-28 December, nobody mentions Christmas; nobody wishes anybody else a happy New Year.

But why should they? Little in life seems worth celebrating or saving. As the graceful young divers in the photograph prove, nothing lasts. Archer's dream, in Chapter 24, of a hermit who lives "in a landscape of crumbling stones," defines the condition. Images of fog, damp, and chill pack the end of the book, matching Isobel's mental disorder. The symbolic source of life, the sea, exudes corruption. Carl Stern's corpse is found floating in it. In Chapter 31, Isobel, speaking, perhaps, as the madwoman who has the truth, addresses the "muttering" ocean as "Dirty old cesspool." As usual, sex helps spread the taint. *Coast* contains many kinds of sexuality: the overage marriage of the Graffs, the onage one of the Walls, the patient, sentimental tie of Isobel and Bassett, Graff's adulterous tie with both Hester and Gabrielle, the incest joining Gabrielle and her cousin Lance, and the homosexuality of Lance and Carl Stern. All of these run to grief. The grief acquires vividness from Ross Macdonald's precise, bevelled prose. Few writers today can impart depth, clarity, and judgment through style. To speak of hair "splashing out like fire" or "pouring like black oil" is to reorder reality in the way of Baudelaire or Emily Dickinson. It also deepens the novel's pessimism. The magic of style is limited; though synesthesia can transform physical substances, it can't ease strife, dignify motives, or lend sparkle to the bleakness rolling in with the gray, wintry sea.

Rich in character, setting, and style, *Coast* is a strong book. But its strength lacks coordination. Ross Macdonald's marvelous material suffers from vagueness and lack of dramatic follow-through. Notably weak is dramatic selection. We don't move close enough to the characters to imagine ourselves capable of their crimes. Instead of finding pieces of ourselves in the book, we examine the motives of strangers. Isobel doesn't act out her neuroses before our eyes; nor does Ross Macdonald put her before us long enough for us to ponder her behavior. Instead, we must rely on the clinical diagnosis of her psychiatrist. Bassett, her would-be lover, also leads a shadow-life. A killer and a blackmailer he is. But what leads him to crime? Archer taunts him about his age, and Dr. Frey explains him psychologically. But is his crime that of the finicky, ageing bachelor? the Ivy Leaguer? the man with a mother-fixation? *Coast* is a driving good novel. Had Ross Macdonald sharpened its motivation, he could have supplied the conviction to make it a memorable one.

II

The Doomsters (1958) breaks more artistic ground than its predecessor, both in technique and subject-matter. In 1964, Ross Macdonald spoke of *Doomsters* as a pioneering work: "This novel marked a fairly clean break with the Chandler tradition, which it had taken me some years to digest, and freed me to make my own approach to the crimes and sorrows of life."[6] The book brings back some structural props used in other works of the 1950s. Like *Victim,* it opens with Archer helping a needy stranger; it takes place in a small town whose leading law enforcer is corrupt; it includes in its cast a young hoodlum who recalls Archer's own hoodlum past. As unsolved murder casts long shadows on recent events; but whereas *Morgue* and *Coast* only sprouted one corpse apiece, two murder cases reopen in *Doomsters.* Psychiatric nurse Rina Campbell of *Coast* returns with sharper thematic contours as Rose Parish, a psychiatric social worker. No lookalike sister dragooned to save a plot, Rose comes in early, alerting us with her professional insights that *Doomsters* is a psychological novel, and re-enters the action often, never pretending to be someone else. Dramatic as well as choric, she also loves the novel's runaway protagonist.

The runaway launches the action: "A very large young man in dungarees," mudstained and unshaven, knocks at Archer's door at daybreak. Carl Hallman has been running all night, since escaping from the State Mental Hospital. All Carl's troubles, it comes out piecemeal, stem from his family. First, he blames himself for the supposed suicide of his mother three years before: "He saw her death as a direct result of his disloyalty to her, what he thought of as disloyalty," summarizes Rose Parish: "He felt as though his efforts to cut the umbilical cord had actually killed her." Then, because he quarreled with his father, a state

Senator and rich rancher, the same night his father drowned in the bathtub, Carl blames the drowning on himself. But his problems don't stop with his parent-killing fantasies. His older brother Jerry, a non-practicing lawyer, who helped commit Carl to the sanitarium, controls his share of the family estate so long as he stays a mental patient. And though Carl doesn't know it, his wife Mildred is being assaulted with sexual overtures from a local sheriff, forty years her senior.

Archer cooks his haggard visitor a breakfast of eggs, toast, and coffee while learning of his guilty past. Good listener as well as kindly host, he assures Carl that he takes him seriously. Carl's boyish candor recalls George Wall of *Coast,* who, at twenty-four, is Carl's age. This candor steps up the action. Agitated by digging so deeply into his troubles, Carl knocks Archer out and steals his car when the detective tries to drive him back to the hospital. The runaway is on the run again.

To do anything, Archer first needs his car. This task sends him to the hospital, where, though finding no stolen car, he seizes upon a name from the past. Time is a closed circuit, often generating guilt or shame, in *Doomsters.* Heroin addict Tom Rica had broken out of the hospital with Carl Hallman and, before going his own way, sent Carl to Archer for help. Why does Tom recommend Archer? Archer had gotten him early parole about ten years ago, after a conviction for car-theft jailed Tom. Then Archer looked after Tom, counseling him and teaching him how to box and shoot. For these troubles, Tom idolized him before dropping out of sight. Archer goes to Rose Parish to find out about these missing years and also about Carl Hallman's recent past. "Tall and generously made," Rose recounts more than clinical history. She calls Carl "a sweet person," and, when Archer challenges her judgment, protests hotly. Her outcry and stormy looks, coming in her first interview with Archer, help establish the novel as psychological, as has been said. Rose, her chief, Dr. Brockley, and the mental hospital where Chapters 4 and 5 take place all invite us to turn our responses inward. Rather than smuggling the psychology in at the end, as in *Coast,* Ross Macdonald irrigates *Doomsters* with it from the outset. The chapter ends with Archer, who knows how emotions work, making an insight applicable to both Rose and Carl: "Carl Hallman was a handsome boy, and a handsome boy in trouble was a double threat to women, a triple threat if he needed mothering."

Archer's next stop is the imaginary town of Purissima, California, where Carl's wife, Mildred, is living with her mother in a rundown neighborhood. The wino mother, Mrs. Gley, receives Archer amid threadbare carpeting, stained, fading wallpaper, and furniture splitting and sagging with age. Mildred, "young and small, with a fine small head" that brightens this domestic squalor, tells him that Carl has been spotted walking around his family's citrus ranch, carrying a weapon. She and Archer go to intercept him before anybody gets hurt. But they're stopped near the gates of the ranch by the local sheriff—smirking, boar-eyed Duane Ostervelt. The sheriff's snide references to Archer as "boyfriend" anger the detective, and he drives away defying Ostervelt's wish to take Mildred to the ranchhouse himself.

At the ranchhouse, Archer meets Carl's beautiful sister-in-law, Zinnie, and her little daughter, Martha. Then another new character moves to center stage. Pulling into the driveway soon after Archer's arrival with Mildred is the silver-gray Jaguar of svelte, gray-clad Charles Grantland, M.D. It is obvious from the start that he and Zinnie are lovers. Zinnie's husband, Jerry, already dumpy, defeated, and middle-aged at thirty-five, enters the action just out of view of the embracing lovers. Jerry, we remember, helped get his brother Carl committed in order to gain control of the family estate. This act makes us distrust him even before meeting him. Yet our hard impression softens as soon as he steps into the book. Her lipstick smudged, Zinnie tells him that Carl wants to kill him and, driving the prod still deeper, that she set down his staying away from the ranch to cowardice. Ross Macdonald's reason for setting Zinnie so cruelly on Jerry, thus making him the underdog we automatically side with, soon emerges: no detective writer wants a corpse his readers don't care about. After snapping his garden shears at Dr. Grantland, calling him a "cod," and ordering him to leave Zinnie alone, Jerry turns up dead, "a defunct teddy bear." Carl, who had come out of hiding briefly to be with Mildred, becomes the chief suspect.

The next chapter introduces the Hallmans' Japanese groundsman, Sam Yogan, Ross Macdonald's first (and, given the high Oriental population of California, long-overdue) characterization of an Oriental. Yogan's quiet self-possession contrasts well with the manic bustle of the others: the racist, proto-fascist Sheriff Ostervelt begins his questioning of Yogan thus: "Come here. . . . I ought to kick those big white teeth down your yellow throat, but I'm not gonna." Yogan identifies the small pearl-handled revolver found near Jerry's body as belonging to Alicia Hallman, the Senator's wife. The interest shifts from the dead to the living and also from the details of detection to motives and meanings. In a taut, well-paced interview, Archer tricks Zinnie into confessing her affaire with Dr. Grantland. That Zinnie is crudely sketched, though, drains much of the interview's force. Her transparent lies and her attempt to win Archer with her "never-say-die eroticism" call into question her attraction for Grantland. What can Zinnie offer an educated, accomplished man like Grantland besides sex and money? Why should a doctor in middle life with an established practice risk scandal with a member of the town's leading family?

Ross Macdonald knows the dramatic value of making the reader curious and then making him wait before slaking his curiosity. Thus he returns to matters of crime and detection in order to sharpen the issues. Who killed Jerry Hallman? Mildred, Zinnie, Carl, and Dr. Grantland all had a motive and an opportunity. Carl remains the leading suspect; no case can be made against anyone else till he explains himself. Archer places more importance on his explanation than do most of the others. Resisting the tide of opinion building against him, he presumes him innocent till proved guilty. He assures Mildred, marshaling his solid, middlebrow faith in justice, that he plans to go on working for Carl. Carl needs this help more than he suspects. Mildred tells Archer that, six months before, Ostervelt had agreed to shut off his investigation of Senator Hallman's drowning if Mildred slept with him. Archer feels the blasts of this sexual fever himself. "A sudden hot dream" that Carl's death would free Mildred for another man ignites him briefly before drenching him with guilt.

Guilt floods other lives as well. A deputy coroner explains that Alicia Hallman had tried to shoot herself in Dr. Grantland's office a week before she died and that Grantland could have prevented the death by referring her to a psychologist. Incriminating evidence against him mounts. No autopsy was done on either of the elder Hallmans after he pronounced them dead. The deputy coroner's recitation stops when Ostervelt troops in, his jaws working and his little eyes "dirty with dismay." Archer soon feels the sting of this consternation. When he parries Ostervelt's threats, he is pistol-whipped unconscious. Waking up to find his face contused and his ear torn, he drives to the avocado ranch of his friend, Glenn Scott. Scott, the police officer, now retired, who investigated Alicia Hallman's death by drowning, produces the sort of information Archer usually gets from Peter Colton while working in Los Angeles. Echoing *Coast*, *Doomsters* displays Archer's now-famous practice of solving a fresh case by reopening a related one from the past. Scott tells Archer that Alicia tried to shoot herself because Grantland had refused to step up her dosage of barbiturates; he adds that her son Carl, a victim of "apronstring trouble," was suspected of drowning her to free himself.

This suspicion bears investigation. The middle chapter of the book, Chapter 18, takes Archer to Grantland's clinic, ostensibly to get his torn ear mended. Besides dressing the ear, Grantland gives evidence that restores Carl Hallman as the Most Likely Suspect. He says that Carl came to the clinic several hours ago and stole the pearl-handled revolver that killed Jerry and that Alicia had taken to herself three years before. The chase motif invests this disclosure with suspense. Archer waits for Grantland to leave his surgery and then follows his Jaguar two miles out of town; here, Grantland has a hurried meeting with Tom Rica, ex-high-school athlete and reformed car thief gone to ruin on hard drugs. Still harboring a fatherly protectiveness toward Tom and anxious to know

Tom's place in the Hallmans' lives, Archer trails him to a hotel.

In the meantime, the manhunt for Carl has stepped up. Though the evidence against him makes us distrust Carl on rational grounds, our natural prejudice for underdogs—especially when tired, hungry, and badgered—makes us side with him emotionally. We also admire Archer's ability to resist the mob psychology bred by the manhunt. Carl's only chance lies with Archer. The need to find Carl before the local vigilantes, who have been talking about lynching and shooting on sight, sends Archer to the cottage of Mrs. Hutchinson. Formerly the nurse of Alicia and now the all-purpose babysitter-nanny of Zinnie's small daughter, Martha, Mrs. Hutchinson has looked after three generations of Hallmans. Thus her mention of a "bad-luck house" and a "family curse" overhanging the Hallmans carries the weight of long personal experience. Like the psychology introduced in Chapter 5, Mrs. Hutchinson's touching-in of important background data here in Chapter 26 strengthens the book's intellectual fiber. Build and drive also come from Ross Macdonald's ability to swing smoothly between present time and past time and between talk and action. A posse of seventy riflemen have started beating the creekbeds, culverts, and woods of Purissima's back country in hopes of ferreting Carl out. Now since Archer usually plays the hunter rather than the hunted, Ross Macdonald rarely recounts the psychology of pursuit or of entrapment as do John Buchan in *The Thirty-Nine Steps* (1915) or Geoffrey Household in *Rogue Male* (1939). But with all of Purissima ready to convict Carl of homicide, he does show some of the hysteria of his pursuers. The manhunt, quickly degenerating into a bloodchase, brings out the worst in everybody. Ostervelt, the rural demagogue, cries out for swift, simple Old Testament justice. Hearing this battle cry, witnesses who have seen Carl recently, however casually, describe him as a monster. His stalkers, fanning over the Hallman acreage in futile pursuit, give vent to aggressions they normally suppress as their frustration rises.

Almost three-quarters done, the novel, in Chapter 28, needs a spurt of energy to provide home-stretch momentum. Jerry Hallman was found dead in Chapter 11; his parents both died mysteriously before the book began; Carl, his brother, suspected of having a guilty hand in all three deaths, has been out of view since Chapter 4. But he has also stirred such a frenzy in Purissima that Ross Macdonald has no reason to bring him out of hiding. Instead, he turns ironically to his hunters. For all its zeal and firepower, the posse of seventy can't stop the killing of Zinnie Hallman, who appears stabbed to death in her red station wagon. Archer re-enters Mrs. Hutchinson's cottage, outside of which he had found Zinnie. Mrs. Hutchinson, perhaps Ross Macdonald's only sympathetic quoter of Scripture, tells how Jerry married Zinnie after picking her up in an L. A. nightclub and how Zinnie asked her, about three months ago, to testify against him in divorce court. Ironically, Zinnie, a victim of verbal attack, lies stretched out dead less than ten yards from her attacker's door. Wanting more information, Archer sees no reason to enlighten Mrs. Hutchinson. When he turns the talk to Charles Grantland, she says she saw Grantland take Alicia's pistol to the Hallman ranch the same morning. If she's speaking the truth, then Carl didn't steal the pistol from Grantland's clinic, as Grantland claimed. Nor did he kill his mother; according to Mrs. Hutchinson, he was out of town the night she drowned. These revelations give the assembled evidence new meanings. Having possibly explained an earlier death, Archer applies his findings to a recent one.

The action takes a strange spin when he finds his ex-protege' Tom Rica trembling on his hands and knees outside Grantland's clinic. Rica's intrusion into the plot adds spontaneity and surprise without slackening the plot. Whatever brief distraction he causes is erased by his words. Rica has been getting heroin from Grantland in exchange for keeping quiet about Grantland's murder of Alicia, which he saw take place. These words send Archer to Grantland's new home. Seeing the doctor rubbing bloodstains out of his carpet with a gasoline-soaked cloth, Archer tells him, "The big dream is over now." Grantland does admit that Zinnie had visited him a few hours ago but adds that he left her to treat an emergency patient and then found her blood all over his bedroom when he came back home. Archer only believes part of the story. He identifies Grantland's emergency patient as Tom Rica and then accuses Grantland of giving Rica a fatal overdose of heroin. Self-protection, Archer's accusations runs, also led Grantland to stuff Zinnie's corpse into her station wagon and then drive the wagon to a street where Carl Hallman had been recently spotted.

Now Archer's unravelling of the evidence and his confronting the felon with his felony five chapters from the end looks premature. But the well-planned structure of *Doomsters* assures a rich forward flow. Plenty of action follows the naming and cornering of the culprit. First, Grantland starts to carry out Archer's order to telephone the police. But, somewhat implausibly, since Archer is armed, ten to fifteen years younger, and in better physical shape, Grantland smashes him with the telephone base. Then, helped by the gasoline he had been cleaning the bloodstains with, he starts a fire and drives away, leaving Archer to burn. The fire leaps through Grantland's house, snapping at Archer's legs "like a rabid fox." Ross Macdonald's ability to create the leap, surge, and flapping destructive power of fire shows such high inspiration that his decision to build a novel, *Underground Man,* around a fire thirteen years later can surprise nobody.

Archer escapes the blossoming, zig-zag flames in time to follow Grantland's car to an unexpected destination—the seedy cottage of

Mildred Hallman's alcoholic mother. He arrives too late to stop Grantland from shooting Carl twice in the chest, but does protect Mildred from gunfire. Bullets continue to stitch the air. Attempting escape, Grantland is shot to death by Sheriff Ostervelt, who then sends for an ambulance to rush Carl to the hospital. But Ostervelt's motives aren't entirely humane. Standing in the shadows. Archer sees him kissing Mildred, stroking her "from breast to thigh," and, despite a forty-year age difference, asking her to live with him.

The rest of the chapter and the two subsequent ones comprise the longest murder confession in Ross Macdonald. Mildred, the Least Likely Suspect, admits killing her four in-laws—Alicia and Senator Hallman and then Jerry and Zinnie. Showering her with great moral charity, Archer treats her less as a killer than as "a human being with more grief on her young mind than it was able to bear." "Nobody ever knew me," muses Mildred, citing money as "one of the dreams" that turned her to murder. But motives more primitive than money drove her knife into Alicia. Disapproving of Mildred, pregnant by but not yet married to her son Carl, and fearing her family's "ancestral curse," Alicia had talked her into having an abortion. But as soon as she came out of the anesthesia, Mildred stabbed Alicia fatally. Grantland, the abortionist, agreed conditionally to keep the murder a secret. His conditions? Mildred had to give him sex and then marry Carl in order to slip him, Grantland, some of the family fortune.

These closing chapters do a great deal. Besides naming the killer, tracing the network of guilt, and probing Mildred's psyche, they also declare Carl the book's hero. Carl has combined precept and action; Christian existentialism first convinced him of life's goodness and then led him to study for a medical missionary. But going with this high-mindedness was the instability that made him quarrel with his father and then put him in a sanitarium. The climax of *Doomsters* is verbal rather than dramatic: the unhoarding of such thematic riches through movement and action would have extended the novel to twice its present length. Ross Macdonald makes this economy work. The finale dispels some of the gloom cast up by the misunderstanding and bloodshed. Carl, still anesthetized, stands a fair chance of recovering from his bullet wounds; Tom Rica will live, although with such heavy odds against him that his doctors may not have "done him any great favor." The situation of Rose Parish is also one of grudging half-victory. Duty requires her to try to rehabilitate Mildred so she can go back to Carl; yet Rose's own love for Carl runs so strong that she'd gladly wait ten years for him. Her heart works against her reason. But reason and resolve bring little comfort. She must use all her skill and experience to divide herself from Carl's love, the thing she wants most.

No moral uplift crowns the ending, either. Abiding by the dark motives and deeds coloring the action, Ross Macdonald dims the few shreds of light that gleam over the Hallman family drama. Snapping, snarling Tom Rica mocks the trouble Archer took with him ten years before, both in his wasted body and his cynicism ("Only suckers work. And . . . Tom Rica is no sucker"). Archer isn't allowed to forget his failures. Another setback, his broken marriage, confronts him in the closing pages. His last reconciliation with his former wife, Sue, having failed, he braces himself for another of time's cruel jests (Thomas Hardy, who supplies the novel's title, presides over the action), like the setting of Sue in his path again.

The false gleams of hope stippling the novel's surface recall Ross Macdonald's 1964 critique of the first good private-eye novel, Hammett's *Maltese Falcon* (1930):

> *The Maltese Falcon* is a fable of modern man in quest of love and money, despairing of everything else. Its murders are more or less incidental, though they help to give it its quality of a crisis novel. Its characters act out of the extreme emotions of fear and guilt and concupiscence, anger and revenge; and with such fidelity to these passions that their natures almost seem co-terminous with them.[7]

Though also clawed by crisis, Ross Macdonald's people sound greater moral depths than those of Hammett's novel. Tempering the shrillness of their hopes, first of all, are the Doomsters of Hardy's poem, "To an Unborn Pauper Child," that supply the book's title. Inexorably, the Doomsters maintain their hold on the woeful Hallmans. But they grip others, too. Archer feels the pressure of their irony in the closing pages. Rose Parish's having to work against her most cherished hopes also has the grimness of a Hardy joke. As in Hardy, the joke is too serious and comprehensive to make anyone laugh. Invoking universality, Adam, Cain, and Abel are all mentioned in Chapter 18, the midpart of the book. The Oedipus myth adds *its* usual dread and inevitability: Carl looks blind when shot by Grantland, his cuckold, in Chapter 32; after Ostervelt's sexual arrogance in the next chapter, Mildred looks like "a blind person in a ruined house." These references to Oedipus invoke Barnes's remark about eyes: "In no way do his [Archer's] subjects reveal . . . their duplicity, or their innocence, their fears and anxieties, more than by their eyes."[8] Eyes both mirror and express reality. The eyes of Mildred and Carl also show how a good novel like *Doomsters* can bounce symbolism and realism, data derived and firsthand, off each other to create a believable picture of life.

Believable but also stark and severe: except for a few lashings of red, Ross Macdonald's obsessive color, most of *Doomsters* takes place in a black and white glare. Though the characters have both psychic and historical depth, they move like sheet tin figures against contrasting backgrounds. Charles Grantland claims to be "bled white" by Tom Rica's demands for heroin, which incidentally, is colored white. Rica's eyes, though, are "puddles of tar," and his arms are peppered with black marks from the hypodermic. Grantland's lover, Zinnie, is wearing a white nylon robe when she finds Jerry dead under the "white painted glass roof" of a greenhouse in Chapter 12. Jerry's mother, Alicia, says Mrs. Hutchinson, was a "black devil" at times, and blackmail haunts the action: Tom Rica blackmails Grantland for drugs, and both Grantland and Ostervelt practice sexual blackmail on Mildred. Sometimes, Ross Macdonald mixes his colors ironically. For instance, Jerry dies in a greenhouse, a place of fertility and growth. His brother Carl, his name darkened by rumors, hides in darkness most of the way to avoid being arrested and possibly lynched. Yet Carl's convictions, as described by Mildred, have clothed him in radiance all along; Ross Macdonald, it must be said, doesn't buy Carl's vision outright. Though important, it is only a part of the author's vision. Ross Macdonald subsumes it in the same way he subsumes Archer's morality:

Carl said he looked up at the Sierra, and saw an unearthly light behind it in the west toward Purissima. It streamed, like milk, from the heavens, and it made him realize that life was a precious gift which had to be justified. . . . He decided then and there to study medicine and devote his life to healing.

That the suspected killer never harmed anyone certifies the book's moral maturity. *Doomsters* avoids absolutes; irony and ambivalence keep its ideas from flattening into direct statement. Zinnie, who has her own burdens, comforts Mildred and advises her to rest after the conflation of Carl's escape and Jerry's murder within one day wipe her out emotionally. Ostervelt's lecherous designs on Mildred show brilliantly in his symbolic first words to her: "Why hello, Mrs. Hallman, I didn't see you at first. I must be going blind in my old age." The Oedipal foreshadowing justifies itself in Ostervelt's asking Mildred to live with him the very day Carl goes to the sanitarium, in his having already bedded her before the book opens, and in the zeal with which he organizes the vigilante force of seventy rifles to find and, if needs be, kill Carl. Ostie is Ross Macdonald's wickedest character. Yet, as has been said, he radios for an ambulance to rush Carl to a hospital, and he voices his regret over killing Grantland, in the same chapter, with quiet dignity: "I . . . don't like to kill a man. It's too damn easy to wipe one out and too damn hard to grow one." Coming from Ostie, the declaration moves us less than it might. Our reaction, like that of Archer, is mixed: "I liked the sheriff better for saying that, though I didn't let it run away with me." Dr. Grantland also repels and attracts. A healer, he dispenses death by giving Tom Rica heroin and Carl Hallman, first, his mother's pistol and, then, two bullets in the chest. Grantland has several forebears in the canon, like Albert Graves of *Target* and Dr. Samuel Benning of *Grin*. He is the good man—

self-made, serious, and humanitarian—who goes bad and, in his ruin, drags others down with him. Mrs. Hutchinson speaks admiringly of his early hard work and dedication:

I remember him when he first moved to town, an up-and-coming young doctor. There was nothing he wouldn't do for his patients. He told me once it was the great dream of his life to be a doctor. His family lost their money in the depression, and he put himself through medical college by working in a garage. . . . When his patients couldn't pay him he went right on caring for them. That was before he got his big ideas.

This dedication persists in his weakness as well as in his strength. When Archer catches him, literally red-handed, rubbing Zinnie's blood from his carpet, he feels "a flicker of sympathy" he must repress.

As well he might, considering the shakiness of his moral credentials. *Doomsters* takes a more jaundiced look at Archer than any earlier book. Its judgments are usually covert, impromptu, and on-the-wing. Thus Archer calls Grantland "brother" while accusing him of terrible crimes in Chapter 30. And he lusts after Mildred as hotly as either Grantland or Ostie. En route to the Hallman ranch in Chapter 8, she momentarily looks like a young girl; this visual trick excites the middle-aged Archer so much he has to remind himself that she's married. His principles do bend, though. In Chapter 32, seeing Ostie stroke Mildred lasciviously, he doesn't interrupt, admitting, "he was doing what I had wanted to be doing." His attraction to her goes beyond sex. He and Mildred communicate well; while not pardoning her, he showers more moral charity on her than on any other killer since teen-aged Cathy Slocum in *Pool;* her long confession of guilt, extending over two chapters, ends with her and Archer crying in each other's arms. But why does he react so livingly to this killer of four? Archer mentions a universal network of guilt that rules out facile moral distinctions: "Mildred was as guilty as a girl could be, but she wasn't the only one. An alternating current of guilt ran between her and all of us involved with her. Grantland and Rica, Ostervelt and me." Yet behind this stated, or avowed, morality lie Archer's covert feelings. Grantland and Ostervelt, though less guilty than Mildred, receive less of Archer's compassion. A victim of sexual blackmail, Mildred is forced by the punishing father-figures Archer hates. The killer and the private detective have an ongoing quarrel with authority. But by killing her powerful parents-in-law, Mildred does in fact what the anti-institutional Archer only dreams of doing. Given the psychological context, he can only admire her.

Wish-projection also joins Archer to her husband, Carl. He sees Carl, hounded, misunderstood, and symbolically crucified by vested authority, as his double. Having married Mildred, Carl has also done something in fact that Archer can only fantasize doing. No client could have a trustier retainer. The muted pre-dawn half-glow of their first meeting

Hollywood-Ontario Shuttle

blurs differences between the two men, who chat amiably enough over breakfast. This amiability foreshadows the fusion of their outlook and interests. The only two people who have had sex with Mildred, besides Carl, are the much-older authority-figures, Ostervelt and Grantland, both of whom want to kill Carl and his champion, Archer. That Carl, a younger brother and the son of rich, dominating parents, also wins the love of the two best women in the book, Mildred and Rose, tightens the symbolic tie between client and detective. Once Mildred is remanded, Archer talks as naturally with Rose as he did with Mildred in the previous two chapters. But both women remain out of his reach for the same reason; they love Carl. Archer's failure to bring his dream to life comes home in his having to confront his two worst failures of the past decade, Tom Rica and Sue, at the end.

Related to this situational psychology is the creed of moral interdependence voiced both by Archer ("we're members of each other") and, more fully, Rose:

Since I've been doing hospital work, I've pretty well got over thinking in terms of good and bad. Those categories often do more harm than—well, good. We use them to torment ourselves, and hate ourselves because we can't live up to them. Before we know it, we're turning our hatred against other people, especially the unlucky ones, the weak ones who can't fight back. . . . And Christian love and virtue go down the drain.

This rare attempt at Wisdom Literature fails because it ignores the book's moral theme. Rose is saying what Ross Macdonald thinks should be said rather than amplifying what he has already described. The gap between what he believes and what he claims to believe can produce unrealistic dialogue. In particular, he allows Mildred to speak like a novelist writes, as these scraps of her talk from Chapters 8 and 34 show:

A building can soak up emotions, you know, so that after a while it has the same emotions as the people who live in it. They're in the cracks in the walls, the smoke-stains on the ceiling, the smells in the kitchen.

*   *   *

That's all there was, the outside. There wasn't any inside, at least for me. It was like a ritual which I made up as I went along. Every step I took had a meaning at the time, but I can't remember any of the meanings now.

But why does Mildred, and nobody else, talk with such poise and polish? No longer Ross Macdonald's stand-in, Archer acts and talks independently; he has his own will and his own way of exercising it. His sexual and anti-authoritarian identification with the killer, Mildred, also narrows the rhetorical distance dividing *them*. Though the style is the man, it can also encroach on the woman when the magnetism between her and the man who loves her pulls hard enough.

Mildred fools both Archer and Ross Macdonald when she says that she killed for money. She is speaking for the plot, not for herself. Money is usually a poor motive for murder in the canon. It works badly in *Doomsters,* not only with Mildred but also with Charles Grantland. Archer accuses Grantland of engineering the deaths of the Hallmans in order to get their five-million-dollar estate for himself. He is wrong, misreading Grantland's needs as badly as he did Albert Graves's in *Target.* Grantland isn't "living modestly on the profits from pills," as Archer claims. He drives a new Jaguar, owns a new, fully carpeted home in a good residential neighborhood, and sports an elegant wardrobe. These, he maintains with a thriving practice. If Tom Rica has been bleeding him white, why didn't he retaliate before now? And how could he buy so many expensive things with such short funds?

Elsewhere, the motivation rings true. Ross Macdonald introduces a surprise when he describes a verbal sparring match between Mildred and Rose in Chapter 25. Though he usually avoids this kind of social comedy, the dialogue between the threatened wife and her would-be love rival has the snapping bitchiness of conversation from Ivy Compton-Burnett:

"I'm so glad to see you, Miss Parish. Forgive me for keeping you waiting. I know how precious your time must be, with all your nursing duties."

"I'm not a nurse." Miss Parish was upset.

"Let me get you something to eat."

"Oh, no."

"Why not?" Mildred stared frankly at the other woman's body. "Are you dieting?"

"No. Perhaps I ought to." Large and outwitted and rebuffed, Miss Parish sank into a chair.

Dialogue like this reveals Ross Macdonald expanding his artistry. The crimes and sorrows of life hit hard in this farewell to hard-boiled writing. But, thanks to his integrity they don't overwhelm. The form of *Doomsters* gives meaning to the violence the action records. Without having first tested his new rhetorical skills, Ross Macdonald couldn't have written *The Galton Case.*

III

The writer was right to view *The Galton Case* (1959) as both "a turning point" and a personal favorite among his books. Though he had already written about exile and semi-recovery, two of the crucial problems of his own American-Canadian life,[9] he hadn't given them the power that pulsates through *Galton.* The novel, the only one Ross Macdonald has singled out, in "Writing *The Galton Case,*" for critical discussion, sustains a higher level of inspiration than any previous work from his pen. Though well planned, it doesn't look preconceived, alternating smoothly between California and the northern Midwest, rich and poor characters, simplicity and complexity: a mystery swathing three generations and two thousand miles resolves itself in a tatty boardinghouse in rural Ontario. As in *Doomsters,* Ross Macdonald uses more than one stand-in; besides Archer, there are John Galton and, more subtly, Tommy Lemberg. This elaborate dialectic, no technical self-indulgence, imparts truths too sheer for straight-forward presentation. If not an attack on reason, *Galton* has little faith in intellectual systems. Characters with formalized plans for the future meet bad ends; recurring blunders by Archer and the police break with the assumptions of the Sherlockian tradition; also humanizing the cosmopolitan scope of the book is the primitivism underlying it: people want families they can call their own.

The craving to belong is an issue from the outset. Archer gets more than he bargained for when his old friend, lawyer Gordon Sable, whom he hasn't seen for four years, calls him to Santa Teresa. First, Sable has been married for two years to Alice, "a pretty blond woman about half his age," whose morning drinking and petulance ("You don't love me at all. . . . You don't care a thing about me") speak badly for the marriage. Next, Sable's houseman, Peter Culligan, "his face . . . seamed with the marks of the trouble-prone," treats Sable with joking arrogance. The importance of Sable's domestic problems, borne out later, shows in Archer's first driving to Sable's office, the normal place for business talk, before he finds his old friend at home. The planned and the acci-dental mix well in this opening chapter. Sable tells Archer that Maria Galton, a rich local widow, wants to find a son who disappeared some twenty-three years before. Poet and social crusader gone wrong, roughly like Charles Singleton of *Grin,* Anthony Galton walked away from both family and university (he was a year away from an engineering degree at Stanford) after impregnating a working-class girl of eighteen or so. The widow's reason for wanting Tony found? To square accounts with the past and to heal old wounds. As with the mother, Mrs. Osoborne, in Margaret Millar's *Beyond This Point Are Monsters* (1970), who also denies her son is dead, reunion with the prodigal, another only child, will wipe out years of misunderstanding, indifference, and cruelty. *Galton* not only delves into the past more doggedly than any earlier Archer, seat-ing its central mystery twenty-three years before the time of the action; it also tells us, in Chapter 1, of the importance of Tony Galton's dis-appearance. By contrast, Alicia Hallman died only three years before the time of *Doomsters;* and not until the novel's halfway point do we learn that her death bears on the crime at hand. Ross Macdonald's later novels will follow the historical scheme blocked out in *Galton.*

Besides giving its clues an historical thrust, the first chapter mingles past and present. Time doesn't die in *Galton* any more than in *Doomsters.*

Maria Galton's wish for her son entails resurrecting the past; the Sables' home, "so new it hardly existed," has sprung up in the "old settled city" of Santa Teresa; Sable's white wavy hair gives "an illusion of youth." Then the second chapter introduces a physician, balancing lawyer Sable, who entered in Chapter 1. Sable takes Archer to Maria, who has just been examined by Dr. August Howell, "a big man in his fifties, who carried himself with unconscious authority." Howell tells Archer that Maria's hope of reclaiming her runaway son has become obsessive. To avoid upsetting her, he also advises Archer to "go through the motions but don't do any real investigating." Chapter Three takes Archer into her half-lit, heavily draped sitting room. As Howell had said, the blood-tie with her son rules Maria; amends must be made to it. Before she dies, she wants to forgive the son who left her to live in a San Francisco slum with his pregnant bride. But she will never forgive him. Tony stole several thousand dollars before disappearing with Theodora, or Teddy, in October 1936. His mother's disclaimer, "His real interest was dirt for dirt's own sake," squares with Howell's sour judgment, "what he was really good at was boozing and fornicating." Yet this grab-and-run rake has shaken several lives in Santa Teresa.

Despite his skepticism ("I think it's a waste of time and money"), Archer agrees to look for Tony. A 1936 poem, "Luna," which Tony published pseudononymously as John Brown provides the first slim lead. What looks like a routine exercise soon hurls Archer into the eye of danger. Murder flares out, presumably to the side of the main plot when Gordon Sable reports finding his houseman, Peter Culligan, stabbed to death. The action continues to branch out. On his way to investigate the death, Archer has his car stolen by an armed hitchhiker, "a thick young man with shoulders like a bull." Then he is arrested in connection with Culligan's death. *Galton* controls its emotional rhythm well. Having twice threatened Archer with danger, it now restores him to his investigative role. Back at Sable's, he notices a tattoo on Culligan's hand like those used as insignias by California gangs. Other leads follow. Among the effects in Culligan's faded canvas suitcase is a letter from San Mateo exhorting Culligan to leave the writer alone and to "Remember L. Bay."

Continuing to dismiss the Galton search as "money down the drain," Archer forgets Tony to fly to San Mateo. But Tony remains a lively issue. Surprisingly, the flight to northern California links him to Culligan. The possibility of yoking the "L. Bay" of the letter, the Luna of Tony's poem, and the town of Luna Bay, near San Francisco, has roused Archer's hopes; the detective likes nothing better than making connections. He gets Marian Matheson, the writer of the letter to Culligan, to meet him in a coffee shop. The meeting unearths some important findings: Racetrack tout and small-time racketeer, Pete Culligan, lived the dream of quick and easy riches. Marian, who married him after nursing him for injuries received in a gang fight, lived the dream of reforming him. But her dream fell apart, she divorced him fifteen years ago, and, a couple of years later, married a steadier man. Her interview with Archer brings into play the detective's best interrogating techniques; Ross Macdonald recounts the fluctuations of tone, the slackening and tightening of tension, and the veiled threats comprising Archer's efforts to find out what happened in Luna Bay in 1936. Though he doesn't want to frighten Marian into silence, Archer needs facts. But Marian has her own needs. As willing as she is to help apprehend Culligan's killer, she won't jeopardize her marriage. "The bitter forces of her will" quiet her, and she leaves Archer to do his own work.

The dead hands of Culligan and Galton (legally dead after vanishing for seven years) keep steering the action. Archer goes for the first time since *Way* to the city. Chad Bolling, editor of the poetry magazine which printed "Luna," is reading his poems to modern jazz accompaniment in a San Francisco nightclub. After hearing him perform at the Listening Ear, Archer shows Bolling some photos of Tony Galton. These jog him into remembering a visit he paid Galton, his wife, and a baby son around Christmas 1936. Ross Macdonald continues to scatter his clues openly. Though unable to recall the name of the baby's nurse, Bolling does mention the nurse's "remarkable eyes"; when Marian Matheson said in the previous chapter that she worked as a practical nurse in Luna Bay, her eyes "pointed like flints." This connection draws the reader. On the other hand, to identify Marian a scant fourth of the way into the book would be premature. The hint strikes the correct balance between doubt and certainty. Ross Macdonald has said enough without making a positive identification: the detective must be allowed to detect. Chad Bolling's curiosity, like ours, has stirred. The poet agrees to drive to Luna Bay the next morning to look for the house the Galtons lived in more than twenty years before.

The "dingy formless . . . sprawling" coastal town turns up more revealing evidence than a house. Archer meets George Dineen, the doctor, nearing retirement, who delivered Teddy and Tony Galton's baby son. Educated, suitably, in the Midwest, seedbed of most of Ross Macdonald's plots and source of many of his personal experiences, Dr. Dineen merits his role as life-bringer. He shocks us by announcing that Tony's son also came to his clinic recently to look for information leading to his father. Yet the page following this announcement threatens to snatch the promise away. Dineen wants information about John Brown, Jr., that Archer can't give. Even the news that the lad stands to inherit several million dollars doesn't budge the doctor's resolve. Dineen does explain, though, that several months ago a headless human skeleton was dug out of the ground under the house in which John Brown, i.e., Anthony Galton, lived in 1936. Like several other buried corpses in Ross Macdonald, Galton's remains, refusing to stay underground, take life. This life blossoms in Chapter 10. Whereas the gas-station in an Archer usually gives information, here he *is* the information. Epiphany-like, John Brown, Jr., materializes pumping gas on the outskirts of shapeless, overbuilt Luna Bay.

Archer and Bolling agree on the spot that the lad looks just like Tony Galton. But rather than surrendering information, the detective teases some self-disclosures out of twenty-two-year-old John Brown, Jr.— that he is a University of Michigan graduate, that he grew up in a Cleveland orphanage, and that he acts in plays. This last bit invites suspicion; as with Ruth Esch in *Tunnel* a good actor can fabricate convincing impersonations and impostures. Ross Macdonald keeps our curiosity aglow. He also continues to wheel in the cycle of the family. Whereas the daughter-search ruled *Doomsters,* with Mildred, Rose, and elderly Mrs. Hutchinson all mothering little Martha Hallman, the search for a father pushes to the fore of *Galton:* John needs a father to rid himself of the onus of being a nobody. Tony Galton's headless torso brings this search to the attention of the police. Chapter Eleven introduces Deputy Sheriff Mungan. Strong, manly, and capable, Mungan, whose name, oddly, is an anagram of Gunman, works smoothly with Archer. We like and respect both him and his colleague, Sheriff Trask, as much as we scorned Sheriff Duane Ostervelt in *Doomsters.* Featuring scurvy lawmen in two straight novels would mislead readers as to Ross Macdonald's usual friendly opinion of the police.

Mungan produces the bones of the headless corpse, noting a mended fracture in the right humerus. A call to Dr. Howell in Santa Teresa confirms that Tony Galton broke his right arm above the elbow while a prep school student. The police, meanwhile, have traced Culligan's suspected killer's getaway car to one Roy Lemberg of San Francisco. Under the pretext of wanting to buy the car, Archer goes to Lemberg's hotel and begins negotiating with his wife. Besides giving the plot breadth and variety, the scene brings out a new aspect of Ross Macdonald's ontology— that the fraternal tie is stronger than the marital; this, rather than existing autonomously for the Freudian novelist, gets its dynamism from infantile sexuality. Tommy Lemberg was paroled from jail in the custody of his elder brother Roy. Fran Lemberg can't produce the car Archer presumably wants to buy because Roy loaned it to Tommy for the day: "Tommy could talk the fillings right out of his teeth," the neglected Fran says of her husband. (In Chapter 26, after Archer sends Roy home because "Your wife could do with a piece of you," Roy clutches Tommy's head "possessively against his shoulder.")

Before she can say any more, Roy walks in, looking like "a man who has lost his grip and is sliding." The Galton case leans heavily on facial resemblances. Archer sees in hangdog Roy an older version of the man who stole his car in Santa Teresa. Cued by Fran's words, he shocks Roy by telling him that Tommy killed a man. Without further explanation, he leaves, giving the hotel's room clerk ten dollars to keep track of all the Lembergs' phone calls and visitors. Then, using shock tactics again, he goes unannounced to the Matheson home in nearby Redwood City. Again, the ordinary reveals the extraordinary. Her love for her husband prompts Marian to improvise a brilliant excuse in order to be alone with Archer. She admits having worked for a John Brown in late 1936. Further pressure gets her to add that an escaped convict and friend of Culligan, Fred "Shoulders" Nelson, probably killed Brown. Marian talks freely, anxious to divest a burden of guilt that has pressed on her for twenty years. Her guilt has a basis. Marian had mentioned her employer's steel money case containing thousands of dollars to Culligan, who, lacking heart, brought in Nelson to steal it. Touched by and grateful for her recitation, Archer assures Marian that her family won't be hurt by his investigation.

More strands of the plot, meanwhile, have knitted. Police records indicate that gang enforcer Fred Nelson escaped from San Quentin Prison the same month John Brown, Jr., was born, December 1936, and that he is still at large. Before Archer pursues this thread of inquiry, he calls the Lembergs' San Francisco hotel and learns that Fran and Roy checked out after phoning a Reno car-dealer named Generous Joe. Two sentences catapult Archer from Luna Bay to Reno. A page later, at one of Generous Joe's car sheds, his eyes are sprayed shut with blue paint and he is knocked out. Another drubbing later, he sees standing over him the young man who stole his car in Chapter 5. Hampered by a broken jaw and smashed nose, he speaks an "inimitable patois" both funny and sad. This pathos dissolves with the entry of Tommy's chief, Otto Schwartz. Though Schwartz has a gun and two helpers flanking him, Archer charges him. The beating he gets, his fourth in the chapter, rocks him into "the red pounding darkness" of sleep.

He wakes up in the accident ward of a Reno hospital, where he spends the next days. This convalescence is not only essential to his recovery; Archer must be kept away from Santa Teresa to give young John a chance to know Maria Galton. The ten days also bring John together with Dr. August Howell's pretty eighteen-year-old daughter, Sheila. En route from Santa Teresa's airport to the pool club where Archer, back in harness, has a luncheon meeting with her father, Sheila tells him that she and John love each other. Howell's disapproval of the romance soon surfaces. But Ross Macdonald first wants to establish a dramatic context. Archer tells Howell that the murders of Tony Galton and Pete Culligan, though twenty years apart, are related; he believes that some racketeers, hungry for the Galton millions, searched out, briefed, and hired John because of his likeness to Tony. Howell, a gifted sleuth in his own right, points out that the Cleveland orphanage where John allegedly lived for five years burned along with all its records three years ago; that its superintendent died, leaving nobody connected with the home to identify John; and, last, that John speaks more like a Midwestern Canadian than an American. Howell then hires Archer to further research John's background. His aim? To discredit John to Maria Galton and to end John's romance with Sheila. Motives clash. Maria won't hear her grandson run down, so happy has she been since his arrival in Santa Teresa. Since scotching her happiness could kill her, Howell, her physician, is undoing somebody he has been paid to comfort and strengthen. His motive lies close by. He is threatened. Maria's wish to leave all her money to John robs Howell of both an inheritance and the well-paying executorship of her will. Most important, a new will would also give John the cash to marry Sheila. The chapter's closing scene dramatizes this fear. Seeing Sheila poolside with John, Howell storms away from his lunch and orders him to leave the club. The chapter ends with the fuming Howell telling Archer from between his teeth to put John behind bars.

Howell's locating John's origins in central Canada gains credence from newly received prison records. Pete Culligan was jailed in Detroit after entering the country from Canada about five and a half years ago, i.e., the same time John appeared in Ann Arbor. That John may have crossed the border with Culligan links the Galton impersonation to the two murders. A couple of days of legwork in Ann Arbor uncover facts that support this assumption. John enrolled in an Ann Arbor high school two days after Culligan's arrest. After graduation, he attended the University of Michigan as John Lindsay, in honor of his new protector and substitute father, guidance counsellor Gabriel Lindsay. John's college career wasn't typical. Though making few friends, he acted in a number of plays and, just before graduation, received a big acting offer from a visiting Hollywood producer.

Archer's sojourn in the Midwest reaches a crescendo in a trip to the lakeside family lodge of John's former sweetheart, Ada Reichler, in Kingsville, Ontario. "Several years older than John," Ada admits that she chased him, even proposing marriage. Other disclosures follow. Ada insists that he never cared about money; had he been mercenary, he'd have accepted her proposal. Next, John's real name is Theodore Fredericks; after he jilted her to go to California, Ada visited his mother, "a hideous fat pig of a woman," at her boardinghouse in Pitt, Ontario. Mrs. Fredericks, her voice croaking "like a kazoo," said that her son ran away with one of her boarders five years before. This revelation enforces the belief that John, or Theo, came to the United States with Pete Culligan to defraud Maria Galton. But before Archer can act on his belief, he and Ada feel the emotional shock waves emanating from her disclosure, from the thick July dusk, and from the fragrant blooms nearby. Losing control, Ada cries out, "I betrayed him. Nobody could love me." Archer, "never

Hollywood-Ontario Shuttle

. . . angrier," ends the lakeside garden talk by tumbling Ada.

The sexuality is dramatically valid. The frenzy created by discussing long pent-up thoughts about John, the aphrodisiac scent of the clamoring buds, and Archer's conviction that Ada deserved more from John than he gave her transmit enormous power. This power asserts itself in line with the Oedipal sexuality prevailing elsewhere in Ross Macdonald: Ada, about twenty years younger than Archer, runs "blind" to the end of the garden, "her eyes . . . bright and heavy as mercury." Their love-making, an act of heat in the hot July gloaming, looks back to Archer's parting glimpse of another couple with a twenty-year age difference—the Sables, whom the detective left sitting shoulder to shoulder at twilight two chapters before.

Hearts release their treasures after the Ada Reichler incident: it is nearly as if the heavy moist summer night gave birth to the answers to the mystery of John's identity. After leaving Ada, Archer drives to Pitt (i.e., the southern Ontario town of Chatham, named for the English statesman Pitt). The "patchily furred leather" face, scrawny chest, and washboard ribs of boardinghouse manager Nelson Fredericks give a shocking picture of alcoholic waste. The hunched, bony Fredericks is the father his step-son, Theo, or John, can't accept. Theo's father-search stems from a real need. His mother talks about his wild boyhood dreams and visions of romantic destiny. Archer carries the fantasies forward. The impression-able Midwestern boy's ambition to rise above drab, dingy Pitt, he explains to Mrs. Fredericks, now includes posing as the prodigal heir of a rich California family. But the talk slews sharply away from Theo when it comes out that the Culligan's suspected killer, Tommy Lemberg, has been staying with his brother Roy for the past two weeks in the Frederickses' boardinghouse. Luck has given Archer a case-breaking lead. Tommy was sent to Santa Teresa by Reno gambler Otto Schwarta. He admits throwing his weight around to scare Alice Sable into paying Schwartz what she owed him; he also admits scuffling with Culligan, whom he didn't expect to find at the Sables'. But he insists that he left Culligan alive after the scuffle.

Then who killed Pete Culligan?

Archer and the Lembergs board the next plane west to find an answer with the Santa Teresa County police force. They have to do without John Galton's help. No sooner did John learn of Archer's visit to Pitt (from Ada Reichler?) than he left town, taking Sheila Howell with him. His troubles spread. The day he loses the protection of Maria Galton's name and wealth, he becomes a suspected killer. John's wish to sever his partnership with Culligan could have driven his knife into Culligan once the Galton millions came within reach. But even though John had already stabbed one rejected father figure, the wino Fredericks, as a boy, supporting evidence is thin. Culligan's murderer is still both unknown and at large, and Archer must act fast to bring him to heel. Where is the best place to look? As usual in Ross Macdonald, murder and adultery walk together. The Lemberg brothers' testimony that Alice Sable lived with Culligan while separated from her husband sends Archer back to the Sables' new home. Painfully disoriented, Alice admits killing her former lover. But, even when cued, she can't remember details. Now, if murder mkaes a beautiful woman ugly, as with Galley Lawrence in *Way*, it both desexes and denatures a man. Just before Alice's confession, Gordon Sable looked like "an old woman peering out through the fringes of a matted white wig." This detail, Alice's memory lapse, and Sable's avoidance of Archer's eye help disclose that Sable killed Culligan: as Clarence Bassett did to Isobel Graff in *Coast*, Sable, to protect his skin, talked Alice into believing herself a murderess.

General exhaustion and relief from mounting nervous strain bring on Sable's confession in Chapter 30:

Culligan picked her [Alice] up in Reno last summer. She went there to divorce me, but she ended up on a gambling spree with Culligan egging her on. No doubt he collected commissions on the money she lost. She lost a great deal, all the ready money I could raise. . . . I had to go there and beg her to come home with me. She didn't want to come. I had to pay him to send her away.

Alice wasn't Culligan's only link with Sable. Culligan had also known both Tony Galton and the Fredericks family of Pitt, Ontario; needing a helper in Santa Teresa with his prodigal grandson scheme, he approached Sable. The need to raise $60,000 for Otto Schwartz made Sable league with Culligan. He flew to Ann Arbor as a Hollywood producer and, by stages, got Theo to do the Galton imposture. Sable can't be condemned out of hand. Ross Macdonald judges him shrewdly but also sympathetically. Deserving of punishment Sable is—for attempting to defraud, for blaming Culligan's murder on Alice, and for his intellectual pride: "They talk about the greatest crime of the century. . . . This would have been the greatest of all—a multi-million dollar enterprise with no actual harm done to anyone." On the other hand, Alice's gambling spree and her rut with Culligan, both of which have cost her husband plenty, soften Sable's moral guilt. Though Archer apprehends him, he does permit Sable— curiously, the only person in the book who tries—to call him Lew.

This open-mindedness carries into the last chapter. Wanting to close the case himself, Archer goes back to Ontario in order to capture Theo, whom he now speaks of as "a small-time crook . . . with a record of violence," The moral charity softening his judgment of Sable, though, he also extends to Theo. Delving into Theo's deprivations helps Archer understand, even help, him. Like Carl Hallman in *Doomsters*, Theo emerges from the shadows of disgrace into the healing warmth of self-acceptance and belonging. Beginning at three o'clock in the morning, "the darkest hour of the night," and lasting till daybreak, the last chapter stirs more hope than any other last chapter in the canon. Like an imaginative artist, a madman, or a god (Theo-Deus), Theo has created a character and melted into it. But the ability of art to edge into and overtake life is not at stake, as in Pirandello. John is no role-player. Self-discovery, not simulation nor the profit-motive, took him from Pitt to Santa Teresa. That Nelson Fredericks hangs himself in the last chapter doesn't lessen Theo's moral achievement. The whipped, cringing Fredericks is the same Fred "Shoulders" Nelson who killed Tony Galton and then forced his teen-aged widow. Nelson had threatened to kill John/Theo if Theodora told anybody about the murder; so she married him to spare her little son's life. Thanks to her sacrifice, that son can live happily in the California sun.

His happiness costs a great deal. Ross Macdonald's calling *Galton* "a breakthrough novel" refers not only to aesthetic distance and control; the book also probes the deep meanings of the author's life. In a letter to the present writer, 3 June 1974, he called Ontario, "the place where everything first happened to me: family, love, writing, teaching, scholarship, friendship, and suffering. All my forebears were Ontarians." Speaking of the novel's genesis in 1969, he said, "My half-suppressed Canadian years, my whole childhood and youth, rose like a corpse from the bottom of the sea to confront me." This highly personal novel cried to be written. Coping with the deprivations of not-having and not-belonging, it confronts "the poverty and brokenness" of Ross Macdonald's "worst days." He never dug deeper for material than in *Galton*. The threat of dispossession and displacement lurking behind the action shows in early ideas for titles like "A Matter of Identity," "The Castle and the Poorhouse," and "The Impostor." Ross Macdonald's "Preface to *The Galton Case*" yokes this alienation to the Oedipus myth. The essay repeats the workpoint from his notebook that was to give shape to the novel: "Oedipus angry vs. parents for sending him away into a foreign country." The essay continues:

This simplification of the traditional Oedipus stories, Sophoclean or Freudian, provides Oedipus with a conscious reason for turning against his father and suggests that the latter's death was probably not unintended. It rereads the myth through the lens of my own experience, and in this it is characteristic of my plots.[10]

Subjects like dual citizenship and the lost father (Kenneth Millar's father left the family when Ken was three) makes *Galton* a landmark for Ross Macdonald both as a writer and a person. The novel did for him what *Sons and Lovers* did for Lawrence, allowing him to face and understand his past. Similarities between him and John Brown, Jr., "an imaginary boy whom I recognized as the darker side of my own remembered boyhood," abound: "John Brown, Jr.'s life is a version of my earlier life: the former could not have existed without the latter," said the writer in 1969. Novel writing is an adventure for writers like Lawrence and Ross Macdonald because, self-realizationists both, they discover reality by writing about it; fiction-making gives them both an inlet to and criticism of experience. Thus Ken Millar and John both came dangerously close to being stowed in an orphanage at age four; both took degrees at the University of Michigan after spending fifteen years or so in central Canada; both experienced poverty (Ontario), gentility (Ann Arbor), and material comfort (southern California) in the same order. ("We were poor among the poor," said Ross Macdonald of his Ontario childhood in a July 1974 interview for *People*.)[11] John and Archer, the writer's other self, both tumble the same girl. Red, the writer's obsessive color, splashes the action—sometimes as fire and blood, its most vital, radiant forms.

But the exuberance is contained; *Galton* is less of a parade of Ross Macdonald's obsessions than an artistic expression of them. Craftsmanship tempers feeling throughout. Resisting any temptation to identify the auctorial self with young John, Ross Macdonald scatters bits of himself into other characters. Archer mirrors him as accurately as ever; in fact, the detection done by Dr. Howell, relieving Archer of some mechanical sleuth-work, lets him live more fully and generously; Tony Galton, whom we never meet, was born in 1915, the same year as the author; and, though he studied engineering, his real work was the writing of imaginative literature. Finally, Ross Macdonald has explained how Tom Lemberg both foreshadows and serves as an opposite number to John, his own boyhood double: Archer's meeting with Tom in Chapter 5, when Tom steals the detective's car, "prefigures Archer's confrontation with the boy impostor John." The parallels continue:

Tom serves an even more important purpose at the beginning of the book, when he is held responsible for the murder of Peter Culligan. The structure of the story sufficiently identifies Culligan with the wino father [Fredericks], so that Culligan's death parallels and anticipates the final catastrophe [of Fredericks's suicide by hanging]. Like the repeated exile of Oedipus, the crucial events of my novel seem to happen at least twice.[12]

The ability to express deeply felt subject matter would go to waste unless Ross Macdonald worked John smoothly into the plot. Again, artistry modulates obsession. Ross Macdonald only puts John before us long enough to certify his reality; the youth has no marked personal style, quirk, or skill other than his acting. He is kept colorless for a reason. His character is developed from the outside, through the complex reactions of others to him. Maria Galton, Ada Reichler, and Dr. Howell, all having a vested interest in him, read their needs into John; he expresses their hopes and fears. Had he been portrayed with psychic depth, he would have blocked this variety. The plot thrives on his indefiniteness. Ross

Hollywood-Ontario Shuttle

Macdonald hides his identity as long as possible. Even Archer can't make up his mind about John—doubting, challenging, being both puzzled and impressed. At the start of Chapter 16, he says inwardly, "I'd made a moral bet with myself that John Brown was telling the truth." Yet in the next chapter, he barks, "That Galton boy is a phony." Ross Macdonald keeps changing Archer's mind and bringing in new evidence in order to mystify us. The more we learn about John, the less we know. Our curiosity rises accordingly. His shifting role amid several developing dramas keeps us wondering and, what is more important for any writer, reading.

Mellowing the surprises that spring up around John are the repetitions mentioned in "Preface." Many of these center around Nelson Fredericks. The scars on the thighs and rearparts of Theodora Galton Fredericks reappear in the hundreds on John's back, "like fading cuneiform cuts." All were inflicted by Fredericks, who has "a hatchet profile" and a voice "like a knife." In addition, John had taken a knife to Fredericks as a high school student, and Culligan, another rejected father-surrogate, does die from knife wounds. The false father must die by stabbing before he runs the son through—as he did (Culligan instigating the murder) with the true father, Tony Galton, axing his head from his body for good measure. John's fear and revenge imply a castration threat. Freud's famous case history of Hans and the castrating father depicts the father as a horse—plunging, strong-thighed, formidable. The novel alludes to Hans's plight. Not only did Tony Galton break his arm falling from a horse; the poet Chad Bolling also mentions Icarus, famous father-defying son from antiquity. In keeping with the metaphor of the knife, John, like Jack the giant killer, must cut down all false fathers before coming into manhood. A sure sign of this growth and self-being is his engagement to Sheila Howell. Ada Reichler also loved him; was, according to Archer, "worth five of him"; came from a rich family; and, several years John's senior, excites a maternal-erotic attraction missing in the breathless teen-ager, Sheila. John's rejection of marriage to Ada, despite her assets, prove his unreadiness. The ordeals he goes through in the novel make him a man.

Another well-conceived and well-executed character is Marian Matheson's eleven-year-old son, Jimmy, whom we meet in Chapter 13. Like four-year-old Jamie Johnson of *Morgue* and six-year-old Ronnie Broadhurst of *Underground Man*, little Jimmy attests to Ross Macdonald's knowledge of the behavior of small boys: their love of animals, shows of athletic skill, and boasts of bravery and physical strength. Though Jimmy doesn't serve as dramatically as his two counterparts, he convinces us that the Matheson family is worth saving. Also mirroring other characters in the canon is Gordon Sable. Like Albert Graves, he is an old lawyer-friend of Archer who calls the detective into the case for selfish reasons; he marries a much-younger woman; he kills for money. Excessive love for a faithless wife from greater Chicago leaves him as shattered as it did Dr. Samuel Benning in *Grin* (whose wife, Bess, came from Gary, Indiana). The condoning of adultery always brings down the sky in Ross Macdonald. Alice had left Sable a year before the time of the novel and then showed up in Reno with Pete Culligan. Sable found her and, agreeing to pay her heavy gambling debts, talked her into coming back to Santa Teresa with him. Then he moved Culligan, her ex-lover and his confederate in crime, into his home, leaving him alone with Alice for hours at a stretch. *Galton* is richer than either *Target* or *Grin*; the love triangle that emerges at the Sables' has a far more complex effect, both dramatically and structurally, than anything like it in the past; its three participants struggle blindly to bring on the calamity that destroys them.

Archer also helps make *Galton* the writer's most moving and intense work to date. He doesn't let what he might be, the ideal, blot out what he is—a fallible person working at a hard job. He makes the mistake of frightening the Lembergs into going to Canada, beyond the range of California law. Vindictively, he smashes Tom Lemberg's jaw "with all my force" for stealing his car two weeks before, even though Tom's arm is in a sling. The fresh, funny look he takes of himself when he tries to talk with a broken jaw in Chapter 16 and his sexual bout with Ada Reichler eight chapters later both lend him humanity. His impulsiveness gains our imaginative commitment; not only Ross Macdonald's stand-in, he is also our man, as capable of surprising us as of trying out patience. Ross Macdonald's skill in deploying him shows in his never eavesdropping on a conversation; Archer can create his own opportunities for detection. The same coward who punches a defenseless man will rush a gangster ringed by armed henchmen or break bad news as gently as possible. The reason for this new humanity? Ross Macdonald challenged himself deeply in *Galton* and, thanks to the introspective effort the challenge posed, grew as an artist. Another explanation for his growth stems from the near-absence of organized crime in the book. The introduction of Otto Schwartz and his thugs in Chapter 16 opens the possibility that Culligan's death was a gang killing. Ross Macdonald's keeping this possibility alive imparts terror to the action; where will the sinister monolith strike next? But Sable killed Culligan, and the gang Culligan and "Shoulders" Nelson worked for disbanded over twenty years ago. Ross Macdonald has maximized his options: he energizes his novel with the animal dread and large-scale intrigue of underworld fiction; at the same time, he avoids the tough talk and hard-boiled stances, i.e., the clichés, hobbling the form.

Appropriately, the book that made Ross Macdonald an important novelist quivers with renewal and rebirth. In Chapter 16, after Archer's eyes are sealed shut by spray paint, the detective wakes up to find his cheeks dripping with olive oil "like tears," symbolic of the anointing, or anealing, of Catholic ritual that precedes spiritual rebirth. Then he eats baby food while the broken bones in his face mend. Still acting symbolically as well as realistically, he makes love to Ada in a garden. Most of the remaining rebirth motifs in the novel center on John, called "a tough little egg to start with" by a former high school teacher. The cracking of the shell of deprivation encasing him releases new life. First, his play-acting lets him become many different people. Similarly, he uses several names: raised as Theodore Fredericks, he went to high school and college as John Lindsay, arrives in Santa Teresa as John Brown, Jr., and leaves the action as John Galton. Why is this multinymity important? Because names don't only stand for reality; they're real in their own right. The taking of a new name invites self-renewal. But renewal and refreshment don't require new names. Other characters besides John expand into fresh new life. Both Maria Galton ("She's becoming much more active") and her friend Cissie Hildreth ("She looked more feminine. . . . Something had happened to change her style") gain vitality from John's being in Santa Teresa. Sheila Howell will renew herself through marriage. Nor does Ross Macdonald slight the negative side of this rejuvenation: Culligan and Fredericks both die, and Alice Sable slips mentally into childishness.

But a killer she isn't, despite her husband's efforts to prove her one. Waste, madness, and cruelty darken the book. Yet the gloom lifts. The action ends at dawn with its leading players making ready to follow the sun west to California. This optimism isn't cheap. *The Galton Case* builds its cautious hope and cheer upon Ross Macdonald's investigation of his troubled past. The bravery and honesty of his effort confirms both his artistic integrity and manhood.

IV

An apposite successor to *Galton, The Ferguson Affair* (1960) contains many moments worthy of Ross Macdonald's later work and none of the easy cynicism riding his early fiction. The book, a non-Archer, is deeply imagined: it probes the anxieties of Ross Macdonald's life as doggedly as *Galton;* it delivers action, suspense, and atmosphere; it balances hidden fears and ingenious warmth.

The action starts quietly on the women's floor of the county jail servicing the fictional California town of Buenavista. The relay system by which attorneys are picked to represent defendants without funds has paired Ella Barker and lawyer Bill Gunnarson. Ella, a local nurse, has been jailed for selling a stolen diamond ring. Denying any knowledge of jewel thieves (like *Galton,* the novel keeps gang crime at a distance), Ella claims she found the ring on the sidewalk. Then, changing this feeble story quickly, she admits having fears; these stem from her having been warned not to testify against the burglars. Frightened for her life, she remains tight-lipped. Her refusal to talk nettles not only Gunnarson but also the local police. Buenavista has had seventeen burglaries in recent months, more than half of which took place at the empty dwellings of hospital patients. Crime courses through the chapter. Gunnarson's talk with a likeable detective-lieutenant ends with the news that somebody has just assaulted a junk dealer on Pelly Street in Buenavista's lower town, or slum district. Gunnarson and Lieutenant Wills pull into Pelly Street just as the victim, Hector Broadman, is being taken to the hospital. The two ambulance men who've come to collect Broadman attract as much notice as their patient: these are Ronald Spice, "a slightly shopworn cherub," and Whitey Slater, a "willowy . . . middle-aging man who can't give up the illusive airs of youth." Another compelling presence, Sergeant Pike Granada, "a powerful bull-shouldered" ex-lower town thug turned policeman, helps Broadman into the ambulance. Two pages later, a phone call from the hospital declares Broadman dead on arrival.

Various strands of the plot have begun to knit. Back at the prison, Ella Barker admits having dated Broadman several times despite a large age difference. But the dead man didn't give her the stolen ring. That dirty trick was played on her by Larry Gaines, a lifeguard at a nearby swimming club. Until recently, Ella and Gaines had kept close company. She met him through Broadman, liked him better than her older friend, slept with him, and even talked marriage. But their romance ended when she caught him with another woman at his apartment; the woman, Ella throws in, looks like movie starlet Holly May. The offhand reference takes hold. Calling his wife to say he won't be home for dinner, Gunnarson hears from Sally that Holly May has left Hollywood to live with her husband, a Canadian oilman, right in Buenavista. To learn about Gaines's part, if any, in the jewel heist that produced the ring Ella tried to sell, Gunnarson goes to the Foothill Club. Like its name, the exclusive club, where Holly May and her husband belong and where Gaines worked till recently, is "monumentally unpretentious." This restraint doesn't intimidate Gunnarson. But before he enters the club, he hears Holly May's name again. A Miami businessman named Salaman, looking for information about Holly, stops him in the parking lot. Gunnarson isn't delayed long. A crack about Holly's alleged affaire with a lifeguard kills his interest both in the brief conversation and in Salaman. Inside the club, he finds out that Gaines was fired recently for paying too much attention to a member's wife. Gaines's photograph describes the same sexual pirate women all through the canon can't resist:

He was slim-hipped and wide-shouldered. He held himself with that actorish air, self-consciousness pretending to be self-assurance, which always made me suspicious of a man. His crew-cut was handsome, but there was a spoiled expression on his mouth, something obtuse in his dark eyes.

These barbered animal good looks have threatened the club with a major scandal, club manager Arthur Bidwell reports: the previous night, Holly May Ferguson marched out of the dining room and drove away with Gaines, who was waiting for her in the parking lot. Ferguson, her jilted husband, has been drinking heavily in the bar. Like George Wall of *Coast,* another Canadian newlywed with a runaway wife, Ferguson blames his wife's disappearance on the cowardly manager of an exclusive pool club: Bidwell had called Holly to take the phone call that sent her to the parking lot. Colonel Ian Ferguson storms into the novel by kicking in Bidwell's door. He is imposing. "A big man in his fifties, shaggy in Harris tweeds," the gaunt, bulky Colonel has already downed a fifth of whisky without passing out. But the alcohol *has* furred his reflexes. Gunnarson, acting decisively, knocks him out while he is reaching for his pistol. Escorted by the club's bartender, Tony Padilla, Gunnarson drives the craggy, grief-rocked warrior home. Padilla, who knew them both, doubts that Holly and Gaines were lovers: "She isn't the type to play around. If you ask me, I'd say she loved her husband," the street-smart Padilla, another lower town old boy, explains.

Her husband doesn't seem lovable. Once awake, he starts another row, showering with his clothes on, guzzling a quart of coffee, and smashing a mirror with his fist. These antics end when Holly's abductors call, demanding $200,000 for her return. Rejecting Gunnarson's advice to call in the police, Ferguson agrees to pay the ransom. Padilla then drives Gunnarson to the local police station. The path between here and Pelly Street is well worn, both by lawmen and those the law doesn't protect. Violence has broken out again in the lower town. Detective Sergeant Pike Granada, the reformed thug, has shot his ex-running mate, Gus Donato, after catching him with some recently burgled loot. The shooting raises questions. For years, Granada has loved Gus's wife, Secundina. (Secundina's snubbing Granada for Gus, the bent Donato brother, rather than for Manuel, the straight one, whom she also could have had, fits the masochistic pattern of female sexuality in Ross Macdonald.) Did Granada kill Gus to get her for himself? Did she help set up the killing?

Shifting elsewhere on the map of love, Chapter 9 gives one of the writer's rare attempts at domestic realism. Sally and Bill Gunnarson move and speak naturally, superbly unconscious of the reader. The sarcasm, vaguenesses, and muffled resentments they exchange could describe an evening in any marriage when the husband forgets to call ahead of time to warn that he'll be late for dinner. The marriage has a meaning and a style apart from the plot, and the realistic alternation between affectionate byplay and evasive self-protection captures this dynamism. Yet the endearments, the communication lapses, and the guilt occupy but little space. *Ferguson* is a novel of crime and detection, not a domestic novel. Ross Macdonald need only make the Gunnarsons' marriage believable; showing Sally and Bill together for long stretches would distract from the main plot. Thus, worn out both by the late hour and her advancing pregnancy, she falls asleep soon after he comes home, and he wakes up early the next day without disturbing her to get back to work. Ross Macdonald has authenticated the marriage without sidetracking his plot.

The trim plot resumes course smoothly. Fear of endangering Holly, who is pregnant, still keeps Ferguson from calling the police. A stroke of unexpected luck has also given him hope. The news that Gaines both studied drama and acted in plays supplies a slim, but useful, lead. Ella Barker sends Gunnarson to her apartment for a copy of the newspaper review of a high school play one Harry Haines starred in some eight years ago. But another outbreak of crime on Pelly Street stalls the investigation. Both Pike Granada's stowing of Hector Broadman into an ambulance just before he died and the gunning-down of Gus Donato have made Granada the Most Likely Suspect in the lower town subplot. The mysteries have multiplied. Where is Holly? Why did Broadman die? Did Granada kill him? Gunnarson's attempts to solve these problems end, together with Chapter 15 and the first half of the novel, with a crash: Ferguson has run his car into a truck.

The action continues to release a rich lode of incidents and ideas. Gunnarson drives to the scene of the crash and takes the reeling Ferguson to a local bar. Here Ferguson hires him as a legal adviser and makes some key disclosures. Crossing the border into the United States has muddled the stubborn Alberta oilman as much as did his much-younger counterparts from Ontario, George Wall and John Galton. He feels awkward about marrying for the first time at age fifty-six; about having a pregnant wife thirty years his junior; about living in southern California. His latest ordeal? His wife was seen driving the car Larry Gaines used to pick up the ransom money a few hours before. Thus Holly, no kidnap victim, is conspiring to rob him. Why? As often happens in the novels, the chapter beginning the second half of *Ferguson* touches a sensitive spot in the past. This structural device propels the novels backward and forward at once. The device works as neatly in *Ferguson* as it does anywhere else in the canon. Having agreed to represent Ferguson, Gunnarson needs information obtainable only through close personal questioning. The answers to his questions not only furnish a backcloth to the drama; they also bring Ian Ferguson to life. Ferguson dominates the second half of the novel, partly because of the self-revelations made here.

Though vague on supporting details, Ferguson sees his present trials as just punishment for his misdeeds in the past. Specifically, he always believed that his early sins would bar him from succeeding in love. Yet a year or so ago, he was passing through Vancouver, British Columbia at the same time a Holly May movie was playing in a local film festival. The ageing, duty-ridden Scots-Canadian fell in love with Holly's photo and used his clout to meet her. His urge to know Holly lay deep in his private past. She reminded him of a girl he had loved but then dropped twenty-five years before, while attending Harvard Business College. "It was like being given a second chance at youth," he claims. The chance both to erase the mistake of rejecting love and to admit beauty and wonder into his life had released all his hidden romantic dreams: "I'd been going through the motions for twenty-five years, piling up money and acquiring property. Suddenly, Holly was the reason for it, the meaning of it all." The dream has been livable. Holly's pregnancy symbolizes her thriving glowing happiness; Ferguson has been loyal, loving, and realistic ("I'm not a handsome man, and I'm not young").

But if marriage makes sense of his past, it devastates hers. Gunnarson must dredge up this past in order to help her marriage. As time rolls backward in the second half of the book, two ideas first stated in *Doomsters* come forth: the persistence of the past and the retributive power of time. Nothing is buried; the past can't be ignored. Ferguson's willingness to piece together the shards of the past make him heroic—both in his moral aspiration and his suffering. What is more, Ross Macdonald perceives the distinctions that makes this heroism live. Gunnarson, who had silenced Ferguson's outburst in Chapter 6 with a punch to the jaw and who usually calls Ferguson by his last name, addresses him respectfully as "Colonel" at the end of their long talk in Chapter 16. Ferguson's dream has gravitated to Hollywood, home of manufactured celluloid hopes. The oil baron married a beautiful screen actress of whose past he knew nothing; just as dreamerlike, she left him, a millionaire husband who loves her, for a wanted criminal. The weird logic governing her act—if, indeed, she is self-acting—lies somewhere in the past. But to explain her motives prematurely would drain much of their force. Ross Macdonald wants to establish more justifications and spring more surprises before turning his lens on Holly.

Alternating different plot-levels, he carries the action to the local morgue. Here, two new developments surface: that Hector Broadman died from suffocation, curiously showing no signs of strangulation, and that Secundina Donato is also dead, apparently from an overdose of barbiturates. In one stroke, Ross Macdonald introduces a new mystery while deepening an earlier one. Meanwhile, the moist electric air of sexual attraction continues to shoot sparks. Tony Padilla, bartender at the Foothill Club and Gunnarson's guide through Pelly Street, also loved Secundina. Sexual love and death keep fusing; the lower town beauty, nicknamed "Sexy" and loved by three men, dies in her twenties.

The dangers of sexuality recur in Gunnarson's next painful talk with

Ferguson. At the Colonel's home, Gunnarson finds the Florida business-man he had met in the parking lot of the Foothill Club in Chapter 5. Like Alice Sable of *Galton,* Holly seems to have run up heavy gambling debts while away from her husband; Salaman has come to Buenavista to collect the $65,000 she owes a Miami gambling firm. On the rack, Ferguson can't dodge the probability that Holly is carrying Gaines's baby ("I don't know the sort of woman I married"). Yet he stands by her —because he loves her and also because he believes her betrayal of him to be what he deserves. The Old Testament justice that has finally caught him out finds voice in a maxim from his boyhood:

My father used to say that the book of life is like a giant ledger. He was right. Your good actions and your bad actions, your good luck and your bad luck, balance out. Everything comes back to you. The whole thing works like clockwork.

But what is the bad action he must pay so heavily to expiate? Why should he be robbed of love just when he learns that love, not money, is life's greatest boon? Ferguson admits having discarded the Boston girl he knew twenty-five years before, fobbing her off with a thousand dollars after learning of her pregnancy. His crime and his punishment mesh. Having deserted one pregnant woman, he is now deserted by another. In the interim, he was undone by success; riches and the pursuit of more riches had kept love out of his life. Now he is paid out in kind for degrading love and its fruits into another financial deal.

While Ferguson keeps hope alive, Gunnarson drives to Mountain Grove, California. This development combines the epic hero's traditional descent to the underworld with the obligatory journey to the prodigal's humble origins. But why Mountain Grove? By checking the names of the cast-members in the play-review of Chapter 6 against old out-of-town phone books, Gunnarson finds this small inland city worth an exploratory visit. And worthwhile the visit proves. One moving scene follows another in this crackling good novel. First, the novel has two prodigals. Next, as in *Galton,* the seedbed of the action is a neglected, out-of-the-way dwell-ing. Larry Gaines's mother, Mrs. Adelaide Haines, depicts the shabby and the run-down lodging the fantastic. Obsessed by the Puritanical fear that the flesh will conquer the spirit, Mrs. Haines is one of Ross Macdonald's wildest originals. Her former piano and voice students have all stopped taking lessons from her; this decline tallies with the lower-class neighbor-hood she lives in, suitably, by herself; like the cobwebbed corners of her living-room ceiling, her mind has grown foggy. This alienation manifests itself in sexual fixation. Sex colors all her responses. Doused with per-fume, she flirts with Gunnarson, condemns Hilda Dotery (son Harry's fellow cast-member in the high school play and long-term sweetheart) for corrupting Harry, and uses her cat as a surrogate son-lover: the castrated cat, who even has her son's name, can't betray her with other females. Her thoughts are painfully scrambled. She blames everyone else for the crimes that sent her son to reform school ("It's the same old story—after all, they crucified Christ"). While worrying the pitiless past, she calls her cat "lover" and squeezes him so tightly he jumps from her lap. The gesture strikes home; this leap both expresses futility and puts her beyond blame. Like Eliot's nonspringing cat in "Prufrock," Harry the cat lives in a slum. Both he and his human namesake are only children of a possessive mother. Both leap ineffectively. At the end of the chapter, the cat is again being stroked and cooed to by "his muzzers"; son Harry, we shall see, has also kept within the shadow of Mrs. Haines's hand.

Gunnarson's visit to Hilda Dotery's, i.e., Holly May's, family reveals as strong a tie as the one linking Adelaide and Harry Haines. But Kate Dotery's maternal influence—avoiding any overlapping of dramatic function—works differently from Adelaide's. Immediately noticeable to Gunnarson is the facial resemblance between Holly and Kate, whom the lawyer finds "very good-looking and well-preserved." Her alcoholic husband safely out of the way at his local bar, Kate answers Gunnarson's questions freely and honestly: her eldest daughter Hilda ran away from home five or six years ago. Then she turned up unannounced a month ago regaled in jewelry and expensive clothes; these she claimed to have bought with her earnings as a movie star. When the talk turns to Hilda's friendship with Harry Haines, Kate, protesting her daughter's innocence, slanders Haines as viciously as Adelaide had slandered Hilda: Haines started the trouble that drove Hilda from town. But Hilda, rather than blaming Haines for her disgrace, as her mother does, prefers him to her rich oilman husband. To the best of Kate's knowledge, Hilda and Haines are still running together.

The surmise is borne out straightaway. Hiding behind the driver's seat of Gunnarson's car is Harry Haines. As soon as the engine turns over, Haines points his revolver at the back of Gunnarson's head and tells him where to drive. Haines's late first appearance (Chapter 24 in a thirty-chapter novel) squares with Ross Macdonald's usual practice of delaying the prodigal's entry as long as possible. But here the practice also has another meaning. The previous two chapters had centered on mothers—Adelaide Haines and Kate Dotery. Analagously, narrator-hero Gunnarson's first act in the new chapter is to call his wife, an expectant mother. Sally doesn't answer. Fear and guilt that she went to the hospital whets Gunnarson's need for her. Just as this jolt raises his stake in life, he runs afoul of Haines. Form and content have knit brilliantly. Haines, ironically, is no desperado. A stammering misfit with a "painfully high" voice, he is an easy mark for Gunnarson's sarcasm. The glamor and scowling heroism of crime come a cropper again when the two men reach their destination. Holly and Haines, both of them nervous, tired, and bored with each other, have been living rough in a decayed house miles from civilization.

The chapter ends wildly. A spat between Holly and Haines ends with his smashing her on the side of the head with his gun. Catching him off his guard, Gunnarson charges in. But just as he knocks the gun to the floor and starts to take on Haines in hand-to-hand combat, Holly picks up the gun and shoots him twice. The shells that rip into his shoulder, no mere show of violence, help the book's realism. It is time for Gunnarson to get these knocks. Archer rarely goes so long without getting hurt: unless the detective, especially a narrator-detective, tastes danger personally, he can't make danger live for the reader. *Ferguson* doesn't go flat. Not only has Gunnarson been shot; like Archer, after Dr. Grantland knocks him out in *Doomsters,* he is also left to die in a burning house. Again, the flapping, chewing fire materializes with roaring brilliance. But unlike Archer, Gunnarson awakens to find another potential victim alongside him—Holly. Sure that she has just shot him, he still hauls her, unconscious, from the blaze. Action continues to dominate. What looks like help soon comes in the form of an ambulance. The same two men who took Hector Broadman from Pelly Street to the hospital, chubby-jowled Ronald Spice and the pale, limp-wristed Whitey Slater, find the wounded pair.

Needle tracks on her arm make it likely that Holly has been drugged. But no sooner does Gunnarson wonder how an unconscious, drugged woman could fire a pistol than his attention is yanked elsewhere. The two ambulance men have been preparing to dress his wounded shoulder. Then "a sense of survival deeper than consciousness" grips him, as his wrists are strapped and a black rubber mask pressed to his face. He understands in a flash that the drivers want to drug him just as they had done Broadman and Secundina Donato. Though contrived, the melodramatic scene promotes some rich human insights. While holding his breath—the one thing he can do to stay alive—Gunnarson is saved by the policeman he had charged with graft and murder, Pike Granada. Slater and Spice had been using the radio in their ambulance to learn, from their contact in the hospital, which patients' homes would be safe to burglarize. Granada's stopping them before they can kill or rob any more ends the local crime wave. What remains to be done includes solving the riddle of Holly/Hilda and catching the ineffectual Haines. The melodramatic soon gives way to the human. A cadenza of hope comes from the foregoing violence. Life and death fuse for Gunnarson: we live most intensely in the shadow of death. The same night he nearly dies three times (from bullets, fire, and suffocation), he becomes a father. Danger renews him. Pike Granada not only saves him from smothering; he also gives him a pint of blood. This infusion of Chicano blood and policeman's blood will bring Gunnarson closer to the people he serves. The glow spreads. Granada, whose redemptive role began when he saved Gunnarson from falling through a trap door early in the novel, clears both himself and the police. The mysteries echoing from Pelly Street to the police station have been solved, and solving them has made Gunnarson a better man.

But other mysteries remain. In the hospital, Holly's doctor says that the kidnapers drugged her as soon as they abducted her and then kept her heavily sedated so she couldn't identify them. As has been mentioned, this account clashes with her controlled, deliberate actions of the night before. Ferguson doesn't know what to believe. Gunnarson tells him that Holly went with Haines voluntarily and that Holly shot him while he was brawling with Haines. Ferguson's reluctance to accept her guilt makes Gunnarson furious. Stunned by being called "morally stupid" and "trouble that walks like a man," Ferguson finishes telling about his family in Alberta, his education, and, finally, his impregnation and desertion of the Boston salesgirl. The narrative structure of *Ferguson* shows a new confidence and control. Delaying important background data till Gunnarson comes back from Mountain Grove shows the same technical skill as does Ferguson's piecemeal confession. The book's organization is tight and clean. As in Ross Macdonald's other novels of this middle period, time in *Ferguson* is a closed circuit generating a strong charge. Grounded in Ferguson's deepest loyalties, its blasts shock the Colonel into humankind. Until he accepts his guilt, Ferguson can't accept himself. Years of suppressing the guilt have given it tremendous force. Gunnarson introduces the probability that Holly is Ferguson's natural daughter: Kate Dotery, the lawyer explains, came west with her illegitimate baby daughter from Boston some twenty-five years ago. This news unleashes more madness than any other disclosure in the canon. Convulsed by horror, his eyes glowing "in their deep cavities," Ferguson begs Gunnarson to keep this information from Holly.

His unselfishness sparks a hope that gleams to the end. Holly's denial, in the next-to-last chapter, that she has ever seen either Gunnarson or the Miami dun, Salaman, reveals, eventually, that somebody has been impersonating her. As usual, the key to the mystery lies in the prodigal's immediate family. Holly isn't the former Hilda Dotery, as we had believed, but Hilda's younger sister, June. Thus she and Ferguson aren't father and daughter. The lifting of the incest taboo steers the novel temporarily into the groove of literary detection. Gunnarson holds a crucial interview with Holly's former screen-agent, Michael Speare of Beverly Hills. Speare tells how Haines talked Hilda into having plastic surgery and cosmetic dentistry to make herself look just like her movie-star sister. Morally trapped, Speare also admits engineering a scandal with the newly doctored Hilda to wreck the Fergusons' marriage and, hopefully, restore Holly to the films. Though despising him, Gunnarson agrees to protect Speare from the police in exchange for Hilda's address.

This he hands over to Ferguson, extracting, in return, the promise to get Hilda the best psychiatric and legal help available. But his fatherly love is never to be. To end the novel on a happy note would deny the years of guilt leading up to it. On the road to Hilda's hiding-place, Gunnarson spots Speare's car. Suddenly, Hilda steps into the road, holding a raised pistol. Though Speare tries to avoid her, he can't swerve quickly enough. His car smashes into Hilda. Not only does he kill her on impact; his careening car also takes away Ferguson's chance of settling accounts with the past. But Ferguson won't repress the truth any more. He holds Hilda's corpse in his arms and acknowledges her before others as his daughter "in a clear voice." His declaration takes effect right away. The last page of the novel carries a report that Harry Haines burned to death near the disused house of Chapter 24. The chief threat to the Fergusons' marriage has been routed. Bound by sorrows as well as love, Holly and Ian Ferguson deserve their chance for happiness.

This blend of loss and hope comes partly from the care that goes into the characters. Spice and Slater, the murderous corpsmen, suffer from direct moralizing: they seem to be lovers; furthermore, as if ageing, and, more pointedly, the refusal to age gracefully, constituted a crime, Ross Macdonald keeps branding Slater with epithets like "no lad" and "the tall old youth." He and Spice aren't permitted a kind act from the time they step into the book. But in this they are alone. None of the other characters exist to point morals or to create a sociology of distinctions. One who serves the plot particularly well is Tony Padilla, bartender at the Foothill Club. Padilla's function as a mediator fits both the plot and the underlying pattern. First, he bridges the gap between the law-abiding white establishment and the crime-prone Chicanos of lower town; agile and unpretentious, he does this as Gunnarson's guide and translator. His person also brings the two worlds together. Like Pike Granada, who injects Chicano vim into Gunnarson along with his blood, Padilla expresses the vocational mobility of the early 1960s; though Chicanos couldn't join exclusive clubs, they could work in them. Padilla's special attraction to Ferguson has another source—Ross Macdonald's obsession with crossing borders. Padilla likes Ferguson; he speaks well both of him and his wife, tries to stop him from making trouble with the club's manager, drives him home, and makes him coffee. He knows that Ferguson needs kindness. Both men are outsiders; the Chicano feels as dispossessed as the Canadian amid southern California gentry. Their coming from above and from below the border counts less than their dislocation. Padilla plays the good squire to Ferguson's knight (he is described twice as doglike, designating loyalty, in Chapter 20) because he knows firsthand the alien's pain and lostness.

Ferguson shows how completely, if unconsciously, a writer can reveal himself in his work. The likenesses between him and Ross Macdonald's forerunner, Raymond Chandler, are too glaring to overlook. Both men directed oil companies, served in the Canadian army, drank heavily, and married out of their generations. The likenesses continue at different levels. Like Holly May, Chandler's Philip Marlowe was knocked out, drugged, and held captive for two days in *Farewell, My Lovely;* Ferguson's father was the same kind of Scots-Canadian outdoorsman and husband-*manqué* as John Macdonald Millar, the author's father. Chandler and Ross Macdonald both set their novels in greater Los Angeles, use Oedipal materials, and couch their rhetoric within the hard-boiled literary tradition. But Ross Macdonald had all but given up hard-boiled fiction in *Doomsters.*[13] Why should Chandler exert such a strong spell on him two novels later? The laying-to-rest of the literary father looks pointless. Ross Macdonald had to make the gesture, even though he did it without malice. Chandler influenced him more than any other writer. He also disliked the results of his influence, attacking *Target* in a 1959 letter for "stylistic misuse of the language."[14] More graciously, Ross Macdonald praised Chandler in "The Writer As Detective Hero" (1964). Chandler could have also been on his mind, together with other aspects of the resurrected past, in 1959, when *Ferguson* was being written. Having published a feeble last Marlowe, *Playback,* the previous year, he died in 1959. (Ross Macdonald's next novel, *The Wycherly Woman,* uses the word, playback [Chapter 27].) The ambivalence caused by the combination of his snipe at *Target,* the inferiority of *Playback* alongside *Doomsters* and *Galton,* and the resentment permeating the leader-follower relationship all come through vividly. For most of the 1950s, Ross Macdonald was a better writer than the more celebrated Chandler. Knowing this, he lets Ferguson, whom he likes, gain his hopes, but only after putting him through the direst ordeals inflicted on anybody in the canon.

Some of these ordeals filter through Bill Gunnarson, who resembles Ferguson closely enough to understand his failings. Both men, whose names end similarly, have forsaken love for work. Both have pregnant wives who go to the same obststrician; Dr. Trench's name, moreover, echoes the domestic struggle besetting the two men at different times. Gunnarson can't correct in himself the traits he dislikes in Ferguson. His ambition (he works non-stop) reflects the same hunger for money and power that has driven Ferguson for the last thirty-five years. Tempering it somewhat is a dislike of authorities and institutions. Sitting at his father's roll-top desk in Chapter 9, he says, "It's oddly pleasing to sit at your father's desk. Diminishing, too." The diminution outpaces the pleasure in a man anxious to get ahead. Gunnarson never mentions his father again. Whenever he can, he defies the establishment, the social embodiment of the father. He holds back information from the police; without a scrap of evidence, he accuses Pike Granada of murder and robbery; he riles Ferguson whenever he can. For general, as well as personal, reasons, Ferguson is his favorite whipping boy. After silencing his drunken rant in Chapter 6 with a knockout punch, Gunnarson says, "I had always wanted to hit a Colonel." Though a good twenty-five years younger, he insults Ferguson, lectures him, and usually calls him by his last name. Nor does he, a man unworthy of a faithful wife, spare any brutality stating his suspicions (later disproved) that Holly is deceiving Ferguson with Harry Haines.

But the person Gunnarson resembles most, down to his mannish name, is that other enemy of the establishment—Lew Archer. The institution that frets both men most is that of marriage. Some of Bill and Sally's chats could well have taken place between Sue and Lew Archer. Sally will scold Bill for neglecting her for his work. Her first words to him, when he comes home at midnight, some six hours late for dinner, are, "So you finally decided to come home." On the next page, she accuses him of deliberately avoiding her. The accusation has force. Work counts more with him than marriage, comfort, or security. Early in the novel, he has qualms about subduing his marriage to his job:

We had been married for nearly three years; tonight for the first time I was fully aware of her preciousness to me. But I was more determined than ever to stick with the case and do my duty in it. The problem was to know where my duty lay.

Later, he forgets these struggles of duty and conscience. Though guilty about not standing by Sally during labor and childbed, he makes her a promise he intends to break when she asks, reasonably enough, "Promise me you won't take criminal cases and rampage around the countryside and all." Right before this, his surgeon asks him jokingly if his wife shot him. The surgeon speaks truer than he knows. Far be it from Ross Macdonald to rule out an acausal link between Gunnarson's absence from Sally and the dangers that rock the lawyer the night Haines abducts him. The issue of work-fixation keeps looming before Gunnarson, even though he tries to suppress it. His marriage threatens to crack under the same strain that undid Sue and Lew Archer.

Gunnarson resembles Archer in his triumphs as well as in his domestic troubles. Though untrained, he investigates crime with both the flair and the mechanical aptitude of a skilled detective. Like Archer, he is a decent, intelligent man with a sketchy personal background: all we know of him is that he was born in Pennsylvania, served in Korea, since which time he attended both college and law school, and married Sally some three years before the time of the book. The similarities between him and Archer mount. Neither man speaks with the elaborate casualness of the hard-boiled dick; neither is afraid to stray far afield of his original purpose in a case. Once on the hunt, the two men use the same investigative techniques—checking leads, examining physical evidence, cross-questioning witnesses, and, above all, relying on a highly developed historical sense to

Hollywood-Ontario Shuttle

relate incidents in the past.

But *Ferguson* stands closer to traditional detective fiction than do most of the Archers. Many of the riggings of the sleuth novel are here—the legwork, the red herring (Pike Granada), the laborious but necessary work of checking old out-of-town telephone books, the all-purpose secretary: Bella Weinstein, Gunnarson's Girl Friday, nearly emerges as a Della Street (lawyer Perry Mason's secretary) or a Bertha Cool (secretary of Donald Lamb, the lawyer turned detective in the novels of A. A. Fair, or Erle Stanley Gardner). The book also includes scientific detection. The coroner reports his examination of Hector Broadman's corpse in highly technical language:

I've found no evidence of strangulation. The neck structures are intact. There's no sign of external violence at all, apart from the injuries to the back of the head. But the internal evidence points conclusively to asphyxia: edema of the lungs, some dilation of the right side of the heart, some petechial hemorrhaging of the pleura. There's no doubt at all that Broadman died from lack of oxygen.

Later, Gunnarson's eagle eye and good memory prove that Holly didn't shoot him after his scuffle with Haines:

She removed the harlequin glasses and let me look at her. The bruise was an old one, already turning green and yellow at the edges. She couldn't have received it within the past fifteen hours. Besides, it was on the wrong side. Haines was right-handed. The woman in the mountain house had been struck on the left side of the head by his revolver.

Ferguson is a rich, robustly told novel that exerts force at several levels. Gunnarson allows Ross Macdonald to include things that wouldn't fit into an Archer. Yet because the book has too much material, some of these things lack definition. The domestic subplot doesn't fuse with the main action. Some events occur out of view—Pike Granada's mounting and then executing his plan to catch the killers, Ella Barker's release from prison, Sally's lying-in, and Ferguson's visit to Kate Dotery in Mountain Grove. The ending is clogged and contrived. Michael Speare shouldn't have explained Hilda's impersonation of Holly/June. Though a purveyor of celluloid dreams, this Hollywood screen agent doesn't deserve to resolve the book's last puzzle. The unveiling of criminal motives counts as much in detective fiction as the catching of the criminal; the one wouldn't make sense without the other. Structurally, Speare plays a role as bogus as that of the *deus ex machina* of classical drama.

Most of the way, the structure is trim and smart. Though the novel ends badly, it has a strong start. That Hector Broadman appears alive for a couple of pages makes him more than a corpse around which to string a murder-puzzle. His brief appearance rouses feeling, and his death en route to the hospital provokes thought. Though his "fair" physical condition in Pelly Street implies foul play, the head wounds that sent him to the hospital were serious enough to cause death. This ambiguity shows how Ross Macdonald stirs both our minds and our hearts. Bright rips of insight refresh the action everywhere. An awareness of the incongruities of speech relieves tension when Salaman, the enforcer of a Miami gambling syndicate, asks with comic helplessness, "Why are the ones with the most the hardest to collect from?" Sometimes the comedy veers into the unexpected. At one point, Ferguson resembles "a Himalayan holy man"; in this light, his marriage to Holly, who has the same name as the sacred plant of the Druids, creates a powerful unity. Other examples of name symbolism extend the process. Holly May makes up a literal half of a May-December marriage. Yet her husband's name (Ian-Jan[uary]) carries the marriage into the new year, whose powers to renew and refresh intensify with the advent of the Ferguson baby.

The symbolism isn't always this esoteric. Ross Macdonald roots some of his best effects in everyday life. What symbolizes a needy and neglected wife better than a pregnant woman who has been ignored, along with the special dinner she cooked him, by a work-raddled husband? The book's symbolic range keeps pace with its stylistic variety. The terse, graphic idiom of the Archers governs the action. Yet the tone and the vocabulary can shift, as in this extract from a Hollywood gossip column:

Rumor hath it that ex-movie-tidbit Holly May, who was too sweet-smelling for movie-town, is trying to prove the old saw about the Colonel's lady. Her partner in the Great Experiment is a gorgeous hunk of muscle (she seems to think) who works as a marine menial in her millionaire hubby's millionaire clubby. We ordinary mortals wish that we could eat our fake and have it, too. But gather ye sub-rosas while ye may, Mrs. Ferguson.

A good ear for journalese in its different corruptions shows in the review Gunnarson finds in the high school newspaper from Mountain Grove. The cliches, the amateurish sentence structure, and the breathless desire to praise everybody connected with the production make the review a triumph of impersonation:

Dorothy Drennan was her usual charming self in the role of ingenue. Claire Zanella and Marguerite Wood were charming as the bride's-maids. Stephen Roche and Hilda Dotery performed excellently as the comic servant couple and had the large audience of friends and parents in stitches, as did Frank Treco and Walter Van Horn with their usual live-wire antics.

A different, but equally brilliant, rhetorical effect comes in Ross Macdonald's fusions of mental and sensory data. Ella Barker's fear smells "like sour fermentation" in Chapter 3; likewise, "the thought of Speare intruded like an odor" in Chapter 19. Releasing their magic as similes, these fine examples of synesthesia clinch the new inside the homey frame of the tested and the achieved. This verbal strategy mirrors the form of *Ferguson*. In its way, the book breaks as much new artistic ground as the more admired *Galton Case*. Strewing its red herrings discreetly and using solid police work to unravel the mysteries, *Ferguson* relies heavily upon the conventions of standard literary detection. These it rubs to a deep, mellow gloss. The detective novel has more sinew and suppleness thanks to *The Ferguson Affair*.

6

"SECURITY: THE GREAT AMERICAN SUBSTITUTE FOR LOVE"

The books from *The Wycherly Woman* (the earliest and least success-ful of the group) to *Black Money* deal with tragic sexual passion. Some of the tragedy is caused by money; money cuts across the passion in all the books. Catherine Wycherly's lover works for her husband; a man in *The Chill* lives off of much-older wife he no longer loves; characters in *Black Money* use a wife and daughter to pay their gambling debts. In each case, love is checked by mercenary impulses. In no case is a relationship or commitment inviolable. Price tags appear on human hearts everywhere; the sacred and the precious becomes items for barter.

Sometimes, tragedy comes from suppressing facts. A character in *The Wycherly Woman* says, "The truth is supposed to make you free, but it doesn't. The less people know of the truth, the better for them." Wrong. Living with appearances and ignoring the truth only foment crisis. Once to the fore, the crisis can whip across generations to lash those least able to cope with it—the innocent and the unsuspecting. Archer scolds a man in *The Far Side of the Dollar* for hiding his son's origins: "You had no right to cheat him of the facts, whether you liked them or not. When the facts finally hit him, it was more than he could handle." Suppressing the truth also hurts the suppressor, inviting black-mail. Threat of exposure informs both Ross Macdonald's narrative struc-ture and motivation. People murder both to protect themselves and to shore up the faulty substructure of their lives. Because the truths they want to keep hidden often lie deep in the past, these people are middle-aged rather than young: they have parents as well as children who could be touched by calamity.

The plots raise both moral and sociological questions, with characters of all backgrounds joining in the investigations. This inclusiveness pro-motes a realism usually reserved for the mainstream novel of manners and morals. Yet Ross Macdonald holds his ground. Literary conjurer as well as psychologist of repressed feelings, he builds plots expressive of the tensions undergirding them. The works published between 1961-66 grow more elaborate and complex. Red herrings abound; options spring open and slam shut; characters surprise us while acting in line with their ruling passions. Some of these, it needs saying, are women. As he gains artistic seasoning, Ross Macdonald imparts new depths and shadings to his female characters; women bear more and more of the narrative burden. What is more, the killer in three of the five novels in the group is female.

The years have brought other changes. Titles like *The Chill* and *Black Money* show Ross Macdonald's vision darkening with the years. Reality has become tougher; experience offers more pain than it does joy, and we feel the pain more keenly. Desperation becomes more common. Middle-aged and elderly women now kill as well as adolescents (*Pool*) and wives in their early twenties (*Way* and *Doomsters*). Whereas the soldiers and sailors in the four pre-Archers were men of derring-do, their older counterparts in *The Wycherly Women, The Zebra-Striped Hearse,* and *The Far Side of the Dollar* all invite pity. The harshness of routine living also accounts for Archer's frequent mistakes, hesitations, and acts of compassion; the recent works are both tougher and more tender-hearted than their predecessors. One reason why people need compassion and charity is the growing danger of living a dream. In the earlier works, a fantasy might become a fact without causing widescale damage: John Galton and Ian Ferguson find happiness or at least a chance for it. The fantasies spun by the heroes of the novels published between 1961-66 end in isolation or death. No longer livable, the dream bursts, its fragments, often storing a twenty-years' charge, shattering violently. Dreamers use up their options quickly in these dark novels. The past tears away their disguises and smokes them out of their hiding places; in *The Wycherly Woman* and *The Far Side of the Dollar*, the killers end up as suicides.

But gloom and waste don't engulf all. To recognize darkness is not to sink into it. The later works of Ross Macdonald express more than despair. Resisting cynicism and moral quietism, he maintains moral balance, stylistic flair, and control of his characters. To write about evil constitutes an honest attempt to cope with it. Unlike most American novelists, he improves with the years. Evil bores, inhibits, and confines. On the other hand, the Archers published between 1961-66, broadening their human base, display new strengths, with *The Chill* and *Black Money* pushing to the top of the canon.

I

The Wycherly Woman (1961), the first Archer set mainly in northern California, begins in the imaginary valley town of Meadow Farms. Homer Wycherly has just come home from a two-month luxury cruise to Australia and the South Sea islands. "A weak sad man in a bind," Wycherly needs help because his daughter has been missing since the day he sailed. Like most of Ross Macdonald's fathers of only daughters, Wycherly sees Phoebe unrealistically, it turns out, describing her both as "a well-conducted girl" and "a complete innocent." She was last seen with her mother, his recently divorced wife, the day of his voyage out. Wycherly blames himself for Phoebe's disappearance. But he won't say why. Nor does recent history produce a good lead. She had transferred from Stanford University, where "she had a little academic trouble," to nearby Boulder College. She had also been upset by her parents' divorce. The divorce, though, Wycherly rules off limits to Archer together with his former wife, Catherine, who, we discover later, had boarded the vacation liner "much in her cups" and left "howling out obscenities." Wycherly insists that Catherine had nothing to do with Phoebe's disappearance and, changing the subject whenever Archer mentions her, blocks an important line of investigation.

Used to working around obstacles, Archer sets out for Boulder Beach and the apartment of Phoebe's former college roommate. The apartment manager, Mrs. Doncaster, describes Phoebe as "a spoiled rich brat who cared for nobody." Cared for nobody? Mrs. Doncaster's grudge has its basis in caring. Phoebe had met her only son, Bobby, the previous summer and come to Boulder Beach to be near him. Trouble with mothers keeps breaking around Phoebe. Her ex-roommate tells how she blamed herself for some anonymous letters sent to the Wycherly family a year before the divorce; the letters, accusing the mother of adultery, hastened the divorce. Though Phoebe denied having written them, she did believe Catherine an adulteress and sided with her father during the separation and divorce.

Present and past carom off each other. Archer's next witness, Bobby Doncaster, admits having talked Phoebe into enrolling at Boulder Beach College but, "very much his mother's boy," kept the arrangement a secret. Archer faces handicaps everywhere. That the two most important men in the life of the missing person—her father and her sweetheart—hold back information adds to his burden. Wycherly denies knowing that the poison-pen letters upset Phoebe and claims that he destroyed them after recovering them from a detective he had hired to investigate them. Chapter Five takes Archer to San Francisco and the ocean liner, docked in the harbor, where Phoebe was last seen, wishing her father a happy trip. Thorough and methodical, Archer starts looking for Phoebe at the likeliest place. The master-at-arms repays the effort, recalling Phoebe and Catherine leaving the ship and then boarding a cab for the city. Thin on leads, Archer will use any scrap of information he can uncover. He leaves his name with the dispatcher of the fleet of taxis operating between the harbor and downtown San Francisco. A listing in a local telephone directory then sends him to Catherine Wycherly's home in Atherton, on the Peninsula between Bayshore and Camino Real. A For Sale sign and a straggle of old unopened newspapers on the lawn prompt Archer to scale the wall surrounding the dark house. But he's stopped by an armed caretaker and,

"Security: The Great American Substitute for Love"

after looking down the barrel of "a nasty little gun," drives away.

He doesn't drive far, observing, instead, his usual practice of interviewing the family and close friends of the missing person. Helen Trevor, Wycherly's stiff, forbidding sister, says that Catherine barged into her brother's stateroom both to extort money and to spoil his farewell party. "A thin woman of about fifty with a face like a silver hatchet," Helen also tells how much Phoebe's disappearance has upset her husband: "She's been like a daughter to us, especially to Carl." Returning to his original plan of seeking the daughter through the mother, Archer goes to the realtor in charge of selling Catherine Wycherly's home. Ben Merriman isn't at his office, located in "a gap-toothed section of rundown houses and vacant lots and struggling businesses" in Camino Real. But his wife, "a thirtyish blonde . . . [who] had seen better days," admits Archer. Just as he steers the talk to the house in Atherton, a bearded young blond man bursts into the office. His purpose: to beat up Merriman for making a pass at his girl-friend. Sally Merriman retorts by accusing the absent girl-friend of making passes at Ben. Her retort draws the sting from the young man's attack. Within a page, the quarrel is over, and Archer is fitting a key into the door of Catherine Wycherly's home.

The door conceals murder. A page later, Archer is looking down at the smashed, mangled face of Ben Merriman, "a mask of blood behind which no life bubbled." Back at Merriman's office, where he rushes to report the murder, Sally tells him that a Captain Mandeville had come looking for Ben the previous week with a gun in his hand. Following a recent tendency to use at least one ex-naval officer in his books, Ross Macdonald introduces Theodore Mandeville (USN, ret.) in Chapter 9. "A lean brown old man with white hair," Mandeville claims that Merriman cheated him on the sale of his home in Atherton. Having bought the Mandeville home for $50,000, Merriman sold it straightaway to Catherine Wycherly for $75,000; the legality of the transaction is being studied by the Real Estate Commission. The case has also put Mandeville in touch with Catherine. Eager to help, he sends Archer to the seedy Champion Hotel on the fringe of a Sacramento slum.

Pretending to be Homer Wycherly, Archer learns from the room clerk that Catherine checked out of the Champion an hour before to move into the elegant Hacienda Inn. The novel's intricate plot darts between different social levels. Leaving the squalor of the Champion, Archer finds a heavily-made-up blonde in dark glasses seated at the bar of the Hacienda; the glasses and the make-up are intended to cover facial bruises. When the woman, whom he believes is Catherine Wycherly, discovers that he has a gun, she invites him to her room, moves close to him on the bed, and, pressing the "soft bombs" of her breasts against him, asks him to kill a man. The man is Ben Merriman. The plea gets Archer to unload some bombshells of his own. He explains that Merriman was clubbed to death a few hours ago, that Phoebe Wycherly has been missing for two months, and that Phoebe's father has hired him to find her. But before he can learn her part in all this, he is knocked out from behind by a man wearing a silk-stocking mask.

The blow with the tire iron concusses Archer and opens a cut requiring six stitches. Then the manager of the Champion Hotel advises him, still believing him to be Homer Wycherly, "Look to your lady." Though he has seen many "sad" women, the manager continues, he never saw one "sadder" than Mrs. Wycherly; during her stay at the Champion, she locked herself in her room, refusing to see a doctor, and emerged four or five days later looking a decade older. This news takes Archer to San Francisco and the offices of the Wycherly Land and Development Company, managed by Wycherly's brother-in-law, Carl Trevor. Archer tells Trevor that Ben Merriman beat up Catherine Wycherly and then turned up dead in her empty house in Atherton. Are the events related? Archer suspects that Catherine, out of pocket, killed Phoebe for her insurance money and then killed Merriman to rid herself of a blackmailer: Catherine had already spent a large sum, perhaps to buy Merriman's silence, moved from a fine home to a cheap hotel, and even asked Archer to kill Merriman for her. Trevor and Archer call Homer Wycherly for permission to hire another detective to look for Catherine while Archer keeps searching for Phoebe. But Homer, "a foolish man full of passions he couldn't handle," rejects the idea, slamming down the phone. Unexpected help and moral strength come from Trevor. His belief that "in-laws never really like each other" and that Homer Wycherly wants an excuse to fire him doesn't stop Trevor from authorizing Archer to bring in another detective. Helen Trevor's remark about Carl's great love for his niece Phoebe is thus borne out. An executive in his mid-fifties with a history of heart trouble, Trevor risks his livelihood by defying his chief.

Archer's dinner with San Francisco detective Willie Mackey, "a flat-faced man in his late forties with black eyes that had never been surprised," produces copies of the anonymous letters charging Catherine Wycherly with adultery: Mackey is the detective Wycherly had retained briefly to investigate the letters. The harvest of letters surprises Archer with its rich yield: the two crank letters and Wycherly's cover letter were typed on the same typewriter. But Mackey has had his fill of letters and missing Wycherly women. Having already gotten fired for moving close to a solution, he refuses the job. Archer has more luck with Nick Gallorini, the cabdriver who took Phoebe from the docks the day she vanished. More to the point, Nick also saw her ten days later when he found her standing dazed in a rainstorm without a raincoat. Phoebe broke down in his cab and needed to be helped to her flat.

Archer has Nick drive him to her San Mateo address, the Conquistador Apartments, where he poses as a would-be tenant. He learns that a

"Security: The Great American Substitute for Love"

Mrs. Smith had left her flat soon after furnishing it and that the flat is now available. Letting himself in, Archer notices in one of the pink bedroom walls a hole plugged with white plaster. The possibility that the hole was made by a bullet sends him to the next-door flat, where another hole along the baseboard and some electronic equipment suggest that the Smith flat had been wired for sound. The use of electronic surveillance in crime and detection—the first in Ross Macdonald—doesn't wrench the plot; Ross Macdonald is sparing in his use of gadgetry and, playing fair, grants both lawman and lawbreaker one go apiece with a hidden microphone. Archer and Nick Gallorini drive to the stereo shop of Mrs. Smith's neighbor. The drive brings results: Nick recognizes the store manager as Phoebe's next-door neighbor, and Archer remembers him as the bearded man who barged into Ben Merriman's office the night before. Accused by Archer of hiding a microphone in Phoebe's bedroom, Stanley Quillan produces an automatic pistol from under the counter and orders the detective out of the store. He then drives, ignorant that Archer is following him, to the Merriman cottage in Atherton. Pressing his contact microphone to a door leading into the cottage, Archer hears Quillan talking to Sally Merriman. He is asking his sister for money. When she pleads poverty, he reminds her of a recorded tape Ben had stowed in his office safe for purposes of blackmail. But Sally refuses to have anything to do with blackmail and sends Quillan away.

He merits close watching. But no sooner does Quillan become a leading suspect than he gets killed. Archer finds him shot to death in the next chapter near a satchel of hundred-dollar bills. Melodrama gives away briefly to analysis; the next chapter finds Archer, "somewhere between witness and suspect," discussing Quillan's murder with a local police captain. Suspecting that Archer is hiding information about the dead man's partnership with Ben Merriman, the captain jails him on an open charge. But he's permitted one phone call before going to his cell. His talk with his client, Carl Trevor, serves him well. As soon as it surfaces that Archer is working for the influential Trevor, the captain releases him. The action speeds ahead. Out of jail, Archer is summoned to Medicine Stone, where Phoebe had recently summered with the Trevors; a car resembling hers has been found in the sea bordering the resort town. This discovery sets another drama into motion. Helen Trevor, a woman of "furious maternality," doesn't want Carl to go to Medicine Stone; he had a serious heart attack two years ago, and his doctors have warned him that he mightn't survive another. Discovering Phoebe dead inside her drowned car, Helen fears, could induce the fatal coronary. With her fear come reasons. Because Helen was barren, Carl has always lavished his fatherly love on his niece.

Denying that his heart is still weak, Carl hears Archer suggest that Catherine Wycherly killed both Quillan and Merriman to remove a black-

mail threat. The supposition encroaches on certainty when Trevor identifies the corpse inside the drowned car as Phoebe. Ross Macdonald's
handling of this difficult scene is masterful. Avoiding graphic descriptions
of physical decomposition, the writer only gives the corpse two sentences.
Yet these both make the corpse believable and justify the shock the corpse
transmits: "The sea-change she had undergone had aged her rapidly and
horribly. She was beaten and bloated and ravaged." The shock occurs
immediately. As soon as Trevor makes his identification, tears burn
Archer's eyes, as they had in *Victim* and *Coast*, when he discovered the
corpses of two other young women he had never met. Carl Trevor is
racked more deeply. Going blue in the face, he falls to the ground with a
heart attack. The local sheriff rushes him to a hospital, but not before
Archer admits having erred by bringing him to Medicine Stone.

Could the calamity at Medicine Stone—the drowning and the coronary—stem from Ross Macdonald's having spent a year of his unhappy
boyhood in Medicine *Hat*, Alberta?[1] How much of the author's long trek
from British Columbia to his mother's family in Ontario gets into the
canon? The trapped woman, the stricken man, and the well-meaning
detective, who worsens a predicament he had set out to improve, all suggest strong psychological undercurrents. Yet these are easier to recognize
than to verify. Archer leaves Medicine Stone straightaway to interview
Phoebe's former landlady, the mother of Phoebe's boy-friend in Boulder
Beach. As she did in her first talk with Archer, Mrs. Doncaster wants
desperately to shield Bobby from harm. She does admit that Bobby had
left Boulder Beach the weekend of Phoebe's disappearance. He is also out
of town now, having left last night after taking a long-distance phone call.
Archer traces the call to Palo Alto. Then he notices, from a sociology
term-paper belonging to Phoebe's ex-roommate, the e's on the typescript
to be askew in the same way as on the crank letters sent to the Wycherly
family. Archer takes all his bad news to Homer Wycherly. He tells his
client, first, that Catherine probably typed the upsetting letters. Then he
does a much harder job; with delicacy and tact, he explains that the dead
body stuffed in the car near Medicine Stone was probably Phoebe.
Though called crazy, insane, and a "garbage raker," Archer keeps hope
alive while discouraging false hope. Competing with the story that Phoebe
went into the sea the night of 2 November is the one, supported by three
witnesses, that she was living in the Conquistador Apartments in San
Mateo through the next week. Undermining the probity of this story,
though, are Carl Trevor's positive identification of the corpse and the
confirmation supplied by his heart attack.

In order to fan the dim hope, Archer goes to the gas station in Palo
Alto from which last night's phone call to Bobby Doncaster was made.
After getting his tank filled, Archer asks the attendant if he remembers a
woman making a long-distance call from his pay phone at six o'clock the

"Security: The Great American Substitute for Love"

evening before. But Archer isn't the first person to ask these questions. A few hours before, the attendant sent a dignified middle-aged man to a motel the telephone-caller had asked about. Archer also goes to the hotel, where he finds, not Catherine Wycherly, but Bobby Doncaster. Bobby tells how he and Phoebe had planned to marry but how Phoebe changed her mind. Surprises pepper the interview. Archer accuses Bobby of pushing Phoebe off the bluffs near Medicine Stone for breaking the engagement. Bobby denies the charge. The car he tipped into the sea was empty; what is more, Phoebe is still alive.

Waiting until Chapter 24 of a twenty-eight chapter novel to bring his prodigal to life was already standard practice for Ross Macdonald by 1961. But bringing Phoebe to life and then keeping her hidden from us argues technical growth. Phoebe killed her mother on 2 November and then got Bobby to dispose of the body. Bobby has good reason to keep Archer away from Phoebe. Speaking with tormented eyes "from a blind face," he wants to protect her from the ordeal of a police investigation. Combining moral strength and gentleness, Archer convinces him that he's on Phoebe's side and that he'd never force her to stand trial if she weren't up to it. But Archer isn't alone in his suspicions that Phoebe is mentally unfit. Bobby identifies her other caller at the motel as a Dr. Sherrill, director of the sanitarium she escaped from before calling Bobby last night.

At the sanitarium, Archer tells Dr. Sherrill his belief that Phoebe killed Merriman and Quillan along with her mother. Bobby shifts the focus of the case by suddenly announcing that he impregnated Phoebe the previous summer in Medicine Stone, site of her mother's death. But he can't explain why Catherine had no clothes on when pulled from the sea. All that makes sense is that Ben Merriman, Catherine's blackmailer, found Phoebe and Bobby in the Atherton house and then forced the girl to pose as her mother. His motive was money. He wanted, first, to keep Catherine's alimony checks coming, so he could take his usual cut and, next, to sell the Atherton house in Catherine's name, thus assuring himself a fat realtor's commission. Phoebe also had reasons for cooperating with Merriman. Her guilty need to resurrect the mother she killed explains her putting on weight and wearing Catherine's clothes. Just as important as all this, her impersonating Catherine entails her own symbolic death; the moral account squares. Archer blocks this drive to self-annihilation by revealing that the gangster Phoebe claims to have hired to kill both Merriman and Stanley Quillan was—himself. Phoebe never issued a contract on the two blackmailers: Merriman was already dead when she met Archer in the Hacienda Inn, and Quillan probably died by the same hand that took his partner's life.

Phoebe comes into the novel in her own right in Chapter 26, two chapters from the end. Her entrance is robbed of drama; so sunken in spirit is she that she needs the help of a uniformed nurse. The doldrums persist. Still punishing herself, she again confesses to killing Merriman and Quillan. Archer gives her false security, mentioning the poison found in Merriman's stomach and the shotgun that blew off Quillan's head. Duped by his improvisation, she gives the case a strange new twist. Why has she been confessing to murders that never happened? Before Archer can find out, Dr. Sherrill stops him. Phoebe *is* living a dream, he agrees; but she has also set up a false guilt to blot out a real guilt she can't face:

I don't like the quality of her lies. They're very important to her. If we take away the whole structure at once, I can't predict the consequences. She's been living for weeks in a half-world where lies and truth are all mixed up.

The doctor has explained her need to unload false guilt. On the next page she tells why she blames herself for her parents' divorce. About a year ago, she had seen her mother and her uncle, Carl Trevor, embracing in a taxi, and she made the mistake of telling her Aunt Helen, Trevor's wife, what she saw. The next day brought the first of the crank letters.

Moral guilt keeps pouring from Phoebe. Her mother was already dying when Phoebe reached her. Though blinded by the thrashing inflicted on her, Catherine named Phoebe's father as her attacker. The tempo of *Wycherly*, counterpointing its worn, haunted characters, keeps fresh and lively to the end. Options stay alive: Homer Wycherly gives the novel a new leading suspect; he had threatened to kill Catherine, and his ship, delayed by engine trouble, didn't leave port till 3 November, the day after it was scheduled to sail. All along, Phoebe has taken the blame for the three killings to protect her father. (Impersonating Catherine came easily to her, since it converted her, the loving daughter, into the faithful wife Wycherly deserved.) But, besides playing variations on Oedipal sexuality, Ross Macdonald has effectively misdirected our attention. A visit to the ship's steward in the next chapter reveals Wycherly's guilt to be a red herring. Though his ship did spend the night of 2 November at anchor, he couldn't have driven to Atherton, killed his wife, and then driven back to the ship without making his absence known.

As in Roderick Thorp's *The Detective* (1966), which also relies heavily on tape recordings and psychology, the killer is named on the playback of a tape. Prodded by Archer, Sally Merriman removes from her husband's safe the tape her brother Stanley had tried to pry from her in Chapter 17. The taped conversation, a lover's quarrel between Catherine and Carl Trevor, gives Archer all he needs to solve the case. Catherine pleads with Trevor to give up his job and his "goddam frigid wife," Helen. Trevor, handicapped by poor health and advancing middle age from starting anew, temporizes: "We have to keep the situation as it is," he advises. But twenty years of hidden facts and feelings recoil on him. Surprises come in *Wycherly* when least expected. The always crucial next-to-last

"Security: The Great American Substitute for Love"

chapter gives the reason for Trevor's heart attack at Medicine Stone. It also realigns the book's motivation. Ross Macdonald had all but eliminated Trevor as a suspect—rousing our pity for him as a cardiac victim; our admiration for him as a brave, loving uncle who overrules his powerful brother-in-law; and our trust for springing Archer from jail.

A bed-ridden coronary patient, Trevor personifies helplessness. Archer's cornering and then pouncing on him takes on, momentarily, a sadistic look. Archer accuses Trevor of having identified Catherine's corpse as Phoebe to foil the investigation. What clinches his guilt for Archer is Catherine's naming her killer to Phoebe as "your father." Crime continues to hew to the blood-tie. Phoebe naturally thought her mother was speaking of Homer Wycherly, but the taped conversation from the Conquistador Apartments confirms the reference to Trevor. Archer promises to keep the blood-tie a secret. He also puts forth, through Trevor's confession, a psychological vision of forgiveness. Nobody chooses evil in Ross Macdonald. A desperate last option, evil is what people clutch at to fend off harm. As Trevor says, "You start out with an innocent roll in the hay, and you end up killing people." His affaire with Catherine, or Kitty, started twenty years ago when, at age eighteen, she came to live with the Trevors. Helen and Carl were already sleeping in different rooms owing to her having lost a child early in the marriage. Frustrated and normally sexed at thirty-two, he turned to Kitty. When Kitty missed a period, she married Homer Wycherly, later convincing him that Phoebe was born prematurely. (The background of the plot closely resembles that of *Pool*.) Giving the marriage every chance, she also ended her liaison with Trevor. For nearly twenty years she and Trevor never made love. But Helen's coldness and Kitty's frequent brawls with Wycherly reunited them.

Why did he kill her? Her divorce destroyed the structure of her personality: she drank more; her demand that Trevor get a divorce and marry her grew shriller; she threatened to tell Phoebe that Trevor was her father. This pressure had to be lifted. In Trevor's words, "The sheer involvement became too much for me." Catherine was found naked, he adds, because she had undressed. "It was one of her means of persuasion which had worked on me in the past," Trevor admits with candor. The finale of *Wycherly* reveals a new moral maturity. In mitigating Trevor's guilt, Ross Macdonald extends him a compassion he had heretofore reserved for young female killers, like Cathy Slocum (*Pool*), Galley Lawrence (*Way*), and Mildred Hallman (*Doomsters*). He also validates Archer's last act in the novel. Though a sexual outlaw, Trevor is no tomcat. Nor does he kill for profit; his two murder victims besides Catherine were blackmailers, whose deaths sadden nobody. Thus Archer can respond tenderly to his plea for mercy. Trevor doesn't want a court trial because his certain conviction would shackle Phoebe with the knowledge that her father killed her mother. To spare Phoebe, he asks Archer to bring him his coat, which contains enough digitalis pills to kill him if taken all at once. Archer offers to trade this gift of death for a written murder confession.

Trevor agrees. The last paragraph in the book shows Archer placing the signed confession on a bureau beyond the invalid Trevor's reach, saying nothing. Does he keep his bargain with this killer of three? Or does he renege, denying the killer all right to fair play? Though the book ends before Archer takes action, it implies no betrayal. The last sentence, "we didn't speak again," shows that no more words are needed to show Archer where honor lies. Profiting the most from his bargain with Trevor will be Phoebe. Though Trevor will also gain, Archer is no Old Testament scourge—matching crimes to their appropriate punishments. Humane and charitable, he lightens Trevor's suffering while giving Trevor the chance to help the daughter he has always loved.

The novel's title, referring obliquely to the silent partnership of Archer and Trevor, looks beyond the reported action: thanks to the deal, Phoebe will grow into womanhood, marrying Bobby Doncaster and having his baby. Archer has already reached full growth. Tough, mobile, and quick to react, he admits in Chapter 3, while talking to Bobby, "I hadn't been handling him with any tact, and I changed my line of questioning." He interviews witnesses with more conscious technique in *Wycherly* than heretofore—improvising subjects, changing pace, and giving the witnesses the impression of not incriminating themselves; forensics establish Phoebe's innocence in Chapter 26. At other times, he talks and acts like a private eye in a crime novel. In Chapter 14, fellow detective Willie Mackey asks about his bandaged head. Archer changes the subject quickly. To dwell on one's knocks and aches would violate a professional code that sometimes looks like a manly cult. (Archer later tells Helen Trevor, speaking as a coterie member addressing an outsider, "A man has to do what he has to do.") The tough casualness of his response, when he is asked about his experience with missing girls, suits his deadpan elitism: "They turn up counting change in Vegas, or waiting table in the Tenderloin, or setting up light housekeeping in a beat pad, or bucking the modeling racket in Hollywood." But he will drop his knowing airs. Carrying over from *Galton* is the self-irony designating both control and balance in times of stress. Even when hurt, he avoids the sour and the glum. His head swathed in a towel after Trevor smashes him with a tire-iron, he calls himself "an Indian holy man who had run out of holiness and just about everything else."

Also recurring from *Galton* and ultimately from *Oedipus Rex* is the use of repetition to shape the action. Many of the events of *Wycherly* occur twice. Some of these recurrences are trivial. San Francisco cab-driver Nick Gallorini and Mr. Clement, purser of the ship on which Homer

"Security: The Great American Substitute for Love"

Wycherly took his cruise, both have daughters. The manager of the Champion Hotel and Wycherly are both divorced, as is Archer. The detective visits an empty house in Chapter 6 and an empty flat in Chapter 16; Catherine Wycherly had lived in both places, and both are ready for a new occupant. Moving closer to Oedipal themes, Bobby Doncaster dreams of killing his mother, while Phoebe accepts the guilt for killing hers. The mother-daughter identity switch looks ahead to the doubling at the end involving Phoebe's legal and natural father. Glancing off the planes of this many-sided Oedipal prism are two Sophoclean themes—hidden parentage and the killing of the parent in order to supplant her.

Where does *Wycherly* fit in Ross Macdonald's development? Though some fifteen percent longer, it has four fewer chapters than *Ferguson,* implying that the restoration of Archer brings a new maturity of design and execution. Not true. *Wycherly* offers less than either *Ferguson* or *Galton.* This lack is felt in different ways. Homer Wycherly's sailing date is given in Chapter 3 as Friday, 2 November. Yet 2 November didn't fall on a Friday in the four years between 1958-61. This trifle wouldn't deserve a mention if Ross Macdonald himself hadn't gone to the trouble of matching dates with the days of the week in his later books. More damaging to the novel are its contrivances and improbabilities. Ready at hand to serve the plot, Stanley Quillan complains to Sally Merriman about her husband Ben just when Archer happens to be present. Sally and Stanley can't talk out of Archer's earshot; in Chapter 17 the detective eavesdrops on them for five pages, during which they reward his pains with some key leads. Equally implausible and, what is more, out of joint with his moral charity are some of his *machismo* pronouncements. He tells Homer Wycherly in Chapter 23, "Nothing is impossible in this case" and "Suspicion is my occupational hazard." Then there is the crudely moralistic, "Life. It's a course that goes on and on. You never graduate or get a diploma. The best you can do is put off the time when you flunk out." A good novel doesn't need these splashes of hard color; a weak one can't be freshened by them. Archer will reflect their triteness. For all his jaded street sense, he is duped by twenty-one-year-old Phoebe Wycherly's impersonation of a frowsy, faded matron of forty. Plotting rather than plausibility also explains Catherine and Trevor, middle-aged lovers acquainted for twenty years, embracing in a taxi just when Phoebe's car pulls alongside.

Many other scenes are vivid and intelligent. The book's incalculability promotes both shock and imaginative participation. Surprises come from all sides and from all characters. Its beauties and its strengths make *Wycherly* a transitional work. Like *Victim* and *Ferguson,* it owes something to Wilkie Collin's *Woman in White,* in which a woman is drugged, held prisoner, and believed dead while her lookalike sister takes her place. The novel also breaks new ground. Its portrayal of the collapse of traditional notions of marriage and the family prefigures *The Far Side of the Dollar, The Instant Enemy,* and *The Goodbye Look*, works which link crime to the loss of security in the home.

II

Ross Macdonald judged well to rank *The Zebra-Striped Hearse* (1962) among his favorites.[2] The action is crisp, the atmosphere fully realized, and the ideas stimulating. This stylish, intelligent novel is also the first by Ross Macdonald to open at Archer's Sunset Boulevard office since *Grin,* published ten years before. Isobel Blackwell, a suburban woman from nearby Bel Air, has come to talk with the detective before his appointment, scheduled for half an hour hence, with her husband, Mark. Isobel doesn't want to belittle her husband, but to protect him. Speaking from "a face that had known suffering," she explains that Mark wants to stop the forthcoming marriage between his twenty-four-year-old daughter Harriet and an artist she met about five weeks ago while visiting her mother in Mexico. Isobel would like to see Harriet get married. Assessing the future honestly and clearly, she rates her step-daughter's chances for happiness with Burke Damis, the artist, high:

He [Damis] does have artistic talent—a great deal more talent than Harriet possesses, as she knows. And, after all, she'll have money enough for both of them. With his talent and—virility, and her money and devotion, I'd say they had the makings of a marriage.

Colonel Mark Blackwell doesn't share Isobel's views. His objections to the marriage test Ross Macdonald's craftsmanship. For parental disapproval of young lovers marrying is usually a subject for comedy; Colonel Blackwell's accusations—that Damis, a fortune-hunting nobody, has bewitched innocent, unsuspecting Harriet—have antecedents in the *commedia dell'arte*. But the Colonel's suffering and the relentlessness with which it infects others border on tragedy. Blackwell has already ended several of Harriet's romances; possessive and domineering, he has always believed her an easy mark for upstarts and frauds. The object of his rage now, though, is his wife. Having seen her car in a nearby parking lot, he barges into Archer's outer office and shouts for Isobel to come out. His shouting, "brown outdoorsman's face," and "ramrod dignity" don't faze Archer, who outmaneuvers and then quiets him.

Once calmed, Blackwell takes his wife to her car and comes back to Archer's office muttering about "the combined force of the females in my life." The female he has come to discuss is Harriet, but his words tell more about him than about her. Convinced that she is offering Damis love, comeliness, and loads of money (she will have half a million dollars outright on her next birthday) in exchange for nothing, he asks Archer to

"*Security: The Great American Substitute for Love*"

investigate Damis. Archer suspects that Blackwell's urge to manage Harriet springs from secret fears:

> Blackwell was a sad and troubled man, hardly competent to play God with anybody's life. But the sadder and more troubled they were, the more they yearned for omnipotence. The really troubled ones believed they had it.

He will only work for Blackwell on his own terms. No lines of investigation may be blocked, and no compromise made with his reputation, license, or honor: "I'm not going to cook up evidence, or select it to confirm you in your prejudices. I'm willing to investigate Damis on the understanding that the chips fall where they fall."

His first stop is the Blackwells' beach house, near Malibu, where Damis is staying temporarily. ("They're not even married, and he's already scrounging on us," growls Blackwell. "I tell you the man's an operator.") Posing again as a prospective renter, Archer inspects the house, noting, during his reconnoiter, a shaving kit in the bathroom bearing the initials, B. C. He also discovers an emotional truth—that the love of Harriet and Damis is one-sided. Before leaving the house, he sees Harriet kissing a trapped, unreciprocating Damis: "She leaned toward him . . . and kissed him on the mouth. . . . He was looking past her at me. His eyes were wide open and rather sad." Harriet, an outsize blonde with her father's bony features, doesn't suspect Damis to be an unwilling lover. But she has suspicions of a different kind about Archer. Catching him before he can drive away, she accuses him of spying. To the argument that her father wants to spare her unhappiness, she replies that Blackwell is insuring her unhappiness. Archer has a hostile witness on his hands, and he must shift his approach. But the recognition comes too late. By pressing her too hard for information about Damis, he has already lost her trust. The interview ends badly. Accused of rushing into marriage to spite her father, she calls Archer "an insufferable man" and walks away from him.

As has been seen in his talks with Galley Lawrence Tarantine in *Way*, Archer is unimpressive when prying into the loves of young women; he tells Harriet, "You're making me look like a slob," and admits, "I was trying to do a job. I bungled it." Chastened, he goes to a local diner to think of a way to recover his losses. He is soon yanked from his thoughts. His window seat at the roadside diner gives him his first look at the zebra-striped hearse of the novel's title. Symbolizing the fusion of youth and age that organizes the action, the hearse contains six teen-aged surfers (six being the usual number of pall-bearers at a funeral). Archer's attention turns quickly from the surfers, who have entered the diner, when Harriet's car drives by. Archer follows the car to Colonel Blackwell's hill-top house, where he finds the colonel and Damis quarrelling hotly. Humane, decisive, and poised, he wrenches Blackwell's shotgun away with the rebuke, "Shooting never solved a thing. Didn't you learn that in the war?" His reply, "A daughter isn't exactly a possession," to Blackwell's charge that Damis is stealing his "most precious possession" confuses the colonel. It also puts him in the background while his wife re-enters the action. The following scene excludes him.

Though many of his women do harm, Ross Macdonald values the healing, comforting glow connected with the female principle. This shows vividly in his portrait of Isobel Blackwell. First, the usual rivalry between step-mother and step-daughter is absent from Isobel's encounter with Harriet. The women treat each other with friendly dignity. Speaking affectionately, Isobel asks Harriet to treat her father more lovingly, adding with self-effacing frankness, "You're more important to him than I am. You could break his heart." Ross Macdonald handles the encounter with the moral delicacy it deserves. Though Harriet rejects Isobel's plea, she is grateful for the honesty and warmth underlying it. Embracing Isobel, she says, "You've been the best to me—better than I deserve." The touching scene, brilliantly countervailing the brutal one between Damis and Blackwell, ends with a restoration of life's complexity. Harriet and Damis drive away, neither of them looking back; Colonel Blackwell roars into the house after another tirade; Isobel and Archer find themselves much as they were in the first chapter—anxious to help a bad situation but feeling weak and confused.

Isobel explains her husband's wildness. While the Army was preparing to retire him "very much against his will," his first wife divorced him, remarried, and settled with her husband in Mexico. A lead of a different sort appears in the next chapter. Back at Blackwell's Malibu beach house, wedged into a loose-fitting glass door and its frame to stop the door from rattling, is a much-folded set of Mexicana Airlines flight instructions for one Q. R. Simpson. A little legwork reveals that Harriet and Simpson, not Burke Damis, flew Mexicana from Guadalajara to Los Angeles a week ago. A check through police files gives the case a new dimension. Archer learns from his old friend and former Army commander, grizzled Peter Colton of L. A.'s criminal investigation branch, that Simpson was reported missing by his wife two weeks ago. Wasting no time, Archer flies to Simpson's wife, Vicki, in Redwood City, near San Francisco. "A striking beauty," Vicki hasn't seen her husband for two months. Simpson's absence fits a pattern common to Ross Macdonald's losers: "Hopeful beginnings and nothing endings," Vicki says of her husband's many projects, which number jobs as a short-order cook, bartender, houseboy, and, most recently, amateur detective.

Vicki's rehearsal of her husband's dreams ends with a phone call reporting his death: Simpson was disinterred by a bulldozer clearing land for a new freeway in Citrus Junction, near L. A.; physical evidence indicates that he was buried two months before. Vicki and Archer fly south to look at the cadaver, which Ross Macdonald displays tactfully. Though he takes us into the morgue, he avoids all concessions to gore and decay: "The dead man lay on an enameled table. I won't describe him. His time in the earth, and on the table, had altered him for the worse." He does materialize the local coroner, who says that Simpson was killed by an ice-pick (Ross Macdonald's first icepick murder since *Morgue*). Vicki identi-fies the dead man as Ralph, tenderly confirming her identification "by stroking his dusty hair." But she identifies nobody else. Her denial that she knows Burke Damis, the man who used both her husband's name and passport to cross into Mexico, sends Archer home to "a hot shower . . . a cold drink and a dark bed."

The possibility that the airline instructions he found at the Malibu beach house tie in with Harriet's disappearance sends Archer the next morning to Guadalajara—the place where Harriet met Damis. Her mother, a new character type in the canon, the neglectful, sybaritic parent, notes the difference between Damis's good looks and Harriet's plainness. But she assigns no vicious motives to Damis. Another new character, Anne Castle, Damis's former sweetheart and the manager of a crafts shop in Ajijic, keeps the plot moving. Like Harriet's mother, Anne is a new kind of character study for Ross Macdonald. She is "smallish," and small women ignite the same erotic-paternal explosion in Ross Macdonald as waiflike ones do in Graham Greene. Anne's saying on the page she is introduced, "I work all the time," strikes home. "So do I when I'm on a case," Archer replies. But their similarity of outlook and Archer's im-mediate liking of her lead nowhere. Anne's work, weaving, symbol of sexual fidelity since Homer's Penelope, shows that her relationship with Archer will be strictly professional; she loves somebody else.

The object of her heart's trust? As her regal-sounding name suggests, she has maintained her queenly passion for Burke Damis even though he left her for another woman. Damis had come to her shop some weeks ago looking for a place in which to paint, and she rented him one of her studios. An artist herself, Anne was amazed at his dedication and drive: "He'd paint himself blind," Anne says revealingly; "I never saw a man work so ferociously hard. He painted twelve and fourteen hours a day. I had to make him stop to eat." Like Ada Reichler in *Galton*, another attractive, well-bred loser in love, she doesn't resent the torment her erratic lover put her through; what saddens her is that the torment has stopped. Scathingly, she calls herself, "the classic case of the landlady who fell in love with her star boarder and got jilted"; two pages later, after giving Archer a sketch Damis had done of himself, she adds, "Jilted landlady betrays demon lover." Anne is running down her best womanly qualities—her tenderness and devotion; her hurt stings her so deeply be-cause of her openness to love. Archer's favorable first impression with-stands her self-reproach, and he leaves her regretting that he probably won't see her again.

He flies out the next morning. The evidence he collects in Los Angeles after his arrival incriminates Damis. First, a local art critic identifies Damis's self-portrait and the photographs Archer took of Damis's other pictures as the work of a young California artist named Bruce Campion. The critic adds that a local news bulletin has reported Campion wanted by the police for killing his wife: Dolly Stone Campion was found strangled to death with a silk stocking. Ross Macdonald's throwing the runaway together with the Most Likely Suspect and then putting them both beyond the reach of the law sharpens the danger threatening Harriet. Already suspected of killing his wife, Campion, clearly not in love with Harriet, may have already murdered her, as well. Colonel Blackwell's reaction in the next chapter keeps us wondering if Campion is a sex-killer. Blackwell, hearing that his daughter is traveling with a suspected killer, shows "the pale insides of his mouth" in dumb gaping horror and then faints. The sly allusion to Othello, supported by his earlier accusation that Campion bewitched Harriet, belittles Blackwell, who had a mediocre military career. The chapter adds little; rather, it builds tension out of pre-existing materials. This treatment is typical. Nearly every touch in *Hearse* tells; nearly every sentence either tightens or advances the action.

The next scene introduces several rapid shifts. Archer tells Blackwell that he has co-opted a Reno detective, Arnie Walters, and, now that murder has entered the investigation, gets his client's permission to call the police. Captain Royal of San Mateo County's homicide force explains that Dolly Stone Campion was already three months pregnant when she married Bruce last September. Hope pierces the growing gloom with Royal's unexpected announcement that Harriet and Bruce were seen yesterday near the Nevada-California border. This hope, though, isn't allowed to spread. Touchy, scandal-fearing, and generally uncooperative, Blackwell fumes over what he heard while listening in on an extension to Archer's phone conversation with Royal, namely, "Harriet has been living under military occupation. She's a fugitive from injustice." He fires Archer. Fortunately, two pages later, Isobel Blackwell, who has come home in time to learn of the falling-out, rehires the detective.

Both financed and morally fortified by a client, Archer flies to Reno, where he tells Arnie Walters his fears about Campion. These take on a new urgency when Archer finds Harriet's hat in the lake near her father's lodge. A smear of blood on the lining and a swirl of long blonde hair torn from the roots drain Walters's hope: "Looks like we're too late," he says sadly. Archer, pluckier in the face of grief, asks Walters to get the Reno Police Department to test the blood-smear and to drag the lake for Harriet's body. But new evidence saddens Archer. Already suspected of killing two people, Simpson and Dolly, Campion is now reported by a local man to have quarrelled with Harriet yesterday. The local man adds that

"Security: The Great American Substitute for Love"

Simpson worked as a houseboy at the Blackwells' lodge the previous spring. *Hearse* builds suspense through strong, vivid supporting details. Given both a personality and an adventure, Ralph Simpson comes to us as a person we can care about rather than as a corpse. The local man recalls his gambling, his bizarre ideas on subjects like nuclear war, space travel, and reincarnation, and, though Simpson was married, a romantic fling he had with a beauty operator named Fawn.

Archer traces Fawn King to her apartment, where he learns that Simpson took a job with the Blackwells in order to investigate the death of his good friend, Dolly. Fawn also mentions a package Simpson had left with her, cautioning her at the time not to open it. Hanging fire on the question of the package, Ross Macdonald ends the first half with a different sort of disclosure—that Dolly Campion came from Citrus Junction, Simpson's murder-site. But other excavations must take place before the action returns to this bulldozed, scooped-out place. The second half of the book opens with Archer going to the Tahoe cabin where Campion lived the previous summer. The first of many surprises igniting the second half comes quickly. A man feeding his pet hawk at the cabin introduces himself as Burke Damis, a University of California art professor who loaned Campion his cabin while on sabbatical. Archer just missed Campion, in fact, who returned to the cabin a couple of hours ago looking "perfectly ghastly" and asking to borrow Damis's car. Though upset that Campion left the cabin in disarray, Damis loaned him the car. Ross Macdonald's keeping Campion out of the action makes him an outlaw at large, capable of any crime. Keeping him beyond Archer's eager reach also creates the opportunity to bring in testimony and evidence against him. His wet clothes and scratched face increase the likelihood that he killed Harriet the night before.

More incriminating evidence follows when the blood on the hat fished out of Lake Tahoe fits Harriet's blood group. Again, Campion stays a step ahead of his pursuers by leaving Saline City an hour before Arnie Walters traces him there. But he is finally caught. In a scene brilliantly expressive of life's incongruity and complexity, Archer finds the desperado "sleeping peacefully" by the fireplace of his sister's comfortable suburban home. Archer's capture of him fuses professional pride and skill. Conceding that he should turn the job over to the police, he nonetheless takes Campion himself—luring him to his sister's garage by jamming a car-horn and then hitting him on the head with a hammer as he enters the garage; characteristically, Archer hits him hard enough to knock him out but gently enough to avoid serious injury.

Now here is where most crime writers would start to resolve the novel. The action has already provided a family crisis, a love triangle or two, a chase, and both geographical and sociological sweep; an apprehended killer of two has shown himself a flase friend (to Damis) and a false lover (to Anne Castle). Ross Macdonald only needs a chapter to fill in the motivation and to get Campion to say what he did to Harriet. Except for the absence of these explanations, Chapters 1-18 could stand as a good adventure novel.

The book sets itself other artistic challenges and goals. The rest of it, Chapters 19-32, comprises a *tour de force* of gyrations. Just when somebody seems ready to confess his guilt, he bounces the suspicion off himself to somebody else. Besides offering ingenious plotting, the novel also bids to become a sentimental journey through different law enforcement agencies from the earlier Archers. In addition to restoring Peter Colton, *Hearse* brings back Captain Royal of *Wycherly* and Deputy Sherrif Patrick Mungan from *Galton* (where he had no first name). Ross Macdonald's aim? To carve out a familiar fictional context; also, to bring in new evidence and then to ponder its meaning from a professional standpoint. Records show that Ralph Simpson gave Bruce and Dolly Campion money; the couple's welfare check stopped coming when the county found that Campion was using most of it to buy paints. That Simpson introduced Dolly and Campion invites several questions. Could he have impregnated Dolly, as well? Could Campion have found out about the liaison and then murdered Dolly and Simpson in revenge, stolen Simpson's passport, and bolted to Mexico? Campion's story that he scratched his face walking through some bushes loses in credibility. The weight of circumstantial evidence, braced by a set of matching motives, presses against him.

But the pressure is lightened. Mungan, whose late entry into the case gives him a clairty Archer may lack, says, "There's some doubt . . . that Campion killed Dolly" and "We don't have any firm evidence that Campion did it." These insights are important. If Campion didn't kill Dolly, he'd have little cause to kill Simpson. Mungan believes that had Campion not run, he'd not have been arrested. He's still far from being convicted; his unsupported account of his whereabouts the night Dolly died Mungan calls "the kind of story you can't prove or disprove." Mungan, as objective outsider, has done his job of keeping doubt alive. The investigation must move elsewhere.

The emergence of new evidence reawakens the hopes of finding Harriet and of naming the killer. Several hours after Dolly's death, a neighbor found her baby in a parked car holding a brown leather button in its small fist. Archer goes back to Citrus Junction to match the button to the coat it came from. Vicki Simpson tells him of a brown tweed topcoat with a missing button that her husband brought back from Tahoe. Allowing himself to be led by a little child has given Archer a case-breaking clue. Though he lacks the button, he does remember seeing the coat Vicki described on one of the surfers in the zebra-striped hearse. Using the tide-tables kept in the hearse, one of the surfers supplies the exact date the brown, salt-stained coat washed ashore. Archer takes both coat and

"Security: The Great American Substitute for Love"

information to Police Sergeant Wesley Leonard of Citrus Grove. The interview between the two lawmen continues to shrink the moral distance between investigator and suspect in Ross Macdonald. Earlier, in his office, Archer had tried on the coat, which "hugged him like guilt." Leonard, convinced that he has "something hotter than the coat," produces Simpson's murder weapon—an icepick from a bar set a local hardware dealer had sold to an old friend of Leonard's wife. The imaginative tension between the icepick and Leonard's "something hotter than the coat" introduces exciting possibilities.

Thus the next development in the plot merges with the novel's underlying pattern. The purchaser of the bar set was the mother of Dolly Stone Campion; the Stones had bought the set as a wedding gift for a widowed neighbor named Mrs. Jaimet. ("She was *wonderful* to Dolly, a second mother," says Mrs. Stone. "Dolly used to call her Aunt Izzie.") Mrs. Jaimet and her second marriage interest Archer. A few more questions reveal that, after leaving Citrus Junction, she married a Colonel Mark Blackwell. This breakthrough is followed by another, a mile or so away from the Stones' house. Sergeant Wesley Leonard continues to draw on his experience both as a policeman and a long-term resident of Citrus Junction. He denies that either Isobel or Ronald Jaimet, "the best principal we ever had at the union high school," killed Dolly. Keeping his own counsel, Archer drives to the Blackwell house. But Ross Macdonald tightens some more screws before letting the detective face Isobel. Arriving at the Bel Air mansion, Archer finds that the case has coaxed Harriet's mother, Pauline Hatchen, from Mexico. Pauline says that Isobel's first husband, Blackwell's cousin and close friend, died accidentally while hiking with the colonel in the mountains.

The chapter includes still more exposition, which, coming late on, helps create an even realistic flow of action. Disinclined to speak well of a former husband whose blunders may have lead to her daughter's death, Pauline describes Blackwell as a hollow wooden soldier:

He wasn't interested in any woman, and that includes me. . . . Mark was a mother's boy. I know that sounds like a peculiar statement to make about a professional military man. Unfortunately it's true. His mother was the widow of the late Colonel, who was killed in the First War, and Mark was her only son, and she really lavished herself on him, if "lavish" is the word. "Ravish" may be closer.

This fixation Blackwell foisted on Harriet, another only child of the opposite sex: "He got her so confused that she didn't know whether she was a girl or a boy, or if he was her father or her lover." This confirmation of Blackwell's shakiness makes sense of his motivation; his uproars mask a painful void: he only knows sexual love as a function of the parent-child relationship. Archer uses Blackwell's guilt to explain his past. But no sooner is the Colonel smirched than he is redeemed. Archer's talk with

Isobel, spanning the next two chapters, lifts a great deal of moral guilt from Blackwell. Full of chloral hydrate, which acts like a truth serum, Isobel admits having virtually adopted Dolly Stone when Dolly was a girl. But she denies knowing that Simpson was killed with her icepick or that he was buried in back of her former home. Seconding Sergeant Leonard, she also denies any sexual tie between Dolly and Ronald Jaimet. Nor will she own to any foul play causing Jaimet's death in the Sierras. Her present husband didn't kill her former one; a diabetic, Jaimet broke his insulin needle after tripping on a steep slope.

Archer doubts the truth both of this story and of Isobel's professed ignorance of a brown tweed topcoat with a missing button. These doubts he phrases characteristically: "The case keeps opening up, and taking in more people and more territory. The connections between the people deep multiplying." Ross Macdonald has introduced complication at a point where most writers would wind the action down. Isobel, Archer implies, may be the coping stone of the case. One event he rejects as coincidence is Campion's marrying her substitute daughter one year and eloping with her stepdaughter the next. What is more, Isobel knew all the putative murderees, three of them intimately—Dolly, Harriet, and Jaimet. Archer's interview with her shows the detective at his finest—both in the questions he asks and in what he makes of the answers he gets. Isobel tells him, "I'm not fond of your objectivity," "I don't admire your methods. They're a combination of bullying, blackmail, and insulting speculation," and "You have a vile imagination and a vicious tongue." These gibes bring on a crisis of conscience in Archer. He likes Isobel, *dis*-likes making her squirm, and, rather than mistreating her, has already helped her by not reporting his suspicions to the police. What happens next proves that he must speak out soon. Going into Blackwell's wardrobe, he turns up the cuff of one of the colonel's suit jackets and finds the same cleaner's mark he saw on the inside cuff of the brown topcoat worn by the teen-aged surfer at Zuma.

The chapter-break only eases tension briefly. If Isobel is to escape jail, she must act quickly. Calling herself "an unlucky woman," she discusses her marriage to Blackwell in terms more damaging to Blackwell than those used by his resentful former wife. As usual in Ross Macdonald, a man's failings reveal themselves sexually; as usual, the sexuality hearkens to the Oedipus myth. Last summer, Blackwell had gotten a much-younger woman pregnant and then begged Isobel to marry him to stop his moral deterioration. She didn't know that the girl was Dolly Stone. Nor could she stop him from killing Dolly. Archer's reaction to this news conveys more sympathy and understanding than rancor. The mellowness of Chapter 27 of *Hearse* counterpoints the stabbing staccato rhythm of Chapter 26. Archer's tender feelings for Isobel, strained but not shattered, work discreetly into the investigation. No sooner does the detective ponder Blackwell's killing of Dolly than this happens: "I touched her temple where the hair was wet, she leaned her head against my hand." Under different conditions, these two could have built a loving relationship.

But the investigation must move forward. Blackwell has deposed Isobel, Campion's successor as Most Likely Suspect. Where is he, though? Like Campion, when suspected of killing Dolly and Harriet, he may have gone to Tahoe. Not true. A phone call to Arnie Walters makes him sound more like a runaway killer than a father anxious for his missing daughter. He didn't show up at the lake for the dragging operation; moreover, he hasn't been seen at the lakeside lodge. The chase reasserts itself as the plot's unifying principle. Archer's tracking instinct leads him, not to Tahoe, but to Blackwell's beach house in Malibu. A red trail leading from a bloody towel in the bathroom sink ends with Blackwell hunched on the side of a bed looking so scurvy that Archer hates touching him. Drained of will, Blackwell denies killing Ronald Jaimet: "Ronald was my favorite cousin. He greatly resembled my mother." But he ages and shrinks horribly during the interview, Archer mentioning his "tangled white hair" and "withering neck." This deterioration is understandable; Blackwell's self-disclosures would sink the bravest of spirits. A few moments after saying that he molested Dolly as a child, he admits to a worse crime—that of killing his daughter, Harriet. "I'm a dirty old man," he adds in a dry chuckle that erupts into a choking fit. Two reversals within half a page end the chapter. Bringing Blackwell a glass of water from the bathroom, Archer finds a revolver pointing at him. But Blackwell slams the door between himself and the amazed detective and, rather than escaping, shoots himself. Ross Macdonald phrases the discovery of the dead man in an image that transmits the sexual degradation bristling through the chapter: "Blackwell's gun went off. . . . It was still in his mouth when I reached him, like a pipe of queer design which he had fallen asleep smoking."

Finding Harriet's corpse becomes Archer's first job. Developments elsewhere have strengthened him for this work. Thanks to his efforts, Bruce Campion comes to a good end—leaving jail and reuniting with Anne Castle, who had flown up from Mexico to help him in his ordeal. Campion tells Archer that Harriet clawed him when he told her that her father killed Dolly. But this heavy news didn't cause Harriet's death. Anne Castle reports having seen her the night before in the Guadalajara airport: as he did in *Ferguson*, Ross Macdonald hints at a hideous moral and dramatic resolution to the gathering tensions but then, once the ugliness has snagged the reader's mind, reverses direction. (Blackwell's calling Dolly "my fairy princess" recalls Ian Ferguson's first reaction to Holly May.)

The drama of primitive emotions ends, logically enough, in a primitive setting. The last chapter, Chapter 32, set in a nameless Aztec village, restores the runaway, who hasn't appeared since Chapter 5; but only to reveal her as the killer. Religion permeates the scene. Harriet has spent the day in church praying; unable to confess to the Spanish-speaking priest, she unburdens herself to Archer. Her despised father is resurrected: Colonel Blackwell posed as the killer to shift both the blame and the investigation from Harriet: "He loved you to the point of death," Archer tells her on the last page of the book. Like the strips on the zebra-striped hearse, good and evil alternate sharply in the characters; each character, moreover, embodies elements of both death, conveyed by the hearse's original purpose, and renewal, suggested by the hearse's young passengers. Twice, Blackwell stopped Harriet from killing herself—at the Tahoe lodge and then at the Malibu beach house, where she had slashed her wrists. But she still hasn't forgiven him for Dolly Stone. Dolly's affaire with Harriet's father and her marriage to Harriet's then-lover, Campion, decided matters: Dolly had to die. Simpson also had to die because he had found out about Dolly and Blackwell. Motives of spite and insecurity run deep in Harriet. Most likely, she threw Simpson's corpse in her stepmother's back yard in order to make Isobel, another rival for her father's love, look guilty. Her harshness softens when she decides to waive extradition. Though driven by emotions she can't control, she can get psychiatric care when she returns to California. In the book's last sentence, Archer, her confessor, leads her along the dusty back country road to the airport. For all its twisted passions, secret motives, and technical dazzle, *Hearse* tapers to a peaceful ending.

Archer's humanity keeps the fast-changing plot from slipping into extravagance. Flexible and open-minded, the detective can change his mind in the face of new evidence. He admires skill and dedication. He is humble: in Chapter 25, Sergeant Leonard finds a cleaner's mark in Blackwell's tweed coat in a place Archer forgot to look; Archer's courteous next words, "Do you recognize the mark, Sergeant?" show respect to Leonard for finding a clue he should have found himself. As with the mercy he extended Carl Trevor at the end of *Wycherly,* he doesn't try to vindicate the law on every count. Nor does he worry every mystery he confronts for an answer. His final verdict on the death of Isobel's first husband, "Ronald Jaimet's death may have been something less than a murder, but it was something more than an accident," subordinates accountability to compassion. He doesn't investigate the death. Archer welcomes indeterminacy and charity when they help rout fear. Only once does his judgment flag. His reaction to Blackwell's false murder confession, "I was afraid he was going to talk about his mother. They often did," betrays a knee-jerk smugness he usually avoids.

But he overcomes his moral aversion both to Blackwell and to the vested authority Blackwell represents. He prizes the false murder confession of Blackwell, whom he had loathed so much he wouldn't touch, as an act of love, and he strengthens Harriet by assuring her of her father's love.

"Security: The Great American Substitute for Love"

He also opens his heart to Blackwell's wife. Isobel's interest in him, heightened by her empty marriage, shows in her asking him twice (in Chapters 1 and 27) if he's been married. His own interest in keeping aglow his semi-romantic attachment with Isobel shows just as clearly. First, he insists that younger women no longer interest him. His meeting Isobel in Chapter 1 reflects his maturity, together with a little regret: "She was about my age. As a man gets older, if he knows what's good for him, the women he likes are getting older, too. The trouble is that most of them are married." The trouble is that Archer is trying to talk himself into something. His willpower carries the day, though. Regret, disbelief, and resignation fuse in his parting look at Isobel the next time they meet. As soon as he catches himself estimating her age, he concludes that *both* she and he are over forty.

His dual acceptance of middle life and of Isobel shows in his turning down Fawn King's offer of sex in Tahoe: "You're too young for me," he tells Fawn, combining recognition and moral resolve. Isobel's feelings for Archer also undergo a test. Isobel rehires him after her husband fires him; regrets her decision when he threatens to jail her for a murderess; then tells him, after hearing of her husband's suicide, "You were cruel . . . but actually you were preparing me—for this." What is "this"? Her farewell scene with Archer is noncommittal but tender: "I said I would be seeing her again. She didn't deny it, even with a movement of her head." Whether Archer and Isobel meet again will never be known; we only see Archer at his job, and he rarely discusses his private life. But he needn't soul-search. The business of art is revelation, not explanation. He has been sexually roused, responded like a gentleman, and gained self-knowledge. Whatever happens afterward, this discreet romantic moment is his forever.

If Isobel sheds Blackwell's baleful influence, Harriet, whose relationship with the man goes much deeper, fares less well. Everyone who talks about her brands her a loser. Archer calls her "not pretty"; the Blackwells' maid calls her "a real sad cookie, even with all that money"; Isobel says, "Her talent as a painter will never set the world on fire"; to Anne Castle, Harriet is "an emotionally ignorant girl"; an American painter living in Mexico, whose opinion is more objective, sees her as "a big little blonde" who "hasn't make the breakthrough into womanhood." Underlying this unreadiness is the impurity evoked by her last name. The primitive and the predatory hedge Harriet in; her sharkskin suit and snakeskin purse also depicting the threat lurking within her.

A person she can't subdue, hard as she tries, is Bruce Campion. Her failure is typical; nobody else gains an edge on him, either. Harriet and Anne Castle both fall in love with him. Ralph Simpson idolized him ever since serving with him in Korea ten years before; "He was obsessed with Bruce Campion," says Vicki of her husband. Burke Damis deplores

Campion's ways, and he knows that Campion only comes to him when he needs something. But he can't resist him: "Bruce has an ascendancy over me," he admits. A furious worker, Campion has a splendor that overwhelms the others. He remains, with his intense dedication, Ross Macdonald's portrait of an artist. Nobody can tame his blood. Like Joyce's Stephen Dedalus, he shakes loose from all institutions and dogmas. He says, "I've always hated people standing over me," and Archer rightly calls him "a maverick, an authority hater." He was discharged from the Army for assaulting an officer; his hatred of the police runs so strong that he can't resist mocking them at a time, i.e., his arrest, when mockery works against him; since leaving his native Midwest, he has never worked for anybody. Wisely, Ross Macdonald keeps him in jail through most of the book's second half to keep him from interfering with the plot.

Campion's independence, hot temper, and rabid anti-institutionalism make Colonel Blackwell his natural enemy. Blackwell, who has always regulated his conduct by imposed hierarchies, can't understand Campion well enough either to classify him or control him. His bewilderment isn't unique. Campion, the artist, differs from the gatecrashers of *Galton* and *Black Money*. An outcast to the end, he despises rank, money, and property. His apartness, though, goes beyond social protest. Blackwell's calling him "a man from nowhere" and a "filthy little miracle man" accords with his mysterious origins:

When I asked him where he came from [says Blackwell], he said Guadalajara, Mexico. He's obviously not Mexican and he admitted having been born in the States, but he wouldn't say where. He wouldn't tell me who his father was or what he'd done for a living or if he had any relatives extant. When I pressed him on it, he claimed to be an orphan.

Equally miraculous are his appearance in Mexico, with nothing except his paintbrushes and the old clothes he was wearing, and the speed with which he gains the love of two women. Yet happiness and genius rarely mix. Like Joyce's Stephen Dedalus, another artist-hero, he is misunderstood and badgered. He never stays long anywhere, in addition, and the society he serves keeps him from his work. To protect himself from the Philistines, he needs the aliases of Q. R. Simpson and Burke Damis. But neither these disguises nor his punishing work routine insures his freedom. He's knocked out, arrested, and accused of killing three people. Above all, he never escapes the torment of being himself. Freud said of the artist, "He has not far to go to become neurotic."[3] Bypassing textbook formulations, Ross Macdonald anchors Campion's maladjustment in sex. Campion says of Anne Castle, "I never went to bed with her. I loved to paint her, though. That's my way of loving people. I'm not much good at the other ways." His phallic brushes, with their power to create new life, do the work of normal sex. Why? Could he be impotent or homosexual? His

"Security: The Great American Substitute for Love"

dislike of being kissed by Harriet, his longstanding, sentimental friendships with Simpson and the precious Burke Damis, and his willingness to rear Dolly's child by another man (a cover mechanism?) all suggest abnormality. His calling himself "a moral typhoid carrier," finally, fits him in the tradition, associated with Schopenhauer and Freud, of the maimed artist who uses his art to get back at the society which has excluded him.

Campion's arrest in Chapter 18 doesn't split the novel. Technique overcomes this structural problem for Ross Macdonald. The zebra-striped hearse and the brown tweed coat with the missing button both appear in each half. Archer also goes to the same places both before and after he apprehends Campion—Mexico, the Blackwells' Malibu beach house, the family's hilltop mansion in Bel Air, and the made-up town of Citrus Junction; Anne Castle and Pauline Hatchen each appear twice in the action— once early on and once near the end. Structure promotes balance and variety clear through. The ratio of puzzle to action is healthy, and the two material clues that lead Archer to the killer, the icepick and the button, transmit balanced erotic force. The minor characters, too, have a Dickensian gusto that sustains this excitement. Some of them, in fact, inspire the book's most inventive scenes. Burke Damis's calling his friend Campion a predator upon young women while feeding raw red meat to another predator, his pet hawk, opens a field of speculation. Is Campion the hawk? Does Damis imagine himself the meat being snapped up and eaten? Moments like this occur frequently. Conveyed in clear, bold strokes, they breathe vitality. Ross Macdonald keeps *Hearse* fresh and firsthand. Archer only eavesdrops once (in Chapter 12), and the conversation he hears is summarized, not reported verbatim, like the Stanley Quillan-Sally Merriman exchange in *Wycherly*. Far from lowering dramatic tension, the summary conveys the importance of the overheard talk while concealing the scene's artificiality.

Care with details—selecting, assembling, and combining them—characterizes the novel. Ross Macdonald usually sets his books contemporaneously with their composition. Thus the action of *Hearse*, which was published November 1962,[4] starts on Monday, 17 July. Not surprisingly, 17 July fell on a Monday in 1961 but not in 1959 or 1960; Ross Macdonald probably began writing *Hearse*, feeling confident and content, this very day. But accuracy in assigning dates imparts limited pleasure. Ross Macdonald's device of revealing character through eye-imagery takes on a new intellectual subtlety and emotional depth. Prefiguring his sympathetic portrait of Isobel Blackwell, he describes Isobel's eyes as "intelligent and capable of warmth" in Chapter 1. The muzzle of the double-barrelled shotgun her husband points at Campion in Chapter 5 looks like "a pair of empty insane eyes." Hungry for news about Harriet, Blackwell greets Archer in Chapter 14 with eyes "like a blind man's eyes trying to glean a ray of light." Another reference to the Oedipus legend comes in Vicki

Simpson's response to her husband's death: "The pupils of her eyes had expanded and made her look blind."

Ross Macdonald's dialogue also offers stylistic treats, some of them funny. Archer's verbal byplay can recall that of Hammett's Sam Spade:

"I thought you liked me, that we liked each other [says Isobel]."
"I do. But that's my problem."
"Yet you treat me without sympathy, without feeling."
"It's cleaner that way. I have a job to do."

Or it can sound like the coy sparring of a conversation in Henry James; again, Isobel is his interlocutress:

"Mark needs to be able to trust me. I don't want to do anything behind his back."
"But here you are."
"Here I am." She relapsed into the chair.
"Which brings us back to the question of why."

Style also lends color and mass to the book's portrayal of Mexico, a place Ross Macdonald hadn't revisited since his tinsel-and-neon sketch of Tijuana in *Trouble* (1946). As in Lawrence's *Plumed Serpent*, the Mexico of *Hearse* exudes a rough, but delicate magic: "It's as ancient as the hills and as new as the Garden of Eden—the real New World," says Anne Castle. Anne's description of Mexico as a colony of lost, reeling Americans also chimes with the book's purpose: "This is our fifty-first state," says Anne; "We come here when we've run through the other fifty." The well-documented Mexican landscape Archer scouts in *Hearse* does consist mostly of American expatriates. Mexico means different things to different people, and the sum of their responses makes it a psychic, as well as physical, presence. To Claude Stacy, a homesick hotel clerk, whose dream of quick money has dried out on the glaring mesa, Mexico is an outpost for fellow Americans. Anne Castle uses it as a place to work without distractions. The bizarre Wilkinsons, who buy one of Bruce Campion's paintings, view it differently: ex-film starlet Helen Holmes Wilkinson has made it a refuge from a Hollywood that has forgotten her; her husband Bill, twenty years her junior, also finds it a haven—from legal trouble caused by reckless driving in Texas.

This psychic spectrum typifies *Hearse*. Nothing in the book happens in a vacuum; motives interlace and the present flows unstingingly from the past. The flow, for all its hidden currents, is sure and even. The book poses many problems and solves them in its own good time, amid an impressive show by its narrator-sleuth.

III

A person who only wanted to read one Archer would do well to go

"Security: The Great American Substitute for Love"

to *The Chill* (1964). Most of the standbys of the canon are here, combined ingeniously and rubbed to a fine glaze. An old crime committed in the Midwest surfaces despite the efforts of a rich, powerful family to squash it. Key events recur. Archer's understanding of the past and his good working knowledge of psychology controls an elaborate, richly imagined story. Ross Macdonald continues to portray wrongdoers without malice; unsympathetic characters win our respect, even affection, as their past unfurls. Furthermore, this installment in Ross Macdonald's modern Oedipus legend features two prodigals, both middle-aged, both dispossessed. Each exists chiefly within the context of the parent-child relationship; while one man is searching for his natural daughter, the other is trying to cut loose from his substitute mother. Neither effort has succeeded. The home-ridden man pretends to be summering in Europe, but travels no further than Reno, enclave of the self-exiled. His foil, having been gone for ten years, never appears in the novel with the daughter he craves.

Organizing this interplay is the judgment pervading the action. *Chill* opens in court; it includes two lawyers; at the end, Archer pronounces doom on the killer. A Coleridgean omen gives the action its first push—no surprise coming from an author whose doctoral thesis dealt with the poet who wrote "The Rime of the Ancient Mariner." Archer is stopped, not en route to a wedding, but preparatory to a fishing trip; the man who stops him is a jilted bridegroom, whose sad story Archer hears and takes to heart, like the narrator of Coleridge's poem.

The book's opening also conveys Archer's life-style. No sooner does a long, bitter legal action end than Archer, chief witness for the acquitted defendant, has his nerves and skills tested again. Waiting for him outside the courtroom is young Alex Kincaid. Ross Macdonald's use of eye imagery to describe Alex shows his trouble to be sex-related. His "clean, crewcut All-American look" glazed by "a blur of pain in his eyes," Alex wants to find a wife who left him three weeks ago after one day of marriage. Like Ian Ferguson, Alex married on impulse: his "I don't know too much about my wife" recalls Ferguson's "I don't know the sort of woman I married." His belief in Dolly also recalls both Ferguson and that other dispossessed Canadian with a runaway wife, George Wall of *Coast*. Why did Dolly leave Alex? The events leading to her departure puzzle Alex as much as the departure itself. A bearded man came to the newly-weds' room while Alex had gone swimming, and he stayed about an hour. Soon after he left, Dolly took a taxi on her own to the local bus station but, say transportation officials, never left town by common carrier. Alex answers Archer's usual request for a picture of the missing person by producing a wedding photograph of himself and Dolly. A minor quarrel between the two men causes the photo to tear. A master at yoking feelings to physical acts, Ross Macdonald ends the first chapter with the "flimsy picture" in two halves. Not only does the torn picture summon up the torn marriage (an image of which rests in Archer's hands); Alex's bursting into tears over it also conveys his personal crisis.

The torn photo gives Archer his first lead. In the next chapter, the photographer who snapped it testifies that a bearded man named Chuck Begley, employed by a local liquor store, had ordered a print of the wedding photo but never came back to collect it. Archer traces Begley through the liquor store to a beach cottage, where he is living as a non-paying guest of one of the store's customers. In an irony familiar in Ross Macdonald, Begley, the central figure in the case, opens the cottage door himself when Archer knocks. "A man of fifty or so wearing an open-necked black shirt from which his head jutted like weathered stone," Begley denies knowing Dolly Kincaid. He only visited the Surf House because the picture of Dolly from the newspaper reminded him of a daughter he hasn't seen for ten years. The visit refuted the resemblance in the photo; Dolly isn't his daughter. Now living on Madge Gerhardi, Begley, a widower, claims to have spent the last ten years mining chrome in New Caledonia. The investigation has stalled. Yet to the side of the dramatized action, it refurbishes itself. Though Archer hasn't found out anything about Dolly, his client, Alex, unearths a useful lead. Madge Gerhardi tells Alex that Dolly has been driving an old brown Rolls Royce for a local woman. Archer traces the Rolls to the white colonial house of Roy Bradshaw, a Harvard Ph.D. and Dean at nearby Pacific Point College. Archer is received, not by Bradshaw, but by his arthritic mother. Recalling for a moment an eccentric English widow in Angela Thirkell or Rumer Godden, the gnarled Mrs. Bradshaw says she uses student chauffeurs from the college because of her poor health. Yes, she adds, Dolly is her latest driver, but, no, Archer may not inspect her living quarters.

The refusal sends him to her son's office for information. It also promotes, in passing, some insights into higher education. "An oasis of vivid green under the brown September foothills," Pacific Point College recalls many of the instant colleges and universities which came into being during the 1960s. Buildings "ornamented with pierced concrete screens and semi-tropical plantings" and then furnished in Danish modern fit convincingly with closed-door conferences about budgets: instant higher education. Archer, feasibly enough, gains little going through normal administrative channels in this expensively appointed bureaucracy. Attractive Laura Sutherland, Dean of Women, identifies Dolly as a newly enrolled student, Dorothy Smith, but won't let Archer talk to her. This second refusal to cooperate in two chapters foils him no longer than the first. Chance sets Dolly in his path, "her eyes dark and blind with thought." Chance also brings Archer together with another woman. While waiting for Dolly's conference in the Dean's office to end, he meets Helen Haggerty, a striking-looking language instructor, who has come to

"Security: The Great American Substitute for Love"

Pacific Point College from the Midwest. Her witty talk, stylish clothes, and short razorcut hairdo, popular at that time, attract Archer. But he turns down her offer of a drink, noting, in her reaction to his refusal, that she looks "more disappointed than she had any right to be."

Following Dolly across campus, he gets as little out of her as Helen Haggerty did from *him*. A self-styled carrier of bad luck, she won't go back to Alex. This refusal Laura Sutherland supports; Dolly learned something so awful about herself on her honeymoon that to return to Alex would be a cruelty. What began as a misunderstanding has darkened into a mystery; everybody who knows Dolly tells Archer to keep her and Alex apart. Again help comes from an unexpected source. Out in the parking lot, Archer accepts Helen Haggerty's second invitation for cocktails when Helen asks to discuss the "Dorothy Smith" case. One round of drinks, though, reveals that Helen has deeper reasons for wanting Archer with her. Fearing imminent death, she wants his protection. She was threatened on the telephone by a caller she identifies as "the voice of Bridgeton talking out of the past." Though gone twenty years from her Illinois birthplace, she insists, "You can't run away from the landscape of your dreams," adding, "Bridgeton will be the death of me." Archer's appreciation of the aliveness of the past makes his walking out on Helen one of his worst, and most costly, mistakes. The guilt rising from it hangs over him for the rest of the book.

Developments elsewhere keep Archer from Helen, despite his resolves to look in on her. The rumor that Chuck Begley, whose real name is Thomas McGee, spent the last ten years in jail for killing his wife sends Archer back to Madge Gerhardi. Besides seconding the story about McGee, Madge adds that he packed and left her cottage right after Archer's visit. That McGee was Dolly's maiden name gives Archer his first breakthrough. But hope soon fades. The next chapter, where Dolly and Alex appear together at the Bradshaws' gatehouse, introduces disaster. Screaming and struggling, Dolly reviles herself for causing the death of a friend. To quiet her, Archer calls the psychiatrist who had treated her ten or eleven years before. Dr. James Godwin explains that seeing her father shoot her mother and then testifying against him in the murder trial twisted young Dolly. What he doesn't know is that fate has chosen Dolly to find the freshly murdered bodies of women close to her. The death that has traumatized her is that of Helen Haggerty, whom Dolly had visited earlier in the evening. Archer drives to Helen's with Roy Bradshaw. Climbing the hill to the house, the men are jostled by a young downhill runner. Archer recovers sufficiently from his jolt to give chase. And though he doesn't catch the fleeing man, he does see both the make and the first four numbers of the Nevada license plate on the man's convertible before it vanishes into the fog.

Helen has been shot through the forehead. Appropriately, Archer calls in the local police. But the bullying and bluster of thickset Sheriff Herman Crane put him off. Withholding evidence from Crane, he drives to Dr. Godwin's nursing home, where Dolly has gone for treatment and rest. Dolly first came under Godwin's care, the doctor recalls, when her mother, Constance, noted symptoms of self-withdrawal in the little girl. These symptoms Godwin ascribed to the bad marriage of Dolly's parents. They worsened when she saw her mother get shot to death. Time has altered this experience, though. Whereas she named her father the killer during the trial, she now insists on McGee's innocence. A believer in McGee's guilt, Godwin sees Dolly's confession as a repetition compulsion borne from a need to sidestep a guilt darker than that of killing either Helen or Constance. Before this guilt can be probed, Sheriff Crane barges in, demanding to question Dolly. He doesn't get his way. Arguing that a police investigation would endanger Dolly, Godwin sends the sheriff away emptyhanded—an act that earns him Archer's "unfeigned admiration."

To get a better fix on Dolly, the detective drives to the home of Alice Jenks, the maiden aunt who reared Dolly after Constance's death. What he finds at the end of the seventy-mile drive to Indian Springs makes him doubt Tom McGee's guilt. Shaking his hand with a grip like a man's, Alice Jenks, a senior welfare worker, drips resentment—against Godwin, for allegedly alienating Dolly, and against McGee, for killing Constance. In language ill-suited to a social worker, she calls the McGee family "the scum of the earth," adding that "most of them are on welfare to this day." Archer pierces her moral rectitude by going to the spot on the second story from which little Dolly, the only witness, saw Constance's killer run into the street. A twelve-year-old of Dolly's then-height couldn't have seen the street from the front bedroom, especially if the street was unlit. Dolly lied in court. Yet her aunt rejects Archer's finding. Her reverence for vested authority, her longterm hatred of McGee, and the challenge of questioning a heretofore accepted truth ("It's harder than I thought to rake over the past like this") have closed her mind. A final jet of malice, directed at Dolly for marrying without consulting her, tells Archer to end the interview.

After driving back to Pacific Point, he persuades Jerry Marks, a scholarly young lawyer he had already worked with, to represent Alex Kincaid. But lawyer and detective are soon out in the street. Alex has lost heart. The discovery of the gun that shot Helen Haggerty under Dolly's mattress and the coaxing of Alex's father ("We'll go home and cheer up Mother. After all you don't want to drive her into her grave.") weaken the young man's faith in his marriage. Only Archer can reverse the downflow of personal fortunes. But he can't finance the investigation himself. The search for a new client sends him to the Bradshaws. Amid displays of antique coyness, old Mrs. Bradshaw agrees to hire Archer pending the approval of her son, now attending a professional meeting in Reno.

"Security: The Great American Substitute for Love"

Heartened, Archer moves forward with the case. He collects Helen's mother, Mrs. Earl Hoffman of Bridgeton, Illinois, at the airport and drives her to Pacific Point. What she says about Helen's Bridgeton girlhood sheds light on the murder case. Like Dolly, Helen may have witnessed a murder. A Bridgeton contractor shot himself accidentally while cleaning a gun, runs the police report of a death that took place just before Helen left town. Helen's reaction suggests foul play. A girl of nineteen, she bolted from her father, who, as chief investigating officer, filed the report: she claimed that her father suppressed the truth that somebody (Helen herself? Archer wonders) saw another person shoot the contractor, Luke Deloney.

Other disclosures and conjectures follow. Archer takes what he hears from Mrs. Hoffman to Dr. Godwin. Then, after foiling an attempt by Alice Jenks to wrench her niece from the nursing home, he flies to Bridgeton. The skill and power energizing the Bridgeton section recalls his only other recorded trips to the Midwest, in *Galton*. He goes first to Helen's father, Earl Hoffman, a massive ruin with thirty-four years on the local police force and a heart saddened by Helen's death. Watched over by his ineffectual son-in-law, the big old cop, trundling like "a sick bear" after a day of non-stop drinking, reasserts that Deloney shot himself. He rules out, too, any liaison between Deloney and Helen; Deloney's sexual tastes ran to older women; besides, Helen's heart belonged to a student named George, whom Hoffman got a job running an elevator in the Deloney Apartments. Alternating violence, bleary sentiment, and good street sense, Hoffman denies having hushed up any crimes or indiscretions. Then, rocked with grief, the wild, old bull smashes his face again and again. Ross Macdonald's description of this pounding evokes great moral suffering. The introductory adverbs and the phrases set in parallel after the main clause drill home, along with the stressed syllables in the last two sentences, the thumping, thudding woe Hoffman inflicts on himself:

> Heavily and repeatedly, he struck himself in the face, on the eyes and checks, on the mouth, under the jaw. The blows left dull red welts in his clay-colored flesh. His lower lip split.

Archer's next witness introduces variety, owing to her high social station. Daughter of a former senator and widow of a political boss in Bridgeton, the aristocratic Mrs. Deloney emits power. Conviction infuses both her "unfaded and intelligent" eyes and her insistence that her husband Luke wasn't murdered. Yet her calling Luke's death a suicide and her estrangement from him at his death rouse Archer's suspicions. To get more information, he goes back to Earl Hoffman. En route he sees the broken old bull reeling through the streets and follows him to the Deloney Apartments—the same building, now blistered and watermarked, where Luke died. The purpose of Hoffman's sad mission soon unfolds—to re-enact the Deloney shooting; Hoffman wants another chance to arrest the killer and thus win back his dead daughter's love. Crazy from drink, he frightens a sunbathing couple on the roof. Archer steps in to stop the fantasy from getting out of hand and takes Hoffman away. Anxious to shed guilt, Hoffman admits that he was ordered to close the Deloney case. This is *all* he admits. Before he can say more, he feels his skin acrawl with hundreds of spiders. By the time the police come, he has wrestled out of his clothes. The quietness of the short last paragraph in the chapter counterpoints perfectly the hysterics of the heartbroken old man: "The two patrolmen knew Earl Hoffman. I didn't even have to explain."

From Bridgeton Archer flies to Reno. His reason? To meet the owner of the car that fled into the Pacific Point fog the night of Helen's death. Arnie Walters's wife Phyllis has set up a dinner date for Archer with Mrs. Sally Burke, in whose name the car is registered. After dining expensively, Sally takes Archer, posing as a Hollywood agent, to meet her brother. A failure since his varsity football days at Washington State, Judson Foley impresses Archer as "a man of half-qualities who lived in a half-world: he was half-handsome, half-lost, half-spoiled, half-smart, half-dangerous." A revealing incidental clinches the impression. Foley's "pointed Italian shoes . . . scuffed at the toes" catches both the dream and sad reality of his shadow life. Anxious to clear himself of killing Helen, he proves a good witness. He admits both visiting Helen and then bolting when he found her dead. He adds that Roy Bradshaw, supposedly touring in Europe, spent the summer in Reno with her. Archer learns no more, for the present, about Helen and Bradshaw. Panicking, Foley tries to fight past the detective. But Archer has no trouble outmaneuvering Foley and holding him till the police come.

The dramatic focus shifts. A presumed bachelor whose "good looks were . . . the kind that excite maternal passions in women," ex-Ivy Leaguer Roy Bradshaw surprises us again by registering in a Reno hotel with his wife. At the hotel, Archer learns that Bradshaw and his fellow Dean, Laura Sutherland, have been married for months. Bradshaw urges Archer's silence for two reasons—a regulation forbidding faculty members at Pacific Point College to marry and the umbrage old Mrs. Bradshaw might take over the secret marriage, which could cost Bradshaw money. Archer agrees to say nothing, keeping his ambivalent feelings about Bradshaw to himself: "Having money and looking forward to inheriting more were difficult habits for a man to break in early middle age. But I felt a sneaking admiration for Bradshaw. He had more life in him than I suspected."

During Archer's absence, new developments have broken in Pacific Point: the police have put out an APB for Tom McGee, and Bridgeton has come to town flying unexpected colors. Looking out of a restaurant window, Archer sees Helen's mother with—Mrs. Deloney. Quickly and ac-

"Security: The Great American Substitute for Love"

curately, he explains this strange turn: "Mrs. Deloney's arrival in California confirmed my belief that her husband's murder and Helen's were connected, and that she knew it." Archer follows Mrs. Deloney to the office
of the town's top criminal lawyer, leonine Gil Stevens. Though forty
years of legal practice have taught him how to field embarrassing questions, Stevens does confirm the story that Constance McGee had a lover
in the last months of her life. Another piece of important news comes
when Arnie Walters, Archer's Reno operative, reports that Judson Foley
recently got fired from a local casino for running an unauthorized audit
on Roy Bradshaw's bank balance. Archer's belief that Foley wanted this
information for purposes of blackmail is soon borne out—again by Bradshaw's deceptive masculinity. Bradshaw did spend six weeks in Reno
the previous summer—establishing residence to divorce one Letitia O.
Macready.

While launching Bradshaw into manhood and using his manhood to
propel the plot, Ross Macdonald slyly keeps him out of the action. Archer
drives to Bradshaw's white colonial home and learns from his mother that
he left town three days before. The detective wonders if Helen Haggerty
had been blackmailing Bradshaw with the help of Jud Foley in Reno. He
then lets fly the bombshell that makes Bradshaw blackmailable—his marriage to Letitia. Archer knows from the effect the name has on her that
Mrs. Bradshaw is lying when she denies knowing Letitia:

> She was lying. The name drew a net of lines across her face, reduced her eyes to
> bright black points and her mouth to a purse with a drawstring. She knew the name
> and hated it, I thought; perhaps she was even afraid of Letitia Macready.

Her denial that her son summered in Reno sounds more candid. Mrs.
Bradshaw displays postcards Roy sent from places he had visited on his
European tour. Yet, when the dates on Roy's cards show that they could
have been sent by an accomplice in Europe, she flusters. Loss of grip
makes her admit knowing Letitia—an older woman whose crude, flashy
good looks tricked Roy into marriage soon after she met him in Boston.

Suddenly Bradshaw has become the Most Likely Suspect. He and
Helen knew each other long before their Reno summer. As her blackmail
victim, he had a wallet full of motives to kill her. Archer also suspects
him to have been Constance McGee's lover. But before he can test the
suspicion, he gets a surprise visit from Madge Gerhardi. Tom McGee, hiding out on lawyer Gil Stevens's yacht (aptly named the *Revenant*), wants
to talk to him. "His sky . . . black with chickens coming home to roost,"
McGee names Bradshaw his dead wife's lover. Out of the novel between
Chapters 4-26, McGee shares the distinction with Roy Bradshaw of being
Ross Macdonald's first middle-aged prodigal. Archer likes him better the
longer he knows him, as he does Alex Kincaid, Dr. Godwin, and Bradshaw. Thus his heart drops when three officers who come to arrest

McGee make him think that Archer turned him in. Meanwhile, his daughter, Dolly, out of the action since Chapter 9, has agreed to submit to questioning under heavy sedation. In a pentothal daze, she says that a lady called Tish came to the house the night Constance died, accused her of having an affaire with Roy Bradshaw, and then shot her; Dolly blamed the murder on her father because her Aunt Alice told her to.

Still off the scene, Bradshaw continues to beguile. His mother hasn't heard from him; his wife Laura denies that he was previously married; she received the same European postcards, their messages written almost verbatim, he had sent his mother while secretly living in Reno. Similar greetings aren't all he sends to different women. His poem, "To Laura," is identical to one that appeared over the initials, G. R. B., twenty-two years ago in the Bridgeton *Blazer*, a copy of which Earl Hoffman had given Archer. This putting of poetry into American literary detection weakens the fictional detective's line of ancestry from the frontiersman, who never sets store by the arts. More immediately, meaning flares out for Archer in "a roaring traffic of time": George Roy Bradshaw ran the elevator in the Deloney Apartments while attending Bridgeton City College. This detail sharpens the investigation. Still in Pacific Point, Mrs. Hoffman confirms Bradshaw's long friendship with her daughter, Helen. Then she confirms Archer's belief that Earl shut off the Deloney investigation on orders from above and that Helen left town when she learned of her father's dereliction. Other disclosures follow. Tish Macready was a daughter of Senator Osborne and the sister of Mrs. Deloney. "The belle of Bridgeton in her time," she may have been both Luke Deloney's lover and killer. But she never killed Constance or Helen; Tish died in France in 1940 during the Nazi invasion.

Suspense builds as Archer finds Bradshaw—again in a hotel room with a woman, Mrs. Deloney. Under the pressure of accumulated evidence, it comes out that Tish killed Luke Deloney after Deloney caught her in bed with Bradshaw; that Bradshaw married Tish despite a twenty-five-year age difference; and that he took her to Europe, where she died after he came back to Harvard for his sophomore year. This last detail Archer disbelieves. A French death certificate notwithstanding, Letitia is still alive. Otherwise, Bradshaw wouldn't have tried to divorce her; nor would her sister have come to California. Again, Archer makes Bradshaw change his story. Again, Bradshaw keeps Tish out of Archer's reach; he put his sick, old wife on a plane for South America two days ago, and she is now beyond extradition. Bradshaw does some painful dredging. Having always craved a wife and children, he says, "I'm beginning to hate old women" and then, "I've lived my entire adult life with the consequences of a neurotic involvement that I got into when I was just a boy." Yet he didn't always see his involvement with Tish as neurotic. He loved her once and made her promises. Further, he has come to rely on her

241

"Security: The Great American Substitute for Love"

money. Rather than leaving her, he deceives her. The overage marriage
has also brought out the worst in *her*. Fiercely jealous, she has killed a
real love rival, Constance, and an imaginery one, Helen. A phone call
breaks this flow of information. Laura has called to voice a deep fear,
probably related to Archer's belief that Tish is still in California: "Roy,
I'm frightened. She *knows* about us. She called here a minute ago and
said she was coming over." Before Archer, who had taken the call, can
drive to Laura, he is hit from behind by Bradshaw's flailing poker.

Waking up several minutes later, he has a new Gestalt. The last,
three-page, chapter unleashes the dramatic and intellectual climax the
novel has been preparing for. The ending of *Chill* is the most skilfully
pointed in the canon. Bradshaw dies on the road when his compact car is
smashed by his mother's Rolls Royce. All the ruses and evasions of Mrs.
Bradshaw, the driver, break with his life. She asserts that her sending him
to Harvard and then giving him both money and influence "made all his
dreams come true." But the dreams, causing four deaths, including the
dreamer's, have chilled to nightmare. A real whodunit, *Chill* sets Archer
the double challenge of naming and then slicing through a smokescreen
(fog is the book's central metaphor) of years, miles, and false documents
to find the killer. The book ends with the unmasking of Mrs. Bradshaw as
Roy's wife, Tish. En route to kill Laura, her latest love rival, she kills her
husband instead. But the accidental killing obeys a logic; the sudden
death she inflicts differs only in kind from the slow one she has been
dealing Bradshaw these twenty-odd years.

Part of the shock the finale delivers comes from Ross Macdonald's
strong personal response to the issue. Rearranged and disguised, the
author's life pulses through *Chill*. That the clutching old mother-wife
kills her son-husband with her Rolls Royce sedan projects the Oedipus
myth against the power that England, heart of a sick old Empire, continues to exert on Kenneth Millar. (Tish's first husband migrated to England, reversing the usual westerly direction of migration, as did young Ken
Millar, by going from British Columbia to Ontario.) The title also refers
to sexual fear and the ruined castrating mother. A term for murder and
the customary coldness of a corpse, it can also designate both the erect
phallus and the inextricability of sexual love and death. Bradshaw isn't
the only man in the book whose sexuality thwarts other impulses. Like
him, Luke Deloney and Tom McGee live unhappily off women. Jud
Foley's living arrangement with his sister, Sally Burke, doesn't need the
vividness of sex to identify Sally as a castrating mother figure. For part of
his time with her, Foley supports himself as a gambler. When Archer
meets him he has no job; so fallen is he from his days as a college running
back that, though fifteen years Archer's junior, he loses quickly in a fight
with the detective. Though Ross Macdonald's men through *Ferguson*
deteriorate rapidly when taken from their women, from *Chill* onward the

stay-at-homes, not the bolters or the bachelors, usually risk strangulation.

The book's greatest maternal-erotic threat remains Tish Bradshaw. This threat owes much of its sinister force to its presentation. A master of concealment, Ross Macdonald waits till the last page to tell us that Tish is Roy Bradshaw's wife and not his mother. His narrative cunning recalls Chesterton's pronouncement about hiding a leaf in a tree. In clear view and acting in character all along, Tish represents a marvelous stroke of literary conjury. No mere technical deception, Tish, half-invented and half-observed, packs menace. Her bright dark eyes gleam with fantastic vitality. The classical formality of her front name imparts an authority whose roots, going back to antiquity, strike as deeply into the soil of civilization as does motherhood itself. Letitia's last name at the time of her marriage to Bradshaw, Macready, invokes phonetically the clutching mother (Ma-greedy). In Chapter 29, before her unmasking, she uses the word "greedy" to describe the Tish whom Bradshaw had met in Boston, and Archer says of her on the last page, "She was still greedy for life."

Her deathliness, measured by her murderous deeds, is carefully foreshadowed. Her home has a "towering cypress hedge," symbolizing death, fronting it; officially dead for over twenty years, she enters the novel carrying a pair of garden shears. This emasculating mother-figure lacks ties with life. She spends most of her time alone. Dolly remembers her as having "a big scary voice," and to Helen, the pitch of her voice falls between that of a man and a woman. She has never had a child. First referred to, by a local garage mechanic, as "an old woman," she is not only denatured but also dilapidated. Crumpled with arthritis, she moves on "creaking reluctant limbs." Ross Macdonald's mentioning her decrepitude every time she trudges into the book—her slack throat, "seamed lips," gnarled hands—may spoil his case against her. Is she old and twisted by choice? Are her painful joints and sagging flesh her punishment for being a murderess? for marrying a much-younger man? Her rustling, creaking evil works better as drama than as moral judgment. Tish is a force from start to end. She controls several lives, and it takes Archer's best efforts to find her out.

Her wrath suggests tragedy as Ross Macdonald defined it in a 1974 interview: "Tragedy happens when you lose what is most valuable to you. But that means you have *found out* what is most valuable—and have even *had* it."[5] Tish knows exactly what she wants—to put happiness and love back into her marriage. Bradshaw once loved her, found her exciting, and enjoyed being with her. Though this golden age has ended, its rarity (especially in the canon) makes it worth fighting for. But worth killing for, too? A senator's daughter accustomed to having her way, the headstrong ex-beauty Tish fights savagely when crossed. And like all of us, she sees her existence as timeless: Why should Roy need another woman? Her marriage lives in her heart. Much of its life comes, not so much from

"Security: The Great American Substitute for Love"

her having Roy, than, owing to her insecurity, from her knowing that other women do *not* have him. But his roving eye wrecks her peace. In her anguish, she believes herself in the right to kill her rivals. She bought Roy and, like her pioneer ancestors, defends her claim by bearing arms.

Others reach out less desperately for bygone Edens. Tom McGee changes his name, grows a beard, and takes a low-paying job beneath his talents—all to make things right with a daughter he hasn't seen for ten years. Young Alex Kincaid says in Chapter 1, "Dolly is the only one I've ever loved and the only one I ever will love." In the next chapter, Archer notes of him, "He didn't seem to know if he was a man or not." Ross Macdonald has no easy answers to the questions raised by love's urgencies. What turns Mrs. Bradshaw into a monster and McGee into a fugitive infuses Alex with the stuff of manhood. But only after he undergoes anguish: manhood clenches his face as he peers "into depths he hadn't begun to imagine" until Helen's murder. His moral backsliding when his mother's weak heart lures him away from Dolly shouldn't count against him; smooth, steady growth into maturity isn't realistic for anybody. Nor does his backsliding ease his pain. Commitment and pain walk together.

Ironically, Alex has little reason to complain of hardship. Though under great stress most of the way, he suffers less than most of the others. His wife, Dolly, for instance, had her face rubbed in lies and murder as a child and hasn't recovered. As with Alex, hardship makes a man of Roy Bradshaw; Archer notes that Bradshaw's looking at Helen's corpse "cost him the last of his boyish look." Yet his manhood is short-lived; nor does it make his second marriage any more fulfilling than his first. The last woman he spends time with alive is the elderly Mrs. Deloney, and he drives to Tish rather than to Laura, whom he only talks to on the phone.

Pain lances Archer, as well. Helen's death, giving him a personal stake in the action, because he could have stopped it, upsets his calm. In Chapter 13, he admits, "This case has gotten under my skin. Also I don't know where I'm at." His skin prickles throughout. Mistaken for Dolly's and then Alex's father, he acts from parental as well as professional motives. The tie to Alex is strong. In Chapter 10, Archer says of his client, "I felt vaguely grateful. I was old enough to be his father, with no son of my own, and that may have had something to do with my feeling." Understandably, Archer and Frederick Kincaid, Alex's father, hate each other on sight. (His making Kincaid an oilman shows the author's dislike of him, as well.) In their brief only meeting, Archer calls Kincaid "a bloodless bastard," in perhaps his most open-faced insult in the canon, and Kincaid fires him. Perhaps motives of fatherly moral instruction explain Archer's unique awareness of money in *Chill*. Though he never presses Alex, his client and surrogate son, for payment, he does remind him several times of his debts—both to himself and Dr. Godwin.

What Alex buys in retaining Archer is first-rate skill and experience. Nowhere else in the canon does Archer perform better than in *Chill*. Rightly called "very thorough" and "quite a digger for facts," he goes beyond the stony-jawed academic sleuth. He does look closely at physical evidence: he inspects Alice Jenks's house to investigate a murder which took place there ten years before; he asks about the clothing, hair styles, and looks of suspects allegedly out of view for ten and twenty years. But the Helen Haggerty murder, weighing more heavily on his conscience than he lets on to the reader, prods him forward. Not content to wait either for the transcript of Tom McGee's trial or the bailistics report from Helen's killing, he works over the weekend. As usual, he opposes vested authority. He sides with Godwin over pompous Sheriff Crane; he enjoys telling Mrs. Deloney that the clout she wields in Bridgeton can't help her in Pacific Point; on the same page where Bradshaw addresses him as "Mr. Archer," he calls Bradshaw, holder of both a doctorate and a deanship, simply "Bradshaw." Through it all courses his humanity: he works smoothly with Dr. Godwin; sides emotionally with the underdog Dolly; comforts the despondent Earl Hoffman; earns the grudging praise of Mrs. Deloney. His addressing Dolly as "Mrs. Kincaid" and Bradshaw as "George," a name he never uses, may betray a theatrical flair. But his informing these two people by nominal shorthand that he knows their secrets warns them to square with him. Advantages like this he will use. That he pulls Alice Jenks out of Indian Springs and, more improbably, the elderly, powerful Mrs. Deloney out of Bridgeton speaks for his ability to make the most of his chances. Though a hireling, he makes others come to him and act his script.

Ross Macdonald's efforts equal those of Archer. The novel's many delicately nuanced perceptions are couched in a fresh figured style; Tom McGee, for instance, has "the untouchable still quality of an aging animal." The structure of the novel includes, among its strengths, skilful foreshadowing. Ross Macdonald both points the novel's bloody climax and hints at his central mystery in references to "an old woman" and "an old brown Rolls" in Chapter 3. The main issues of the book he sets in clear view as early as he can; Tish reveals her deepest fears in her first appearance when she says, presumably a propos of nothing, "The young ones leave the old ones." Psychology holds strong throughout in that every close relationship affects every other. The stress caused by Constance's death persists in Dolly and undermines her marriage. Having betrayed her father, she doubts her ability to love a man without hurting him. Her desertion of Alex she explains as an act of mercy: "*I* don't want to hurt *him* . . . Tell him to congratulate himself on his narrow escape."

But where to escape and how? The fog that rolls through the novel inhibits, isolates, and plays tricks with distances; fugitives escape into it,

"Security: The Great American Substitute for Love"

and it hides evil. Curling into the groins of the coastal mountains and hanging in the valleys, it touches all. Even a flying owl is a "traveling piece of fog," and the fog gives Archer "the queer sensation that the world had dropped away." Blurring countours, the fog foils brightness and clarity (as it does in Margaret Millar's *The Fiend*, also set in southern California and published in 1964). The characters must grope. But fog doesn't cause the crash that kills Roy Bradshaw. The fog had broken in Chapter 26, which opens on a brisk Monday morning. Confronted with her guilt at the end, in Chapter 32, Tish can't slip into the fog or behind her money.

A specialist in coping with fog is Dr. James Godwin. Ross Macdonald's first full-scale study of a psychiatrist, Godwin probes his patients' murky minds and trouble-clouded pasts. Bradshaw calls him "the best we have in town," and Archer, stressing other qualities, compares him to "a weary king." His kingliness encroaches on the metaphysical: literal-minded Alice Jenks accuses him of being "a little tin god"; his voice sounds "like the whispering ghost of the past," as if ignoring barriers of time. His swinging and shaking of his keys in Chapter 18 also symbolizes both his access to secrets and his ability to keep the secrets from prying eyes; Sheriff Crane, we remember, has no luck forcing his way into Godwin's nursing home. The trust Godwin's job exacts goes beyond the written law. Here he is on the subject of Constance McGee: "I loved her. I loved her the way a doctor loves his patients, if he's any good. It's a love that's more maternal than erotic." Like that of most divinities, Godwin's will is usually done; his ability to inspire trust gets others to obey him, even when not wanting to. His habit of spreading his large hands shows him blessing the creatures he controls and loves. Godwin's godliness can also assert itself in action. To him, wrongdoers belong in hospitals rather than in prisons. Observing the spirit rather than the letter of the law, he takes risks for his patients. Besides refusing to let Sheriff Crane question Dolly or the politically powerful Alice Jenks remove her, he probably also sent Bradshaw's European postcards to Tish and Laura; his wife brought a dress in Paris in his company while Bradshaw was living in Reno. He shows particular affection for young children. During his discussion of Dolly's childhood, he shakes with emotion, and, before Alex rehires Archer, he considers paying for the detective's flight to Bridgeton.

A novel which has a character named Godwin and which mentions *Waiting for Godot* needn't have only one god-figure. Tom McGee, called by Archer "a sort of twisted saint," invites comparisons with Christ. After a long absence, he materializes, not at a wedding, but during a honeymoon. Carrying "some of the stigmata of the trouble-prone," he spreads his arms in Chapter 3 "as if for instant crucifixtion." Crucified he is, having sacrificed himself for his daughter. McGee spent ten years in prison to spare Dolly the ordeal of cross-examination during his murder-trial. His lawyer Gil Stevens also rises to the divine. Alice Jenks labels him "an old fox"; attorney Jerry Marks, who can better judge his mettle, refers to him more respectfully as "the local old master" and "the most successful criminal lawyer in the county." Like McGee and Godwin, he exercises his divinity through charity; he lets his former client, McGee, hide out on his yacht, and he buries his clients' secrets. But he will discuss his own faults and failings. Though forty years of legal practice have taught him many shifts and dodges, he admits having blundered twice in the McGee murder trial—by excusing Dolly from cross-examination and by trying for an outright acquittal. Readiness to admit failure helps overcome failure. It also teaches Stevens compassion: having failed himself, he opens his mind and heart to failures less lucky than he.

These will need all the help they can get. One of Ross Macdonald's darkest books, *Chill* portrays deceit, betrayal, and the exploitation of people. Broken relationships abound. Once things go wrong, they rarely correct themselves. What happens to the marriage of Dolly and Alex Kincaid is never told. For Ross Macdonald to bring them together would falsify the sexual calamity pervading the action in the broken marriages of Helen Haggerty, Sally Burke, Archer, the Macreadys, the Deloneys, and the McGees. Yet parting the newlyweds would sadden most readers and, what is more important, lower reader involvement before the exciting last scene. As it stands, Archer's best reasoning performance states its case with flawless precision.

IV

The Far Side of the Dollar, named the best crime novel of 1965 by the Crime Writers' Association of Great Britain, homes in on the dangers of burying the past. Danger erupts when a youth tries to piece together the shards of a troubled past his parents had hidden from him. George Grella summarized the plot tersely in *Contempora* in 1970: "In *The Far Side of the Dollar* . . . a hunt for a runaway boy becomes a multiple search for identity; the boy runs off to find his real parents, his real name, while Archer seeks not only the boy, but also a murderer, an answer to a puzzling series of events in the past, and the son he himself never had."[6]

Nearly a year has passed since the Kincaid-Bradshaw case; *Chill* took place in September, and *Dollar* opens with Archer driving through an August rain. His destination: the Laguna Perdida School, a private reformatory located between Los Angeles and San Diego. Dr. Sponti, the school's director, has sent for Archer because a student has decamped. After less than a week at Laguna Perdida, seventeen-year-old Tom Hillman told his fellow students that the school was violating their rights. The dormitory supervisor, called by a colleague "our local Marquis de Sade," knocked Tom out to restore order; the same night, Tom left the school.

"Security: The Great American Substitute for Love"

His outbreak helps set the book's tone. Like the workhouse in *Oliver Twist*, Laguna Perdida, "a kind of prison" with high, heavily screened windows, haunts the action. (Kenneth Millar spent two years in a boarding school, St. John's in Winnipeg, as a young adolescent.) Its harsh discipline, jerrybuilt facilities, and poor leadership depress the students. But apart from its operation, the fact of Laguna Perdida is both a blight and a judgment. Leaving home and being stashed in a boarding school for maladjusted youths replaces the confrontation with a dead parent in works like *Chill, Instant Enemy,* and *Sleeping Beauty* as the archetypal childhood trauma. Archer's hardest job, when he finds Tom, is convincing him that he won't be sent back to the school. Archer's assurances also apply to Tom's parents: enrolling a child in Laguna Perdida (lagoon of the lost), a desperate last resort, spells out parental failure to provide love and guidance in the home.

Archer doesn't shrink from Laguna Perdida. Instead, for the first time in his recorded career, he takes on a school as a client; Sponti hires him to find Tom Hillman before the boy's father, "a very proud and very angry man," sues the school for neglect. Captain Ralph Hillman's pride and wrath both flare out soon after his taxi nearly runs Archer down. The detective's summary of this "large, impressive-looking man" recalls another vain patrician with a military past, Colonel Mark Blackwell of *Hearse*:

His face had the kind of patrician bony structure that doesn't necessarily imply brains or ability, or even decency, but that generally goes with money. He was deep in the chest and heavy in the shoulders. But there was no force in his grasp. He was trembling all over, like a frightened dog.

Like Blackwell and Ian Ferguson before him, Hillman's money has made him the target of other people's malice—in the form of kidnaping, poison-pen letters, and blackmail. What is more, it has exposed him to temptations he lacks the moral courage to resist. Yachtsman, ex-sea captain, and prominent industrialist, Hillman specializes in authority. And authority is the natural enemy of intelligence and independence. Like Colonel Blackwell, Hillman is hurt by his power-lust. He prefers a "handsome, healthy, empty" local youth over his introspective son. Having sold his freedom to marry into a rich New England family, he believes money and influence can solve all his problems. His recognizing, much later, that Archer's honesty can't be bought constitutes his readiness, both as a father and a person. This recognition again links him to Blackwell; both men turn out well. Yet each is treated differently. Ross Macdonald and Archer both like Hillman throughout, despite his arrogance, whereas they only open their hearts to Backwell after he dies.

This maturity comes to light early. One of Tom's kidnapers has demanded $25,000 from Hillman in ransom money. Then Archer asks why he sent Tom to Laguna Perdida. Tom had stolen a neighbor's car, kept it overnight, and then wrecked it. The next morning he refused to discuss the incident, adding that Hillman had no right to an explanation, since he wasn't Tom's father. The recitation breaks Hillman down. The ugly, cawing sounds tearing from his throat humanize him. Broken by loss and pain, he is more of a loving father than a heartless tyrant, in spite of his brusqueness.

Archer takes his cue from this suffering and drives Hillman home, down the "palm-lined central road" dividing his housing estate, "one of those rich developments whose inhabitants couldn't possibly have troubles." Like the unseasonal summer rain, troubles have invaded the Hillman hearth against long odds. Archer continues to suspect that they stem from sources Hillman won't disclose. Greeting him at the heavily ornamented Spanish mansion is Hillman's wife Elaine, "a beautifully made thin blonde woman in her early forties" who exudes "an aura of desolation" like a "faded doll." The faded doll fades quickly into the background. Besides insisting that the police be kept out of the case, Hillman also forbids Archer to question Elaine. The day is one of frustrations. Hillman's refusal to let Archer go through Tom's room strengthens the impression that Hillman is hiding information. On the subject of Tom's disappearance, his wishes are clear: "We've got to keep it in the family. The more people know, the worse—" Before he finishes his sentence, the extortionists call. Listening in, Archer hears the caller say that Tom came freely to him and his friends. Why? Tom's tight-lipped father again provides no insights. Like the handicapped sleuths in John Dickson Carr and Ellery Queen, Archer needs all his wits to puzzle out the background of Tom's disappearance.

As often happens in his cases, the way out of his quandary lies within reach. Posing as an insurance adjustor, he visits the white colonial home of the Carlsons, owners of the car Tom wrecked the previous Saturday night. Rhea Carlson says that the car was smashed on purpose to repay her and her husband for discouraging Tom's romance with their sixteen-year-old daughter, Stella. When Rhea says that Tom took the car without Stella's knowledge, Stella, who had been eavesdropping, contradicts her; Stella, in fact, gave Tom the keys to the car. Archer seems to be standing at the center of another plot from the *commedia dell'arte*, in which the young lovers defy their curmudgeonly elders. This impression fades when Stella, "a slender girl with lovely eyes," gives Archer some information on her own. She took the keys to her parents' car because Tom had an urgent errand and his parents had grounded him. This announcement brings in a new mystery—the all-night errand. Though Tom called it "the most important thing in his life," he wouldn't say anything else. Is the errand related to his disappearance? Is he in danger? Is he helping somebody extort money from his parents?

Perhaps some answers to these questions will surface from the wreck-

"Security: The Great American Substitute for Love"

age of the Carlson's automobile. Again posing as an insurance adjustor, Archer visits the auto yard where the totalled-out car was taken after the crash. The visit justifies Archer's trouble. Jammed behind the driver's seat is a motel key joined to a plastic name tab: Dack's Auto Court. But Archer has some stops to make before going to Dack's. A local jazz musician recalls Tom's visiting a night club with a blonde woman "practically old enough to be his mother." The musician adds that he heard the woman, who called herself Mrs. Brown, ask for money to get away from her husband. This report Archer takes to the Hillmans, where he meets a new character, Dick Leandro. A handsome, athletic-looking youth in his early twenties, Dick has brought the ransom money from Hillman's office, where he works, and has joined his chief to await instructions for delivering it. Archer's disclosure that Tom has been out with an older woman provokes a violent response—from Elaine Hillman rather than her husband. With horror-strickened eyes, she accuses Archer of lying. A ringing telephone redirects her emotion. The extortionist has called to state his demands.

Hillman leaves to deliver the money, and Archer, fighting the urge to follow him, goes to Dack's Auto Court. The motel room corresponding to the key found in the Carlsons' automobile contains the book's first corpse—Mrs. Brown, her bruised face suggesting that she was beaten to death. Before reporting the murder, Archer searches a nearby suitcase for clues. Tucked in the breast pocket of a coat is an old, creased business card reading "Harold 'Har' Harley, Application Photos Our Specialty." While reading the card, Archer hears somebody park a car and come to the door of the motel room. He recognizes the voice of the man asking to be let in; it belongs to the extortionist who talked to Hillman on the telephone earlier in the day. When Archer rushes the man, a bullet rips into him and knocks him unconscious. At the hospital where he is treated and questioned, he receives a visit from his client, Dr. Sponti. Sponti is peeved; Archer's going to Dack's has frightened Tom Hillman's abductors; now Tom is out of his parents' reach. Sponti takes Archer off the case. The detective leaves the hospital several hours later in spite of concussion and a bullet-creased skull. Still holding most of Sponti's fee after paying his hospital bill, he decides to investigate on his own. Work begins immediately. He co-opts Arnie Walters for the third straight novel, and, failing to find a telephone listing for a photographer named Harold Harley in any out-of-town directories, makes an appointment with the officer investigating the case, a Lieutenant Bastian.

Bastian and Archer team well, Ross Macdonald continuing to portray policemen carefully. Just as he followed scurvy Sheriff Duane Ostervelt of *Doomsters* with the decent, energetic Detective Mungan in *Galton*, so does Bastian blot out some of the stain spread by Pacific Point's Sheriff Herman Crane in *Chill*. Basically friendly to the police, Ross Macdonald won't put nasty law-officers in two straight novels, other than in a minor role.   Bastian believes that Mrs. Brown's husband beat her to death. Archer disagrees.   Why should Brown, he asks, kill his wife and knock on her door a few hours later?   Bastian sees merit in Archer's reasoning.   "Co-operation breeds cooperation," Archer notes, as the lieutenant hires him to identify Mrs. Brown at the standard wage paid private operatives by the police.

Fruitless visits to the Los Angeles Police Force, the Hollywood press, and the burlesque circuit give Archer the idea of going to ageing Joey Sylvester, a once-famous screen agent.   Miraculously, Sylvester recognizes in Mrs. Brown's death photo the face of a would-be starlet from Idaho he helped find work for in the 1940s.   He also remembers that the person who introduced him to Carol Harley was Susanna Drew, now a Hollywood television producer.   This news stuns Archer, who was romantically involved with Susanna about ten years ago, before "a bad passage" divided them.   The past grips Archer as inexorably as it does those he investigates. A page later and Archer is in Susanna's office in Television City.   "Forty-ish . . . and not exactly pretty," Susanna nonetheless compels Archer with eyes "furiously alive."   Her recitation compels as much as her gaze: at sixteen, Carol eloped with Mike Harley, a prize fighter, inveterate gambler, and AWOL sailor of twenty.   The couple stayed at the Barcelona Hotel in Santa Monica before the Shore Patrol arrested Mike.   Susanna then moved Carol, already pregnant, into her apartment in the hope of starting her on a screen career.   Chapter Twelve takes place at the defunct Barcelona, "a huge old building, Early Hollywood Byzantine," and now a gutted wreck of flaking paint, broken windows, and threadbare furnishings.   Reeking of liquor and carrying a revolver he looks anxious to fire, the hotel's watchman, Otto Sipe, denies knowing any photographer named Harold Harley.

Archer's luck changes quickly.   The operator of a service station across from the hotel both remembers Harley and supplies a lead that puts Archer on Harley's doorstep in Van Nuys three pages later.   Luck continues to favor the detective.   In Harley's garage, he spots a car with Idaho license plates and a registration tag made out to Robert Brown, Mike Harley's alias.   Haggard and hangdog, brother Harold has always taken the blame for Mike's misdeeds.   His inability to resist Mike perpetuates the pattern.   The previous night, Mike talked him into exchanging cars; driving a different car would put Mike out of the reach of some sailors whose money he had won playing poker.   Though unable to stand up to Mike, the sharp schoolboy who steals the prize and lets somebody else take the blame, Harold has resented him for years.   He tells how Mike once stole a camera from a troop ship, sold it to him, and then blamed him for the theft when questioned by his ship's officers.   Tension mounts as Archer starts to open the trunk of Mike's maroon car: anybody who

"Security: The Great American Substitute for Love"

would steal a camera and then try to pin the theft on his brother wouldn't scruple to dump a corpse on the same brother. "My brother," Harold says, "is a sickness that never passes."

Tom Hillman's body isn't in the trunk. But Tom may have spent time there; caught in the lock is a snag of black yarn which could have come from the sweater he was wearing when last seen. Mike Harley remains Archer's best lead to Tom. But where is Mike? His gambling fetish makes Nevada a likely choice, especially now that he has Ralph Hillman's $25,000. Archer relays his surmise to Arnie Walters in Reno together with information about the car Mike took from Harold. Sad, broken Harold has still more to say about Mike. The Harleys' father, an Idaho farmer, religious fanatic, and occasional mental patient, beat his sons so violently that he drove them from home. The more adventurous Mike left first, running away to Pocatello, where he lived for a couple of years with his high school football coach and mentor, Robert Brown; Mike needed the guidance and loving security supplied by a father, and Brown craved a son. His craving did him in. Along with Brown's name, Mike took his daughter, Carol; now Carol is dead. Archer takes this information, together with $500 Mike had given Harold, to police headquarters. Lieutenant Bastian surprises him by saying that Carol was stabbed, rather than beaten, to death. But the murder weapon is still missing. Still cooperating with Bastian, Archer produces the knitting yarn taken from the lock of Mike Harley's car trunk.

The two men go with this evidence to the Hillmans' where Elaine pronounces it identical with the yarn from a sweater she had made Tom. Like her, her husband grasps the meaning of this identification: Tom may have ridden in Mike Harley's car trunk as a corpse. This grim possibility releases forces buried too deeply within Hillman for direct speech. The averbal communication that follows between Hillman and Archer signals further artistic growth for the author. Moving with the "somnambulistic precision" of somebody driven by his unconscious, Hillman takes Archer into his library and shows him a picture of his last command, the escort carrier, *Perry Bay*. His motive for showing the picture, though unstated, is clear: Mike Harley also served on the *Perry Bay*. Furthermore, Hillman recommended Mike for an undesirable discharge after his conviction for stealing the Navy camera. (Mike is the first sailor who steals Navy property since Kerry Snow, or Smith, did it—again, years before the recorded action in *Morgue*.) Could Mike have been waiting eighteen years to take revenge on his former commander? Hillman wants to know, and, to back up his wish, hires Archer. The first half of the novel ends with the detective no closer to the missing person but provided with both the incentive and the financial backing to keep looking.

His enthusiasm comes quickly to the fore. Chapter Fifteen, which opens the second half, shows him covering a great deal of ground. He spirits from Los Angeles to Las Vegas and then to Pocatello after tracing the car Mike took from Harold to the car's new owner—the gambler who won the car from Mike at poker and then slipped him $100 with which to get back to Idaho. Did Mike use this money to go home? The possibility must be checked. Like the parents of the truant lovers in *Ferguson*, the Harleys and the Browns have widely differing values and life styles. The self-appointed divine scourge, Mr. Harley, runs Archer off his property with a pitchfork, ironically, a device associated more with Satan than with God. The forces ruling Ralph Brown are also irrational, but more secular than supernatural. As has been stated, Brown let Mike Harley, a budding football star, live with his family as a substitute son. His attractive wife has never forgiven this folly. Brown, a guidance counselor who needs counseling himself, launches a verbal counterattack, and the scuffle goes on till Archer asks to inspect Carol's room. (The novels contain an implausibly high amount of marital bickering in Archer's presence.) His inspection turns up a surprising lead. In a suitcase, he finds an old letter sent Mike by Harold; the letter mentions both Mike's grudge against Captain Hillman and his friendship with the current caretaker of the Barcelona Hotel, Otto Sipe; Sipe took Mike to California after being sacked from the Pocatello police force for taking bribes.

Surprises assault Archer. Back at his West Los Angeles flat, he discovers sixteen-year-old Stella Carlson parked on his studio couch. Stella adds to the exhilaration carrying over from Archer's case-breaking finds in Idaho: she spoke to Tommy Hillman on the phone a few hours before Archer's return. Though unhurt and out of danger, Tom sounded upset, Stella says, mostly over the threat of being sent back to Laguna Perdida. His duty clear, Archer promises to do his best to keep Tommy out of Dr. Sponti's school. But first he must take Stella to Susanna Drew's for the night in order to forestall a kidnaping charge.

Working with his usual non-stop flair, Archer resumes his investigations as soon as he leaves Susanna's. He drives to Santa Monica and lets himself into the unlocked Barcelona Hotel. Back in his caretaker's room sprawls Otto Sipe, "his ugly nostrils glaring and his loose mouth sighing at the ceiling." Being shaken, slapped, and splashed with water don't awaken him. But the visit isn't wasted. An important piece of evidence appears during a random inspection of the room adjoining Sipe's—a grease-smeared black sweater with a raveled sleeve. Along with Tom's phone call to Stella Carlson, the sweater indicates that Tom is still alive. Archer locks the sleeping Sipe in his room and, though it is four o'clock in the morning, calls Ben Daly, owner of the gas station opposite the Barcelona Hotel. Daly recognizes Tom's picture. But he doesn't know anything about Tom's connection with Sipe. To learn about the connection, he and Archer head for the Barcelona. They must work quickly. Once Sipe is arrested for his part in the kidnaping, Archer won't be able to question him.

It appears that he won't question him at all. Sipe has fled his room. But he hasn't gone far: he is soon found digging a grave-like trench in back of the hotel. The grave-digging, like similar rites in *Blue City* and *Victim*, ends in gore. Mike Harley is lying near the trench with a knife handle jutting from his chest. And he isn't death's only victim. While Archer is examining the corpse, Sipe, attempting to escape, smashes Daly with his spade. In the fracas, Daly kills Sipe with the gun Archer had given him to hold over the caretaker. Archer's efforts have recoiled. His two best witnesses, Harley and Sipe, are both dead. Still worse, he has pulled Daly, an innocent witness, out of his bed at four a.m.—to kill a man; in spite of the justifiable homicide plea which will stand up in court, Daly must live out his days with a murder blackening his heart.

Misfortune occurs again at Susanna Drew's. Stella Carlson's announcement that Tom plans to be at a local bus station only gladdens Archer briefly. His joy sours when Stella says that Tom's father, Ralph Hillman, visited the apartment early that morning and, after some private talk and even a failed try at a kiss, took Susanna out for breakfast. This development frets Archer more than he would have imagined. "Susanna and I cared about each other in ways I hadn't even begun to explore," he admits with an aching heart. His attempt to soothe the ache tells a great deal about him. He invites Stella to have breakfast with him at the same time Susanna is breakfasting with Hillman. But work routine, that defensive standby against emotional setback, intervenes. Instead of eating with Stella, he skips breakfast and goes to Laguna Perdida School. The trip proves worthwhile. One of the boys says that Tom bolted because he had learned that he was adopted and wanted to find his natural parents.

This reference to the Oedipal story establishes a new set of motives. Archer takes these motives to the Hillmans. What dominates his talk with Elaine, though, isn't Tom but Susanna Drew. Hearing that her husband spent time with Susanna that morning crumples Elaine's "delicate blonde face . . . like tissue paper." What cruel trick of time could undo her like this? Elaine reports that her husband has been having an affaire with Susanna for twenty years despite promises to end it. Here is the background of the affaire, as Elaine understands it: While his ship was being repaired after a Kamikaze raid at Midway Island in 1945, Hillman often came up to Los Angeles from San Diego to visit Elaine, his then fiancée. But he also spent time with Susanna, often whole weekends. The sea fight at Midway touched Hillman deeply elsewhere, too. The battle killed twelve members of his squadron, and, perhaps to compensate for the disaster, he persuaded Elaine to adopt a son after learning that he was sterile. Reliving a military battle, even psychologically, can produce casualties. The sterile captain of the twelve dead sailors wanted a son so badly that, when he got one, he never told him he was adopted. Perhaps as retribution, the father-son relationship has languished. "A sensitive, artistic, introverted boy," Tom didn't take to the "lusty gusty things" the outdoorsman Hillman enjoyed. The clash in temperaments turned Hillman to the local boy, Dick Leandro, as soon as Dick took Tom's place crewing on Hillman's sloops.

The drama of substitute fathers and sons steps up when Archer gets the name of the M. D. who delivered Tom. After making an appointment with Dr. Elijah Weintraub, Archer has speech with Lieutenant Bastian. Evidence shows Carol Harley and her husband Mike to have been killed by the same knife, probably by the same person. But since neither was killed for money, both motive and killer remain a puzzle. At Susanna Drew's in the next chapter, Archer speaks as both a detective and a wounded lover. Susanna (her black hair ruling out an identification with Archer's red-haired ex-wife Sue, though not denying an imaginative tie) admits having slept with Hillman. But she also insists that, till today, she hadn't seen him for eighteen years. The interview forces Archer to dredge deeply. Standing over her like a predator, he accuses her of hiding the truth. He would have been happier biting back the accusation. For his pains, he hears that Susanna loved Hillman because he was "handsome and brave and all the other things." By comparison, Archer is something less than a sexual voyeur: "You're not interested in people, you're only interested in the connections between them. Like a . . . plumber." But ten years can breed affection and patience as well as anger. Susanna's heart softens; the mood of her talk with Archer relaxes. And when she explains that Hillman proposed to her that morning, she adds, "her dark meaningful eyes" resting on Archer, that she's waiting for a better offer.

Before Archer can answer, the telephone rings: Tom Hillman just stormed into Dr. Weintraub's office demanding to know if Carol and Mike Harley are his parents. Edging closer to the action, Tom finally shows his face in Chapter 25. It is a tired, unwashed face. Having lived rough for nearly a week, he comes to us wearing a dirty white shirt and a pair of rumpled slacks. His entry point, the Santa Monica bus station, is as drab as his looks. Ross Macdonald wisely robs this long-awaited entrance of high color. That plenty of issues need resolving is seen straightaway; when Archer introduces himself to Tom as a private investigator working for his father, Tom snaps back that Ralph Hillman isn't his father. He also speaks his mind on other subjects. He did ride in the trunk of Mike Harley's car, but only to escape Laguna Perdida School. The extortion was Mike's idea; neither Carol nor Tom knew about it. Archer convinces the lad to go back to the Hillmans. On his way there, more background data emerges. Carol had called Tom several weeks ago, identified herself as his mother, and asked to see him. But no sooner did a warm glow form between mother and son than it was snuffed out.

When Tom arrives home, Hillman, a stranger to plain dealing and straight talking, can't cope with his bitterness. Elaine, a genteel New

"Security: The Great American Substitute for Love"

Englander, outdoes her husband in graciousness, thanking Archer for bringing Tom home and letting him take her to her son. But the son won't forgive his adoptive parents either for hiding his parentage or for putting him in Laguna Perdida. The falsity that comes from suppressing the past has spread. "This is a dismal household," says Hillman in weary disgust. His wife's agreement deepens the gloom: "I've been aware of it for many years. I tried to keep it together for Tom's sake." Lieutenant Bastian's arrival only clears the gloom briefly. Showing Hillman the murder weapon, Bastian then charges him with having bought it from a local hardware dealer named Botkin (a bodkin from Botkin, runs the silent word game). At first, Hillman denies buying the knife. Then he admits having bought it for Tom. Is he protecting Tom? Ross Macdonald has implied that Tom killed his parents and that Hillman has guilty knowledge of the fact.

The implication builds both horror and suspense. Tensions relax when Hillman tells why he sent Tom to Laguna Perdida. Tom had come home the previous Sunday morning after staying out all night and threatened to shoot his adoptive parents for hiding his genealogy. His outburst was borne of moral crisis; for Tom tried to kill not only his parents but also himself, using the Carlsons' car as a suicide weapon. Here is Archer's explanation of Tom's crisis; he is speaking to the Hillmans:

You might say he was lost between two worlds, and blaming you and your wife for not preparing him. You should have, you know. You had no right to cheat him of the facts, whether you liked them or not. When the facts finally hit him, it was more than he could handle. He deliberately turned the car over that morning.

Ralph Hillman has one more secret. Tom is his natural son with Carol Brown Harley. Carol slept with Hillman, her husband's commanding officer, to thank him for keeping Mike out of jail after the camera theft. Carol was a virgin: Harley, a sexual masochist, gladly used Tom to hide his impotence from the world. Hillman and Archer go to Elaine. Again, she taunts her husband; "You never faced up to anything in your life," she says, her knitting needles clicking angrily. Her anger threatens to explode into violence. But just as she flings Susanna Drew's name in his face, the telephone rings. Lieutenant Bastian has called to report that Dick Leandro drove somebody the previous night, i.e., the night Mike Harley and Otto Sipe were both killed, to the Barcelona Hotel.

Leandro's business at the Barcelona? Called to the Hillman home, Leandro admits that his passenger was Elaine. What develops is that Elaine, like her captain-husband, has been piloting the family to disaster. She went to the Barcelona to pay Mike Harley another $25,000, which she had in her knitting bag. But instead of giving him the money, she stabbed Mike to death. The third Archer in a row has a woman as the killer. Elaine murdered Carol because Carol didn't want Tom hurt by

Mike's extortion plot.   What rankled Elaine here was that Carol was protecting her own son. Elaine's deathliness fuses with her anti-sexuality. Her opposite number in the novel isn't Ralph Hillman but Mike Harley. Accused of acting as if her husband was murdering her on her wedding night, she resembles Mike, the novel's other false parent and foe of normal sex.   She says that her knife "slipped in and out" of Carol when she killed her. Showing no mercy, Archer keeps the sexual metaphor alive by asking her, of her next murder victim, "Why did you have to stick it into him [*viz.*, Mike] ?"

Cornered, Elaine asks Archer to let her take an overdose of sleeping pills rather than be arrested and stand trial. His denial of the break he gave Carl Trevor in *Wycherly* prompts her, out of the wastes of her sexual phobia, to call Archer "very hard."   She reaches her deathly consummation in spite of Archer. Sighing "like a woman in passion," Elaine jabs her knitting needles into her breasts; anything long and pointed will kill her if it enters her body, we recall from her response on her wedding night: dream, or nightmare, has merged fatally with reality.   Elaine's suicide reaches beyond itself into our cultural history. Her knitting, her suicide, and her patience with her husband's infidelities all put the Penelope-Ulysses story in a modern key. But the classical story points up Elaine's wifely failings rather than her devotion. She put up with Ralph's rutting because it spared her from giving him sex herself. The mythical echoes reverberate.   Archer's tracing the black strand of wool from the sweater Elaine made Tom through the byways of the case likens her not to Penelope, but to Ariadne, a woman done in by sexual abandon. This likeness, both apt and off the mark, captures Elaine's confusion and complexity. She both condemns and envies the normally sexed; though she loves Tom, she hates both the act that gave him life and, with a still greater moral loathing, his parentage. Elaine Hillman is a character Ross Macdonald wants us to ponder rather than condemn, and he introduces paraphernalia in order to incite thought.

Some of the minor characters also stir our minds and hearts. The work-raddled dormitory supervisor at Laguna Perdida, Mr. Patch, suffers more from his strictness than do his charges. "When I hit them, they go down for the count," says Patch. But they also get up and eventually leave the school, whereas Patch, who knows no other life, must stay. Mrs. Mallow, the sad, tippling housemother, is probably as unfit as Patch for life outside the school, despite her compassion for the student-inmates. Unable to find anyone to love her, she settles for institutional relationships and solitary sessions with the gin bottle. The name of Otto Sipe exudes a Dickensian malevolence justified by Sipe's forays into blackmail and bribery. His occasional partner in crime, Mike Harley, whose death occurs within hours of Sipe's, also grips our imaginations. Yet this thief and gambler, sexual masochist and false brother, appears but once—as a

"Security: The Great American Substitute for Love"

voice heard on the telephone. This treatment shows first-rate artistic judgment. Anybody capable of scattering as much dirt as Harley, if allowed to appear, would divert the plot. On the other hand, his misdeeds provoke as much response occurring off-stage as they would on. The mainspring of much of the action, Mike—a perfect candidate for Laguna Perdida, staff or student body—shows narrative technique building both an issue and a crisp story-line.

He also shows Ross Macdonald's moral charity. *Dollar* contains many human insights. Rather than fixing moral blame, it portrays characters whose secret grievances run away with their judgment. Repeated beatings by his father twisted Mike Harley. His inability to love stems from his father's knotted-wire whip rather than from personal failing. "The old man was a terror when Mike was a kid," says brother Harold; "Maw finally had him committed for what he did to Mike and her." Harold's withholding of moral judgment invites us, who have less to complain of in Mike, to follow suit. Another character we are meant to understand rather than condemn is Ralph Hillman. Mannish, hard-drinking Hillman ignores his family's deepest problems, bullies people with his money and influence, and deceives his wife. Yet he risks his life by delivering the ransom money to Mike Harley. "I'd rather take a chance with my own life than with my son's," he tells Archer when warned of the dangers facing him. Even Elaine, who has good cause to resent him, calls him "a tragically unhappy man." Though his vanity and evasiveness block the drive of tragedy, they don't exclude him from manhood. He works hard, he tries to keep his family intact, and he deflowers three virgins (Elaine, Carol, and Susanna). Archer justifiably fears him as a sexual rival. Complex enough to do evil and dynamic enough to make women love him against their better judgment, Hillman radiates force.

This force gains contour from the book's descriptive flair. No earlier Archer describes the physical effects of emotional stress as well as *Dollar*. When Bastian bridles his anger after being accused of double-talking, "white frozen-looking patches" bracket his nose and mouth. Ross Macdonald never says that Archer is afraid of pitchfork-wielding Harley, Sr.; instead, he translates Archer's fear into nervous recoil: "My shirt was wet through now, and I could feel sweat running down my legs." Two pages later, the handshake of Carol's mother, Mrs. Brown, seems "less like a greeting than a bid for help." Passages like these, which describe, create, and speculate all at once, achieve what most fiction aims for—the impression that the reader is living an experience, not reading a book. The prose of *Dollar* is both smooth and restrained. Only rarely will a conceit make us blink: Archer says of the Hillmans' huge Spanish chandelier, "Its bulbs protruded like dubious fruit from clusters of wrought-iron leaves." The American hard-boiled detective novel had never attempted baroque wit of this kind. Yet such verbal brilliance doesn't disjoint

Dollar. Stabilizing its rhetorical flourishes and quick-paced action is the motif of recurrence. Like the other Archers from *Galton* onward, *Dollar* emphasizes repeated experience. Instances come quickly to mind. Both Ralph and Tom Hillman use the Barcelona Hotel as a hideaway; both neglect Elaine for Carol Harley. Trouble happens around cars: Carol takes her father's car to elope in with Mike; Tom steals the Carlsons' car some eighteen years later as a result; Mike trades cars with his brother and then loses Harold's in a poker game.

This rhythm of recurrence includes Archer. Like Oedipus, he's part of the process he investigates. He addresses Susanna as Sphinx and she calls him Oedipus in Chapter 18. Suitably, she is also the one who sweeps him into the emotional currents of the action. Her affaire with Ralph Hillman in 1945 may have influenced her romance with Archer eight or ten years later; the "bad passage" she and Archer suffered implies sexual trouble, traceable, possibly, to Hillman, her first lover. At any rate, the affaire with Hillman colors Archer's view of Susanna at the time of the action. Only when he learns of the affaire does she come to life for Archer. Could the prospect of supplanting the authority-figure Hillman give her the new luster? It puts Archer closer to the Hillmans than he finds comfortable. Not only does it weld him in a love triangle of sorts with his client; it also gives him and his client's wife, who is also the killer, a common cause. Archer doesn't hide his emotional susceptibility. Though baffled by the teenagers at Laguna Perdida, he remains tolerant and non-judgmental. When he does pass judgment, he hides behind his license. The knowing last sentence of his description of Stella Carlson's homecoming smudges the restrained delicacy of the moment:

Her father came out of the house. . . . He put his arms around her. With a kind of resigned affection, she laid her head neatly against his shoulder. Maybe they had learned something, or were learning. People sometimes do.

On the other hand, so poorly does he control his own feelings that self-inventory leaks into self-pity:

I had about three hundred dollars in the bank, about two hundred in cash. I owned an equity in the car and some clothes and furniture. My total net worth, after nearly twenty years in the detective business, was in the neighborhood of thirty-five hundred dollars. And Ralph Hillman, with his money, was letting me finance my own search for his son.

Archer's shakiness weakens the joints of the novel. The structure of *Dollar* lacks the strength and confidence of those of *Hearse* and *Chill.* Complicating details pad the plot—the possibilities that Elaine is deceiving her husband, that Tom is on drugs, and that Tom is working with the kidnapers to bleed Hillman of money. Contrivances rescue the plot several times; Chapter 17 introduces Harold Harley's letter, which links Mike to

"Security: The Great American Substitute for Love"

the Hillman family; a last-chapter reversal lays bare the prodigal's hidden paternity; telephone calls help Ross Macdonald out of three tight spots. A spot where no help is forthcoming is that occupied by Dick Leandro, Hillman's stammering yacht hand and substitute son. Though Leandro fits into the plan of the novel, he spurs little dramatic interest. He makes very little happen, and, though Ross Macdonald needs him to take Tom's place in the Hillman home, he doesn't give Dick much to do there. Most of the time, Dick stands around looking suspicious. The ease with which we can imagine the novel without him shows how little he adds. One last objection: the plot corners too tightly. Narrative structure conveys both value and idea, as it should. That Archer's ladylove was once his client's bed-partner rules out life as a series of random interludes. But it also loads the novel with more improbability than it can bear. *Dollar* has some excellent characters, and it probably says more about Archer than any book since *Doomsters*: Susanna Drew is in the novel to test and draw out the detective. Its structure, though, puts these people, Archer included, in situations that resist belief.

V

Like most of the Archers since *Galton*, *Black Money* (1966) explores the struggles of not-having and not-belonging. But it explores in a unique way. Set in May 1966 but published four months earlier, in January,[7] it is the only Archer whose action postdates its writing and publication. Ross Macdonald set *Black Money* in the future deliberately. Though neither prophetic nor utopian, the book has a distinctly contemporary ring. Readers coming to it in 1966, noticing the time-setting, might apply the characters' search for security amid rampant change to themselves. Again, the search has as its goal beauty and riches; the happy American has a thick bankroll and a beautiful wife. The searcher, a man whose cravings outpace his credentials, wears the familiar garb of the gatecrasher. Ross Macdonald has compared the outsiders in *Galton* and *Black Money* to his own situation as a Canadian-American only child of a broken marriage. In an autobiographical sketch written for *Mid Century Authors* (H. W. Wilson and Company), he called the two novels "probably my most complete renderings of the themes of smothered allegiance and uncertain identity which my work inherited from my early years." The 1970 *Time-Life* film, *Ross Macdonald "In the First Person,"* directs these themes to the author's obsession with crossing borders: "Both Francis and John [the anxious gatecrashers in the two novels] had crossed a border, as I had, into the United States, and attempted to start radically new lives in California. California was movieland where anything could happen."[8]

Though the action isn't set in Hollywood, celluloid values predominate. These both run around and through everybody, including Archer. Brilliantly coordinated and nuanced, *Black Money* ranks high in the canon. Ross Macdonald lists it as one of his favorites,[9] and his novelist-wife, Margaret Millar called it (during a conversation at the Santa Barbara swimming club that supplies the model for the Tennis Club in *Black Money*) her very favorite. This high praise suggests antecedents other than *Galton*; the shaping of a masterpiece includes many years and many unconscious sources of strength. Strength does flow into *Black Money* from some of Ross Macdonald's best novels. Together with *Hearse*, with its Mexican setting and characters, *Black Money* comprises a Latin-American group. With *Chill* and *Dollar*, it also comprises an academic trilogy. All three works take place on school campuses; all include students, teachers, and administrators.

As in most of the Archers, membership in different institutions overlaps, and the path between the institutions is well worn. The action begins at the Tennis Club, whose modest name, like that of the Foothill Club in *Ferguson*, masks its elegance and exclusiveness (the Bradshaws' white colonial mansion in *Chill* was also located on Foothill Drive). Archer has come to the club, located in Montevista, an imaginary community just south of L. A. County near Pacific Point, to talk to a prospective client. Peter Jamieson, Jr., is easy to spot, too much food and too little exercise having given him the "puffy and apologetic . . . face of a middle-aged boy." The fat post-adolescent who eats too much, a familiar figure in English writers like Huxley, Waugh, and Amis, is new to the Canadian-American Ross Macdonald. The satire asserts itself quickly. Twenty-four-year-old Peter meets Archer outside a snack bar, a double malted in his hand, and, while introducing himself, suggests having lunch. Taking only coffee, Archer listens to Peter's muddled plea. First, Peter wants his former fiancée back. When reminded that the fiancée, a local girl his age, can't be forced to return to him, Peter shifts his stance from that of spurned lover to one of protector: Ginny Fablon must be stopped from ruining her life. Ruination to Peter means marrying Francis Martel, a dark Frenchman who may be wanted by the police. Peter explains his urge to control Ginny as concern for her welfare. His calling her "innocent" and "undeveloped for her age" recalls many unrealistic parents in the canon. Like them, he defines proper conduct for Ginny as doing what he wants rather than what she wants, and he blames her moral lapses on others.

Archer agrees to look into Martel's background and drives to where he is living. Preceding him there is a would-be sleuth named Harry Hendricks. Archer shows his mettle right away. His ability to gain the upper hand over the cocksure Hendricks also spells out a truth apparent in *Coast* and *Hearse*: detection takes more skill, nerve, and training than the amateur realizes. Danger can explode anywhere. When Hendricks takes a picture of Martel, his expensive camera is grabbed and smashed.

"Security: The Great American Substitute for Love"

The next time Hendricks appears, he, too, will have been smashed under Martel's heel; so cruel is this beating that it sends him to the hospital and keeps him there for the rest of the novel.

Archer leaves Hendricks and his broken camera to do some legwork. His first witnesses, as usual, are the parents of the leading figures. From Marietta Fablon, Ginny's widowed mother, he hears that Martel came to the United States as a political exile from his native France. Marietta's next-door neighbor, Peter Jamieson, Sr., has also been widowed for many years. But unlike most of Ross Macdonald's widowed parents of only children, he has *not* tried to do the work of his dead spouse along with his own. The family's powerful housekeeper Vera raised Peter, Jr., while the father was slipping into an alcoholic blur. Both elective and unconscious affinities support the novel's tensions. Jamieson says that ex-varsity athlete Roy Fablon, his former roommate at Princeton and Ginny's father, drowned seven years ago by walking into the sea. Jamieson also speaks out on the subject of Archer's present errand. Harboring no illusions about his fat son, he says that Ginny felt sorry for Peter but never loved him. Her dashing Latin promises a fuller, more exciting life than any she could have had as Peter's wife.

The dashing Latin returns to the scene in Chapter 5, his re-entry dispelling none of his romantic aura. Annoyed by having his privacy invaded by the club's manager, whom he caught listening to one of his conversations, he is giving up his cabana at the Tennis Club. Has he something to hide? Archer is baffled. Of Martel, a "compact and muscular" thirty-year-old, he says, "He had the controlled force and reticence of an older man. I didn't know what to make of him." He also doesn't know what to make of Martel's plans. Is he leaving town? Is Ginny going with him? If she is to have the facts on which to decide responsibly either for or against Martel, she must get them from Archer. Thus Archer, working methodically, makes his first job the discovery of Martel's lineage—specifically, whether Martel is a French aristocrat, as he claims. To expedite the job, Archer and Peter, Jr., go to the seedy stucco cottage of one of the French professors at nearby Montevista State College. Professor Tappinger, who remembers teaching Ginny Fablon, leaves his chores to help the investigation. Martel, he explains, is "one of the ancient names in France." Archer leans on Tappinger's expertise to find out if Martel descended from this pedigree. Tappinger, or "Taps," will prepare a short quiz based on French culture which nobody but an educated Frenchman or a graduate student in French could pass. But the role of expert witness is too limited and arbitrary for a realistic novel. Ross Macdonald isn't ready to home in on Martel; better to linger with Taps, who does have a life outside of academe, which isn't always happy. He flusters quickly when his wife Bess, twelve years his junior, comes into his makeshift study calling him Daddy. Is Bess vexing him for a reason? As soon as he leaves the study to prepare Martel's quiz, she makes it clear that she has both noticed and responded to Archer.

Ignoring her enticements, Archer drives to Martel's house with Taps's five questions:

1. Who wrote the original *Les Liaisons dangereuses* and who made the modernized film version . . . ?
2. Complete the phrase: "*Hypocrite lecteur. . . .*"
3. Name a great French painter who belived Dreyfus was guilty. . . .
4. What gland did Descartes designate as the residence of the human soul . . . ?
5. Who was responsible for getting Jean Genet released from prison . . . ?

Standing in the doorway of the house, Ginny explains that she and Martel got married two days before. Composed, dignified, and aristocratic, Martel not only confirms Ginny's report but also scores a hundred on the quiz. The novel could end here: Peter has lost his girl to Martel, who has proved himself worthy of her. Having answered the Sphinx (which Archer was called in *Dollar*), this Latin Oedipus deserves to be let alone. Archer, too, having earned his fee with diligent legwork and skillful questioning, can close the case. But doubts remain. "He has an answer for everything," Archer says of Martel, calling his aplomb and readiness to supply information "too convincing." These doubts are soon justified. The Washington, D. C., family Martel used as his *entrée* into Montevista society has never heard of him. The manager of the Tennis Club, a French-speaking Swiss immigrant, also smirches Martel's credibility. Though Martel speaks perfect French, he speaks with a provincial accent; he isn't the Parisian he claims to be.

Archer keeps digging. His next witness is George Sylvester, an erect, handsome M. D. Ginny Fablon Martel worked for as a secretary after dropping out of college. Ginny's physician as well as her former employer, Sylvester doubts her chances for marital happiness. What he questions is her ability to fulfill herself sexually. Her father's death blunted her interest in men; instead of dating, she has been spending most of her spare time in recent years studying French. Her willingness to settle for safe Peter, Jr., also indicates poor emotional preparation for the mysterious intruder, Martel. But Archer's investigation of Ginny must wait. Parked on the side of the road less than a mile from the club is Harry Hendricks's car, its keys in the ignition. The novel continues to wheel in a tight frame. Knocking on the door of Hendrick's hotel room, Archer meets the missing man's pretty wife. Kitty answers the description given Archer of a redhead who tried to coax a local photographer into snapping Martel's picture. The case is moving forward. That Kitty's husband also wanted a picture of Martel clinches the identification of Kitty. Both Hendrickses want something from Martel. Archer asks what. According to Kitty, Martel stole some bonds she and Harry are trying to recover for their chief. But she hasn't seen Harry all day.

Together, she and Archer drive to the stranded car. Kitty says that, though still married, she hasn't lived with Hendricks for years. Like Peter, Jr., Hendricks hopes that the woman he loves will come back. Also like Peter, Jr., he may have had his hopes dashed by Francis Martel. Now he and his car are both gone. Kitty's fears mount. Crying out that Archer brought her to this lonely spot in order to kill her, she runs hysterically into the night. She soon reasserts herself in Archer's mind, though. At the studio of the Tennis Club's photographer, the detective looks at a negative made seven years before: wearing a bathing suit, Kitty is sitting alongside a powerful-looking older man in a striped suit; behind the couple a mustached busboy is holding a tray. Archer orders some prints to be made from the negative and then goes back to the Tennis Club, where he gleans some good new leads. The club's veteran bartender says that Roy Fablon didn't kill himself, strengthening Archer's belief that an athlete like Fablon wouldn't walk into the water clad in a raincoat. The past revives again when a club-member identifies a picture of Kitty as Mrs. Ketchel. Archer begins to organize his findings: a Mr. and Mrs. Ketchel took a cottage at the Tennis Club shortly before Fablon died. If these events are related, then the connection between them must be found.

Archer tries a long shot. Dr. Sylvester, a heavy gambler, once gave Marietta Fablon $5000, and he has been spending so much time with her lately that his wife Audrey believes the two to be lovers. This drama calls for a visit to Marietta, even though the hour is past midnight. Looking "thinner and older" and as if "she was having a bad time," Marietta lets him into her house. Ketchel she identifies as the gambler who took her husband's money and probably caused his death. This identification opens two possibilities—that Dr. Sylvester played a part in Fablon's death and that Fablon's death is linked to the present case. Supporting evidence for Archer's hypotheses comes from the ancient device of a rediscovered letter. Ross Macdonald, unapologetic about resorting to well-used plotting devices, responds well to the structural demands of Black Money. The old letter fits so smoothly into the plot that its worn edges hardly show. Audrey Sylvester's suspicions about her husband and Marietta have a basis in imagination, if not in fact. A few days before the present investigation, Marietta happened upon a love letter written to Roy three months before his death by Audrey. The affaire, besides prodding Sylvester into an affaire of his own, also gave him good reason to throw Roy to the lion Ketchel: "After seven years," says Marietta, "I understood why George Sylvester introduced Ketchel to Roy and stood by smiling while Ketchel cheated Roy out of thirty thousand dollars which he didn't have. . . . He may have even planned it all. He was Roy's doctor."

Once again, Archer goes to the Jamiesons after visiting their next-door neighbor, Marietta. "Transparent and withdrawn," Jamieson drinks as compulsively as his son eats. Yet he has the grip to give Archer some important information, culled from a banker-friend: when Martel came to Montevista, he deposited close to $120,000 in a local bank from a Panamanian bank draft. This money he has just withdrawn. But Archer doesn't have time to think about why Martel wanted so much cash. Marietta Fablon crawls into the house bleeding from a bullet wound. "Her eyes . . . as wide and blind as silver coins," she identifies her assailant as "Lover-boy" before she dies. Marietta's death, coming at the end of Chapter 15, is one of the latest first murders in the canon. The postponed murder creates the chance to generate motives and suspects: Sylvester, Ketchel, and Martel have all been actuated by sex; all have had motives to hurt Marietta. The investigation fans out. Back at Marietta's, Archer finds a letter from the same Panama City bank Martel had invested with; the letter tells Marietta that no more money will be sent to her.

On his way back to the hotel, he finds another surprise—Harry Hendrick's car has been driven back to the spot from which it disappeared a few hours before. This time, though, the front end of the car is caved in, and the front seat spattered with blood. Archer takes the key from the ignition and opens the trunk, a favorite spot for the disposal of corpses in the novels. Harry Hendricks is, in fact, hunched inside the trunk. But he isn't dead. Freeing him gives Archer the sensation of "delivering a big inert baby from an iron womb." Then he refreshes Hendricks with a sea-moistened handkerchief. This symbolic rebirth and baptism culminates in Hendricks's going to the hospital. A capable young patrolman, Ward Rasmussen, gets Hendricks admitted to a private hospital, and Archer pays the admission charges. The next morning, the photographer from the Tennis Club brings Archer the pictures he ordered. An incidental, nearly overlooked, has created a major breakthrough. The mustachioed busboy standing in the background of the picture of Ketchel and Kitty Hendricks is Francis Martel.

The club's manager confirms that Martel worked as a busboy at the club for two weeks in September 1959 under the name of Feliz Cervantes. The date is important; within days of the time Martel/Cervantes quit his job, the Michigan gambler Ketchel also left the club, and Roy Fablon drowned. Martel/Cervantes also lasted only a couple of weeks at Montevista State College. But his short stay left an impression. One of his former instructors is Professor Tappinger, and Taps remembers him as a brilliant student who spoke French better than he did English. Archer's luncheon party at Taps's brings other discoveries, some of them with roots in the Midwest. Trying to get rid of her "boxed-in tension," Bess explains that she met Taps as his student at the University of Illinois and married him soon after, at age seventeen. But the brilliant, charming young scholar has become, in his wife's words, "a talking machine, with a computer instead of a heart." Before Bess's self-pity thickens into sexual longing,

"Security: The Great American Substitute for Love"

Archer leaves her. His destination is the student quarter near the college—that area "of explosive growth and feeble zoning" where Feliz Cervantes lived as a student.

Like most of Cervantes's other local acquaintances, his former landlady remembers him. She also remembers his leaving town with Kitty and Ketchel in a Rolls Royce. Prefiguring his behavior seven years later, when he posed as an enemy of Charles de Gaulle, Cervantes had claimed, in his student days, to be a political refugee from Spain. In his vexing way, he has grown more transparent and more opaque at the same time. He also told his landlady that he would return to Montevista a rich man and marry "the only girl for him," Ginny Fablon, whom he had only glimpsed. What will the dreamer do now that he has attained his dream? The question takes Archer to a man whose dream of love has shattered—Harry Hendricks. Hendricks says that Ketchel, alias Leo Spillman, won Kitty from him at poker; Kitty only rejoined Hendricks to get back some money Cervantes had stolen from Ketchel/Spillman. But how did Cervantes gain access to Ketchel/Spillman's exchequer?

A person close to all the actors in the drama is George Sylvester. Archer tries another shot in the dark by seeking information at Sylvester's clinic. His shot hits home. Archer accuses Sylvester of introducing Spillman to Roy Fablon; as Marietta believed, Sylvester had good cause to make trouble for his wife's lover. But revenge wasn't his only motive. Like Harry Hendricks before him and Roy Fablon after him, Sylvester had already lost a large sum to Spillman, a Las Vegas casino owner. When summoned to discuss the debt, Sylvester noticed signs of acute sickness in Spillman. The arrangement the two men made to clear the debt is nearly as bizarre as that of Spillman and Hendricks. Sylvester agreed to pay half of the $20,000 he owed; to discharge the other half, he would treat Spillman for his acute hypertension and also get him a cottage at the Tennis Club.

Action follows talk. Ginny calls Sylvester to report that her husband was just shot to death. Though he kept no clock—a revealing incidental, chiming with his heroic self-concept—time ran out on him in Brentwood, a suburb of Los Angeles. The death of the arch-romantic's timeless world promotes revelations that blanket a wide expanse of time. These come from Ginny; the sudden loss of a husband and a mother within a day hasn't blurred her memory. She tells Archer that, a few hours before her father died, he took her to lunch with Spillman, who offered to send her to school in Europe. Everything in Montevista has a price; Fablon was bartering his daughter to Spillman as Hendricks had bartered his wife. Though Fablon's death cancelled the deal, Spillman liked the idea behind it. The following year, he sent somebody else to a French school—Feliz Cervantes. This arrangement hurt everyone. It cost Spillman the millions his courier Cervantes later stole from him, and it cost the greedy courier his life. More information comes from Los Angeles. A friend of Taps's, Allan Bosch of Los Angeles State College, identifies his ex-student Cervantes as Pedro Domingo, a Panamanian. Domingo entered the United States illegally in 1956 and studied under a false name at both Long Beach State and Los Angeles State before coming to Montevista. What also comes to light is the squalor underlying Domingo's grandiose dreams:

Pedro's dilemma can be stated quite simply: he was a poor Panamanian with all the hopes and troubles and frustrations of his country. His mother was a Blue Moon girl in the Panama City cabarets, and Pedro himself was probably illegitimate. But he had too much gumption to accept his condition or remain in it.

More background information flows in, this time from Washington, D. C., concerning Domingo's diplomatic ties:

Until a few months ago he was a second secretary at the Panamanian Embassy. He was fairly young for the job, but apparently he's very highly qualified. He has an advanced degree from the University of Paris. Before they transferred him to Washington he held the post of third secretary in Paris.

But being a career diplomat didn't satisfy Domingo's romantic destiny: to merge with his self-concept, he needed Ginny Fablon as fiercely as Gatsby needed Daisy Buchanan (Fitzgerald is mentioned in the book). Also like Gatsby, he couldn't go to his dream girl without all the riggings of success. These riggings stretch over a moral void. Living a dream wipes him out as remorselessly as it did Gatsby.

But *who* wiped him out? Leo Spillman is the leading suspect. Some legwork and astute questioning direct Archer to familiar Santa Teresa, where Spillman is living. His disused-looking house, nestling in "an established neighborhood of well-maintained older houses," contains a real shock. Nursed by Kitty Hendricks, who hates him but won't betray him, Spillman has wasted into a helpless, drooling wreck: "His face was moon-shaped and flaccid, his body loose. Only his black eyes held some measure of controlled adult life." The money factory is in serious danger: Domingo has taken all the syndicate's ready cash, and his once-powerful chief, "a poor little sick old man" unable to speak or write, can't realize his investments. Also, like that of Leo Durano, another defanged lion, in *Grin*, Spillman's sickness must remain secret to stop his fellow racketeers from taking over his empire. The scene is dominated by chattering Kitty. Confused, resentful, and threatened, she tells Archer that Marietta knew about Roy's dealing Ginny to Spillman. But Marietta didn't know, adds Kitty, that Ginny had already gotten pregnant by a local man her father was trying to steer her away from. This attempt may have led to Fablon's death. Kitty (her surmise recalling the death of Gabrielle Torres in *Coast*) thinks that Fablon fell into the salt-water pool of the Tennis Club scuffling with Spillman and that Domingo threw the drowned body in the

"Security: The Great American Substitute for Love"

ocean to make the death look like suicide. Though this explanation by-passes Ginny's pregnancy, it does account for Domingo's meteoric rise in the Spillman galaxy.

Domingo served his crooked paymaster well till he betrayed him. He hept his chief's name out of the police investigation of Roy Fablon's death; as a diplomatic courier, he smuggled both goods and money to Spillman in his search-immune pouch. But once Spillman fell sick, Domingo skipped with his ready cash. Other insights into Domingo come from the person best qualified to make them. His mother, a Señora Rosales, has come from Panama City for his body. On his way to meet her, Archer lunches with her son's former French instructor at L. A. State, Allan Bosch. What Bosch says helps Archer understand both Domingo and his ex-B-Girl mother: Domingo had "a good mind, rather disordered but definitely brilliant"; though he never knew his father, he set store by the fact that his maternal grandfather was French:

Pedro got quite a decent education in French. You can understand why the language obsessed him. He was a slum boy, with Indian and slave blood in his veins as well as French. His Frenchness was his only distinction, his only hope of distinction.

This exposition, boldly introduced three chapters from the end, changes both the direction and meaning of the case. For Domingo isn't Bosch's only topic of conversation. It comes out that Taps, Bosch's former colleague at the University of Illinois, impregnated a student at Urbana and then married her. This one-time sophomore prodigy of seventeen is Bess Tappinger. While this disclosure lodges in our minds, the action swings elsewhere. Ross Macdonald is following his usual practice of springing a key fact and then, rather than developing its importance, moving away from it. What he gains, besides suspense and reader interest, is a fresh perspective from which to assess the fact. Events and issues count less on their own in Ross Macdonald than when mixed and shuffled. The tight, clean organization of Black Money makes for a swift execution of plot. The writer's ability to make us live with his data and respond to them imaginatively puts his best work where we'd least expect to find detective fiction—close to the refined social comedy of Jane Austen and Henry James.

Bosch stays in the action long enough to translate for Archer in his interview with Domingo's mother. "Still handsome in spite of her gold teeth and the craterlike circles under her eyes," Mrs. Rosales believes her son to have been a budding national hero: "My son had nothing to do with gangsters. He was a fine man, a great man. If he had lived, he would have become our foreign minister, perhaps our president." She believes nothing Archer says (somewhat heartlessly and stupidly, given the context) about his criminal tie with Spillman. Communication between detective and witness has broken down. Archer refuses to take her to

Ginny, arguing that Ginny's heart is too heavy with loss to bear such a meeting, and Mrs. Rosales leaves him. Her place is taken by Bess Tappinger, whom Archer visits next: women dominate the last chapters. Bess confirms Kitty's story; Ginny Fablon did get pregnant seven years ago—by Taps. In fact, Taps is probably with her now; Ginny called several hours ago to ask whether Taps killed her parents. Speaking quickly, with eyes "wide and blind, like a statue's," Bess, who had listened in on the phone conversation, adds that Taps took his revolver to Ginny's. Suspense grows as Archer arms himself before confronting Ginny and Taps in the last chapter.

The lovers' only appearance together emits little love. Ginny and Taps had plotted to kill Domingo for his money after Ginny married him, but, having fallen in love with him, she changed her mind. The harrowing finale releases the accumulated tensions, with Archer, the detective-catalyst, standing by passively. Taps admits having done the murders; then he shoots himself—offstage, like most of Ross Macdonald's gunfire victims. The shot takes Ginny to his side, Archer following quickly. The novel's sharp-cut last image establishes the lovers as mirror-images:

> She was lying on the sitting room floor face to face with Tappinger, their profiles interlocking like complementary shapes cut from a single piece of metal. She lay there with him, silent and unmoving, until the noise of sirens was heard along the road. Then she got up and washed her face and composed herself.

This ending, a *tour de force* of contained terror, quietly restores the mystery of the everyday. The verb, "composed," in the novel's last sentence implies creation and artifice as in a musical composition. As her reaction to the deaths of her mother and husband proved, Ginny, no well-meaning innocent as Peter Jr., claims, shakes off adversity quickly. The police sirens dispel the soul-searching caused by Taps's suicide. Defensively, she improvises a social self. As her father, her husband, and her lover all proved, caring entails heavy penalties. She won't follow their example. Instead, she prepares a face with which to face the investigating policemen. Perhaps she has already started to think about marrying Peter, Jr.

During the recorded action, Ginny must have already regretted opting for thrills and danger over the dull safety represented by marriage to Peter. As well she might: spectacular characters burn out in *Black Money*. What lasts is the safe and the dull. Amid the speed and boom of southern California, casualties crop up everywhere; one scene in the novel even takes place in a hobo jungle, or tramps' bivouac. Ross Macdonald's Scots-Canadian suspicion of brilliance touches all. Taps, "the white hope of the French department at Illinois," settles into a mediocre job and dies at forty-one. The second-rate teaching post sustains Taps. What undoes him is passion and excitement. Glamor and romance kill you dead in *Black Money*. This lesson applies indirectly to Roy Fablon. Handsome, dashing

"Security: The Great American Substitute for Love"

Fablon, with the kingly Gallic first name, gambles away his wife's money, his daughter, and his own life rather than taking a regular job. Cervantes, called "a tropical Hamlet," goes to defeat because of his romantic self-image. The failure of Leo Spillman, the powerful Las Vegas gambler, is conveyed technically. Though strong enough to have wrecked several lives, Spillman appears for less than half a page; the leaking-away of manhood suggested by his name also refers to him. This ex-boxer from Michigan who took his ring name from Stanley Ketchel, "the Michigan Assassin," has dwindled into a vegetable subsisting on hydrotherapy.

But his slow decline doesn't seize us like the sudden downfall of Pedro Domingo. A gutter brat from below the border, Domingo looks back to John Galton, Ross Macdonald's gatecrashing indigent from north of the border. A comparison between what happens to the two outsiders shows how the author's attitude darkened between 1959 and 1966. This pessimism accompanies artistic growth. *Black Money* is a better book than *The Galton Case*. First, Ross Macdonald writes more objectively about the Panamanian Domingo than about his fellow Canadian, John Galton. By not leaning upon his Canadian past, he can better criticize his adopted society. The Spanish-Americans are the persecuted people in southern California, not the blacks. A gifted non-white from Central America, Domingo stands for a whole spectrum of non-white Latins. The strong impact he makes on those around him gives him a power and a radiance beyond those of Caucasian outsiders like Galton, Holly May Ferguson, Bruce Campion (*Hearse*), and Dick Leandro (*Dollar*). Everyone who meets him remembers him; nearly everyone is charmed. Though the bartender at the Tennis Club calls him "just another paisano," the club's most prominent members lease their home to him. Marietta Fablon finds him "a fascinating person"; Peter Jamieson, Sr., says of him, "There's not much question that he's a cultivated European"; speaking as a sex-starved woman of twenty-nine, Bess Tappinger calls him "hot-blooded . . . aggressive, the kind of man you imagine a bullfighter might be." Domingo wins admirers at all levels. His former teacher, Allan Bosch, calls him "the best student I ever had," and Taps, following suit, praises him as "a brilliant student, one of the most brilliant I ever had," even though he only taught Domingo for a week or two.

Anybody capable of impressing so many people should have a good chance at happiness. What blocks Domingo from his hopes is his extravagant imagination. He models himself on romantic stereotypes—making a mission of winning the girl he loved at first sight, posing as a political exile, and hiding a sword inside a bamboo cane. He is as silly to us as to Archer: "I didn't know what he wanted from Virginia," the detective says in Chapter 20; "it was probably something that didn't exist." His values reflect Hollywood, America's dream factory. Yet he has both feelings and brains. No empty space, he tries to be human. He has a

degree from the Sorbonne; he marries the girl he loves; he has the knowledge to score a hundred on Taps's quiz in Chapter 7. His energy and his
commitment make him more of a courtly knight than Ginny is an innocent maiden. Even Archer cheats him by continuing his investigation
after Domingo makes a perfect score on the quiz.

But Domingo dies too early to be the novel's thematic center. The
heart of *Black Money* is the love affair of Ginny and Taps. Though it
only moves to the fore in the last two chapters, the affaire regulates
nearly everything and everybody in the case. Taps is a pale, sad, cranky
man who keeps getting turned down for the full professorship he deserves.
Yet real fire surges within his tame, tepid exterior. Even his familiar name,
i.e., Taps, belies him at first glance. The name denotes gentleness and
caution, as in the tapping of a blind man's cane. But it also indicates
probing—in the quasi-sexual sense of an oil drill tapping the supine earth,
universal symbol of the female, for her dark stored riches. Sexuality is a
large part of his life. Women like him. His wife speaks of his "Scott
Fitzgerald good looks"; the assistant dean of women at the University of
Illinois "had a crush on Taps"; a dean's secretary at Montevista State also
wants him for herself. Finally, in Bess and Ginny, he gets two exceptional
young women to fall in love with him; the affaire with Ginny lasts seven
years despite handicaps imposed by her parents, his marriage, and a seven-
teen-year age difference. Nor is his surge narrowly sexual. He understands his love-rival, the slum-child Domingo, because he, too, clawed his
way up from the gutter. Ex-rifleman and combat infantry soldier, "the
rising young man in the department" at Illinois, and, says a colleague at
Montevista State, "one of our most brilliant scholars," he deserves more
of life's prizes than he has won. His friend and former colleague Allan
Bosch summarizes Taps too conservatively when he says of him that he's
"not a negligible man."

To counterweight the fantasy-lives led by the dreamers Taps and
Domingo, Ross Macdonald gives Archer little to do besides detect. No
Susanna Drew probes his heart; his passiveness in the last scene falls far
short of the brilliance he showed at the end of *Chill*; except for a brief,
ineffectual flurry by Peter, Jr., he isn't attacked: nobody shoots him,
knocks him out, or points a weapon at him. Ross Macdonald limits him
in order to study him. As he did in *Victim*, his first sustained investigation
of Archer, Ross Macdonald studies the detective by means of reflectors—
characters who simultaneously resemble and differ from him. *Sui generis*
in the canon is Archer's younger alter ego, Ward Rasmussen. This efficient
young policeman, who reminds Archer of himself as a rookie cop, has
Archer's blue eyes, energy, and "slightly fanatical look." Also, he never
went to college, carries a notebook, and works on his own time. If his
dedication is connected with his ambition to move out of his father's
house, then he may also share Archer's uneasiness with authority. His

entry into the novel rolls time backward. Introduced in the same chapter with him are the photograph of Domingo taken seven years before and also Harry Hendricks's symbolic rebirth, i.e., his being lifted from the car trunk where he had been left to die. A link between Archer and Rasmussen has been forged. The morning after the two men take Hendricks to the hospital, they discuss the case over breakfast, Archer buying his younger counterpart his own favorite breakfast of ham and eggs and coffee.

But if Archer calls to mind honest, effective Ward Rasmussen, he also resembles the piece of work who brought them together, Harry Hendricks, self-styled "the biggest failure west of the Mississippi." Archer and Hendricks, neither of whom can keep a wife, register in the same hotel, show up at Domingo's house the same morning, browbeat witnesses. *Black Money* doesn't show Archer at his most kindly. He bullies Peter, Jr., about overeating and neglecting physical exercise. He may dislike questioning Ginny the same day she learns that her mother and her husband were both murdered; yet even though he feels "like a tormenting devil," the questions keep coming. In the next chapter, he's told, "You make everything sound like an accusation," and Ginny says in Chapter 30 that he has "a horrible imagination." She may be right. Archer *is* menacing, perhaps even murderous; Kitty Hendricks accuses him of wanting to kill her in Chapter 12. But he controls his murderous impulses, here and elsewhere. He also snubs a bribe of $5000 to lead some Las Vegas gamblers to Leo Spillman, who means nothing to him. Archer can be cruel or gentle. Turning Spillman over to the mob wouldn't have cost him a scruple. He yanks information out of reluctant, evasive George Sylvester; yet once he learns what he wants, he protects his witness. Ross Macdonald's novels aren't production-line items. In formula writing, the formula determines all. Archer, on the other hand, has moral conflicts that wouldn't fret Philip Marlowe, a man with fixed ideas about right and wrong. By testing Archer in order to know him better, Ross Macdonald emerges as a more modern novelist than Raymond Chandler. The novel's references to European culture also take American literary detection beyond the frontier individualism that survives in Hammett, Chandler, and the early Archers. Works like *Black Money* bring detective fiction into the dovecote of serious modern literature.

The vehicle for this modernism is often irony. What is serious and straightforward in Chandler becomes ironic in Ross Macdonald. Kitty Hendricks struggles to get a picture of somebody, namely, Domingo, she was once photographed with. Taps makes out a quiz for his former student, again Domingo; then, rather than rewarding him for scoring perfectly, kills him. Any discussion of Ross Macdonald's modernism must turn on *Black Money*, his most literary thriller. References to French culture abound. What is just as important, the book, which mentions James

Joyce (in Chapter 27), crackles with Joycean wit and verbal byplay. As in Joyce, *Black Money* fuses literature and life. The book includes a paragraph from a scholarly essay on Stephen Crane. Pedro Domingo is both "a tropical Hamlet" and a quixotic Latin who calls himself Cervantes. The presence of famous lovers from literary history, like Pyramus and Thisbe and also Dante and Beatrice comments wryly on the love triangles of Bess, Taps and Ginny and of Taps, Ginny, and Domingo; just as wryly, these triangles form during a *Cercle Francaise* production of a play about a love triangle—Sartre's *No Exit*. Other characters join the word-romp: Patrolman Ward Rasmussen finds Harry Hendricks a room in a hospital ward. In Chapter 25, Rasmussen and Archer turn up at the same place for the same purpose; their walking toward each other makes their confrontation a mirror meeting, which foreshadows the book's stunning final image—Ginny lying face-to-face with her dead lover Taps, "their profiles interlocking like complementary shapes cut from a single piece of metal." Contributing his share to the narrative pattern, Leo Spillman has a lion's head knocker on his front door. But the person behind most of the structural pranks is the one who stimulates Ross Macdonald most—Pedro Domingo. Having entered the United States at San Pedro, Pedro dies on a dead-end street called Sabado Avenue, or Avenue of the Sabbath—an apt death-site for one whose name translated into English means Sunday. Others enter this linguistic web. Domingo's first name is the same as that of Ginny's previous fiancé, Peter, Jr., and the initials Ginny knew Domingo by, F. M., duplicate those of her mother, Marietta Fablon, in reverse.

This intricate doubling pattern includes psychology, specifically, the mechanism of repetition compulsion: Taps impregnates two brilliant students of seventeen; Domingo tells the same lie—that he's a European political refugee—on both his sojourns in Montevista; Kitty Hendricks either falls in love with feeble men or finds that men she loves go feeble: "I always get stuck with feebs and cripples," she says in Chapter 29. Finally, Bess Tappinger complains about being married to an older man; yet she wants to leave her older husband for the still-older Archer. This compulsiveness, in Kitty and elsewhere, has sexual roots. Its literary ancestor is Dante, whose tormented souls in the *Inferno* must re-enact their earthly sin; its focus in the novel is not the authority on Dante, Bess Tappinger, but Ginny Fablon, whom Domingo loved at first sight as Dante did Beatrice. Involved in three love triangles, she causes the death of those closest to her—her father, mother, husband, and lover. This deathliness is sexual. That her parents are killed by Domingo and Taps puts their death within the Oedipal orbit. That the short version of Ginny's nickname, Gin, also means an animal trap defines the orbit. Sexual fear runs through *Black Money.*

It runs in trim, well-honed grooves. The motivation in *Black Money* is first rate. In Chapter 1, for instance, Peter, Jr., makes Ginny's father,

"Security: The Great American Substitute for Love".

Roy, the basis of her attraction to Domingo: "it's all mixed up with her father and the fact that he was part French." This explanation does apply —yet less strictly to Domingo than to Taps, Ginny's ex-French teacher and much-older lover. All along Ross Macdonald hides the truth that her love for her "dark and dashing" French-speaking father carries into her choice of Taps. Here as elsewhere, Domingo is the odd man out. Yet his deprivation and exclusion is general. Though not the main figure in the plot, he does dominate the pattern. Nobody in the book achieves free-standing human identity. Some are uprooted, some bereft. Marietta and Peter, Sr., are widowed; Archer is divorced; the manager of the Tennis Club is a dispossessed Swiss; Bess, Taps, and Spillman are Midwesterners who run the reefs of Montevista. Then there are the characters' carefully chosen names. The Jamiesons have the same first and last name; their house-keeper Vera has no last name; Taps has no first name; Kitty Hendricks keeps Harry's name but lives as the wife of Leo Spillman, who, as Kayo Ketchel, has two names. Domingo/Cervantes/Martel uses three names; the non-white can't afford to settle into a single identity. Yet he doesn't differ greatly from the others. False claimants all, these others lack the credentials for the prizes they covet. Nick Carraway's parting words to Gatsby echo through the closing pages of *Black Money*: Pedro outshines the whole damn bunch of Montevistans he strives to impress. The novel touches on many subjects—the rackets, international politics, psychology, and the Class Game. Informing them all is the outsider, Pedro Domingo. Like the tragic hero, he lives in our imaginations, reminding us, in his struggles, of both our fallibility and good luck. He deserves the serious, sympathetic attention Ross Macdonald gives him.

7

The thriller is an action story, a narrative with a drive and moral simplicity lacking in most mainstream fiction; suspense, movement, and the intellectual exercise of naming the killer replace character analysis and subtle moral discriminations. Ross Macdonald's contribution to the genre consists of bringing depth and resonance to plots depending on swiftness of execution. In thrillers, action usually supercedes character. The Archers maintain a brisk tempo without allowing the crisis to dominate. They keep action and character in healthy balance by seating many of their key events in the past; channeling a dramatic event through a twenty-year shaft of time creates intensities that safeguard rather than blur individuality. The presence of psychiatrists, social workers, and policemen helps create a forum where the meaning of these intensities is debated. Because detection isn't an exact science, it thrives on discussion and debate; the detective writer's need to conceal both the killer's motive and identity till the end intives speculation, much of it historical or psychological, in the Archers.

Murder brings the tensions undergirding the Archers into the material world. Ross Macdonald said in a 1972 radio broadcast in London that his books try "to take the psychic event which has occurred in all of us, the guilty loss of togetherness and innocence, and put it back in the external world where it has had its repercussions."[1] One of these repercussions is a craving for security, which usually translates in the late Archers to an urge to find and then reunite with a lost parent. The shuttle between chaos and order forms one of Ross Macdonald's basic narrative rhythms. "In the detective novel," said the writer in July 1974, "I found a form that corresponds to the form of my own life and the times we live in—on the one hand, violent destruction of order and meaning; on the other, unrelenting effort to put the world together again."[2] Murder energizes the rhythm. Unlike killing, which is often accidental, murder has roots in relationships that go back in time. Because it usually happens close to home, its solution will lie in the home life of the murderer. But this life depends on secret ties. The detective's discovery of these ties includes both intellectual challenge and bodily risk. Murder taking place in a close-

Urban Apprehensions

knit social structure becomes harder to detect because, based on motives deeper than money or political differences, it is more desperate.

Archer's job in Ross Macdonald's four latest books is his usual one—that of finding the connection between the people, places, and motives informing the crisis. In Chapter 12 of *The Instant Enemy*, the detective assumes a typical investigative stance: "Coincidence seldom happens in my work. If you dig deep enough, you can nearly always find the single bifurcating root." Archer's practice of digging in mined terrain has made Ross Macdonald, the miner, an object of some unfriendly criticism: That rather than enlarging his narrative world, he keeps presenting the same world—that of the runaway, the fresh murder tied to one committed some twenty years before, the hidden marriage or blood-tie—in each of his books; you know beforehand what you're going to find in an Archer. But you don't know where, why, or how. And here is where the drama comes in. What happens counts less than the reasons it happened; the how and the why express humanity—people's longings, fallibility, and courage. Rather than describing reality realistically, the Archers are metaphors for crisis. Ross Macdonald doesn't inform so much as he creates and communicates the shatter-effects of crisis.

The four latest Archers maintain the sharpness of their predecessors while broadening and strengthening their thematic base. The forest fire in *The Underground Man* and the oil spill in *Sleeping Beauty*, by fusing moral guilt and ecological disaster, bring Ross Macdonald's inventiveness new scale and dignity. The lesson of these last two works hinges on the dangers of urbanization: cutting yourself off from nature causes almost all your troubles. Links can be heard snapping all through Ross Macdonald's work and life—the broken family, the ambiguous national tie, the experience of living in a cold, empty outpost of an empire whose capital lay 5000 miles away. Realities like these touch everybody; all of us have lost something vital. The environmental calamities of the last two novels slant the loss we all know to the urban sprawl polluting our air, stunting our crops, and poisoning our wild life. Rattlesnake, the fire chewing through the coastal timberlands of southern California, recalls primordial evil in its name. It also joins the serpent of Eden to a truth just as ancient—that our worst ills are self-inflicted; we can hurt ourselves much worse than others can hurt us. The self-undoing often comes from an ignorance of the environment. Birdwatcher, Sierra Club and National Audubon Society member, and conservationist, Ross Macdonald, in a 1973 interview, set forth the suicidal dangers of cutting our ties with nature:

I just feel that man's connection with nature is indispensable to him. And a society or an individual literally goes insane if they lose touch entirely with natural rhythms and natural forces, both exterior and internal. And the two are in touch with each other. They speak back and forth to each other. . . . And the destruction of nature is a serious moral crime because it destroys man and his ability to live in the world.[3]

I

The opening paragraphs of *The Instant Enemy* (1968) find Archer doing familiar work—driving his car. He is taking the Los Angeles Freeway into the Valley. Keith Sebastian, a public relations officer for a bank, has asked him to come to his home in the good residential suburb of Woodland Hills. The reason for the conference? Sebastian's seventeen-year-old daughter Sandy has decamped with her boyfriend, taking along a shotgun and a box of shells. Her decampment doesn't surprise Archer. During recent months she has been neglecting her school work and her family for Davy Spanner, a nineteen-year-old parolee Archer later summarizes thus:

Davy Spanner, son of a migrant worker, orphaned at three or four and institutionalized, then taken by foster parents; a violent dropout from high school, a wandering teen-ager, car thief, jail graduate.

What probably drove Sandy from her parents happened two nights ago, when her father followed her and Davy to "a weird joint" and warned Davy that, unless he kept away from Sandy, he'd blow the lad's head off—with the same shotgun Sandy and Davy drove away with.

Many of the standard plot ingredients of the canon have emerged by Chapter 3. The Sebastians hire Archer to find a missing daughter whose innocence they overrate and who has cut and run with a young man they resent; the parents blame each other for their daughter's outbreak; their desire to save face prompts them to hide important information about Sandy from Archer. Also apparent by Chapter 3 is Ross Macdonald's ability to put well-worked matierals to new uses. Even though runaways or prodigals have appeared in the last five Archers, they all differ from each other. In *Black Money*, twenty-four-year-old Ginny Fablon is the former fiancée of Archer's client; Tom Hillman of *Dollar* is a reform-school student of seventeen; Dolly Kincaid is a young bride in *Chill*; Harriet Blackwell, though missing during most of *Hearse*, turns out to be the killer; Phoebe Wycherly, Harriet's junior by five years at age nineteen, is fleeing both the pain caused by her parents' divorce and the responsibility of her own pregnancy.

High school senior Sandy Sebastian differs as sharply from these earlier missing persons as they do from each other, Ross Macdonald working creatively within the tight discipline imposed by his basic framework. Pocketing two days' pay plus expenses, Archer goes looking for Sandy at Davy Spanner's apartment in Pacific Palisades. The red-haired manageress of the apartment complex, Laurel Smith, reacts angrily to Archer's ques-

Urban Apprehensions

tions. "Davy Spanner's a good boy," she insists, demanding wearily, "Why don't you people leave him alone for a change?" What happens next could well make Archer wish he had taken her advice. Now plausibility requires that he meet Davy and Sandy. Ross Macdonald had to produce the runaways in order to make us care about them, as he did with Harriet Blackwell and Bruce Campion in *Hearse*; it's hard to care about somebody you've not met. But Davy isn't just paraded before us. The surly, heavily muscled young man takes charge as soon as he walks on. Opening his door himself, he grants Archer a minute's talk with Sandy, who has been staying at the apartment. Archer acts the gentleman, perhaps to counter Davy's brusqueness, addressing Sandy politely as "Miss Sebastian" and, rather than advising her to go home, says that her parents want to know her plans. Only when Davy orders him to leave does Archer lose his poise; he calls Davy "a psycho" and claims that, when he does leave, Sandy is leaving with him. This ill-tempered outburst recoils immediately. Davy's right-left combination of punches knocks him down— "balancing the wobbling sky" on his sore chin and rapping his head on concrete. The case has started badly. At the end of Chapter 4, Archer feels old, tired, and lonely. He admits defeat and, after plucking up the vim to follow the runaways, tastes defeat again when he loses their car in traffic.

Short on leads, he rides dejectedly back to Davy's apartment, where Laurel scolds him for scaring Davy away. Her attitude softens when Archer says that, by fighting, Davy broke one of the rules of probation. A bargain is in order. Laurel will help find Davy; in return, Archer won't report Davy, provided that Davy let him take Sandy home. "Her parents could hang a rap on him that would put him away until he's middle-aged," Archer clinches the bargain. Laurel gives in. She lets the detective into Davy's apartment and allows him to examine it. Then the cooperation stops. Archer gets more bribes in *Enemy* than in any other work, and the first comes in Chapter 5, when Laurel offers him $1000 and her body to "lay off" Davy (her eyes, curiously, revealing nothing worth reporting). But he doesn't lay off. From Davy's parole officer, his next witness, he learns that Davy grew up in an orphanage. "A boy who never really had anybody or anything of his own," Davy took easily to crime. His career as a criminal faltered when a conviction for car theft led to a six-month prison term. But Laurel asked his parole officer to waive the jail sentence in lieu of Davy's working part-time in her apartment complex. The parole officer agreed to Laurel's suggestion, explaining himself to Archer, "I think she's a woman who wanted someone to help."

Talks with other witnesses follow. In the next chapter, Archer meets his client's chief, Stephen Hackett, "a well-kept man of forty or so." Keith Sebastian sums up the background of Hackett's business career:

He inherited a fortune from his father. Mark Hackett was one of those fabulous Texas oilmen. But Stephen Hackett is a moneymaker in his own right. Just in the last few years, for example, he bought out Centennial Savings and put up this building.

Sebastian also identifies a crude map found at Davy's apartment as corresponding to the Hackett ranch. But he denies that the map, done in Sandy's scrawl, and the shotgun Sandy stole infer trouble. Only reluctantly does he direct Archer to Hackett's place, where the detective goes straightaway to prevent a shootout.

The fenced-in estate contains some threats Archer hadn't foreseen. He is met at the gate by Lupe Rivera, a "lean Spanish type" with "dark and ageless eyes" and a revolver in his belt. Hackett's Bavarian wife, Gerda, "handsome but a little flat and dull," takes offense at the way Rivera, manager of the Malibu estate, talks to her. But because he has the backing of Hackett's mother, Ruth, Gerda's complaints count for nil. Gerda's frustration gives the plot momentum. No sooner is Ruth Marburg mentioned that she pulls up to the house with her son. Ruth gives off a rank sexuality. Gerda believes her to be "too close" to Stephen, who is older than Ruth's present husband, Sidney Marburg. Then Ruth looks at Archer "with the arithmetical eye of an aging professional beauty: would I be viable in bed?" Archer's refusal to be impressed either with her charms or with her son's taste as an art collector ends the visit abruptly. Interchange has failed. Archer won't concede to social rank, and the Hackett circle has ignored his danger warning.

What the detective confronts next heightens the negative, bitten-up mood—Laurel Smith slugged unconscious and left bleeding in her bath. After making the necessary phone calls, he dismantles a portable television set Laurel had won recently in a telephone contest. His suspicions prove correct; the set contains an electronic surveillance device. Somebody has been spying on Laurel. But who? Following his leads well, he learns that, a few weeks ago, a man moved some radio gear into a building near Laurel's. The man, who has since left Los Baños Street, is a retired sheriff from Santa Teresa named Jack Fleischer. But developments elsewhere keep Archer from questioning Fleischer. Sandy Sebastian and Davy Spanner have invaded the Hackett estate, smashed Lupe Rivera's skull with a tire iron, and then kidnaped Stephen Hackett at gunpoint. Strands of irony lace the melodrama: the Hackett's, so high-handed with Archer a few hours ago, now need his help.

Again, developments at the Malibu estate surprise Archer. Hackett's mother, Ruth Marburg, offers him $100,000 to bring back her son. But Archer, always suspicious of large offers of money, boggles. "That's too much," he says, knowing that large bankrolls buy people as well as their services. His foreknowledge of the abduction, inferred from Sandy's rough map, doesn't mean that he had a part in the abduction, he makes clear. Besides, he already has a client in Keith Sebastian. He can't let a richer offer break this compact. "His daughter is missing, remember," he tells Ruth of Sebastian; "He feels about her just as strongly as you do about your son." This argument doesn't change her mind. Archer isn't allowed to control the investigation. Using her money and influence as leverage, she gains the upper hand over her son's hireling Sebastian: "Your precious daughter has stolen my son," she says: "She drove in here with her bully-boy hidden in the trunk of her car. Knocked out our manager with a tire iron. Walked into the house with bully-boy and marched Stephen out to their car and took him away." As in Edgar Wallace's most famous book, *The Four Just Men* (1905), a foreseeable but non-preventable crime has occurred. Even though Sandy's map, the stolen shotgun, and the testimony of Sebastian made Hackett's abduction inevitable, nobody could stop it.

But Hackett and his young captors are still within reach. Just before he left for his chief's estate, Sebastian had a phone call from Sandy; she dialed him from Santa Teresa to ask to come home. The drive to Santa Teresa takes him and Archer two hours. Hope and fear oscillate. The manager of the gas station from which Sandy placed the collect call remembers a girl telephoning from his office and then being taken to her car by a young man before finishing her talk. The manager also recalls the young couple's saying that they had a large dog in their car-trunk. The best way to Hackett and his two abductors seems through the retired Santa Teresa sheriff and electronic bugging specialist, Jack Fleischer. In fact, Archer will spend the rest of the novel pursuing Fleischer—his person or his leads or his recorded tapes. Chapter Twelve introduces Fleischer's wife of thirty years. Mrs. Fleischer says that Jack and Laurel Smith have been lovers for fifteen years and that Jack is traveling north, having only stopped at home long enough to book a room in a Palo Alto motel.

Archer doesn't give chase right away. Before leaving Santa Teresa, he visits Davy Spanner's former high school counselor, Henry Langston, "a large, homely, sandy-haired young man with sensitive eyes." Langston admits having involved himself so deeply in Davy's problems at one time that the involvement nearly broke up his marriage: "There were times when our identities seemed to get mixed up. I could actually feel his feelings and think his thoughts, and I felt this terrible empathy." A deep need created this empathy. Like Tom Hillman in *Dollar*, Davy wanted to find out where he came from and who he was. What he found did him no good. Langston's digging into his past brought an appalling discovery— from Deputy Sheriff Jack Fleischer. When Davy was three, his father fell under a moving train and was decapitated; little Davy spent the night sitting alongside the headless corpse. Hearing this childhood story and knowing it to be true drove him berserk. He attacked Langston and, still raging, smashed his office. The school expelled him and, but for Langston's intervention, would have stowed him in a reform school.

Davy hasn't forgotten his father's death since being reminded of it three years ago. In fact, he came to Hank Langston a few hours before Archer to learn the exact place where his father's body was found. Archer has Langston drive him to the death-site. On the trip north, Langston explains that he visited the site about three years ago with Deputy Fleischer, who had already spent twelve years working on the case. Unexpectedly, the travelers spot Sandy Sebastian near a lonely gravel road. Sandy tells how Davy tied Stephen Hackett to some train tracks nearby. But she adds that she left the scene before learning if he went through with the murder; nor does she know why he chose Hackett as his victim. It is past three o'clock in the morning when Archer returns her to her father in Santa Teresa. Here, the fear and confusion she displayed earlier disappear. She treats her father with contempt—blowing a cloud of cigarette smoke in his face, telling him that she uses marijuana as well as tobacco, and trying to run away again. The case has spread and deepened. Archer advises psychiatric help for Sandy and then co-opts San Francisco detective Willie Mackey, out of view since *Hearse*, to watch Jack Fleischer. While awaiting Mackey's report, Archer drives back to the Hackett ranch, where the case takes on still a new complication: Stephen Hackett's father Mark was shot by an unknown assassin about fifteen years ago.

The search for the relation, if any, between this shooting and Stephen's abduction must wait, though. The local police report that Laurel Smith died from the beating given her in her apartment. Then another phone call: Willie Mackey says that Fleischer had breakfast with an Albert Blevins in the Mission district of San Francisco. This news puts Archer on the next jet to the Bay area; Laurel Blevins was the name on the social security card he found in Laurel's flat. In a letter to the present writer, dated 11 March 1972, Ross Macdonald said he liked the scene at the pensioners' hotel where Archer and Albert Blevins talk. His friendly recollection is well judged. The economical scene combines atmosphere, strong motivation, and deft plotting; Blevins's faded, worn possessions, like those of Pete Culligan in *Galton*, characterize Blevins as the lonely old transient Ross Macdonald connects with his absentee father. Also bespeaking the outdoorsman-loser are Blevins's eyes: "His clear blue eyes had the oddly innocent look of a man who had never been completely broken in to human society." No mere excuse for the author to indulge his past, Blevins plays a key role, uncovering, for Archer's benefit, some important leads. Rummaging through his effects, he produces a marriage license which says that he married Henrietta R. Krug in March 1927. A recollection goes with the license: never stable or socialized enough for marriage, Blevins only married Henrietta, or Etta, because she was pregnant. The farm the Blevinses lived on—a wedding present from Etta's parents—failed after three dry years. What wrecked the marriage, though, wasn't failed crops but Blevins's temper. Etta divorced him because he beat her. Their little son, Jasper, whom he also beat, Blevins stashed with his in-laws in L. A. before selling the farm and making for the open country. Blevins shows Archer a letter, dated December 1948, which says that Jasper married a pretty seventeen-year-old Texan named Laurel Dudney and that Laurel just had a baby boy named David. In a post-script, Mrs. Krug says that she never hears from Etta. The various strands of the case knit tightly as the novel reaches the midway mark: "Davy's father had died a violent death. His mother had died in violence. Davy the child of violence was roaring down the trail which led back to Albert Blevins."

This reordering of time through the causality of violence doesn't explain the sexual protest symbolized by Jasper Blevins's decapitation. Archer seeks an explanation in Jack Fleischer's now-empty motel room, where he finds a newspaper in the wastebasket with the story of the Hackett abduction torn out. The pattern of *Enemy* holds; Archer chases another investigator rather than going straight for the criminal or missing persons. The trial still leads to the past. Some legwork takes him to elderly Alma Krug, Albert Belvins's ex-mother-in-law, Jasper's grandmother, and Davy's great-grandmother. Living in a Santa Monica convalescent home, Mrs. Krug hasn't heard from Albert Blevins for twenty years. She does help Archer, though, by recalling that Jasper and his wife Laurel lived at the same ranch his parents had deserted years before; Jasper wanted to paint the rough countryside rather than farm it. Accepting no substitute for firsthand experience, Archer asks to see the tired, disused ranch. Then the chase underlying the novel's structure reverses. On his way out of the convalescent home, he sees Jack Fleischer asking an orderly to see Alma Krug. When told that visiting hours are over, Fleischer, worn out by long hours and long pulls at the bottle, hits the orderly. Archer reacts quickly, taking Fleischer's pistol and immobilizing him with an armlock. Stunned and helpless, Fleischer calms down. After discussing the case with Archer, he agrees to drive to the Krug ranch with the detective.

The partnership of the two men is short-lived. On the drive north, Fleischer hits Archer with his pistol-butt and dumps him, unconscious, on the lonely highway. Only by flattening himself under an oncoming truck does he escape death. The driver of the truck takes him to the outskirts of Santa Teresa, where he phones Hank Langston. With Langston's help, the case renews. The two men follow the coastal highway to the imaginary town of Rodeo City; then they turn inland to Centerville. The northern reaches of the county are wild and open like the old west. Rain pelts Langston's car as it buckets along the dark, poorly made road to the Krug ranch. Gothic horror permeates the trip to the dark back country. The aptly named Buzzard Creek overflows; to cross its dangerous waist-high currents, Archer must wade.

The paragraphs that show him wading through the flood read as fast as any in the canon. Nor does the excitement slacken when he crosses the creek. To the side of the creekbed, he sees "a grayish bundle" that turns out to be Stephen Hackett, badly beaten in the face and soaked clear through. Once helped to safety, Hackett explains that, besides pounding him and leaving him to die, Davy Spanner also shot Deputy Jack Fleischer. Horror continues to dominate, as an owl flies out of a sagging, deserted barn into the storm. Ross Macdonald, who has an extraordinary gift for describing the weathering of old buildings, equates the blasted corpse of Fleischer with the dripping, dilapadated place where it is found: "Jack Fleischer . . . had become a part of the general ruin. In the weak flashlight beam, his face and head seemed to have been partly rusted away. Water dripped down on him from the leaking roof." The writer includes one more Gothic touch before leaving the Krug farm—Archer's easing Fleischer's car along the floor of the flooding creek: "I eased the car slowly into the water . . . trusting there were no curves. . . . For one frightening instant in the middle, the car seemed to be floating. It shifted sideways, then jarred to rest on a higher part of the invisible road."

The cinematic heightening of the Krug farm episode gives way to psychology when Archer drives Stephen Hackett home. Hackett's wife glowers as Ruth Marburg, his mother, runs at Hackett, Jocasta-like, "crying and exclaiming over his wounds." Ruth controls the scene even after she stops hoarding her son. She gives Archer a postdated check for $100,000 for bringing Stephen home and then makes a sexual pass. This Archer rejects politely but firmly. Embarrassment and bitterness are averted. The arrival of a local police captain redirects everybody's attention to the unsolved case. The captain produces evidence showing that Mark Hackett was killed the same week in May 1952 that Jasper Blevins died headless under a train some sixty miles away. Sex and detection mingle at the Hacketts', Ross Macdonald again using blindness as an Oedipal shorthand for sexual trouble. In the next chapter, Gerda Hackett has a go at Archer, thanking him politely for his troubles and then pushing her tongue into his mouth "like a blind worm looking for a home."

Archer leaves the ranch with relief. Talks with several witnesses indicate that his best chance to solve the mystery lies with the tapes Fleischer made of Laurel Smith: though dead, Fleischer still directs the chase. His widow gloats over the news that he and Laurel are both dead. Unfortunately for Archer, she also refuses to turn over the tapes. The detective must find another way to break the case. The possibility that Fleischer killed Jasper Blevins to get Laurel for himself and then kept her hidden till public interest in the case waned sends Archer back to the frontier wilderness of Santa Teresa County. The scene at ex-brothel madam Mamie Hagedorn's, where Laurel stayed after Jasper's death, is one of the most vivid in the book. The uniformed Spanish-American maid, the Victorian trappings, and ancient Miss Hagedorn, wearing an iridescent wig and conjuring up "the past itself . . . in its shroud," fluster Archer. Though Miss Hagedorn, a sagebrush Miss Havisham, knew Laurel well, she shrinks from naming the headless murder victim of 1952 as her husband. But she does supply some unasked-for information about Jasper's mother. Before marrying Albert Blevins, Etta Krug had another husband. This man, a business tycoon, and not Blevins, sired Jasper. Mamie unearths still another long-hidden family secret: Jasper wasn't Davy Spanner's father. Once more, money cuts across a sexual tie. Laurel became pregnant by a rich Texan, who gave her some money and sent her to California. Eager to grab this money, Jasper married her in spite of her pregnancy. Like Mike Harley of *Dollar*, Jasper had been sexually twisted by a cruel father. Laurel took Jack Fleischer as a lover after spending a few years with a husband who never reacted to her normally. But the affaire couldn't make up for a worsening home life. Unable to put up with Jasper's abnormal demands, Laurel killed him.

Mamie's story of Laurel's marriage has little bearing on the present case: Laurel and her lover Fleischer are both dead; Jasper, though nobody will swear to it, probably died under the moving train in Rodeo City. Somewhat discouraged, Archer goes back to square one, the Krug ranch, "where all the trouble has started . . . where Jasper's marriage had ended in murder, where Davy Spanner was born and Jack Fleischer died." Archer rarely chases down a lead in *Enemy* without finding that somebody else did the job first. Thus he sees Hank Langston's car parked near Buzzard Creek. Langston has found the Fleischer murder weapon—the shotgun, now sawed-off, that Sandy Sebastian took from her father before running away with Davy. But Langston doesn't fire the shotgun at Davy after finding him at his home later in the chapter. When his pregnant wife Kate runs out of the house bloody-thighed and shrilling that Davy is making her lose her baby, Langston (thinking that Davy tried to force Kate?) shoots out Davy's eye with a pistol.

The killing, for which the local police won't prosecute Hank, frees Archer to go looking again for Laurel's murderer. But he's foiled. Mrs. Fleischer has already sold Jack's tapes for $10,000 and is preparing to leave town. She isn't the only one who wants to flee southern California. Bernice Sebastian says that her husband is taking Sandy to Mexico City to spare her from being tried for kidnaping Stephen Hackett. Bernice also admits that Sandy wrote in her diary that she had sex with Lupe Rivera while in an LSD daze the previous summer. Hidden sexual ties continue to order the action. In the next chapter Archer learns from Alma Krug, at the convalescent home, that the rich Texan who impregnated Laurel with Davy was Stephen Hackett. Laurel's pregnancy ignited a series of events. Stephen's father, Mark, who was later to die within days of the Jasper Blevins killing, sent Stephen to Europe; he also paid Jasper, a struggling barber at the time, a large sum for marrying Laurel. Mrs. Krug remembers her ex-son-in-law, Jasper, with mixed feelings:

He was a Tartar. He stole and fought and tortured cats and got in trouble at school. I took him to a head doctor once and the doctor said he should be sent away. But I couldn't bear to do that to him, the poor boy wasn't all bad. . . . He had some artistic talent.

Her daughter Etta Mrs. Krug prefers to forget: "She's ashamed of the life she leads, with young men half her age. I might as well not have a family." She does say, though, thanks to Archer's deft prodding, that Henrietta/ Etta dropped her first name altogether and began using her middle name, Ruth, and also that she married not only Mark Hackett but also Lupe Rivera before her much-younger present husband, Sidney Marburg.

Skipping meals and sleep, Archer intercepts Sandy and her father leaving the Hackett ranch. Sandy runs into the sea; then Archer, testing his mettle as a swimmer for the first time since *Hearse*, catches her and tows her back to the beach. A series of well-naunced questions unearths key facts—that Keith Sebastian bought the Laurel Smith tapes for his chief, Stephen Hackett, and that Hackett is financing the Sebastians' trip to Latin America. For the third time in forty years, a Hackett has tried to squash a problem with a wad of cash and a one-way ticket out of town. For the third time the problem is rooted in sex. Sandy reveals that Hackett as well as Lupe Rivera entered her, front and rear, during her LSD summer. Her confession explains other events. In early fall, Sandy met Davy Spanner; hearing of Davy's wish to lay hands on Stephen Hackett, she helped gladly. This piece of news stirs Archer. Always wary of the contaminating effects of money, he heads straight for the Hacketts' to return the $100,000 check Ruth Marburg gave him for finding Stephen. He walks into the library without waiting to be announced, interrupting the family at the exact time they are listening to the Laurel Smith tapes. For one mad minute, hearing Laurel's voice from outside the library had made him believe Laurel to be still alive. But, recovering grip quickly, he enters the panelled library wearing a friendly smile. When Ruth Marburg, assuming that he can be bribed, reminds him that she postdated her check to him, he displays a check of his own—the one the family gave Keith Sebastian to leave town. Having their guilt thrown back in their faces confuses the Hacketts. Archer maintains the advantage gained by producing the Sebastian check; he takes away the revolver Ruth threatens him with and then coolly switches on the tape recorder.

The playback closes the case. Archer and the others hear Laurel identify herself to Davy Spanner as his mother. Then Stephen Hackett interrupts the tape to say that he killed his half-brother Jasper Blevins for murdering Stephen's father, Mark. The playback contradicts his story. A last-chapter identity switch, the first since *Chill*, reveals Stephen as Jasper

Urban Apprehensions

and also as the killer of Laurel, Mark, and the real Stephen Hackett. Jasper murdered the two Hacketts fifteen years ago with his mother's help; Mark knew about Ruth's affaire with his employee, Sidney Marburg. Before he could disinherit her, by divorcing her and then willing all to Stephen, he had to die. But the action continues after Archer sets forth his evidence and names the killer. He shoots a charging Jasper Blevins in the leg, the revolver blast bringing in a police captain posted outside. The last two paragraphs find Archer back at his office, where he tears Ruth Marburg's check, throws the pieces out the window, and watches them drift to the street below.

The extraordinary plot of *Enemy* shows different kinds of artistic growth. The novel peoples the urban inferno astutely. Willie Mackey's co-operative in San Francisco, "an earnest crew-cut young man named Bob Levine," gives the canon, along with Captain Perlberg of *Black Money*, its second Jewish lawman in two novels. Also, the novel's elderly people play an active role: Archer gets his best leads from Albert Blevins, who is over sixty, and from Mamie Hagedorn and Alma Krug, who are both in their seventies. The novel's social map, including a spread of characters from the down-and-outer Albert Blevins to his millionaire ex-wife Ruth, generates overtones. Both fixed and free, the characters fuse mystery and genetic forces beyond their control. Hank Langston explains Davy Spanner psychologically. Without ruling out his psychological explanation, Ross Macdonald also presents Davy as the last outcropping of a causality embracing three murders, forty years, and a stretch of miles that goes from southern California to London, where Stephen Hackett was studying at the time his father was shot. No wonder Davy acts madly.

Learned allusions also strengthen the novel. The Oedipus myth keeps grazing the plot. Also evident is the use of poetic devices like symbolism. Not only does Ross Macdonald use symbols effectively; his discussion of his symbolic strategy also shows both a knowledge of literary history and an ability to scoop fresh literary ore out of tired seams:

> The thought of the girl [i.e., Sandy] was heavy on my mind. She was swinging through all the changes of the moon. The moon was white and shining, the very symbol of purity, but it had its dark side, too, pocked and cold and desolate and hidden. The girl could turn either way.

Returning from *Galton* and *Money* and ultimately from *Oedipus Rex* is the device of repetition or doubling. The repeated experiences in *Enemy* cover a broad spectrum. Both Davy's adoptive father, Edward Spanner of Santa Teresa, and his natural father, Jasper Blevins, have cut hair for a living. Jack Fleischer's wife looks like an older version of his lover of fifteen years, Laurel Smith. Laurel also manages the Laurel Apartments in Pacific Palisades. When Archer revisits the apartment court, feeling tired and old after his trouncing by Davy, he notes that it is located on Elder

Street. A more subtle use of place names occurs in the chapter (Chapter 4) where Archer, after watching Laurel douse Davy with a hose to cool his anger, finds himself half a page later on Los Baños Street (i.e., Street of the Baths).

This Joycean word comedy comes less frequently in *Enemy* than in *Money*. More notable is the care the later novel takes to tune its dialogue to the spoken idiom of the late 1960s. Its dialogue brackets *Enemy* linguistically with the Children's Crusade, popular rock musicals like *Hair*, and Vietnam. Terms like "escalations and negotiations" and "credibility gap" refer to phrasing made popular by Washington's handling of the Vietnamese war. Sandy Sebastian, whom Davy calls a "chick" and, with a nod to Carnaby Street, "a bird," smokes pot and takes LSD. These pastimes she discusses with jargon terms like "freaked out" and "blew my mind." The novel's ability to reproduce the speaking habits of its junior readership prefigures other insights into contemporary trends. Published the same year as John Updike's *Couples* and the year before Roth's *Portnoy's Complaint*, *Enemy* deals more openly with sex than any Archer to date. First, the novel refers freely to the sexual functions. Hank Langston says of his pregnant wife Kate in Chapter 30, "She's concerned about losing the baby. . . . She was bleeding a little before I left last night." In Chapter 5, when Laurel Smith says of Sandy and Davy, "I can't tell if they were sleeping together," Archer, usually evasive about sex, snaps back, "I assume they were." Laurel is more frank about her own sexuality than about Davy's, at least according to her lover's wife, who says of her, "The only crime *she* ever witnessed was Deputy Jack Fleischer taking off his pants."

Others beside Mrs. Fleischer have sexual grievances. These are voiced in different ways. Albert Blevins says that he beat his son Jasper "for cutting off my nooky by being born." In her last talk with Archer, at the Hacketts' summer cottage, Sandy pleads, "Get me out of here, will you. . . ? This is the bed where Lupe and Steve took turns at me. In the vulva and the anus." Now in Freud, neurotic anxiety stems from the sexual life and refers to a blocked libido. The people in *Enemy* have sex often—Ruth Marburg with men spanning some twenty-five years in age and her son Jasper with as wide a range in sadic variations. Yet this sexual freedom fulfills nobody. Alma Krug despises her daughter Ruth's sexual habits; Davy Spanner pays more attention to his genealogy than to the charms of Sandy; that physical cruelty meant more than sex to Albert Blevins leaves Blevins a lonely old man. The Victorian atmosphere of spinster Mamie Hagedorn's house in Santa Teresa County enforces the mood of sexual repression or stress. Helping build the same anxious mood are the novel's many references to Germany. Although Kenneth Millar served in the Pacific in World War II, he also visited Germany as a student in 1936. The Germany alluded to in *Enemy* is the same hive of psychosexuality found in the Berlin fiction of Millar/Macdonald's fellow California transplant, Christopher Isherwood. This Germany looks back to *Tunnel*, Ross Macdonald's first novel, which describes Munich as a seedbed of Nazi cruelty; Ruth Marburg, in fact, has the same first name as the heroine of *Tunnel*, Ruth Esch. American-born Ruth accounts for much of the book's German strain. Her last name, Marburg, is the same as that of a famous German university town; her maiden name, Krug, is the German word for jug. In Gerda, her son Jasper has a wife from Bavaria, the part of Germany Ross Macdonald knows best (in contrast to Isherwood, who lived in and wrote about Berlin). The influence of Millar/Macdonald's 1936 trip to Munich shows elsewhere. In Chapter 11, the Hackett living room reminds Archer of "an underground bunker"; Deputy Jack Fleischer, who isn't German but has a German last name, uses stormtrooper techniques when he insists on seeing Alma Krug at her Santa Monica convalescent home.

Strengthening the book's narrative economy, Fleischer pulls another important thematic load—that of acting as a double to Archer. Archer says of the hard-drinking old cop in Chapter 20, "In a sense Fleischer belonged to me" and "Facing him in the semi-darkness, I had the feeling that I was looking at myself in a bleared distorting mirror." To Fleischer, the last four letters of whose name are the same as his own, he says, "You're case and mine are connected." The connection goes beyond the case. Both men have a strong sense of vocation; matching Archer's willingness to skip food and sleep are the fifteen years and several hundred dollars Fleischer spends on electronic equipment in order to find Stephen Hackett's killer. Countervailing this dedication is a failed marriage; both men have made their wives unhappy. But Fleischer isn't Archer's only double. As he did with Sheriff Brand Church and Leonard Bozey of *Victim*, Ross Macdonald will give Archer a younger as well as an older alter ego. The detective's relationship with nineteen-year-old Davy Spanner is as short-lived and as violent as the one with Fleischer. Other comparisons are more oblique. Both of Archer's opposite numbers beat him up; both die from gunfire. Archer feels paranoid after Fleischer knocks him out and throws him from his car; several people believe Davy a paranoid. Perhaps Davy plays Archer's younger self too well; like Leonard Bozey and also Tom Rica of *Doomsters*, he resembles Archer in his capacity, as a youth, to turn out badly or well. That Archer swung over to the side of the law whereas his younger counterparts led short, nasty lives must have roused guilt. But not only in Archer: The following account of Davy by his ex-high-school counselor conjures up Kenneth Millar's own boyhood: "You don't know what that boy's been through—orphanages and foster homes and getting kicked around. He never had a home of his own." Later Langston says of Davy: "He wanted some information, essentially information about himself. As I was saying, I delved pretty deeply into his case several years ago. . . . I realize now I went too deep." Langston and Ross Macdonald know Davy better than anybody, even his parents. The two men are also a little obsessed with him. In Chapter 14, Hank dreams of his wife, Davy, and himself in bed together; in Chapter 30, playing the punitive father, he shoots Davy's eye out allegedly for forcing Kate. Ross Macdonald had to make Hank's motivation sexual; he also had to use Hank to kill Davy in order to quell his own painful boyhood memories.

Archer feels the shock waves enamating from his psychological complexity. The first chapter finds him atypically stern and reproachful. He tells Bernice and Keith Sebastian, during a minor domestic scuffle, "I didn't get out of bed at five o'clock in the morning to referee a family argument"; when told by the Sebastians that Sandy went hunting the previous summer with the Hacketts, he asks, with unwarranted crankiness, "Who the hell are Mr. and Mrs. Hackett?" In Chapter 3, he questions one of Sandy's friends, but not before reminding the Sebastians of their helplessness: "You can't control the situation. It's out of control. So why don't you go away and let me handle this?" His sullenness causes regret. The Sebastians *are* helpless; they *do* handicap Archer by hiding important information about Sandy. But they're also worried and confused; though Sandy's running away makes sense to the outsider Archer, it gives her parents more grief than they can handle. Considering their plight, they're as helpful and as pleasant as can be expected. Archer's statement in Chapter 23 of Ross Macdonald's next book, *The Goodbye Look*, that he has given up smoking, could explain the detective's snappishness. Archer may have been suffering withdrawal pains while working for the Sebastians. Getting up at five a.m. and then driving miles in the dark by himself wouldn't have soothed his nerves preparatory to meeting his new clients.

But there is more to Archer than his sarcasm. *Enemy* extends the scope of his mind. He surprises us by recognizing a Klee, a Kokoschka, and a Picasso in Jasper Blevins's private art gallery; later, we wonder where he acquired the learning to identify Erik Erikson, Erich Fromm, Paul Goodman, and Edgar Z. Friedenberg as "the freer spirits" in social science today. This learning doesn't enter the investigation, though, as it would in an English detective story featuring a highly informed gentleman-sleuth. Archer does a moral turnabout after Cahpter 3. He helps a rain-sodden Jasper Blevins into a car, gives him his jacket, and wraps him in his car rug, always calling him "Mr. Hackett," after finding him presumably battered by Davy Spanner near Buzzard Creek. His best insight, which owes little either to formal learning or the mechanics of detection, comes when he explains Sandy's leaving her diary where her mother could find it as an indirect plea for help.

But even insights like this can't humanize Ross Macdonald's most ingeniously plotted novel to date. The writer plants his clues fairly, sets forth his subjects clearly, and reminds us tactfully of the shifts and changes taking place in the fast-moving action. But the mixture of events is too rich. Though brilliantly observed and organized, the novel isn't life-like; it has more material than it can assimilate. For instance, it loses by smuggling in a marriage between Ruth Marburg and the Chicano Lupe Rivera twenty-five years before the time of the book. Though adding a rich tint to the self-contained narrative pattern, the detail reveals a tendency to over-explicitness. The book is too thickly worked. Missing is the openness and good-natured indeterminacy that left unexplained the deaths of Ronald Jaimet in *Hearse* and Roy Fablon in *Chill*. The logic of the plot is the only logic the characters obey. Without being rushed or coldly analytical, *Enemy* is all execution. Besides Laurel, who dies early, none of the other murder victims matter to us; Jack Fleischer is a drunken bully, while Mark Hackett and his son Stephen both died fifteen years ago. Nor do the younger characters invite concern; Sandy is restored to safety less than halfway through, and Davy dies for the sake of the plot. Weak characters mean weak resolutions. Archer's last-chapter demonstration of the evidence gives only mild intellectual pleasure. The evidence comes from a tape recording. Furthermore, Jasper Blevins, still affecting Stephen Hackett, is convalescing at the end; the hunt for the killer isn't a race to stop him from killing others.

The narrative curve of the action expresses negation. *Enemy* opens at daybreak, everything looking "fresh and new and awesome as creation." It ends in darkness; Archer is eating cold, stale chicken as he looks out of his office window at "the crowds of night-blooming young people on the Strip." Here is the book's carping last paragraph:

I had a second slug to fortify my nerves. Then I got Mrs. Marburg's check out of the safe. I tore it into small pieces and tossed the yellow confetti out the window. It drifted down on the short hairs and the long hairs, the potheads and the acid heads, draft dodgers and dollar chasers, swingers and walking wounded, idiot saints, hard cases, foolish virgins.

Ross Macdonald hadn't tried this sullen lower-depths journalism for several novels, usually preferring irony or compassion to cynicism or moral anger. The final image of *Enemy* settles nothing. Nor is it meant to. The people who pass under Archer's office window portray urban futility. Archer's floating the torn yellow flakes of Ruth Marburg's $100,000 check onto their heads neither redeems nor blesses them. Solving the Hackett case has drained Archer. Lonely, bitter, and tired, he is one with the passers-by he describes in the urban barrens.

II

The elaborate narrative mode sought in *Enemy* emerges brilliantly in *The Goodbye Look* (1969). The plot runs in tangents and oblique lines; it splits into parallel strands which cross and recross; spanning four generations, it attempts new turns and variations with time (one character accuses Archer of having a tortuous imagination). This flashing silver neither blinds nor tarnishes, thanks to the book's well-regulated style and sensitive, thoughtful narrator-hero. In short, *Look* has found a controlling voice for the intricate narrative technique of Ross Macdonald's maturity. The superiority of *Look* over *Enemy*, in fact, makes the later work the cornerstone of a technical achievement new in the history of crime fiction.

The action starts with a missing box rather than a missing person. John Truttwell, a handsome, "high-shouldered and elegantly dressed" lawyer in his late fifties, invites Archer to Pacific Point to discuss the troubles of his friends and clients, Irene and Lawrence Chalmers. Recalling the neighborly friendships of the Hillmans and the Carlsons in *Dollar* and of the Fablons and the Jamiesons in *Money*, the tie joining the Chalmerses and the Truttwells goes uncommonly deep for today's instant society: "Larry and Irene Chalmers are friends of mine," says Truttwell. "We live across from each other. . . . I've known Larry all my life, and so did our parents before us. I learned a good deal of my law from Larry's father, the judge. And my late wife was very close to Larry's mother." This longstanding tie, strengthened by choice as well as time and proximity, extends into the future, as Truttwell's daughter, Betty, and young Nick Chalmers have just become engaged. More exposition follows. Lawrence Chalmers Truttwell describes as a mandarin rather than a merchant or a professional: "Larry hasn't accomplished much since the war. Of course he's made a great deal of money, but even that was handed to him on a silver platter." Chalmers's ancestry makes him more special than his money: "Larry Chalmers's grandfather fought in the Civil War, then came to California and married a Spanish land-grant heiress. . . . In our instant society that makes him the closest thing we have to an aristocrat." The credentials of Chalmers's wife Irene, though thinner, are impressive in their own right; Irene has earned lawyer Truttwell's esteem as "a hell of a good-looking woman." This highly favored couple have recently fallen into difficult straits. Their house was broken into while they were vacationing in Palm Springs; oddly, the only item taken from them was an old family keepsake, a Florentine box full of letters that had been locked in a safe.

The timing of the burglary, i.e., while the Chalmerses were away, and the burglars' knowledge of the hidden safe's location both infer an inside job. To investigate the inference, Archer goes to the fine old California Spanish mansion the Chalmers family has lived in for sixty years. Recalling the entry of Tish Bradshaw, in *Chill*, beautiful, dark-haired Irene Chalmers comes into the novel carrying a rose and a pair of garden shears. Like so many other first witnesses in the canon, Irene handicaps Archer; she won't let him talk to her twenty-three-year-old son Nick. She does admit, though, that Nick, who may be missing, ran away from home before and that her husband has connected Nick's current absence with the missing box. The contents of the letters inside the box—written by Chamlers to his mother, Estelle, during the war—can be ignored for now. That somebody wanted them badly enough to steal them has set the groundplan for a missing-persons case with roots some twenty-five years in the past.

The mid-January morning takes Archer to Nick's apartment in Pacific Point's university area, "a city where everyone was young." Irene's fears about her son soon confirmed. Though mid-year final exams are being held, Nick, who needs to pass the exams in order to graduate, has disappeared. His loving fiancée, Betty Truttwell relates Nick's disappearance to an older woman, new to the area. This fortyish woman, a Mrs. Trask, Betty calls "a phony blonde with a big red sloppy mouth and poisonous eyes." Missing persons and things rule the book's early chapters. Archer goes from Nick's apartment to Jean Trask's cottage at the Montevista Inn, where Jean is quarrelling with her husband; Trask wants Jean to come home with him to San Diego and give up looking for her long-missing father, Eldon Swain. Flashing an old police badge, Archer halts the quarrel when it threatens to get out of hand. He can credit George Trask's wanting to take Jean back home; in spite of her heavy drinking, Jean looks better than her self-styled junior rival, Betty Truttwell, had let on. Jean surprises Archer a second time. Lying in plain view on her bed is the gold box he was hired to find. He doesn't touch it, though, dismissing it as "just a physical accident of the case." The box has served the action well, both as plot device and as symbol of female sexuality. Like Pandora's box, which is mentioned twice, it has opened and let fly trouble. Some of the effects of the trouble—the Chalmerses' anxiety about the stolen box and Nick's disappearance—are already known. But since good writing is as much knowing what to leave out as what to put in, Ross Macdonald waits before divulging the trouble itself. The box has given the novel a good start, providing both a hunt and a material clue. Ross Macdonald will return to it. Having nuanced his effect carefully, he can dismiss it for now in order to look at some of the issues it has raised.

One of these issues is murder. The book sprouts its first corpse in Chapter 5; found shot to death in an old tan convertible is Sidney Harrow, a roughneck bill collector Jean Trask had brought up from San Diego to help find her father. Archer must use his best energies to solve the Harrow murder. In the next chapter, he turns up information possibly bearing on both the murder and the theft of the gold box. The information comes indirectly. John Truttwell retails his uneasiness over his daughter's coming marriage to Nick Chalmers: Truttwell had to raise Betty, his only child, because his wife died when Betty was a baby; the job of rearing an only child of the opposite sex by himself has made him overrate Betty's innocence and vulnerability. This family drama is commonplace in the canon. What interests Archer more than Truttwell's overprotectiveness for now is the hit-and-run killing of his wife in July 1945 in front of their Pacific Point home. The plot of *Look* is building along the same lines set forth by its genesis: the box now in Jean Trask's possession may have occasioned another burglary and, with it, an unsolved murder that happened twenty-four years ago. At Archer's request, John Truttwell spells out the strange circumstances of his wife's death:

Whoever it was had made an attempt to burglarize the Chalmerses' house. My wife apparently saw them enter the house and scared them out of there. They ran her down when they made their getaway.

This old death is outshadowed by the urgency of an impending one. Clawed by guilt, Nick Chalmers has called Betty to announce his plan to kill himself.

Why is Nick so despairing? His phone call came from the Tennis Club (setting for much of *Money*), where Archer speeds hoping to stop the suicide. The success of his mission must hang fire. Yes, Nick had been seen at the Club's bar, accompanied by a middle-aged woman who had signed the guest register as Jean Swain. But Jean and Nick left the Club after Nick was put out of the bar for his wild conduct. Is there time to save him? Archer tracks him to his apartment, where he sees right away that Nick resents being tracked. Hiding behind wraparound sunglasses, Nick points a gun at Archer. Betty Truttwell, who has been keeping Nick company, saves the day. Acting with decisiveness, moral clairty, and love, she hits Nick's gun arm, which allows Archer both to disarm Nick and record the serial number of his revolver. Next, he answers Nick's lunge for the revolver with a solar plexus punch executed to stun the "mixed-up overgrown boy" without hurting him.

The turbulence continues. Nick flies into a tantrum, striking himself in the face and refusing to explain himself. The closest he comes to consecutive, reasoned statement is a remark muttered with a "scowling baby-face": "We went to the hobo jungle back of Ocean Boulevard. Someone had left a fire burning and we sat by the coals. He wanted me to do a bad thing. . . . I took his gun and shot him." Archer makes no connection between Sidney Harrow's death and a hobo jungle. But Nick's breakdown after his garbled confession of guilt ends the questioning. Archer and Betty take Nick home and explain his behavior to his psychiatrist, Dr. Ralph Smitheram. The investigation has stalled. Ex-battle

Urban Apprehensions

hero Larry Chalmers's trumpeting the military virtues of endurance and manly courage fails to comfort Nick. His failure is not unique. The trouble father and son have communicating is recounted by John Truttwell, who takes Archer aside after driving up in his Cadillac. The reasons behind the communication barrier, as Truttwell outlines them, are both hereditary and personal:

> He's very close to his mother. . . . I think he idolizes his father, but feels he can't measure up.

*   *   *

> I think Nick was picked up by some sort of sexual psychopath. His family got him back in a hurry, but not before Nick was frightened out of his wits. He was only eight years old at the time. You can understand why nobody likes to talk about it.

Truttwell can understand Nick without wanting him to marry Betty. His mind is made up on this subject. Referring to Nick as a "psycho" and "that weakling," he flies into a rage and must be persuaded by Archer not to force an emotional decision on Betty during this time of stress.

The police investigation of Sidney Harrow's murder moves to the fore in Chapter 9. Sacramento has traced the Colt revolver that killed Harrow to Samuel Rawlinson, retired president of the Pasadena Occidental Bank; Rawlinson, who still lives in Pasadena, bought the Colt in 1941 and let his permit for it lapse four years later. His old frame house, with its moldy walls and sagging parquet floor, seems inappropriate for a retired banker. Why doesn't Rawlinson live better than he does? His companion-housekeeper, a dark-skinned woman of sixty called Mrs. Shepherd, takes Archer into the dining room. The scene that follows is one of the book's best. As the past grows more important to Ross Macdonald, old people, who embody more of the past than others, gain in prominence. For, while representing the past, they can also control the rate with which the past filters into the present. Sam Rawlinson is Ross Macdonald's first important octogenarian. "I'm interested in your memories," Archer assures him, as Rawlinson recalls giving the Colt to his daughter Louise in 1945. Just as Estelle Chalmers's gold box, symbolic of female sexuality, dominated the opening chapters, so does the revolver of Sam Rawlinson, who was probably Estelle's lover, control the second quarter of the action. Crime, or rather its investigation, reorders time. The phallic revolver brings the past to strange new life. Like it, Rawlinson's entering the novel over dinner, the bygone affaire with Estelle, and the lip-smacking delight with which he remembers her all bring the eighty-year-old man to astonishing life as a sexual force.

Archer's visit to the book's two oldest characters to date continues to unleash surprises in Chapter 10. In 1954, Rawlinson's daughter Louise's home was broken into and the Colt stolen, most likely by her husband, Eldon Swain. Thus Louise's daughter and Rawlinson's grand-daughter is Jean Swain Trask, Nick Chalmers's new friend and boon drinking mate. Past and present mesh again as Archer goes to see Louise and Jean. Jean confirms the story that twenty-four years ago her father ran away to Mexico with Rita Shepherd, daughter of Rawlinson's housekeeper. Jean also repeats her intention, voiced earlier to her husband, of finding her father. Her declaration of intent, equating her father search with the death wish, is the most overt Freudian statement in a novel bristling with Freudian references:

> I'm going to find my Daddy. . . . I'll find him dead or alive. If he's alive I'll cook and keep house for him. And I'll be happier than I ever was in my born days. If he's dead I'll find his grave and do you know what I'll do then? I'll crawl in with him and go to sleep.

Louise doesn't share her daughter's worship of Eldon Swain. She believes that Swain stole her father's pistol in 1954, adding that he may have even used it to kill Sidney Harrow. The strong feelings his memory rouses in his daughter and ex-wife launch Eldon Swain to vivid life in Chapter 12. Feelings continue to flesh out his profile. As he did, in different registers, with Betty Truttwell and Jean, Ross Macdonald sounds the tragic opposition of father and lover or husband in a woman's heart. He lets Louise, the discarded wife, recount Swain's worst disgrace—the embezzling of over half a million dollars while working as a cashier in her father's bank in July 1945.

The scene at Louise's changes the course of the investigation. Archer says in the next chapter that his case hinges on Eldon Swain: "Eldon Swain had come into the center, pulling his whole family with him." But is he alive? A police captain reports that an unidentified man was shot through the heart in 1954 with the same gun that killed Sidney Harrow. The man has remained unidentified because his hands were placed in a bonfire nearby, evidently to burn away the fingerprints. Spending fifteen years on the case has convinced the police captain that somebody killed Swain for the money he embezzled and then charred his hands to thwart any investigation.

While the past is unfurling, Nick Chalmers yanks us back to the present. Nick has bolted from his parents again, this time having first raided their medicine cabinet. His disappearance varies the texture of the novel. Whereas Chapters 13 and 14 introduced new developments, the next two chapters bring in new characters. The first of these is Moira Smitheram, the handsome, graying wife of Nick's psychiatrist. The husband-psychiatrist comes on next: That Nick may have killed both Harrow and Swain—his confession fits the old killing better than the recent one—calls for a conference with Dr. Smitheram. "Enormous in a white smock," Ralph Smitheram won't cooperate. Ross Macdonald, whose faith in psychiatry has waned since his sympathetic portrayal of Dr. James Godwin in *Chill*, gives the snowy father-figure Smitheram some of the same favorable traits he gave Godwin. But the traits no longer impress him. Smitheram won't discuss Nick, his patient for fifteen years, with Archer or Truttwell, the Chalmerses' lawyer. Instead of praising Smitheram for shielding his patient, Ross Macdonald condemns him for an obstructionist; later, he'll punish Smitheram for his obstructionism.

Being stalemated at the hospital sends Archer to Jean Trask. (The trip to San Diego is Archer's first on record and also the first in the canon since *Morgue* [1953].) Arriving at Jean's at the same time as Archer in a clattering old jalopy is "a big rawboned man wearing a dirty gray windbreaker and a dirty gray beard." Picking the lock on the front door and going inside, the gray-thatched man, identified by the name-tag on his steering post as Randy Shepherd, then rushes back to his car. After he leaves, Archer inspects the house. The reason for Shepherd's flight becomes clear right away: Jean Trask has been stabbed to death, and Nick Chalmers is splayed out in the garage, several empty bottles of barbituates by his side. Archer rushes Nick to the San Diego Hospital, where he reads the following note, taken from Nick's pocket: "I am a murderer and deserve to die. Forgive me, Mother and Dad. I love you Betty."

Archer takes up the chase for Randy Shepherd and finds him tramping a road near the Mexican border. Randy hides in the brush to escape, but the detective, waiting patiently and then moving nimbly in the scrub, catches Randy leaving his hiding place an hour later. The first half of the novel (a book with the word "Goodbye" in its title) ends with a child bidding the two men "Adios" as they walk to Archer's car, the detective having disarmed Randy when he tried to knife him. Randy talks willingly enough. Eldon Swain buried his stolen half-million dollars "in this very area" but died before he could recover it. Did Randy kill Swain? A suspect at the time, he didn't identify the corpse with the charred hands. Other questions spring to mind. Did Randy keep silent about the corpse's identity to protect himself? Perhaps he was driven by motives deeper than those of money. Like Truttwell, another father of an only daughter, he may have loved Rita unwisely; misguided paternal love could have goaded him to kill his sixteen-year-old daughter's married, middle-aged lover. Randy shuts off Archer's investigation with the claim that he hasn't seen Rita since Swain's disappearance and possible murder in 1954.

Withholding belief in Randy's innocence or guilt, Archer gives the old roustabout fifty dollars traveling money and goes back to San Diego Hospital. Here, he questions Chicago-born Moira Smitheram, wife of Nick's psychiatrist. Smitheram's busy schedule gives Moira a free evening, and she agrees to have dinner with Archer. Dining in La Jolla, where she lived during the war, makes her, a neglected wife and "a middle-aging woman groping for a line of continuity in her life," invite some nostalgia.

Moira explains that, while her "superconfident and know-it-all" husband was serving overseas, she lived with a young postal worker named Sonny. A couple of stops with Moira around the city, including one at the hospital, where her husband again keeps Archer from Nick, don't cool the overheated emotional climate engendered by her confidences. After driving her home, Archer accepts her offer of a drink and then, without much conviction, takes her to bed: "She was willing to be taken. We shed our clothes, more or less, and lay down like wrestlers going to the mat under special rules, where pinning and being pinned were equally lucky and meritorious." Ross Macdonald keeps the sexual bout free of romance. "Something less than love but sweeter than self," Archer's night with Moira works better thematically than the detective's only other recorded rut—with Ada Reichler in *Galton*. To begin with, Ross Macdonald allows Archer to express his feelings sexually; his becoming Moira's lover shows that he cares for her. Whereas Ada was a college student, Moira is a graying forty-five; whereas Archer left Ada after tumbling her in the grass, he spends the night with Moira. What is more, preparatory to their night together, Ross Macdonald leaves Moira and Archer alone several times for as long as five or six pages. Their time alone both carries the investigation forward, by bringing in new information, and gives rise to the intimacy which makes sex between them believable. Their conversation, prior to their bedding down, has a delicacy of phrasing and a subtle animal drive that make us wonder why Ross Macdonald hasn't shown more of the turns and changes of sexual love.

The night Archer spends with Moira also chimes with his anti-authoritarianism. Having admitted, "My feeling about Smitheram . . . got in the way of my feeling for his wife," he must have enjoyed setting horns on the man who thwarted him in his work and called him a junior G-man. His motivation doesn't strain the novel's moral tone. Moira enters the action fairly late—Chapter 15 of a thirty-six chapter book. Liking Archer right away, she gives him important background data. In order to make the giving plausible, Ross Macdonald has to involve her with Archer. The involvement was physical, since, with the book half finished, it had to happen quickly. Yet nothing could come of the involvement because a happy ending for Archer would be out of kilter with the waste and loss generated by the various murders.

Thus no sense of beauty or moral resolve touches Archer when he wakes up in Moira's bed alongside her. He leaves without waking her and then drives through the fog to the local police station. The joys of the night neither distract him nor sap his strength. The investigation asserts itself in his mind immediately, as he tells Captain Oliver Lackland that Randy Shepherd used both Jean Trask and Sidney Harrow to find out about Eldon Swain. That Jean and Harrow both died after being used as catspaws makes Randy the Most Likely Suspect. Yet his guilt remains an open question. The deaths of Jean, Harrow, and Swain can also be traced to Nick Chalmers; Nick has already confessed to having killed Swain and Harrow, and his drugged body was found within feet of the corpse of Jean, the third murder victim. Some new evidence brings the case closer to a solution in Chapter 26 when Betty Truttwell displays a sampling of the 200-odd letters Larry Chalmers sent his mother, Estelle, from the Pacific during the war. Through Betty, Ross Macdonald, scrupulously putting all the facts of the case before us, reintroduces Mrs. Truttwell's mysterious hit-run death in the summer of 1945; Mrs. Truttwell feared that Estelle, by that time blind, elderly, and alone, was being robbed, and, crossing the street to help her, got killed by the robbers' car.

The death needs to be looked into. Archer makes his next witness Larry Chalmers, whose Rolls Royce has just pulled up. A stiff, evasive man, Chalmers takes Archer into his study—the same room that held the Florentine box whose theft brought Archer into the case. Believing Mrs. Truttwell's death relevant to his investigation, Archer tries a long shot—the off-chance that the robbers of the box also tried to loot the safe holding the box in 1945. Jean Trask wanted the box because, according to her, it belonged to her family before her grandfather, Sam Rawlinson, gave it to Estelle. Chalmers won't pursue the line of inquiry. The mere suggestion that his mother, whom he remembers daily, had an affaire with Rawlinson, breaks him down. Crying and swinging at Archer, he rousts the detective out into the fog.

The fog doesn't confuse him, though. The more Archer is frustrated, the more determined he becomes. His suspicion that ex-banker Rawlinson's modest life-style stems from the Truttwell killing sends Archer back to Pasadena. Could the old man have robbed his own bank, stowed the cash in the safe of his blind lover, and then lost out when the lover drooped and died after her friend Mrs. Truttwell's killing? These questions give way to more pressing business. A police bulletin says that Randy Shepherd, who has remained the Most Likely Suspect, is heading toward Pasadena. (To heighten our suspicion of Randy, Ross Macdonald gives him a stolen car to drive and puts John Truttwell in the scene to say that his wife's death car was also stolen.) Heading toward? The last sentence of Chapter 28 shows Randy, his hair dyed a florid red, driving away from a pursuing squad car on a Pasadena street.

Archer finds Randy's car parked half a block from Rawlinson's house. Though suspecting the hunted man to be hiding in the house, Archer doesn't seek him out. Instead, he shows Mrs. Shepherd Nick's graduation photo, which Randy had given Jean Trask and Sidney Harrow to help them ferret out Eldon Swain. Mrs. Shepherd denies knowing Nick. Then Randy dashes from the house and, in one of Ross Macdonald's rare on-stage killings, dies in the street from police gunfire. Archer also takes a bullet in the shoulder and must go to the hospital to have it removed. Ross Macdonald always hospitalizes Archer for a good reason, and he follows the practice in *Look*. But he keeps us waiting before divulging the reason. An unlikely visitor to Archer's room, Mrs. Shepherd says her husband's epitaph: "He was a bad husband and a bad father, and he came to a bad end." Archer wants information, not bitterness. Trying to solve a crime that began some twenty-four years ago, in 1945, he presses the Nick Chalmers line. Some verbal capework reveals that Nick's graduation picture belonged to Mrsl Shepherd, who has come to the hospital to reclaim it. And reclaim it she does. Pretending that his talk with her has worn him out, Archer, feigning sleep, watches her, "her face . . . full of love and longing," take the photo from the darkening room.

Once Archer's hospital stay establishes Mrs. Shepherd as Nick's grandmother, Ross Macdonald can release the detective. Wisely, he smuggles in no miraculous recovery. Archer, still weak and dizzy from being shot, needs Betty Truttwell to drive him to the Smitheram Clinic, where Nick is resting. Archer makes an important discovery before facing Nick or his psychiatrist. The date on one of Larry Chalmers's war letters from the Pacific, 15 March 1945, falls exactly nine months before Nick's birthday, 15 December (two days after Kenneth Millar's birthday, incidentally). The book maintains a lively contrast between mood and plot; Archer's discovery, though bringing the case closer to a solution, doesn't brighten the book's somber mood. Driving through "a brown firmament of smog" to the Smitheram Clinic, Archer spends some awkward moments with Moira. Within minutes of their first meeting since sleeping together two nights before, Moira tells him, "I'm the prisoner of all my past mistakes . . . and Ralph is one of them. You're a more recent one." Archer's reply, "We seem to be ending up on different sides," doesn't bring him closer to Moira. As in *Hearse*, his case prospers while his heart grows sad. Right after leaving Moira, he finds some crucial evidence. On a stadium rug inside Larry Chalmers's black Rolls Royce, which is parked outside the clinic, he sees a yellow spillage resembling dried vomit. This froth he scrapes into an envelope to have it tested for chloral hydrate and Nembutal, the drugs pumped out of Nick's stomach after Nick turned up unconscious in Jean Trask's garage.

The unearthing of new evidence in the next chapter brings Archer still closer to breaking the case. Considering his West Hollywood base, it is fitting that a motion picture reel should help solve at least one mystery in the canon: a home movie taken about twenty-six years ago at a swimming party unmasks the dark, elegant beauty, Irene Chalmers, as Rita Shepherd. Accusing Archer of "trying to strip . . . [her] naked," Rita admits that Nick was conceived while her husband was overseas. Eldon Swain, who shot most of the footage of the home movie, also shot the semen into Rita that gave Nick life. The home movie makes other identifications. The screen shows a "hydrophobic boy" being pushed into the pool and then helped to safety. The lad, too frightened of the water to swim in it, is the bogus war hero and father, Larry Chalmers. But more evidence and proof must be marshalled before the plot homes in on him. An obsessive childhood fear—Nick's repressed trauma—is the hidden mainspring of the case. Rita admits that Nick killed his father, Eldon Swain, in the train yard in 1954; the killing of the father, which was put forward and then snatched away in *Enemy*, becomes a reality in *Look*. Rather than sparing our feelings, the later book intensifies them. Surprises keep coming. Eight-year-old Nick didn't burn away Swain's fingerprints. As Archer shows, the person Swain's identification would have hurt most was Rita:

> You were the one with the motivation. . . . If the dead man was identified as Swain, your whole life would collapse. You'd lose your house and your husband and your social standing. You'd be Rita Shepherd again, back on your uppers.

Like Isobel Blackwell, the wife of another coward parading as an ex-battle hero, in *Dollar*, Rita is suspected only briefly. Ralph Smitheram grudgingly lets her, John Truttwell, and Archer talk to Nick. Nick admits killing Swain after Swain picked him up in his car and then started to kiss and paw him drunkenly. But he never put the dead man's hands in the bonfire; nor did he kill Sidney Harrow.

Who did these crimes? And how did a drugged Nick get from his home in Pacific Point to Jean Trask's garage in San Diego? These questions can be better answered when taken together than on their own. Larry Chalmers's war letters clear up much of the mystery. In a scene that recalls Roy Bradshaw's European postcards in *Chill*, Smitheram notes similarities in both phrasing and content between his letters and the ones Chalmers sent his mother. Starting with the home movie, the book's last chapters drain Chalmers of manhood. Smitheram, who treated him during the war years, reports that he not only failed to earn his wings as a naval pilot but even left the Navy within months of his enlistment because of mental imbalance. But this rehearsal of the past recoils painfully and unexpectedly. Like that of Oedipus, Smitheram's discovery of an old truth shatters the things he lives by. After he got Chalmers a postal job, Chalmers began living with Moira. Besides installing him in the place of his idol, Smitheram, this arrangement gave Chalmers access to his idol's letters, which he raided for material in order to keep up the pretense of being a naval hero. (A title Ross Macdonald considered giving the novel was "The Stolen War.")[4]

These disclosures, while saddening Smitheram, reduce Chalmers to a cipher. Besides not knowing how to swim and not siring Nick, he lied about serving in the Navy. What is more, he may also be sterile. Nick is the only child of his marriage, and his two-year affair with Moira—which was given a lift by her pretending to be his mother at times—occasioned no pregnancy. The last chapter whittles him down still more. Again, Smitheram, whose fortunes have been bound up with those of Chalmers for so long, feels the shock waves of his patient's setback. Moira announces she is leaving. She also spurns Archer, accusing him of violating their friendship by making public the war letters. In the meantime, the lab analysis of the dried yellow foam found in Chalmers's Rolls Royce reveals that Nick threw up some of the pills swallowed en route to San Diego.

The last chapter releases many disclosures—some of them implausible. First, Rita and Chalmers followed Eldon Swain to Mexico and highjacked his stolen half-million. Then the two, staging a reverse burglary, stashed the money in Estelle's safe. When Mrs. Truttwell came out to investigate, Chalmers ran her down. This information comes from Rita: inside of a minute she accuses her husband of planning the robbery and then killing Mrs. Truttwell, breaking twenty-five years of silence on both subjects. An improbably heavy load of evil has fallen on Larry Chalmers; and with it, a huge helping of stupidity. Motivation goes to pieces in the last chapter. Rita and Chalmers didn't have to rob Eldon Swain; Chalmers had enough money to live on one of the best streets in town and to found a clinic for Ralph Smitheram. Furthermore, he botched the reverse burglary so badly that he makes us ask how he could have pinched the money from Swain, a much harder job. Taking the half-million to his family estate at night in a stolen car makes no sense; he would have risked less danger, both from neighbors and the highway police, by carrying the cash into the house in grocery bags or a suitcase during the daytime and then hiding it while his mother was asleep.

Chalmers's plot to kill Nick is just as unconvincing. So much does Ross Macdonald doubt the probity of his solution to the mystery that he denies his killer the obligatory last- or next-to-last-chapter confrontation with his guilt. Archer says that Chalmers wanted Nick dead because the latter, helped along by Jean Trask, was getting close to learning the truth about his tie to Eldon Swain. Chalmers had to maintain the fiction that Nick was his son even at the cost of the son's life. This concept of parenthood defies belief. Ross Macdonald himself had already discredited the sanctity of the parent-child blood-tie. In Chapter 25 of *Dollar* he has Archer say, "An adopted son is just as important as a real one to his parents"; three chapters later Archer adds, "It took more than genes to establish fatherhood." In 1971, two years after the publication of *Look*, the writer again argued that many children today have close ties with non-relatives; a parent-child relationship depends as much on temperament, choice, and need as upon blood. The argument ends strongly: "I don't see any particular virtue or magical quality in blood relationships at all. In fact, I think it's been much overrated."[5] The case ends where it began —in the room with the safe that once held the Florentine box. Two pages from the end, Chalmers, out of the action for the last nine chapters, is found behind the locked door of his study, blood from his slit throat blurring the battle ribbons on his naval commander's uniform. ("The Suicide Room" is another tentative early title for *Look*.)[6]

The last chapter is a sad comedown. Ross Macdonald hadn't left a loose thread up to the finale. Except for a couple of overheard conversations and an occasional tendency of witnesses with guilty knowledge to bite back their words mid-sentence, the first thirty-five chapters of *Look* are nearly flawless. The novel resembles *Chill, Dollar*, and *Money* more than it does *Enemy*, which stands closer to it in time but not in quality of performance. *Look* has the elaborate design of *Enemy*, and its plot begins with a childhood trauma. But Ross Macdonald infuses it with more understanding than he did *Enemy*; Archer's greater thoughtfulness in *Look* giving the other characters added warmth and insight. *Look* also has more detection. The only surviving witness to Mrs. Truttwell's death was Estelle Chalmers, a blind woman who saw nothing; the solution to the murders depends on the microscopic investigation of physical evidence— the scraping of vomit found inside Chalmers's car. Archer doesn't shrink from reminding us that *Look* is a whodunit; in Chapter 6 he says, "This is the sloppiest burglary in history. The woman who has the box now keeps it lying around in plain view." To incite thought, he will express confusion over the investigation and its aims. He tells Nick, "I'm a private detective working on your side. But I'm not quite clear what your side is"; several chapters later, he shares his mystification with John Truttwell: "Facts are hard to come by in this case. I don't even know who I'm working for. Or if I'm working."

Archer's alternations between confidence and doubt work in phase with others—the rhythm set going by those who want to hush up the past and those who want to relive it and also the one between material interests, grounded in the missing money, and the human interest. The human drama filters into many areas. More vividly than any of its predecessors, *Look* shows how society works. The daughter of a tramp marries a California blueblood. The fate of Larry Chalmers is tied to that of the psychiatrist treating him for twenty-five years; Dr. Smitheram's marriage breaks together with his patient's life, and for the same reason—the making public of events that happened twenty-five years before. There are no *ex parte* relations in *Look*. Not only is Smitheram bound up with Chalmers: the detective and the killer both sleep with Smitheram's wife. Roles reverse: Betty Truttwell, after some investigating on her own, asks Archer if he's having an affaire with Moira; for a moment, the investigator has *his* private life investigated. Sometimes, the blurring of roles invites moral distinctions. Dr. Ralph Smitheram, the book's most educated character, has the same initials as the vagrant, Randy Shepherd; Randy's initials, in turn, are the reverse of those of Sam Rawlinson, who lives with

Randy's ex-wife and whose coat Randy has on when killed by a police bullet.

Though scarred, dirty, and out-of-pocket, Randy, the outcast-father, controls the action. Both the book's pattern and plot depend on him. First, his theft of Nick's graduation picture revives the interest in Eldon Swain that brings Archer into the case. Next Randy is the irrepressible frontiersman, homesteader, or gold prospector who always calls to mind Ross Macdonald's father—whose wife, like Randy's, worked as a nurse. Like Albert Blevins of *Enemy*, another man of pioneer sinew, Randy doesn't fit in organized society. He tells Archer in Chapter 19, "I want a fair shake for once in my life. And enough money to live on. How can a man help breaking the law if he don't have money to live on?" Archer's inward response, "It was a good question," suggests Ross Macdonald's compassion for the outdoorsman-loser. This compassion comes through contextually rather than through direct moral statement. Randy holds together the family drama. A gardener, he grew beautiful roses for Eldon Swain in the 1940s; Swain enjoys them along with Randy's proudest blossom, Rita, who enters the book (as Irene Chalmers) carrying a rose. More subtly, speech connects Randy to Rita. In Chapter 19, Randy says that "the statute of limitations ran out" on Swain's buried money; Rita uses the same words in a different context in Chapter 36.

Randy's connections go beyond the blood. The person he resembles most is his fellow tracker, Archer. Randy's introduction into the novel points the resemblance immediately:

> An old car that didn't belong on the street came up the hill. . . . A big rawboned man . . . got out and crossed the street. . . . He knocked, *as I had*, on the Trasks' front door. He tried the knob, *as I had*. [Emphasis added]

Not only do the two men arrive together at Jean Trask's house in San Diego; Archer is also shot in the same burst of police gunfire that kills Randy in Pasadena. The only other time the men appear together occurs along the Mexican border. That a writer obsessed with borders and national ties should set this meeting on a frontier denotes the strong grip Randy has on his imagination. A final sign of the unspoken identity between Ross Macdonald and his least favored character comes in Randy's complaint, in Chapter 16, that the sun gives him skin cancer. Like him, Kenneth Millar gets facial cancers from the sun which must be surgically removed. His creator has put more of himself into Randy than into anybody else in the book. But while responding strongly to him, he doesn't let Randy disjoint the plot. His ability to delve deeply into himself while avoiding self-indulgence shows real artistry.

Another restrained character study is that of Eldon Swain. Hearkening to Ross Macdonald's literary, rather than personal, past, this prodigal father of a prodigal son descends from middle-aged reprobates like Ralph

Urban Apprehensions

Hillman of *Dollar* and Roy Fablon of *Money*. His nerve, good looks, and ability to rule the heart of his daughter Jean make him a figure of mystery and romance. He has turned away from the middle-class routine imposed by a regular job and family. Once he rejects these values, though, he must remain an outsider. The arch-romantic can't be human: the girl he loves betrays him, and his son puts a bullet in his heart when he opens his heart to the son. Ross Macdonald's treatment of Swain shows an abiding distrust of dazzle and flash. Like the other glamorous people in the canon, Swain shines but briefly. A snapshot taken of him when middle-aged reveals "a poet who had missed his calling and had had to settle for grosser satisfactions." This natty, barbered athlete with half a million tax-free dollars and the love of a beautiful teenager dies like a tramp—shot to death while dressed like a migrant worker and stinking of alcohol. A career of reaching for things that didn't belong to him ends, suitably, with his getting his fingers burned. Swain appears only once—doing front and back flips off a high board in Louise's home movie. Like the three arching divers in the Channel Club photo in *Coast*, Swain's maneuvers chart his comet-like life. But *Look* needs only one diver, not three; and it shows the diver in motion, capturing the rhythm and stress of his air-cleaving dive. The artistry with which the dive is recorded compared to that of the aquatic trio in *Coast* suggests the difference between a snapshot and a well-photographed movie.

Like Swain's flips off the high board, most of the activity in the novel leads downward. The car, symbolizing fast movement and change in today's open society, continues to be synonymous with death. The first corpse in the novel, that of Sidney Harrow, turns up in a car in Chapter 5; a car takes Eldon Swain and Nick Chalmers to the hobo jungle where the former is killed; in a stunning metaphor expressing the danger of everyday living, Mrs. Truttwell is run down by a car in front of her house. Ross Macdonald plays some accomplished variations on his equation of death and the automobile. All the social forces in the novel meet in Nick Chalmers: one grandfather is a tramp and the other a judge; his natural father is an embezzler, his mother an octaroon, and his adoptive father a sickly offshoot of the California aristocracy. Though reared in luxury, he experienced the most powerful event of his life in a hobo jungle. Though a political science major, he can't govern himself. His temper tantrums, his flights from home, and his flirtations with suicide reflect his self-division. Nick embodies more social flux than he can assimilate. Like the automobile, he proves genetically that rapid change leads to instability, even madness.

The agent of change is usually sex. Here, too, Eldon Swain controls the flow of several lives. Louise Swain and Rita Shepherd were best friends when Randy was the Swains' gardener. At that time, Louise was rich and Rita was poor. Then Swain, fancying Rita, robbed his father-in-law, bought Rita from Randy, and took her to Mexico. These events started a process that changed everything between the best friends. At the time of the novel, January 1969, the woman no longer speak; Louise lives on a poor street, and Rita has married into one of Pacific Point's best families; whereas Louise lives in a racially mixed neighborhood, Rita hides her mixed blood. Louise's home movie contains a bold image depicting reversal of fortune through sex:

> Rita stood spraddled on the diving board and Eldon Swain inserted his head between her legs and lifted her. Tottering slightly, he carried her out to the end of the board and stood for a long moment with his head projecting from between her thighs like the head of a giant smiling baby being born again.

The phrase, "stood for a long moment," alerts us to the passage's importance. Time plays tricks. If mothers, like Estelle Chalmers, are objects of sexual longing, then sexual puppets, like Rita at age sixteen, can take on a motherly look.

Freud and Sophocles are both worked hard in *Look*. Archetypes appear in different combinations. Jean Trask hires Sidney Harrow because "He reminded me of my father when he was a young man"; the only characters who call Chalmers "Sonny" are his mother and first lover, Moira; John Truttwell, imagining himself and Nick as rivals for Betty's love, forces his daughter to choose between them; Eldon Swain, who may have molested little Nick in the hobo jungle, indulged a form of Laius complex by seeking the boy out to begin with. (His shabby, soiled garb, long absence, and moist expressions of love recall Magwitch's London meeting with Pip in *Great Expectations*.) Some of the Oedipal references fuse different parts of the myth. Blindness recurs often in the second half of the book. Randy Shepherd dies on a blind street near Sam Rawlinson's house. The killing occurs three pages after Rawlinson had said, "Eldon Swain robbed me blind" and several chapters after we learn of Estelle Chalmers's blindness. Another Freudian motif worked into the plot is that of the key. *Look* uses key symbolism with the same intellectual verve as *Ulysses*. Twice, Moira Smitheram has trouble fiting a key into a lock, demonstrating both her bad nerves and failure to make sexual contact. Also twice, Randy Shepherd has his car keys taken by Archer. Like Joyce's Leopold Bloom, who has to climb through his basement window because he forgets his latchkey, Randy lacks male force. His impotence, which goes beyond sexuality, squares with his being an outdoorsman in today's corporate state. Nobody will open any doors for him. But why does Ross Macdonald choose Archer to steal his car keys? The answer relates the American death wish to the automobile. Also, Archer is Randy's urban alter-ego; his stealing from Randy amounts to robbing himself. Similar acts recur in the canon. Some characters confess to crimes they never did; others do crimes in order to be caught or punished.

Urban Apprehensions

Stealing a man's car keys is like wearing his shoes. Feeling guilty because he has enjoyed relative comfort while Randy withers on the vine, Archer assumes the identity of his opposite number to redress the injustice. But his effort goes for nil, proving only that the harm people inflict on themselves outpaces that inflicted by others.

Another recurring truth rising from the novel is that of sexual mismating. Nick doesn't deserve Betty Truttwell, of whom Archer says, "I was beginning to understand the girl, and the more I understood her the better I liked her." The parent-child relationship remains the paradigm of sexual choice. As Archer says, Betty's leaving her father for Nick, rather than signifying rebellion, only reinstates Betty's home situation: "Even if you do succeed in breaking away, it won't be into freedom. You've got it arranged so another demanding male will take you over. And I do mean Nick." Weakness rather than strength endears men to women. Rita Shepherd gives up handsome Eldon Swain and his half-million for the weakling Larry Chalmers; Moira Smitheram also calls her years with Chalmers, who needed her more than her capable husband and thus tested her maternal powers, her happiest. What does all this mean? If Moira is right to say that women ignore the solid virtues in men, then evolution through natural selection hasn't a chance. A woman who wants to feel important can't afford a strong mate. Thus the mates either rebel or fixate themselves in a fantasy version of childhood. The emergence of children will put the marriage in more dangerous straits. Played against a dark backcloth of squalor and negation, *Look* exudes pessimism. Taking its cue from the border setting of Chapters 18 and 19, it deals with frontiers. But whereas *Gatsby* portrayed the closing of the western frontier and the death of frontier optimism, *Look* relates the closed frontier to the American psyche: options have dried up within the individual as well as without. Reality is ugly. When Archer finds Sidney Harrow's corpse in Chapter 5, he notes, "The wind spat sand in my face and the sea had a shaggy green threatening look." Two chapters later, the sea, universal symbol of life, gives off "a raw and rueful smell."

Controlling this pessimism is a style that does all the author asks of it. And he makes high demands. The prose of *Look* asserts and suggests, curls into irony and imparts golden auras. Through all, it keeps a sensible, middle-register voice that doesn't distract from the story. The sentences are usually short and simple in movement; the vocabulary isn't exotic or inflated; the discreet images and figures of speech project psychological states as well as local color. Perhaps the noblest sentence of the canon comes in Chapter 28 in Archer's impression of the impact Mrs. Truttwell's death, twenty-four years before, has had on her husband:

He lived with a grief so central and consuming that it drained the energy from his external life, and made him seem a smaller man than he was, or had once been.

III

The Underground Man (1971) is Ross Macdonald's most ambitious book to date and, thanks to both a March 1971 cover story in *Newsweek* and a friendly front-page review in the New York Times *Book Review*, still his most admired. There is no faulting the book's admirers. Serious and thoughtful, *Man* both absorbs and reflects experience with a high degree of sensitivity. Ross Macdonald doesn't merely conjure up emotions but, rather, helps us understand them. *Man* begins where *Galton*, another book with deep Oedipal roots, ended—with the singing of birds. A flock of scrub-jays camped on the lawn of Archer's West Hollywood apartment awaken the detective, presumably for their usual breakfast of peanuts, on this bright Saturday morning in September 1970. (For a parallel to the beginning of the novel, see the first paragraph of Chapter 27 of *Black Money*.) On the glistening lawn Archer meets six-year-old Ronny Broadhurst, who is staying with his mother at the apartment of Archer's vacationing downstairs neighbors. Archer and his new friend feed the jays together till interrupted by a young man smoking a cigarillo. The man, Stanley Broadhurst, has come for his son, whom he has arranged to take to the boy's grandmother in Santa Teresa. He has also brought a troubled heart. He implies that his wife, Jean, and Archer, who have never seen each other before, are lovers; then, relishing the embarrassment he has caused, accuses Jean of installing Archer as the boy's substitute father. Though the wild shot hits home, Archer stops the quarrel it ignites by sending Ronny away with Broadhurst. From his window, he watches the two drive away, accompanied by a girl or woman with long blond hair and a yellow dress.

But he isn't done with the Broadhursts. A couple of hours later, Jean knocks on his door to say she is worried because she hasn't been able to reach her mother-in-law on the phone. A newscast from Santa Teresa reports that a forest fire has broken out locally, and Jean fears that Stanley and Ronny might be trapped in the blaze. Her worries dim only briefly when Archer's direct-dial phone call finds Elizabeth Broadhurst at home: having spent the morning doing volunteer work at a hospital, Elizabeth never invited Stanley and Ronny to spend the day with her. Jean, who left Stanley only yesterday, believes him on a lover's tryst with the blonde, a possible drug addict he brought home unannounced to dinner last night. But where does Ronny fit in all this? Jean asks Archer to drive her to Santa Teresa and help her fetch the boy home. Reason tells Archer to reject Jean's plea: "I was descending into trouble: a pretty young woman with a likeable boy and a wandering husband." But his parental-erotic instincts rule him, and Chapter 3 begins with him backing his car out of its garage.

Once the car starts moving forward, Jean explains that Stanley's

Urban Apprehensions

father left his wife for another woman some fifteen years ago. The leave-taking deserves mention, first, because it was, "the main event of . . . [Stanley's] childhood" and, next, because Stanley may be reenacting it. But his motive isn't sex. "One of those overconfident people who turns out to have no confidence at all," he secretly believes that all his substance and hope left him together with his father; only by finding Leo Broadhurst can he regain promise. Archer wants a clearer picture of this promise. Stopping at the Broadhursts' home in suburban Northridge, he finds some welcome leads. Parked in the garage is a green Mercedes, presumably belonging to the blond dinner-guest, and under the pillow of Ronny's unmade bed, where the blonde presumably slept last night, is a copy of a novel. Ross Macdonald uses the forgotten book to bring in new characters, Ellen Strome and Jerry Kilpatrick, whose names appear on the inside cover. But the plot isn't ripe for them, Archer needing other help first. Before leaving the house, he inspects Stanley's study, the shrine of Stanley's obsession with his father. The contents of a roll-top desk and a steel filing cabinet sound the depth of this obsession; Jean is speaking:

> Stanley keeps a file on his father—everything he's been able to dig up about him, which isn't much. And all the false leads—the dozens of people he's talked to or written to, trying to find out where his father is. It's been his main occupation these last couple of years.

*　　　*　　　*

> Stanley and I spent two weeks in San Francisco last June. Stanley tramped around the city with his pictures. He covered most of the downtown district before he was through. I had quite a time getting him to come back with us. He wanted to quit his job and go on searching the Bay area.

Still another development, possibly related to Stanley's ruling purpose, keeps Jean and Archer from their northbound trip: a man called Al with a scarred face and the pallor of an ex-convict claims that Stanley owes him $1000. But Stanley has left town for the day and Al must take comfort in giving Archer his local address, a nearby motel, where Stanley is to deliver the money as soon as he comes back.

In Chapter 5, Jean and Archer reach Elizabeth Broadhurst's canyon ranch near Santa Teresa. A short talk with Elizabeth on the subject of her son leads Archer to her gardener, Frederick "Fritz" Snow, "a soft-looking man" with a harelip and "emotional green eyes." Fritz gave Stanley the key to the Mountain House, a cabin on the Broadhurst property. On his way to the cabin with Elizabeth, Archer learns the reason for Stanley's day-trip to his mother—he wanted to borrow $1500. Stanley's black convertible is standing, as expected, near his mother's weathered redwood cabin. Then the *unexpected* intrudes. Looking for Stanley on a nearby slope, Archer meets a forester, Joe Kelsey, who shows him a shallow hole in the ground. The hole contains the pickaxed corpse of Stanley Broadhurst coiled like a foetus. Kelsey has traced the origin of the forest fire to Stanley's death-site and, more precisely, to a cigarillo resembling the one Stanley was smoking outside Archer's apartment. When Kelsey connects the fire and murder, we follow suit: "Whoever killed him probably made him drop this in the dry grass. This means they're legally and morally responsible for the fire." But before trying to establish responsibility, Kelsey has to rebury Stanley's corpse to stop it from being burned.

The unpleasantness of finding Stanley dead obliges Archer to do a chore just as unpleasant—telling both Jean and Elizabeth Broadhurst that Stanley is dead and Ronny is missing. The only lead to the missing child is Fritz Snow, who, as Elizabeth's gardener, had custody of the pickaxe and spade found near Stanley's corpse. The moon-faced weeping boy-man lives with his mother, the Broadhursts' former housekeeper. "A quick-moving gray-haired woman," Edna Snow welcomes Elizabeth, Kelsey, and Archer into her old stucco cottage. She is less eager to have her frightened, backward son questioned by the law. Her objections don't stop Archer, though, whose talk with Fritz spills into the next chapter. Under coercion, Fritz admits giving Stanley the garden tools found by Kelsey on the canyon-slope. He also admits lending Stanley's blond friend her car, which she used to flee the murder-site along with Ronny. Archer takes this information to Elizabeth, who is drinking tea in the front room. But he doesn't get to deliver it. Overtaxed by the day's alarms and excursions, Elizabeth gets dizzy, faints, and must be rushed by ambulance to the hospital.

Archer bends his efforts to the green Mercedes found in the Broadhursts' garage in Northridge. He takes the car back to its owners, whose registration papers he had found in the glove compartment. From the Armisteads' Chicano groundsman he learns that a blond girl had climbed the mast of his employers' yacht the other night and then threatened to jump. The girl, identified as Susan Crandall, was visiting Jerry Kilpatrick, a local youth who lives in the *Ariadne* and keeps her trim for its owners. Archer finds the bearded nineteen-year-old aboard the yacht in the next chapter. "Very hostile," Jerry denies knowing either Ronny or Sue. His snarling denial has the beneficial side-effect of stalling the investigation long enough for Archer to have his first meal since morning. But before Archer can digest his food, he is back at work. The sight of the car Sue had borrowed from Fritz Snow sends Archer back to *Ariadne*. In one of the bunks below deck, Sue and Ronny are huddling under a blanket. But Archer doesn't get to find out why they're on the yacht. Jerry has also come into the cabin unannounced and, with a flailing pistol-butt, knocks him unconscious.

Waking up on the marina some time later, Archer finds *Ariadne* gone from its slip. Following his usual investigative practice, he goes to Jerry's father, a prominent builder and developer, for information about his runaway son. Brian Kilpatrick has information to give. Sue Crandall ran away from home a couple of days ago. Jerry, though gone a longer time, hasn't disappeared till now; he moved into the Armistead yacht after failing to make it in college. Perhaps the Crandalls, who have talked to their missing child more recently than Kilpatrick has talked to *his*, have some fresh leads. En route to them, Archer stops at Jean Broadhurst's Northridge home for his car. Breakthroughs keep coming when least expected. The light reflecting from a neighbor's window reveals Jean's front door to be ajar. Walking into the study, Archer discovers the dead body of Al, the man who came to collect $1000 from Stanley Broadhurst that morning. "Like a magician who had pulled off the ultimate trick," Al is wearing a false beard, wig, and mustache. Archer does some investigating on his own before calling the police. From Stanley's burgled roll-top desk, he removes some pictures of a young couple. He also reads a letter from the Broadhurst family pastor gently advising Stanley to stop looking for his father: "Think of your own life, Stanley. You have recently taken on the responsibilities of marriage. . . . The past can do very little for us . . . except in the end to release us."

Then the police arrive. After discussing Al's fantastic knifing death with them, Archer drives to the Crandalls' Tudor mansion in Pacific Palisades. Sue's trim, blond mother, Martha, can't explain the girl's disappearance. Sue always enjoyed living with her parents; her diving and dancing lessons had been going well; she was looking forward to her freshman year at UCLA. Sue's father, Lester Crandall, "a short-heavy-bodied man with iron gray hair" in his late fifties, is also flummoxed; nothing had been troubling Sue enough to drive her away. Yet linkages form to the side of the main story-line: Martha Crandall went to high school in Santa Teresa, and Archer sees a phone directory in Sue's room opened to the page listing the motel Al had given as his local address. Motels, i.e., way stations for the transient, often contain corpses in Ross Macdonald. Though he dies elsewhere, Al is killed while registered at the Star Motel. He had been dunning Stanley for payment in return for information given him about his father. What information? The woman Al lived with at the Star produces the following advertisement placed by Stanley in the San Francisco *Chronicle* (where Ross Macdonald reviewed books in the late 1950s):

> Can you identify this couple? Under the name of Mr. and Mrs. Ralph Smith, they arrived in San Francisco by car on or about July 5, 1955. It is believed they took passage for Vancouver and Honolulu aboard the *Swansea Castle*, which sailed from San Francisco July 6, 1955. But they may still be in the Bay area. A thousand-dollar reward will be paid for information leading to their present whereabouts.

The woman at the motel adds that Al escaped jail recently and that, on their drive south from San Francisco, they stopped in Santa Teresa, where

Mrs. Snow gave him twenty dollars. The next disclosure, from a local police captain, fits with what Archer hears at the motel: a recent escapee from Folsom Prison named Albert Sweetner was once arrested in Santa Teresa.

Exhausted, Archer goes home to sleep. But not for long: he starts the next day by getting up early and driving to the marina where the *Ariadne* was anchored. On the marina are Jerry's father, Brian, and Roger Armistead, the boy's father-substitute and the angry owner of *Ariadne*. Armistead admits knowing that Jerry was taking drugs. Kilpatrick springs a still-bigger surprise—the revelation that the woman in the picture accompanying the San Francisco *Chronicle* ad is his former wife, Ellen: Ellen Kilpatrick ran away with Leo Broadhurst fifteen years ago. Another piece of the puzzle has snapped into place; Ellen's maiden name, Ellen Strome (Ella Strome is the name of the divorced secretary of the Tennis Club in *Black Money*), appeared on the bookplate of the copy of the book Archer found at the Broadhursts' Northridge home in Chapter 3.

The action keeps clarifying and renewing itself. Chapter 18 finds Archer back at Stanley's burial site, where he watches Stanley's second disinterment. Then he returns to Elizabeth's ranch house. While hefting and aiming some pistols belonging to her father, a Harvard-educated ornithologist, he tries to connect Jerry's kidnaping of Ronny to Ellen's affaire with the child's grandfather. Jerry probably loves Ellen and may be using Ronny to hurt the Broadhursts for smirching her. The case turns on itself again; Archer learns that Brian Kilpatrick and Elizabeth Broadhurst, the jilted parties in their mates' romantic adventure, are real estate partners. Could Ronny's abduction be related to this partnership? Before talking to Ellen, a central link joining the two families, Archer stops at the Snows, where he is called a persecutor. Mrs. Snow's anger has a legitimate basis. Archer knows that he deserves to be attacked. But he also knows that he has been hired to find Ronny and must accept moral guilt as part of his job. Timing his questions and teasing out his prior knowledge discreetly, he catches Mrs. Snow in two lies—her claim that she never knew Al Sweetner and her recollection that she gave Sweetner five dollars; Mrs. Snow gave him twenty dollars. The twenty-dollar figure is important because it signals a much stronger tie than a five-dollar gift, especially when the giver is poor, like Mrs. Snow.

Morally cornered, she explains the tie: Albert Sweetner lived with her family as a boy. He left when he, Fritz, and a local girl named Marty Nickerson ran away to Los Angeles in a stolen car. "We took Albert in and did our best for him," Mrs. Snow recalls. "But he was a hard case already—there wasn't much we could do to straighten him out." The three-day joyride to L. A. hurt Fritz more than either of his mates. Albert, "old beyond his years," and Marty, "a pretty thing, but hard as nails" at fifteen, got off lightly, even though the joyride was their idea.

Fritz spent six months in forestry camp, after which he worked for the Forest Service. Fifteen years ago, though, Al Sweetner came back to town and made new trouble for Fritz. He drove off with a tractor assigned Fritz by the Forest Service. The discovery of this misuse of government property led to Fritz's being fired and then, because of the disgrace, to a nervous breakdown. Mrs. Snow's recitation ends with the spectacular news, gleaned from an old Christmas greeting, thet Marty Nickerson is Martha Crandall, Sue's mother.

Sue and Ronny Broadhurst, her young charge, are both in danger. The *Ariadne*, on which the two were last seen, has been caught in a sea storm. By the time Archer gets to the smashed, capsized yacht, its survivors have come safely ashore and ridden away in a station wagon. Archer is able to trace Sue, Ronny, and Jerry Kilpatrick to the Yucca Tree Inn, a restaurant-nightclub near Vandenberg AFB owned by Lester Crandall. Archer just misses his quarry, the three fugitives having left the inn shortly before his arrival to go to San Francisco. Then Ross Macdonald varies the pursuit. Although the three missing persons believe themselves speeding toward safety, by fleeing Archer, they're inviting danger: Ronny saw his father's murder, and the murderer can't afford to let him or anybody he may have told about the murder go on living. Thus Ross Macdonald maintains narrative focus as he steers the action to the north; because catching the killer is the only way to save Ronny, the chase must go on. Archer's efforts gain a boost from a development that looks irrelevant —Lester Crandall's wanting to hire the detective to bring Sue home. Crandall's offer produces conversation that unearths more hidden ties from the past. A Santa Teresa native, Crandall owned the car that Martha, Al Sweetner, and Fritz Snow stole for their three-day whirl; also the three teenagers met while home-room charges of Ellen Kilpatrick, Jerry's mother and the woman Leo Broadhurst allegedly took to Hawaii.

Martha Nickerson Crandall's refusal to say who fathered Sue doesn't stall the investigation. The detail can wait. In the meantime, Ross Macdonald has been preparing for Ellen's entry. A page after Archer leaves the Crandalls, he is braking on the Sausalito street where Ellen lives—as Ellen Storm. The storm has subsided. The first painter in the canon since Bruce Campion of *Hearse*, Ellen, like Campion, has trouble living at full stretch. Archer refers to her as "pleasant but rather lifeless, like wood ash or dried leaves." The reason for this blandness? After divorcing her husband for Leo Broadhurst, Ellen was left stranded in Reno; Broadhurst never took her to Honolulu by freighter in July 1955. In fact, she never heard from Broadhurst again after leaving Kilpatrick and doesn't even know if he's alive. His disappearance accounts for her low profile. A self-styled "dropout from the world," she has lost her flair for life. Painting has replaced people: "Whatever happens to me happens on canvas," she says, referring to her solitary life in the house where she grew up.

(Like the father-search, Ellen's reversion to an earlier state proves the attempt to relive the past a self-imposed death.)

Stasis gives way to movement. Martha and Lester Crandall have followed Archer to Sausalito. Jerry Kilpatrick, his arm broken in the sea squall that took *Ariadne*, then enters the scene. Sensing trouble, he warns Sue to escape, thus instigating the final chase in this drama of missing persons. Archer follows Sue's car to the Golden Gate Bridge. Before she threatens to jump, she releases Ronny, who remembers Archer as the man whose peanuts he fed to some birds. Then our attention turns to Sue. In a phrase anticipatory of *Sleeping Beauty*, i.e., that birds can't live amid sickness and waste, Sue looks "like half a child and half a bird" on her dangerous perch. Archer talks her out of jumping. Without lying, he convinces her that she has a reason to live. He also acts wisely by questioning her before delivering her to her parents.

The answers he gets, spoken in a drugged trance, obey a mad logic. Sue says that Al Sweetner took her and her mother, Martha, to Elizabeth Broadhurst's canyon to show them a little red car. Then, while taking Ronny to the bathroom, she saw a bearded man with long hair and wraparound glasses hit Stanley with a pickaxe. This image dissolves into one of Al Sweetner gushing blood from the head while raping her. Then Sue calls out for her mother. The effort of dredging up painful events has exhausted her. Archer leaves off his questioning to discuss his findings with Lester Crandall. The possibility that Sue was forced by her natural father opens Crandall's memory along with his lips. He admits beating up Al when fifteen years ago, Al threatened to claim Sue legally as his daughter. But Crandall didn't know that Sue was in the Mountain House the summer night in 1955 when Leo Broadhurst was shot. This secret is spoken by Martha. She admits that, having stashed Susan in the loft of the Mountain House, she was having sex with Broadhurst during the fatal shooting, that Broadhurst had booked tickets to take her and Susan to Hawaii, and, last, that Broadhurst probably fathered Susan; Martha was already pregnant before going to L. A. with Fritz Snow and Al Sweetner.

These revelations shift the book's center of interest. Now that the missing children have come home and the genealogy has filled in, Archer can look for the killer. His first helper, little Ronny, says his father's bearded, black-clad killer "wasn't the same size as anybody I know." More direct help comes from adults. Archer and a forester take a bulldozer to Stanley's death-site. Stanley's reason for going to the canyon slope where he later dies follows shortly. Right under the place where he was first buried, the two men find the red sportscar of Sue Crandall's garbled recollection. The car contains the rotting bones of Leo Broadhurst. This discovery calls for another talk with Fritz Snow, keeper of the tractor that probably dug Broadhurst's grave fifteen years ago. Ross Macdonald sends Archer to the Snows' cottage but varies the pattern of the visit. Archer only stays one chapter, and Fritz, rather than his mother, lets him into the cottage. Though Fritz owns to having buried Leo Broadhurst, he denies killing him. Archer doesn't get to hear Fritz's alibi. The strain of telling how the burial led to his being fired from the forest service and then put in a nursing home breaks Fritz down. At that moment, his mother comes in and, hoping to shield him from more suffering, tells what *she* knows of the Leo Broadhurst murder. As the Broadhursts' housekeeper at the time, she had first-hand knowledge of the events of the night: Elizabeth and Leo quarrelled hotly; then Elizabeth, taking one of her father's pistols, followed Leo out of the house. Whether Stanley, who went with her, saw his father shot can't be known. But he did hear the shot that killed Leo Broadhurst, which he later explained as the report from a shell Elizabeth squeezed off to kill an owl.

Archer must now try out Mrs. Snow's story on Elizabeth. His confronting her in a hospital bed creates the same softening as his interview with another bedridden killer, Carl Trevor, did in *Wycherly*. The talk clarifies Sue Crandall's conduct. Like Stanley, Sue had seen the Leo Broadhurst murder and returned with Stanley to Leo's burial site in order to face this childhood trauma. The ritual return to the primal scream, though, rather than purging fear, heightened it. Seeing Stanley killed inspired Sue to save Ronny. But Archer didn't come to the hospital to discuss Sue Crandall. The information he did come for he never gets. Though a relentless questioner at times, he omits defining Elizabeth's role in her husband's death. The truth of mood and the justice of the imagination override any urge to retribution. Having lost her husband and son and then barely escaping the loss of her only grandchild, she deserves charity. Jailing her would prove little and please nobody.

Archer's moral charity is rewarded right away. At the local morgue, the detective learns that Leo Broadhurst wasn't shot but, rather, stabbed to death by a butcher knife, the broken tip of which lodged in his ribs. As often happens in Ross Macdonald's later work, Archer can't investigate this important discovery immediately. A heavy rainstorm has doused the fire tearing across the county, but it has also brought the new menace of floods and landslides; Brian Kilpatrick's patio is already piled with mud. Yet Archer has his own heat to apply. The book ends with his fourth and last visit to the Snows. "Helpless foolish" Fritz admits buying a wig, beard, and mustache to cover his harelip and make himself attractive to the girls browsing Sunset Strip. His statement that his mother doesn't want him to have a girlfriend creates a moment of pathos that sets the scene's moral climate. Ross Macdonald is less concerned with the mechanics of crime and detection than with capturing a deep emotional truth:

"I wanted to chase the chicks on Sunset Strip. And be a swinger."

"Did you catch any?"

He shook his doleful head. "I only got to go the once. She doesn't want me to have a girlfriend."

His gaze moved past me to his mother.

"I'm your girlfriend," she said brightly. "And you're my boyfriend." She smiled and winked. There were tears in her eyes.

Edna Snow's overprotective love isn't the only emotional truth governing her relationship with her son. Fritz's repressed resentment against her flares out in the last five pages. Like the ruinous last interview between Oedipus and his mother, Jocasta, the mother-son encounter ending the novel has the drive of tragedy. Fritz's accusation that his mother removed the disguise from its hiding place under his mattress leads to the disclosure that she wore it to kill Stanley Broadhurst. Her disposal of the disguise suited her other needs. To protect herself, she killed Al Sweetner, her blackmailer ever since Sue Crandall told him that she killed Leo Broadhurst; then she dressed him in the disguise to make him resemble the bearded, black-topped man Ronny saw pickaxe his father. Mrs. Snow's killing of Leo, her only murder not motivated by self-protection, rings true in a morally righteous woman who keeps a Bible in the exact center of her kitchen table. Though she has worked hard and long, both she and her son will always be nobodies. Does she deserve blame for resenting the handsome, high-living idler, Leo Broadhurst? Could her resentment be sexual as well as moral? Edna Snow always refers to Leo respectfully as Captain Broadhurst; she claims that her son loved him like a father; Fritz's own father had the same scorn for work as Leo; several times, Mrs. Snow criticizes Elizabeth for sexual coldness—the only one in the book to do so. That she wanted to supplant her as Leo's wife comes through in her description of the killing. Edna Snow resented Leo for not loving her. Driven by the same passions that sent Elizabeth to the Mountain House after Leo, Edna, his would-be wife, finished the job began by his real wife:

He was half dead already, lying there in his blood. All I did was put him out of his misery. . . . I'd do the same for a dying animal.

*　　　　*　　　　*

You can't call it murder. He deserved to die. He was a wicked man, a cheat and a fornicator.

No self-understanding comes to Mrs. Snow at the end. Her last words, spoken while the detective is taking her to a patrol car, "You'll shame me in front of the neighbors," shows no enlargement of vision. In the low-church spirit of Revelations, this poor, doughty widow of a job-less husband wants to avoid ridicule. Her last words erase the wild revenger in her, restoring her as a social creature. We are left pondering her unspoken dreams. By infusing his novel with tragedy and then leaving out the element of catharsis, Ross Macdonald redirects our unreleased feelings to Mrs. Snow, the book's most amazing figure.

Geoffrey Hartman sees her as the central character: "The murderer turns out to be a murderess, a protective mother with an overprotected son: the real underground man is the underground woman."[7] Hartman's point has merit. A puritan with little love to give, Mrs. Snow tries to subdue instinct to moral principle. She can't endure the difference between human ideals and their physical counterparts. A hater of moral busybodies, Ross Macdonald prefers dirt to a puritan's cleanliness. Hilda Church's murder confession in *Victim* includes the words clean, cleaned, and cleaning five times within three lines; a sin-obsessed woman in *Ferguson* calls her castrated cat "lover" and refers to herself as "Mother" while cooing to it. Mrs. Snow's flesh overwhelmed her spirit when she felt drawn to a man she rejected morally. That Leo, the man her blood rose to, ignored her after she outraged her principles to crave him lowered her self-esteem. Hiding behind her manufactured moral rage, she killed him. She also solved her moral crisis. Her knifing of Leo during the act of sex with beautiful, young Marty Nickerson, with whom she identifies, symbolizes self-punishment. If sex is the great democratizer, erasing differences of age and rank, it also promotes sexual strain and death.

Another candidate for the role of title character is Mrs. Snow's son, Fritz. Like Randy Shepherd of *Look*, he is a gardener; in fact he is introduced into the novel as "the gardener" rather than by name. (Kipling's 1926 story, "The Gardener," also deals with secret passion and centers on a protective mother's love for her son.) A gardener he is. He has a gardener's familiarity with roots; as a forester, he protected the flora and fauna of the Broadhurst ranch; his tractor plants Leo's corpse; he unearths the evidence that brings his mother to grief. If Ross Macdonald equates the word, Underground, with the word, submerged, then Fritz, the book's most submerged figure, becomes the title character. He is held down by his dullness, his ugliness, and his protective mother. The trappings of manhood, the facial hair he never grew, lie buried under his mattress. The apocalyptic symbolism of the fire and flood underscores his importance. Abandoned and alone at the end, he remains bottom dog, the prospective first entrant into heaven on Doomsday, a whiff of which haunts the novel.

Ross Macdonald hints at his religious theme by referring to Fritz in the opening chapters as the gardener, a term used for Christ in the fourth Gospel. From the New Testament, Lazarus is also mentioned, and the Abraham-Isaac story comes in from the Old. The religious references don't always stem from Scripture. A Great Dane belonging to Ellen Storm's neighbor in Sausalito provides an important lead, recalling the scratching dog who unearths suppressed truths in *The Waste Land*, a work strongly supportive of religious tradition. Finally, Stanley's second disinterment occurs in Chapter 18, the book's middle chapter, two pages after a stable is mentioned. This veiled allusion to the birth of Christ carries into Ross Macdonald's account of the disinterment, with its "naked tree" and resurrection imagery:

> The digging man was almost out of sight in the hole. Like a man growing laboriously out of the earth, he stood up with Stanley's body clasped in his arms. He and Kelsey laid the body on a stretcher and brought it toward us through the naked tree trunks.

This compression of birth (the stable), crucifixion (the tree), and resurrection expresses the timelessness of spiritual truth; the movements of Christ's life can be stretched, reversed, or combine, but their meaning never changes. Secular truth is inexorable, too. Though Stanley Broadhurst dies, his death brings his father's killer to justice.

Most of this religious machinery rolls toward Apocalypse. *Man* shows what happens when we cut the tie between ourselves and nature. Hartman relates this disjuncture to the fire: "By combining ecological and moral contamination," he says "Macdonald creates a double plot that spreads the crime over the California landscape."[8] Like the plague crippling the city of Thebes in *Oedipus Rex*, the fire ties in with a murder. There's a causal connection between the human breakdown and the start of the fire. The fire stems from a breakdown of proper moral relationships between Mrs. Snow, who started it, and her social superiors, who mistreated Fritz. The threat is poses to the city of Santa Teresa is an animistic upsurging of the primitive through the social. Eudora Welty calls the fire "a multiple and accumulating identity, with a career of its own, a super-character."[9] It gains strength, speed, and beauty as it destroys. Destroy it does: the wilderness didn't start the fire; the wilderness is merely another victim. The fire rules both Archer's movements and the lives of the local residents. The book opens when a hot wind and a rustle of leaves awakens the detective. This foreshadowing of the fire gives way, in the next paragraph, to the chirping of birds, perhaps the book's only promising note. For the fire entrenches itself quickly. Hearing about it on the radio sends a worried Jean Broadhurst to Archer's apartment. Then she and Archer smell the fire on the road to Santa Teresa. The next paragraph, the second in Chapter 5, describes puffs of smoke hanging in the distance. Along with bringing the fire to life as a sensory datum, Chapter 5 introduces two characters connected with it—Fritz and Elizabeth.

Driving with Elizabeth later in the chapter, Archer feels "as though we were going against nature." Ross Macdonald portrays the fire throughout as nature's enemy. Its smoke conveys "the illusion of war"; the pears hanging from an avocado tree fanned by its heat look "like green hand grenades"; gazing toward the mountains from the marina in Chapter 11, Archer likens the fire's menace to "the bivouacs of a besieging army."

Urban Apprehensions

Chapter 10 describes the fire in its full, red, raging splendor. Here, Archer fights the blaze while hearing it chew through the dry brush; here, people hose their homes and trees to keep the heat down. Here, too, Ross Macdonald's prose takes on the rhythm and intensity of poetry as it zeroes in on the fire:

> The fire appeared at the top of the hill like a brilliant omniform growth which continued to grow until it bloomed very large against the sky. A sentinel quail on the hillside below it was ticking an alarm.

>   *   *   *

> It made a noise like a storm. Enormous and hot and wild, it leapt clumsily into the trees. The cypress that had been smoking burst into flames. Then the other trees blazed up like giant torches in a row.

The blaze is followed by heavy rains, which pour mud, brown water, and sodden charred debris down the canyon. Only rarely is nature friendly to human life. The weather is either too hot or too wet. Because of the fire and the flood, no crops can grow; no flora remains to soak up moisture and hold the soil together against landslides. Thus yards fill with mud, and the houses left standing by the fire get rammed by boulders. Away from Santa Teresa the pounding continues, as boats are smashed by sea squalls. Archer's intimation, "we were going against nature," proves correct. So does its corollary: to go against nature is the best way to undo oneself; like the wrath of God, all forms of evil will thunder down once man snaps the vital link between himself and his environment.

Responsible morally for the big blaze and the damage it causes is Leo Broadhurst, even though he died years before it takes place. Ross Macdonald relates him to the fire throughout. His name refers to the hottest time of the year, and he disappears during the summer; the fire starts at *his* burial site; others respond hotly to him, both before and after his death. Like Eldon Swain of *Look*, Leo represents a new character type in the canon—the late-middle-aged prodigal father of a grown child. As he did with Swain, Ross Macdonald keeps open the possibility that Leo is alive for as long as the plot permits. He also brings Leo to radiant masculine life through the responses of those who knew him. These he scatters carefully and distributes among characters of widely differing backgrounds and personalities. His pastor describes him, a tennis and polo bum who married rich so he could avoid working, as "a sportsman, an active and spirited man who enjoyed life." Others speak of him with more fever. Martha Nickerson Crandall refers to his "pretty face" and "hot little hands." Yet she loved the glowing swindler-charmer enough to run away with him and have his baby at age sixteen. Ellen Storm criticizes him on different grounds: "He couldn't stand to be alone" and "He had no interior life," she says of handsome Leo. But her moral objections didn't stop her from loving Leo any more than Martha's or Edna Snow's stopped them. No teenager but a sensible married woman with the responsibilities of a teacher and a mother, she proves Leo's sexual magnetism. So cast down was she by his presumed jilting of her that she opted out of life, giving up her job and losing interest in her small son, Jerry. Archer's list of Leo's sexual conquests is too short: in Elizabeth, Leo "married the richest woman" in town, and in Marty, "tumbled the prettiest girl"; but he also thawed the wintry heart of Edna Snow and turned the dedicated teacher and artist, Ellen Storm, into a living death.

Finally Leo rules his son. *Man* contains Ross Macdonald's fullest statement to date on the dangers of trying to relive the past. Like Jean Trask of *Look*, Stanley Broadhurst proves that the dead must be forgotten; both characters die trying to restore a dead father to life. Ross Macdonald would agree with the attitude voiced by the Broadhursts' pastor in an old letter: "The past can do very little for us—no more than it has already done, for good or ill—except in the end to release us. We must seek and accept release, and give release." Stanley ignores this wisdom. The person in the novel who clings most stubbornly to the past, he is also the one the past grinds most gruelly. First, he repeats the reversion of Ellen Storm, who, after Leo's death, takes back her maiden name and subsists at the house where she was raised. His Northridge address, a street called College Circle, refers to the circular pattern of his father-search. His going round in circles has put him out of touch: not only is the calendar in his study three months out of date; he also spends most of his nights in the study, neglecting his sexual tie to his wife. The hurt caused by his obsession spreads to others besides Jean. He encourages opportunists and emotional predators like Al Sweetner; disregarding his job, he takes money from his mother; seeing him murdered could mangle his son, Ronny, in the same way his father's murder twisted him.

The worst feature of all this is that Stanley's father-search comes so easily. Delving into one's ancestry in order to achieve stability and self-knowledge makes sense to anyone living in a society ruled by speed and change. But it must be resisted. Stanley's sense of purpose has no place; he is wasted in society and society is worse because of him. Though Ross Macdonald had characters dig their own graves in *Blue City, Victim*, and *Dollar*, he never used the device as effectively as in *Man*. Stanley's father-search had been edging him progressively toward death—killing his sex drive and undermining him as a provider. The scene on the canyon slope completes the process; when he breaks the earth to find his father, he's literally digging his grave. Coiled like a foetus when unearthed, he has reverted as far back as he can. The foetal coil symbolizes reversion. Three chapters after Stanley's corpse materializes, Fritz Snow crouches and pulls his feet under him when hiding in his room; "the dissolving" Fritz also hunches himself into a coil at the end, after betraying his mother. The lesson he points is the same as that of Stanley, his foetal mirror-image.

Life must be lived forward. Fritz is controlled by a life-denying mother, and Stanley pours his energy into the search for a dead father. Between them, they spell out the danger of parent-fixation. Fritz's half-life and Stanley's snuffed-out life both have roots in the Broadhurst ranch. Lacking a healthy source of nourishment, both feed on mud, burnt-out mulch, and hidden murder. Eudora Welty relates the danger of living a fiction to the novel's complex form:

> The plot is intricate, involuted, and complicated to the hilt; and this, as I see it, is the novel's point. The danger derives from the fairy tales into which people make their lives. In lonely, fearful, or confused minds, real-life facts can become rarefied into private fantasies. And when intensity is accepted—welcomed—as the measure of truth, how can the real and the fabricated to told apart?[10]

Elizabeth also cleaves to a dead past; like her son, she has sacrificed the vitality of the present to the memory of a dead father. Also like that of Stanley, her bondage objectifies itself sexually. Her dead sexuality shows in her eyes. After noting her young figure and barely graying hair, Archer observes, "Only her eyes looked older." Can her husband be blamed for stepping out on her? Elizabeth, who called her father "a god come down to earth in human guise," didn't make love to Leo the last ten years of their marriage. "A frozen woman, a daddy's girl," she represents an extreme of coldness no more bearable than the fire and flood rising up around her. The sexual suppression implied by the Victorian trappings of her home tallies with her shooting of her husband, suitably, with one of her father's pistols. As he did with Elaine Hillman in *Dollar*, Ross Macdonald makes her deathly anti-sexuality a function of social snobbery. Elizabeth's blood is both blue and thin. Daughter of a Harvard graduate, she refers to a local family as *nouveaux riches*; she also complains of her daughter-in-law Jean's poor breeding and lack of refinement: "Jean is an intelligent girl but she comes from an entirely different class. I don't believe she's ever understood my son, though I've tired to explain something about our family traditions."

Elizabeth's clinging to a dead past and a death-dealing social code finds its counterpole in her grandson, Ronny, the novel's hope for the future. Eudora Welty says of the six-year-old, "He constitutes the book's emergency. . . . Ronny is the tender embodiment of everything Archer is by nature bound to protect, infinitely worthy of rescue."[11] This insight helps lighten the book's pessimism. Ronny only needs protection from his father's killer. Everybody else tries to help him—Sue Crandall, Jerry Kilpatrick, Jean Broadhurst, and Archer. That Ross Macdonald intended the detective to love Ronny at first meeting comes out in a 1971 interview: "Archer becomes a kind of father substitute for the little boy," said the writer, adding, "Of course, that is what the book is about to a great extent."[12] Like the others who help Ronny, Archer acts out of need. His strong emotional response to the boy always brings out his best. His behavior in Chapter 1 differs greatly from the impatience and know-it-all sarcasm he displayed in the first chapter of *Enemy*: he gives Ronny peanuts to feed the birds on the lawn. He acts with speed, tact, and compassion when he stops an overwrought Stanley Broadhurst from hitting the boy. He knows that dragging a child into a quarrel will worsen the quarrel and, what is worse, hurt the child more than the quarrelling adults. Thus he ends the bickering between Jean and Stanley by convincing their frightened son of his good luck in having a father who takes him places. These loving acts impress Ronny. When Archer sees him again two days later, Sue says that Ronny has been chattering about Archer's peanuts and birds all day. The detective also prints himself on Sue's memory. His interest in her goes beyond using her as a lead to Ronny and the killer. Helping her recover from the traumas of being drugged and raped and then of watching a murder, he advises her parents to get her psychiatric counseling before he moves on to hunt the killer. A good deal of negation shadows Archer. Elizabeth says to him, "You're persistent, aren't you?" Jerry tells him, "You look like the violent type to me," and Archer admits, "I sometimes served as a catalyst for trouble, not unwillingly." Yet his deeds breathe love. Whereas Elizabeth's ornithologist-father killed birds, Archer feeds them. When a painful memory makes Lester Crandall's head throb, Archer's throbs in sympathy. No wonder children remember him and women like him. Both Ellen Storm and the woman staying with Al at the Star Motel ask to go to bed with him. William Ruehlmann's insight into both Archer and Ross Macdonald applies directly to the ripe moral wisdom of *Man*:

> Ross Macdonald is a moralist . . . but his moralism is compassionate rather than vengeful, and his protagonist protects the innocent in place of punishing the guilty. Like the others of his fictive profession, Lew Archer travels territory where no one can be trusted or believed; unlike them, the fact makes him more sad than bitter. What results is a series of . . . novels that do not exorcise guilt but offer a means of dealing with it.[13]

The novel's tight, sure organization provides the context from which this humanity emerges. First, Ross Macdonald abides by the rules of literary detection. In Chapter 1, he shows Stanley smoking a cigarillo resembling the one that started the fire. To hint at the solution to Leo's murder, he has Archer handle the pistol Elizabeth shot her husband with fifteen years before. Ronny's enigmatic statement that his father's killer was "the wrong size" for both a grownup and a child refers to Edna Snow's littleness, which Ross Macdonald had already mentioned several times. The writer also observes his usual practice of playing out and then interweaving several mysteries at once. For instance, Archer learns that Sue Crandall is Marty's daughter in Chapter 22; but intervening duties stop him from acting on his finding till Chapter 25, and, even then, he doesn't seek Marty out. This network of overlapping and intersecting sub-plots keeps the novel in a state of remaking and reevaluating itself. As in Agatha Christie, nearly everyone has something to hide; all are capable of doing evil. Our worries over Ronny complement the intellectual challenge of staying abreast of the fast-moving plot.

Much of this counterpoint is managed through style. Phrases like bad vibes, freaked out, blown his mind, and telling it like it is reveal the same keen ear for contemporary speech that enlivened *Enemy* and *Look*. A newer stylistic development is that of making verbs like diminuendoed, rockinghorsed and divebomb out of active, vibrant nouns. These color-ful verbs, along with the book's many auditory images, one of which opens the book, give Ross Macdonald's sensory, declarative prose a new source of word music. This music helps create a new stylistic world. The proportion of narration to dialogue runs higher in *Man* than elsewhere in the canon; the first three and a half pages of Chapter 6, for instance, con-tain only a three-line speech and a one-liner. This mix imparts a resonance that lends authority to the book's ecological theme; Ross Macdonald has created a reality and then combined its destruction with a serious warning. The auctorial voice reveals more of his moral conviction than could any set of invented characters. Putting himself in the book, even behind the protective interface of Archer, moves Ross Macdonald closer to the reader and thus affirms the sincerity of his warning. His taking the risk of speak-ing out directly makes believers of us. Moving to the suburbs doesn't make us safe. Unless we protect the environment, we will waste every-thing.

IV

The environment moves to the fore again in *Sleeping Beauty* (1973), a sequel to *Man*. Santa Teresa, the setting for most of *Man*, gives way to Ross Macdonald's other favorite imaginary city, Orange County's Pacific Point, which lies the same distance, sixty miles, south of Los Angeles as Santa Teresa does to the north. Called by Ruehlmann "a novel of wounded birds and wounded men,"[14] Ross Macdonald's latest book describes the contamination of the sea by an oil slick. (The initials of the book's title, SB, are the same as those of Ross Macdonald's home town, Santa Barbara, scene of a disastrous oil spill in 1969, which the book men-tions.) The sea and the fish and the birds who live off the sea are victims of the slick in the same way that the wildlife around Santa Teresa suffers because of the fire in *Man*. Its first two paragraphs link *Beauty* and its predecessor. Flying home on a Wednesday afternoon from a week's vaca-tion in Mexico, Archer sees an oil spill, "a free-form slick that seemed miles wide and many miles long," fouling the coastline below. Ross Macdonald brings home the damage the thousand-plus gallons of crude oil does to the ecology of the sea in a sharp, hard-hitting simile: "An off-shore oil platform stood up . . . like the metal handle of a dagger that had stabbed the world and made it spill black blood."

After reading a news release written by Jack Lennox, a chief of the company responsible for the spill, Archer heads for Pacific Point, "one of my favorite places on the coast." Trouble finds him in the form of an emotionally charged image—a beautiful young woman in white wading in the surf with an oil-blackened bird in her hands. Now birds denote health and cheer to Ross Macdonald (in contrast to Alfred Hitchcock and Graham Greene). The greased bird symbolizes the destruction of nature by mechanized industry. Putting the bird in the hands of a beautiful young woman proves that arguments in literature make impact only when individual and particular. Thus Ross Macdonald introduces Laurel Russo as soon as he can. (By coincidence, the nerve-shattered Laurel comes from the family that owns Lennox Oil.) Archer watches her go down the beach and then begins, informally, to investigate the spill. As in *Man*, an evil originating in the social order has infected the natural order. According to local rumor, the refinery did wrong to drill in the quaky substratum near Pacific Point, especially with inadequate casing. Here is a local journalist's explanation for the spill:

The undersea formations here are naturally porous, delicate to fool with. You might say the area is blowout-prone. But in the short run the oil people are to blame. They didn't take the danger of a spill fully into account, and they didn't use the right preventative measures for drilling at this depth.

Archer takes his unconfirmed findings into a seafront restaurant, where he spots a memorable duo—a broadshouldered man of thirty or so with the eyes of a loser and his companion, a shrivelled and scarred old man moving "like a man lost in the world."

Leaving half of his fish dinner uneaten, Archer walks half a mile and finds, "lodged high among the boulders" encroaching on the narrowing beach, white-clad Laurel. Smelling of fear and stiff with shock, Laurel accepts Archer's offer of a lift home. She has confused the detective. Admitting to himself that she belongs at home, he nonetheless drives her to his apartment, where the self-questioning and self-reproach both step up: "I caught an oblique glimpse of myself as a middle-aged man on the make. It was true that if she had been old or ugly I wouldn't have brought her home with me. She was neither." But Laurel has her own worries. "Full of trouble," she dials her husband Tom to find he has a woman with him. Then, following a visit to the bathroom, she leaves Archer. Archer's own visit to the bathroom, some minutes later, reveals that she stole thirty-five or forty of his sleeping pills, left over from a time he couldn't sleep. He reports the theft to her husband of two years, Tom

Russo, a pharmacist working the late shift at an all-night Westwood drugstore. What he hears from Tom augurs badly. The Russos broke up two weeks ago. Further, Laurel has left Tom before. The conversation is broken by a ringing phone; Laurel's parents have come to Tom's house looking for their daughter. Charging Tom a hundred dollars, i.e., a day's pay, Archer agrees to look, too.

His search begins in the "declining middle-class block" where Tom lives. Important background data surfaces right away. Marian Lennox admits that her daughter Laurel, an only child, has attempted suicide. Her oil-magnate husband, Jack, has other fears, as well—that his father, founder and owner of Lennox Oil, might disinherit him if he finds out about Laurel. Jack Lennox can set store by the detective's silence. Archer has come to gather information, not to impart it. Tom's cousin and housekeeper, Gloria Flaherty, who wants to start a restaurant with her fiancé Harry, has some useful leads. Tom's mother died when Tom was two. Could the loss of a mother and a wife form a pattern? Archer needs more information before he can connect the threads. Gloria tells him the name of a friend Laurel lived with while away from Tom before. The friend, Joyce Hampshire, who has known Laurel since the first grade, explains the background of Laurel's latest disappearance. The Lennox family may be caving in. While his oil firm has fallen into disgrace, old William Lennox, Laurel's grandfather, is divorcing his wife of some fifty years in order to marry a woman half his age. In addition, Laurel's disappearances from Tom aren't her first. She ran away to Las Vegas as a high school girl, tricking her parents into giving her and her traveling-mate, a fellow student named Harold Sherry, a thousand dollars in ransom money.

Archer goes to check this information with Laurel's uncle, Ben Somerville, a retired Navy captain and an executive vice-president of Lennox Oil. But he gets other, more urgent information, instead. "Gray and haggard" because of the oil spill, Somerville explains that Laurel has been abducted and that her abductors are demanding $100,000 for her return. Somerville's wife, Elizabeth, enters the scene, her eyes "blue and candid, with depths behind them hollowed out by human feelings including pain." Some of the pain is new. And Beth wants it eased. Because her brother, Laurel's father, Jack, won't discuss the kidnaping over the phone, Beth asks Archer to drive her to Jack's Montevista home. Several important points come to light during the drive. Marian and Jack's marriage, always shaky, has buckled because of the oil spill, as has the Somervilles'. Within four pages, Beth says three things that cast doubt on her love for her husband. Ben has always been disaster-prone. Some twenty-seven or -eight years ago, while he was serving as a naval combat officer near Okinawa, his ship caught fire and some of his men died. The accident ended Ben's career at sea. Luckily, Beth's father took him into the family business after a short term of shore duty. Now another accident threatens his business career. Even though the blowout wasn't Ben's fault, William Lennox will probably blame it on Ben, his son-in-law, rather than on Jack, his son.

Jack doesn't act like a man under reprieve. "His voice . . . thick with alcohol and passion," he greets Archer by pointing a rifle at him. Beth wins Archer's gratitude and trust by disarming her tormented brother. But she hasn't removed Jack's grief and anger along with his gun. Jack calls Archer a "spying bastard" and accuses him of meddling unasked and unwanted in the Lennox family problems. Archer agrees to wait outside while Beth tries to calm her brother. In about an hour, she comes out to say that the kidnapers have called again to restate their $100,000 demand and that Jack will deliver the ransom tomorrow. The money will come from Sylvia Lennox, Jack's mother and Laurel's grandmother. Beth and Archer drive next to Sylvia's palatial home. Tony Lashman, Sylvia's moist-eyed secretary, takes them inside the mansion. Ross Macdonald realizes Sylvia quickly. "A thin elegant woman" in her seventies who looks "rather like an aging boy," she asks Archer to go with her erratic son Jack to deliver the ransom money: "My son has many good points, but he does tend to get excited in emergencies."

His missing persons cases have always made Archer delve deeply into family histories. That Beth Somerville belongs to the family Archer is investigating whips the two of them into hot currents of rising emotion. Ross Macdonald keeps stirring the heat-laden air. In Chapter 13 they read a letter from Tom Russo to Laurel which ends thus: "Laurel. Take your time. All I want is for things to work out for you. If you include me, I will be the luckiest man in the world." Archer's reaction to this candor ("He's a willing man. . . . If I had been half as willing, I could have held on to my own wife") shows the detective flushed by the gathering heat. On the next page, Beth cries tears that not only humanize her but also make her beautiful: "She turned her back on me. . . . Touched by emotion, her back was beautiful. The narrow waist blossomed out into strong hips, which narrowed down again into a fine pair of legs." Her defenses washed away by her tears, she adds to the hot, heavy mood: Beth explains that her father wanted her to marry Ben ("Captain War himself"), first, because of his brilliant prospects and, next, because he was buying Lennox oil for the Navy. In Chapter 13, Beth says outright what she has been implying all along—that her marriage has failed from the start. Ben hurt their chances by keeping a mistress even after the wedding. In fact, Beth met the mistress when she brought her small son to the Somerville house about a month before Ben's ship burned off Okinawa. The wrenching monologue ends with Archer putting his hands on Beth and steering her, unwanting but unresisting, into bed.

As he did in *Look*, Ross Macdonald robs the incident of beauty, tenderness, or moral uplift. Archer wakes up the next morning to find

Urban Apprehensions

Beth, not next to him (as Moira Smitheram was in *Look*), but standing by the window. A corpse is floating on the oil-smeared sea as if the offspring of Archer's rut with Beth. Calling upon his skill as a swimmer, tested last in *Enemy*, Archer drags to shore the body of the little, lost-looking man with the burn scars he had seen in the dockside restaurant. Inside the suitcoat of the oiled corpse, he finds a label bearing the names of both the tailor who made the suit and the suit's buyer. He interrupts his investigation of the jacket's history, though, in order to report to his client, Tom Russo. Tom, who works nights, is sleeping, and Archer enters his bedroom at the precise time he is hallucinating about his dead mother. This section of the novel is motorized by symbolic births, the first of which, the greased corpse bobbing on the sea, we have already seen. "Huddled like a fetus," Tom both thinks and speaks like a small child. Out of his garbled half-waking dream, Archer infers that Mrs. Russo put Tom out of her bedroom in order to sleep with a sailor. (The resemblance to the 1964 Hitchcock film, *Marnie*, is striking.) Artistically, this episode fails badly. Barring the gimcrack coincidence—in a novel already coincidence-fraught —the action does well enough without Tom's hypnopompic ramblings. In fact, Ross Macdonald does use dramatic incident, the testimony of witnesses, and time-glides to make the same points grazed by these ramblings. But he wants to bring the past to life right away. Tom's mother was shot by an unknown killer more than twenty-five years ago. His cousin Gloria adds that Aunt Alison's killer has never been found.

Archer's own efforts to find the killer are roundabout. The next chapter takes him to the apartment of the ex-wife of the original owner of the clothes worn by the drowned man. Middle-aged Martha Mungan, "her mind leached out by drinking, her body swollen," denies knowing the drowned man. But she does remember giving Mungan's old suit to a bedraggled little stranger who came begging at her door some weeks ago. Archer needs a fresh lead to trace the tweed suit any further. From Martha's rundown apartment, he goes to Sylvia Lennox's elegant estate. Sylvia gives Archer and her son Jack the ransom money, and the two men drive to nearby Sandhill Lake, site of a hunting club to which Jack's father once belonged. Curiously, the kidnaper, not Jack, chose the lakefront for the money drop. Archer's mention of this curiosity upsets Jack. His face fills with blood, he loses control of the car, and then, after stopping, sends Archer onto the road at gunpoint. Archer follows the big executive sedan on foot, and, from a distance, sees Jack enter a wooden lookout tower. Then two muffled explosions break the silence, and a flock of birds leaps into the air. A shooting has taken place. Jack crawls out of the tower and falls. He's followed by another gunshot casualty. Carrying Jack's carton of money, this husky young man—who looks like the friend of the lost-looking burn-scarred man at the restaurant—hobbles to an old green two-door and drives away.

The violence brings out Archer's humanity. Forgetting that Jack just insulted and threatened to kill him, Archer runs to help the bleeding, unconscious man. He also has the sense to call the police and an ambulance before reporting the shooting to the Lennox family. Later, at William Lennox's, he looks at a high school picture of Harold Sherry, the boy Laurel ran away with fifteen years ago. The elements of the case are starting to join. "A rather fat-faced boy with an uneasy smile and dark angry dubious eyes," Harold has paid plenty for his joyride to Las Vegas. He was expelled from high school at the prodding of the Lennoxes, never returning to graduate, and put on probation for six years. While in jail, where he went after breaking probation, he learned that his father disowned him and divorced his mother. The mother, who still lives nearby, is Archer's next witness. "A faded woman," Mrs. Sherry produces a recent photo of Harold in which Archer recognizes the broadshouldered man at the restaurant and "almost certainly" identifies as Jack Lennox's foe in the Sandhill Lake shootout. A pattern continues to form. Mrs. Sherry's explanation of Harold's trip to Las Vegas with Laurel, an adventure the ex-schoolmates might be re-enacting now for higher stakes, fills in the picture given Archer earlier:

He wanted to marry Laurel. That's why they went to Las Vegas—they thought they could get a preacher to marry them. But they ran out of money, and Laurel had the bright idea of pretending to her parents she'd been kidnaped. It was Laurel's idea, but Harold was the one who got the blame. Her father . . . gave my son a terrible beating and threw him in jail. Harold was only eighteen, and he never recovered from the trauma.

The next chapter (Chapter 25) brings Archer together with Beth Somerville for the first time since sleeping together. Neither is glad to see the other. Beth greets Archer "without warmth," and, two pages later, he finds himself "furiously angry in a quiet way" because of her coldness. The scenes in *Beauty* are laid out tidily. As he connects Laurel with Harold Sherry, Ross Macdonald also deepens the connection through the statements of people who know Harold. Beth calls him "one of those people who always gets things wrong" and then, supplying a motive for both Laurel's disappearance and Jack's shooting, adds, "He really hates my brother Jack." Harold remains Archer's best lead to Laurel. (In the late Archers, rundown people steal the spotlight from their more highly favored counterparts.) But the search for Harold must wait. Sylvia Lennox's secretary, Tony Lashman, has been found dead on the beach. The same chapter that materializes Lashman's corpse brings in Leroy Ellis, publicist for Lennox Oil and a former officer on the *Canaan Sound*, the carrier that burned in 1945. The corpse that upsets Ellis isn't that of Lashman. Rather, he identifies the greased body dragged from the sea in Chapter 14 as Nelson, communications messenger aboard the doomed ship. Fantastically, Ellis believes Nelson to have drifted toward California from Okinawa, where he was pitched overboard twenty-seven or -eight years ago.

Ellis's fantasy is followed by the nuts and bolts of detection. After visits to a doctor's office, a restaurant, and a seafront liquor store, Archer runs Harold Sherry's recent girlfriend, Ramona, to earth. Like the book's other grotesque, that scorched husk, Nelson, she has fared badly. Too much beer has added weight and years to her, and family worries have burdened her heart. Her former husband, besides throwing her out, has stopped her from seeing her three children. "They live in Rolling Hills. Sometimes I go down and look across the water and pretend I can see them," she says pathetically. Now Harold has left her. Though adding to the breakdown and suffering haunting the action, she has little information to give either about him or the girl he jilted her for. Archer continues his quest for names and whereabouts at the office of Harold's doctor, Lawrence Brokaw, M. D., of Long Beach. Brokaw admits treating Harold's bullet wound and even tells Archer the name of Harold's motel. But he denies that the "nice-looking brunette, rather tall . . . age about thirty," in the room with Harold acted like a kidnaping victim. Who is she? What happens next looks like a distraction rather than a help. A hospitalized Navy vetern, Nelson Bagley, has been reported missing after going out for dinner last night. A Dr. Lampson of the hospital staff, "a tall dark man with a face that had known pain," admits having signed Bagley out when Harold Sherry offered him a home-cooked meal. The news of Bagley's death racks Lampson: "It was the first invitation of the kind that Nelson had had in the time I've been working with him. . . . I could see no harm in trying it. . . . How wrong could a man be? When I signed him out of here, I signed his death warrant." These words speak home. When first assigned to Dr. Lampson for therapy, Bagley was a near-vegetable. Lampson's attempts to bring him to life may have killed him. He told Lampson, during their last talk, both about the blowout on his carrier and a murder that occurred around the same time—that of Alison Russo, Tom's mother. Who else knew about his memory of these events?

Archer takes his deliberations to Tom's house, where he meets Tom's father, "a fairly good-looking man of seventy or so, with a lot of wavy iron-gray hair." Mr. Russo says that Allie left him during the war and came to live in L. A. with little Tom. Not only was she killed after leaving Bremerton, Washington; five-year-old Tom also spent several days in the house after the killing. Mr. Russo believes Nelson Bagley to have killed his wife in May 1945. His motive? Allie had left him for another man. Ross Macdonald has stage-managed Archer's visit to Tom Russo's effectively. Old Russo's account of his wife's murder builds suspense for Tom's entry in the next chapter. The suspense is justified. Harold's fiancé turns out to be Tom's cousin Gloria; Gloria, who referred to her fiancé in

Chapter 6 as Harry, may have also helped Harry kidnap Laurel. Old Russo believes, instead, that Laurel helped her abductors. He tells Tom, who is moving "like a blind man," "You've been . . . making my mistakes all over again. I thought you'd learn from what happened to your mother." When told that he saw his mother shot, Tom, his face whitening "as if a plug had been pulled," attacks Mr. Russo. Archer steps between the men, and Tom, racked by the memories he had tried to suppress, breaks down. He is not so racked, though, that he is beyond helping Archer. The heart-spilling scene ends with an important disclosure: cousin Gloria's mother is hard-drinking Martha, or Martie, Mungan, to whose apartment Harold and Gloria took Bagley for dinner Tuesday night. Thus Aunt Martie lied about giving her ex-husband's tweed suit to a beggar two weeks ago.

Faced with her lie, Aunt Martie talks freely. Though ignorant of her sister's killer, she rules out Nelson Bagley as a suspect; Allie never let "that poor little roughed-up hammered-down ghost" close enough to her to warrant a murderous reprisal. Aunt Martie has little positive help to give. Even though Harold, as Laurel's kidnaper, could be shot on sight if found by the police, she doesn't know where he and Gloria have taken Laurel. Archer shifts his tactics; short on leads and clues, he will try to solve this new crime, Laurel's abduction, by investigating an old one, Allie Russo's murder. He can regroup his energies because many of the people involved in the first crime are also caught up in the new one. Pocketing Allie's high school graduation picture, he again drives from Mrs. Mungan's tacky apartment to the Somervilles' elegant Bel Air mansion. His talk with Beth is even more strained than their last. Beth uses her futile marriage to parry any friendly overtures; Archer, following her lead, questions her without charity: "The point is that you have a life. Allie Russo lost hers," he says, without addressing her by name. Shamed, Beth discloses "the hidden world behind her eyes," identifying Allie from her picture as the woman who came to her house many years ago with little Tom.

Beth's husband Ben walks in a few minutes later, aged and worn by his efforts to clean up the oil spill. Although he admits, privately to Archer, having bedded Allie, he denies killing her: like Mr. Russo, Allie's widower, he blames the murder on Bagley. Somerville only found out about the killing from a newspaper clipping mailed to him anonymously three weeks after the killing took place. But he doesn't shrug off all moral responsibility for the wreckage of spring 1945. With extraordinary candor, he admits misjudging the pressure capacity in the gas tank that blew aboard the *Canaan Sound*. For the second time within moments, he hedges a confession: he didn't cause the fire that destroyed the ship. The explosion igniting the fire came from a gun Bagley had turned on himself after reading a newspaper clipping identical to the one Somerville received. Archer's talk with the captain unearths a rich lode of information. From it, Archer also learns Harold Sherry's reason for taking Bagley out of the hospital. Harold hadn't forgotten or forgiven the damage done him by the Lennoxes because of the Las Vegas joyride. Eager to hurt the Lennoxes, he wanted Bagley to recognize and then help incriminate Somerville, who was talking on television Tuesday night about the oil spill. Making Lennox Oil take the blame for the gasoline blowout of 1945 or today's oil blowout would redress Harold's being beaten up, stashed in jail, and stopped from finishing high school. But how far do Harold's demands for retribution go? Is the murder of William Lennox's only granddaughter one of his requirements of justice and revenge?

Archer has to find Laurel quickly. He returns home in Chapter 38 for the first time in thirty hours to find help from an unexpected source. A message from his telephone answering service leads him to Gloria Mungan Flaherty. But Gloria insists that, though she has been with Harold recently, she hasn't seen Laurel Russo. She doesn't even know how to find Harold, who left her an hour or so ago, remembering to take the ransom money and a revolver. Gloria's mother Martie, "walking in a mist of alcohol," offers help of a different sort. Her recollections, in fact, join several important threads of the plot. Martie's sister Alison had fallen in love with Captain Ben Somerville during the war. But instead of helping her get a divorce, as he had promised, Somerville jilted her for Elizabeth Lennox, a younger woman from a rich, powerful family. The meaning of this disclosure comes to light immediately. Continuing its swing between 1945 and 1973, the plot puts Harold before us in Chapter 39. Still hobbled by the shell fired into his leg at Sandhill, Harold shocks Archer by saying that he hasn't seen Laurel for a week.

Harold continues to shock. What he says in the next chapter changes much of the motivation nourishing the plot. Claiming that he shot Jack Lennox in self-defense, after being fired at first, Harold says that Jack offered him the $100,000 as hush money but then tried to double-cross him. Lennox's secret? Nelson Bagley never shot himself aboard the *Canaan Sound*. The bullet that grazed his skull and then set the ship ablaze was fired by Jack Lennox. Jack had good reason to want Bagley dead: Bagley saw Jack in Allie Russo's bedroom the night Allie was shot. When Harold told this story to Jack, he was offered $100,000 providing that he stage the transaction as a kidnaping. But Jack never intended to give Harold the money. He lured him to the lonely water tower at Sandhill Lake, where, rather than paying him the bogus ransom, shot him. Had it worked, the double-cross would have made Jack a hero, cleared his name from the oil-slick scandal, and removed Harold as a blackmailer. Doubting Harold's story but acknowledging its "weird reality," Archer goes next to Jack's hospital room. The novel, with only two chapters to go, seems to be rolling toward an obligatory scene in which Archer brings a bedridden killer to justice. Yet Ross Macdonald's vision and technique have both sharpened since *Wycherly*, where he first used this plot-device. The ideas in *Beauty* boom from the oil-smeared Pacific coast to the deep places in our heart, where they speak most clearly.

Ross Macdonald hasn't tucked Jack Lennox in a hospital bed to stage a confession of guilt. Speak out Jack does, but in a way that ravels rather than smoothes the novel's lines of tension. He denies killing either Allie or Bagley. Interrupting his denial is the news that his father has died. The news fills him with power rather than grief. "Don't mock me, little man," he snarls, offering the detective $50,000 to walk away from the case. Archer's refusal of the bribe tempts Lennox to buy his silence with a different coin. He explains that the same phone call that told him of his father's death also brought the news that Laurel has come home. He adds that Laurel pushed Bagley off a cliff into the sea. Harold Sherry saw the murder and demanded $100,000 to keep quiet about it. Why did Laurel want to kill Bagley? Typically, Archer forages into the past for an answer. The past in *Beauty* is May 1945. Lennox believes that hearing about Allie's death upset Ben Somerville so much that it made him over-pressurize one of the gas tanks aboard the *Canaan Sound.* Elsewhere on the ship, Lennox was questioning Bagley at gunpoint about his relationship with Allie; Bagley panicked and ran. Unnerved by the ruptured gas tank, Lennox shot Bagley without planning to and set fire to the ship. But the connection between the *Canaan Sound* and Allie Russo's murder, five thousand miles away, remains dark. Nobody can identify Allie's murderer; nobody knows who mailed the clippings reporting the murder to Somerville, Lennox, and Bagley.

The mysteries dissolve in the last chapter. The surprising twists in the closing scenes recall Agatha Christie at her sharpest. Armed with a revolver, Archer goes to Jack Lennox's home. "I envied anyone who didn't have my errand to perform," he tells us without divulging his grim errand. Guns add to the mounting suspense. Let into the home by Marian Lennox, "her hair . . . ragged and streaked with white," he sees a gun propped in the corner which he quickly disarms. Marian confirms her husband's story that Laurel pushed Bagley into the sea. But, like her husband, she can't explain her daughter's motives. Archer turns her attention to May 1945. Her indiscreet reference to Allie Russo as "that filthy woman" leads to the disclosures that Jack spent his last night ashore with Allie and that Marian found him lying drunk in Allie's bed. (*Le crime passionel* is usually done by women in Ross Macdonald.) Confessions pour from Marian. It was she who sent the newspaper clippings to the men of the *Canaan Sound.* Her recent murders she performed to conceal her first. She killed Bagley because he remembered seeing her at the Russos the night Allie died. (Having watched her mother push Bagley into the sea, and not the oiled bird, accounts for Laurel's nervous strain at the outset.) Tony Lashman couldn't live because he had blackmailed

Urban Apprehensions

Marian after learning why Bagley had visited her. The book ends with the obligatory reappearance of Laurel—sleeping in her old bedroom. But no sooner does Ross Macdonald spotlight her than he turns his lens away. While Archer satisfies himself that she is still alive, her mother Marian has climbed the railing of the cantilevered house. He is too far away to stop her. Within a moment of his calling out, she drops and then breaks up on the rocks below.

This finale lacks force because it isn't prepared for. Ross Macdonald hides Marian Lennox most of the way; her murderousness doesn't flow from any observed set of traits or human values. The ending of *Beauty* resembles that of *Coast* more than that of *Chill*, to mention two previous Archers in which a jealous wife emerges at the end as the felon. The ending of *Chill* reminds us that old Tish Bradshaw has been acting like a killer all along; her murderousness, entirely in character with her lies and stalling tactics, hews to the rules of literary detection. Like Isobel Graff of *Coast*, Marian Lennox plays the killer less convincingly. The problem she raises is more structural than motivational. The novel's design is out of tilt. We don't know Marian well enough to care about her guilt. Whereas Ross Macdonald gives her too little attention, he probably gives the red herring, Harold Sherry, too much. Harold bears a disproportionately large burden of both plot and guilt. Archer's saying in Chapter 35 that he "wouldn't put it past" Harold to kill Laurel recalls the groundless assertions made about Hector Lands's guilt for the sake of the plot in *Trouble Follows Me*. Harold's supposed guilt keeps the action hot till Ross Macdonald sees fit to name the real killer.

A character handled with more skill is that of the missing person and eponym, Laurel Russo. Because she is in danger and because nobody reacts calmly to wild, moody Laurel, we share Archer's fascination with her. "The riddle of Laurel" sustains the book's forward drive. Though seen but briefly, Laurel is the book's most magnetic character. Carefully timed comments about her, either hearsay or first hand, by people who have known her for many years, keep her before us as an imaginative force. Smith, Ben Somerville's valet and groundsman, recalls her as a child: "She was a sweet little thing, but also a handful sometimes." Laurel's best friend since the first grade, Joyce Hampshire, agrees that Laurel can make trouble; "quite a headache" to her parents, Laurel "was never a happy girl, and she wasn't very popular with her teachers." One of her former teachers confirms this judgment, claiming, "It's been obvious for at least fifteen years that Laurel Lennox is a schizoid personality." Laurel's marriage also gains life from the responses it evokes in others. Beth Somerville believes that Laurel and Tom have an "unreal marriage" because "It isn't easy for Laurel to be intimate with anyone, certainly not with a man." Yet Tom could make intimacy difficult. From the statement of his cousin Gloria, whom we might expect to take his side, he must have been hard for Laurel to live with. "Very closed-mouth," Tom, says Gloria, "goes in for these long silences; he always has." Perhaps his moodiness helped drive Laurel away. But he also loves Laurel, and he works hard to get her back. Ross Macdonald doesn't worry the ambiguities in the Russos' marriage. Rather than blaming or prescribing, he uses the impressions and opinions of many people to make the marriage live. These guide our responses. Because we believe in the troubled marriage, we also believe in the efforts of Tom and Archer to save it.

As a rule, Ross Macdonald plays fair with the reader, demanding only that he stay alert. Harold Sherry, whose last name is that of a wine and who wants to become a restaurateur, enters the novel in an eating-place. In Chapter 6, Gloria Flaherty mentions wanting to start a restaurant with her fiancé, a jobless food worker named Harry. A high school yearbook Archer reads in Chapter 23 relates Harold to food again, calling him, "World's greatest gourmet." Ross Macdonald takes the same pains with most of the building-stones of the plot. In Chapter 18, Archer lies to Martha Mungan about the whereabouts of her former husband. Justly enough, he is lied to in turn in this scene (about Martha's disposal of the suit), even though he doesn't uncover the lie till several chapters later. Ross Macdonald also knows how to hide structural flaws. In Chapter 2, Archer voices inwardly his disbelief in the coincidence that he and Laurel both live in West Los Angeles. The coincidence is neither the first nor the least plausible in the early going; Ross Macdonald's throwing Archer together with the beautiful heiress-apparent of the family guilty of the oil slick has already strained our belief. But by voicing our own disapproval of his need to resort to coincidence, he throws the disapproval back at us and, in part, quiets it.

No disapproval mars our acceptance of Ross Macdonald's treatment of Archer's sexual bout with Beth Somerville. As in *Look*, the gloom that envelops all the other characters rules out any but the skimpiest gains stemming from Archer's rut with Beth. The writer makes his position clear straightaway. That Archer nearly rapes Beth and then sees a corpse as soon as he wakes up the next morning blocks any hopeful future for the couple. We're not surprised that they say so little to each other the next time they meet. Carefully prefiguring this bleakness, Ross Macdonald leads up to the rut with the same exciting care as he leads away from it. As soon as Beth meets Archer, she has to throw in with him. She scolds her husband's groundsman Smith for shooting a rat. The reaction to her reprimand by Smith and Somerville ("The two men looked past her at each other. . . . I got the impression that their relationship was deeper and stronger than the marriage, and that it shut her out") makes Archer, though a stranger, her only source of comfort and trust. Ross Macdonald's leaving Archer alone with Beth for all of Chapter 10 and most of Chapter 11 both brings to light important currents of the plot and gives the couple

Urban Apprehensions

a chance to know each other. The emergency created by Laurel's abduction, meanwhile, has lowered Beth's reserve; as the family crisis steepens, her talk becomes more personal and more pointed. The sexual crescendo of her confession surprises nobody.

Perhaps Beth and Archer do well to vibrate to this crescendo, the diminuendo following sharply. Ross Macdonald's 1973 comment on breakdown and brokenness, printed within months of the novel's publication, relates directly to his thematic intent in *Beauty*:

> I'm profoundly concerned with broken marriages. I was the child of one. I'm sure that has a lot to do with it. Don't forget, though, that the Archer novels, and mystery novels in general, are about various kinds of brokenness. It's various kinds of social, psychological, and moral brokenness that lead to crime. . . . We seem to be moving away from the traditional concept of marriage. And you write about what's there. Writers don't have much control over their material. It's there. And it's not only outside, but it's in them too.[15]

Set in southern California, land of promise and splintered dreams, *Beauty* presents a litter of shards. Our cue comes from the author's comment on broken marriages. Four Lennox marriages spanning three generations are cracking. Gloria Flaherty, Tony Lashman, Ramona, and Archer are already divorced. Nor is the brokenness limited to sex. Joyce Hampshire's living room is full of mementos which Archer calls "disconnected memories that failed to add up to a life." Later, he notes of Bagley, while towing his dead body to shore, "One of his arms flapped like a broken wing." Much of the brokenness in *Beauty* comes from social organization; Bagley, the most deeply broken character in the book, also has the least social identity. Ross Macdonald's deepest and perhaps best novel tries to weigh the cost of living in a democratic society. What are the penalties of socialization?

Sometimes they are stiff. When the dreams and freedoms of the rich clash with those of the poor, the poor haven't a chance. Ross Macdonald's fascination with the rich goes back as far as Archer. "The ordered palms and Monterey cypress" of an expensive housing estate dwarf the Pacific itself on the first page of *Target*. The cabdriver who takes Archer to the estate says, "This is where the cavemen live." The California rich do comprise a society as rigid and as loveless as that of primitive man. Like the Buchanans in *Gatsby*, they smash people and things with their carelessness. Fiercely materialistic and unimaginative, they rate humane values low. Rank and influence they rate high. Money to them is the great solvent, capable of righting any problem or controlling any person. Their flash appointments, well-bred good looks, and contempt for the middle class make them as fascinating and as deadly as panthers. Both impressed and irritated by them, Ross Macdonald often shows them failing to buy Archer's integrity, as in *Enemy* and *Beauty*. At no time does he prefer them morally to the poor or the middle class. His brother naval officers, who all happen to be well born, Lt. Kenneth Millar (USN, ret.) judges most harshly; any commissioned officer who served on a carrier near Okinawa, as Lt. Millar did, will be handled roughly. Like Ralph Smitheram of *Look*, Ben Somerville is cuckolded by Archer. His brother-in-law, Jack Lennox, must share with him the blame for the fire aboard the *Canaan Sound*. Partners in several senses, the men haven't the courage to stand alone. They deceive their wives with the same woman—Allie Russo. Then they both cheat Allie. "One of those men who need a gun to complete themselves," Lennox is nastier (because more gently born?) than Somerville. He beats up and then tries to kill Harold Sherry; he shoots Nelson Bagley; he lets Marian's killing of Allie Russo go unpunished.

Sex is an upper-class sport—a game played by the rich according to the rich man's rules. One rule decrees that the poor always lose. The poor pay for the crimes as well as the erotic vagrancies of the rich. Jack Lennox's money keeps him out of jail for shooting Bagley and setting fire to the ship. As has been said, Ben Somerville talked Allie into leaving her husband, but, instead of helping her get a divorce, passed her on to Jack Lennox, who insulted her again by keeping quiet about her murder. The person who pays heaviest for the misadventures of May 1945 is "that shriveled little throwaway of a man," Nelson Bagley. Bagley, who never made love to Alison, pays dearly—suffering physically and losing his mind —for doing in fantasy what his officers do in fact. But being shot, scorched, and then pitched into the sea isn't payment enough. Dr. Lampson, his therapist, says of him, "He was my Lazarus. . . . I thought I could raise him from the dead." He is wrong. The Lennox clan can't afford to let him live as a whole man; his memory threatens their security. Only as a vegetable is he permitted to subsist. Because he has learned to speak and to remember, he must be shoved off a cliff, dashed against the rocks below, and, in case any life remains in him, left to drown in an oil-coated sea. Harold Sherry, who tries to revive Bagley's memory, fares only slightly better. Though Laurel talked Harold into running away to Las Vegas, she also let him take all the punishment for the joyride. His attempt to square accounts with the Lennoxes fifteen years later heaps on more punishment. Harold doesn't have a chance against vested power. His sacrifical role comes through in his attempt to resurrect the Lazarus-figure, Bagley; in his age, thirty-three; in his importance in the case ("The way to . . . Laurel is through Harold Sherry"); and, finally, in the many descriptions of Tom Russo's head, which relate Tom to John the Baptist and, by extrapolation, Harold, who probably slept with Laurel before Tom did, to Christ. Ross Macdonald's democratic principles account for the growing importance of working-class or jobless people in the later Archers. Only in *Man*, slightly, and *Beauty*, do these principles encroach on the metaphysical.

But suffering doesn't belong exclusively to the poor; the rich can't buy their way out of all pain. Sylvia Lennox's money, property, and age don't fend off sorrow. Her secretary is killed; the family business may go under; her husband has discarded her for another woman; her son is shot; her only granddaughter is missing. Motion and change shudder through *Beauty*. But the wrongs created by this convulsiveness can't be righted. Amid the rush is a desperate sameness. (The Reynolds Price book, *Permanent Errors*, appears in a character's library.) Connie Hapgood and William Lennox never marry; the oiled birds die; the crimes done to Allie and Tom Russo, Nelson Bagley, and Harold Sherry by the Lennox circle are irreversible. The last sentence of the novel, "I picked up the phone and started to make the necessary calls," makes Archer a functionary rather than an oracle. He won't speak his heart, having just begun to clean up a mess the greater part of which lies outside his scope. He can't resolve the marital problems of the Somervilles or the Russos; indeed, he may have heightened them, in part. Though the fire roaring through *Man* goes out before the book ends, the deadly oil slick and the social pollution it symbolizes both remain. Archer's efforts seem wasted. Ignorance and pain haven't been removed; nobody's outlook has brightened; the ugly, floating globs of oil still threaten the sea. If Archer has learned anything, he keeps it to himself.

The persistent oil slick tells us how close we stand to the primeval ooze. The interdependence theme, first sounded by Ross Macdonald in *Doomsters* ("We're members of one another"), courses through *Beauty*. Mr. Russo helped build the ship his wife's two lovers sailed on and then destroyed along with Allie. More to the point, Lennox Oil needn't take all the blame for the slick. By burning fuel in our homes and cars, we create the demand for petroleum products. We share the guilt for the boldest wildcat schemes. In Chapter 14, Ross Macdonald links the slick to the deathly chill of Bagley's corpse. Archer remarks, after dragging the corpse to shore, "I went back to the guesthouse and took a hot shower. It failed to free me of the smell of oil or the chill that the dead man had left on me." As the seeping, clinging oil spreads, it slimes the hulls of ships, kills birds, and drives into men's hearts. The poetic elements of the book support the idea. Played against a greasy black diorama, the action takes place mostly at night. Though it opens on a Wednesday afternoon, night has fallen by Chapter 2 and the darkness doesn't lift till Chapter 14. When dawn does come, it brings with it the oil-blackened corpse of Bagley. Elsewhere, too, sunlight fails to transmit joy and hope, as is seen in the opening sentences of Chapter 19: "It was nearly noon when I got back to Pacific Point. The harbor was even blacker than it had been in the morning." (Chapter 8 had begun, "The darkness in Bel Air was almost thick enough to lean on.") The heavy Conradian music of the similes in Chapter 1 both define a moral stand and lend the coming action a dark universality: the oil oozing from the Lennox's broken drilling platform on the first page looks like "black blood"; on the next page the slick has spread "like premature night across the sea." After killing some birds and fish, the slick washes a corpse to shore in Chapter 14. By the end, it has seeped to the shoreline. Moral darkness permeates the action.

Archer's failure to wash the residue of oil from his body conveys his implication in the guilt. As he did in *Man*, Ross Macdonald makes several on-the-nose comparisons between his detective-narrator and the other characters in order to certify him as an Everyman figure. Like Harold Sherry's physician, Archer grew up in Long Beach. In Chapter 18, he stands in the same spot in Martha Mungan's apartment supposedly occupied by Nelson Bagley a couple of weeks before. Talking about Bagley with Dr. Lampson then makes him and the therapist "linked mirror images" of each other. Earlier, he had noted a resemblance between himself and Tom Russo; besides being in danger of losing his wife, Tom is about the same age as Archer when he lost Sue. Like Tom, Archer is both cruel and loving, patient and moody. His job he does as well as ever, pushing himself hard and working long hours under heavy pressure. He still works to promote the gentle, the kindly, and whatever serves harmony between people. Chapter 19 shows him—in Ross Macdonald's only mob scene since the Nazi parade in *Tunnel* thirty years before—stopping some picketers from locking horns with Ben Somerville, vice-president of Lennox Oil. He protects the innocent rather than punishing or sermonizing to the guilty. No crusader or avenger, he encourages Harold Sherry to turn both himself and the bogus ransom money over to the police in hopes of lightening the charges against him. Nor have the years jaded his investigative technique. As he closes in on Harold's mother's house, he studies the windows for any sign of movement or glinting metal. He questions Harold and the other witnesses with the same professional skill and feminine sensitivity to atmospheres he displayed in his earlier cases. But he sometimes miscues. In Chapter 38, for instance, he goes wrong twice—by believing Laurel dead and by naming Bagley as Alison's killer.

Laurel is his sternest test. A fellow environmentalist and a Freudian wish-projection of the daughter-lover he has craved since *Doomsters* (1958), she receives more of Archer's energy than any other missing person in the canon. Much of this energy is erotic. Archer is mesmerized by Laurel's feet when he meets her on the beach; he keeps looking at them and the "elegant" prints they make both in the sand and in his apartment, where he later takes her against his better judgment. Unlike Jean Broadhurst of *Man*, Laurel has no small son to increase her value for Archer; she has won the detective's heart on her own. Restoring her to her husband, one of Archer's alter-egoes, symbolizes the mending of his own broken marriage. The depth of his feeling for Laurel is gauged by his response to Beth Somerville. An attractive, high-spirited woman, Beth is worth bedding in her own right. That her husband rose to the rank of Captain in the Navy gives Archer the added fillip of striking out at his punitive male society. But the real force impelling him to Beth's bed is her resemblance to Laurel, his *domaine perdu*. Laurel and Beth attended the same school; Archer likes them both at first meeting for the same reasons. As aunt and niece, they are practically mother and daughter; Beth says herself, "You think I'm like Laurel. . . ? They do say an aunt and niece have about thirty percent of the same genes—almost as close a relation as mother and daughter." Logically enough, he dreams that he is sleeping with Laurel after he has sex with Beth—in a bed Laurel slept in many times. When he does find Laurel asleep, a page from the end, he is stunned. Incredulous, he touches her forehead with his mouth to make sure she's alive. Ironically, the canon's latest dreamer undone by his dream is Archer. What happens to the sleeping beauty when kissed? What happens to the prince who kisses her? While inviting these romantic stereotypes, Archer forgets Marian, who is climbing over the rail dividing her balcony from the cliffs overlooking the sea. If he blames himself for Marian's suicide, he doesn't tell us. Rather, he assumes a defensive business-as-usual attitude toward mopping up the residue of the case. This novel about futility ends perfectly—with the failure of its narrator-hero to discuss, perhaps even to perceive, his worst failure of the book. And Ross Macdonald? In calling the novel *Sleeping Beauty*, in Laurel's honor (the garland of laurel was used to bestow honor in antiquity), he adopts the same attitude toward her as Archer.

One of his most prophetic, socially committed works, *Beauty* is neither "rechewed Macdonald" nor "a blurry effort," as John Skow said in *Time* for 14 May 1973 (p. E3). Ross Macdonald's unswerving eye for detail and fine timing gives the well-turned plot a temporal and spatial structure that adjusts easily to the many changes in the action. This interplay of logic, structure, and incident represents a high-order achievement. At a point in his career when most American writers have slackened in creative drive, Ross Macdonald is challenging himself with new ideas and putting detective fiction to new uses. His imagination grows wilder, stronger, and more mystical with the years. Steady in focus, ever-burgeoning in range, the Archers form a cumulative masterpiece. No student of American detective fiction can imagine the development of the genre without them.

NOTES

CHAPTER ONE

[1] Noel Young, "Foreword," Ross Macdonald, *On Crime Writing* (Santa Barbara: Capra, 1973), p. 5.

[2] Jon Carroll, "Ross Macdonald in Raw California," *Esquire,* June 1972, p. 149.

[3] John Leonard, "Ross Macdonald, his Lew Archer, and other secret selves," New York *Times Book Review*, 1 June 1969, p. 2.

[4] Ross Macdonald, "Cain x 3," New York *Times Book Review*, 2 March 1959, p. 51.

[5] Geoffrey Hartman, "The Mystery of Mysteries," New York *Review of Books*, 18 May 1972, p. 31.

[6] John Skow, "More Than Ten Billion Sold," *Time*, 14 May 1973, p. E3.

[7] "An Interview with Ross Macdonald," *Concept Twelve* (1971), p. 41.

[8] See Verda Evans, "The Mystery as Mind-Stretcher," *English Journal*, 61 (April 1972), 4: 495-503.

[9] Matthew Bruccoli, *Kenneth Millar/Ross Macdonald: A Checklist* (Detroit: Gale, 1971), p. 64.

[10] W. H. Auden, "The Guilty Vicarage," *The Dyers Hand and Other Essays* (New York: Vintage, 1968), p. 149; George Grella, "Murder and Manners: The Formal Detective Novel," *Novel: A Forum on Fiction*, 4 (Fall 1970), p. 30.

[11] Jacques Barzun and Wendell Hertig Taylor, "Introductory," *A Catalogue of Crime* (New York and Evanston: Harper & Row, 1971), p. 12.

[12] Kenneth Millar, "Introduction," Bruccoli, *Checklist*, p. xii.

[13] R. Austin Freeman, "The Art of the Detective Story," in Howard Haycraft, ed., *The Art of the Mystery Story* (New York: Grosset and Dunlap, 1947), p. 11; Dorothy L. Sayers, "The Omnibus of Crime," *Ibid.*, p. 101; Ross Macdonald, "The Writer as Detective Hero," in Francis M. Nevins, ed., *The Mystery Writer's Art* (Bowling Green: Bowling Green, Ohio, 1970), p. 297.

[14] Julian Symons, *Mortal Consequences: A History—From the Detective Story to the Crime Novel* (New York and Evanston: Harper & Row, 1972), p. 9.

[15] Erik Routley, *The Puritan Pleasures of the Detective Story* (London: Gollancz, 1972), p. 205.

[16] Newgate Callendar, "Criminals at Large," New York *Times Book Review*, 25 March 1973, p. 49; "An Interview with Ross Macdonald," p. 37.

[17] Ross Macdonald, "Foreword," *Archer at Large* (New York: Knopf, 1970), p. x; "An Interview with Ross Macdonald," p. 36.

[18] Raymond Chandler, "Introduction," *The Simple Art of Murder* (New York: Norton, 1968), p. xii.

[19] George Grella, "Murder and the Mean Streets," *Contempora* (March 1970), p. 8.

[20] Ross Macdonald, "Foreword," *Archer in Hollywood* (New York: Knopf, 1967), p. viii.

[21] Kenneth Millar and Arthur Kaye, *Ross Macdonald "In the First Person"* (*Time-Life*, 1970), pp. 9, 8.

[22] Modified from Stephen S. Stanton, "Introduction," *Camille and Other Plays* (New York: Hill and Wang, 1957), pp. xii-xx.

[23] John Paterson, "A Cosmic View of the Private Eye," *Saturday Review*, 22 August 1953, p. 32.

[24] Carroll, "Ross Macdonald in Raw California," p. 149.

[25] Millar and Kaye, *Ross Macdonald "In the First Person,"* pp. 24, 13; Carroll, "Ross Macdonald in Raw California," p. 149.

[26] Kenneth Clark, *Civilization* (New York and Evanston: Harper & Row, 1969), pp. 14, 4.

[27] G. K. Chesterton, "A Defence of Detective Stories," in Haycraft, ed., *The Art of the Mystery Story*, p. 5; George V. Higgins, "The Private Detective as Illegal Hero," *Esquire*, December 1972, p. 348.

[28] Carroll, "Ross Macdonald in Raw California," p. 149.

[29] Macdonald, "Foreword," *Archer in Hollywood*, p. viii.

[30] Rollo May, "The Origins and Significance of the Existential Movement in Psychology," *Existence: A New Dimension in Psychiatry and Psychology*, Rollo May, Ernest Angel, Henri F. Ellenberger, eds. (New York: Basic Books, 1958), p. 17.

[31] Sigmund Freud, *The Interpretation of Dreams*, James Strachey, ed. and trans. (New York: Avon, 1965), p. 87.

[32] *Ibid.*, p. 587.

[33] Macdonald, "Foreword," *Archer in Hollywood*, p. ix; Millar and Kaye, *Ross Macdonald "In the First Person,"* p. 4.

[34] Leonard, "Ross Macdonald, his Lew Archer, and other secret selves," pp. 19, 2.

[35] Macdonald, "Foreword," *Archer in Hollywood*, p. ix; Carroll, "Ross Macdonald in Raw California," p. 149.

[36] Ross Macdonald, "Research into the History of Detective Fiction," San Francisco *Chronicle—This World*, 15 September 1959, p. 29.

[37] Macdonald, "Foreword," *Archer at Large*, p. x; "An Interview with Ross Macdonald," p. 39.

[38] Freud, *The Interpretation of Dreams*, p. xxvi.

[39] Carroll, "Ross Macdonald in Raw California," p. 188.

[40] Macdonald, "The Writer as Detective Hero," pp. 300-1.

[41] George Stade, "I've Been Reading Thrillers," *Columbia Forum* (Spring 1970), p. 37.

[42] Hartman, "The Mystery of Mysteries," p. 31.

[43] Millar and Kaye, *Ross Macdonald "In the First Person,"* pp. 6. 7.

[44] Ross Macdonald, "A Preface to *The Galton Case*," in Thomas McCormack, ed., *Afterwords: Novelists on Their Novels* (New York and Evanston: Harper & Row, 1969), p. 159.

[45] Millar, "Introduction," Bruccoli, *Checklist*, p. xi.

[46] Millar and Kaye, *Ross Macdonald "In the First Person,"* p. 23.

[47] Macdonald, "The Writer as Detective Hero," p. 303.

[48] "An Interview with Ross Macdonald," p. 34.

[49] Macdonald, "A Preface to *The Galton Case*," p. 157.

[50] William Goldman, "The finest series of detective novels ever written by an American," New York *Times Book Review*, 1 June 1969, p. 1.

[51] Millar, "Introduction," Bruccoli, *Checklist*, p. xv.

[52] Richard Lingeman, "The Underground Bye-bye: Still Another Lew Archibald Novel by Ross Macdonald," New York *Times Book Review*, 6 June 1971, p. 6.

CHAPTER TWO

[1] Raymond A. Sokolov, "The Art of Murder," *Newsweek*, 22 March 1971, p. 108; "An Interview with Ross Macdonald," pp. 39-40.

[2] Macdonald, "A Preface to *The Galton Case*," p. 156.

[3] Macdonald, "The Writer as Detective Hero," p. 304; Macdonald, "A Preface to *The Galton Case*," p. 156.

[4] Raymond Chandler, "Introduction," *The Simple Art of Murder*, p. xiv.

[5] Macdonald, "The Writer as Detective Hero," p. 304.

[6] [Linda Goodman,] *Linda Goodman's Sun Signs* (New York: Taplinger, 1968), p. 281.

[7] Ralph Harper, *The World of the Thriller* (Cleveland: Case Western Reserve, 1969), pp. 26-27.

[8] Grella, "Murder and the Mean Streets," p. 10.

[9] Kenneth Millar, "Literary Tributes to Proust—And Other New Books," San Francisco *Chronicle-This World*, 14 September 1958, p. 31.

[10] Eudora Welty, "The Stuff That Nightmares Are Made Of," New York *Times Book Review*, 14 February 1971, p. 29.

[11] Macdonald, "The Writer As Detective Hero," p. 305.

[12] Macdonald, "Foreword," *Archer in Hollywood*, pp. vii-viii.

[13] Raymond Chandler, *Farewell My Lovely*, in *The Raymond Chandler Omnibus*, Foreword by Lawrence Clark Powell (New York: Knopf, 1964), p. 163.

[14] Goldman, "The finest series of detective novels ever written by an American," p. 1.

[15] Welty, "The Stuff That Nightmares Are Made Of," p. 29.

[16] Dorothy L. Sayers, *The Nine Tailors* (New York: Harbrace, n. d.), p. 278.

[17] Freud, *The Interpretation of Dreams*, p. 169.

CHAPTER THREE

[1] Millar, "Introduction," Bruccoli, *Checklist*, p. xiii.

[2] *Ibid.*, p. xiv.

[3] Ross Macdonald, "Beautiful Books about Terrible Things," Detroit *Sunday News*, 22 October 1972, p. E9.

CHAPTER FOUR

[1] Macdonald, "Foreword," *Archer in Hollywood*, p. viii.

[2] *Ibid.*, p. ix.

[3] Millar, "Introduction," Bruccoli, *Checklist*, p. xvi.

[4] Wilfrid Sheed, "The Good Word: It All Depends on Your Genre," New York *Times Book Review*, 5 September 1971, p. 2.

CHAPTER FIVE

[1] Gerald Walker, "Who's and Why's of Whodunits," *New York Times*, 1 January 1974, p. 17.

[2] Jerry Buck, "Millar Alias Macdonald and His Detective Hero," St. Louis *Post-Dispatch*, 14 April 1974, p. 8G.

[3] Sam Grogg, Jr., "Ross Macdonald: At the Edge," *Journal of Popular Culture*, VII (Summer 1973), pp. 218-219.

[4] Macdonald, "Foreword," *Archer in Hollywood*, p. ix; Macdonald, "A Preface to *The Galton Case*," p. 156.

Notes

[5] Daniel R. Barnes, " 'I'm the Eye': Archer as Narrator in the Novels of Ross Macdonald," *Mystery and Detective Annual* (1972), p. 187.

[6] Macdonald, "The Writer as Detective Hero," p. 303.

[7] Ross Macdonald, "Homage to Dashiell Hammett," *Mystery Writer's Annual* (1964), pp. 8, 24.

[8] Barnes, p. 181.

[9] "An Interview with Ross Macdonald," p. 35; Millar, "Introduction," Bruccoli, *Checklist*, p. xvii; Millar and Kaye, *Ross Macdonald "In the First Person,"* pp. 14-15.

[10] Macdonald, "Foreword," *Archer at Large*, pp. ix-x; Macdonald, "A Preface to *The Galton Case*," p. 151.

[11] *Ibid.*, pp. 151, 153; Brad Darrach, "Ross Macdonald: The Man Behind the Mysteries," *People*, 8 July 1974, p. 29.

[12] Macdonald, "A Preface to *The Galton Case*," pp. 158-159.

[13] See note 6, above.

[14] Raymond Chandler, *Raymond Chandler Speaking*, Dorothy Gardiner and Katherine Sorley Walker, eds. (Boston: Houghton, Mifflin, 1962), pp. 54-55.

CHAPTER SIX

[1] Millar, "Introduction," Bruccoli, *Checklist*, p. xii.

[2] *Ibid.*, p. xvii.

[3] Sigmund Freud, *A General Introduction to Psychoanalysis*, trans. and rev., Joan Riviere (New York: Liverright, 1935), p. 327.

[4] Bruccoli, p. 40.

[5] Darrach, p. 29.

[6] Grella, "Murder and the Mean Streets," p. 13.

[7] Bruccoli, p. 46.

[8] Miller and Kaye, *Ross Macdonald "In the First Person,"* p. 17.

[9] Bruccoli, p. xvii.

CHAPTER SEVEN

[1] Julian Symons, "The Case of Raymond Chandler," New York *Times Magazine*, 23 December 1973, p. 30.

[2] Darrach, p. 30.

[3] Grogg, p. 216.

[4] Bruccoli, p. 48.

[5] "Interview," p. 40.

[6] Bruccoli, p. 48.

[7] Hartman, p. 31.

[8] *Ibid.*, p. 32.

[9] Welty, p. 28, 29.

[10] *Ibid.*, p. 28

[11] *Ibid.*, p. 29.

[12] "Interview," p. 39.

[13] William Ruehlmann, *Saint with a Gun: The Unlawful American Private Eye* (New York: New York University Press, 1974), p. 113.

[14] *Ibid.*, p. 111.

[15] Grogg, p. 218.

INDEX

FINKELSTEIN MEMORIAL LIBRARY

91 00086 5971

850765

813.
52   WOLFE, PETER
MACDONALD   DREAMERS WHO LIVE THEIR
              DREAMS $13.95

**FINKELSTEIN
MEMORIAL
LIBRARY**

19 South Madison Avenue,
Spring Valley, N. Y.
10977
(914) 352-5700

JAN 30 1985